OPERATION TERRA

A Journey Through Space and Time

Sara Zibrat & The Hosts of Heaven

Published by
CELESTIAL WAY
Hendersonville, NC
USA

OPERATION TERRA
A Journey Through Space and Time
by Sara Zibrat & The Hosts of Heaven

© Copyright 1999-2020 Sara Zibrat. All rights reserved.
Published 2020. Revised paperback edition.

Except for brief quotations in a printed review, a copy of which is furnished to the publisher, no portion of this material may be reproduced in any medium or form that is for sale or used for a commercial purpose without prior written permission from the publisher (Celestial Way).

No alteration of the original spellings, content, or wording is permitted under any circumstances by anyone other than the copyright holder (Sara Zibrat), except with her direct participation and consent.

LCCN 2020903678

ISBNs:
978-0-9711297-6-4 (Keepsake hardcover edition);
978-0-9711297-7-1 (paperback); 978-0-9711297-8-8 (epub);
978-0-9711297-9-5 (audiobook)

CONTENT COMPILATION, EDITING AND DESIGN BY SARA ZIBRAT

Publisher's Cataloging-In-Publication Information

Names: Zibrat, Sara, 1941- author.

Title: Operation Terra : a journey through space and time / Sara Zibrat & the Hosts of Heaven.

Description: Revised paperback edition. | Hendersonville, NC, USA : Celestial Way, [2020] | Features an annotated table of contents in lieu of an index.

Identifiers: ISBN: 978-0-9711297-6-4 (hardcover Keepsake edition) | 978-0-9711297-7-1 (paperback) | 978-0-9711297-8-8 (epub) | 978-0-9711297-9-5 (audiobook) | LCCN: 2020903678

Subjects: LCSH: Prophecy. | Metaphysics. | Consciousness. | Cosmology. | Creation. | Ascension of the soul. | Extraterrestrial beings. | Civilization--Extraterrestrial influences. | Mind and reality. | Telepathy. | Self-consciousness (Awareness) | Self-actualization (Psychology) | Chain of being (Philosophy) | Spiritual life--New Age movement. | Spirituality. | Future life. | Earth (Planet)--Miscellanea. | End of the world. | Eschatology. | BISAC: BODY, MIND & SPIRIT / Prophecy. | PHILOSOPHY / Metaphysics. | BODY, MIND & SPIRIT / UFOs & Extraterrestrials. | BODY, MIND & SPIRIT / Channeling & Mediumship. | SELF-HELP / Spiritual. | RELIGION / Eschatology.

Classification: LCC: BF2050 .Z53 2020 | DDC: 133/.93--dc23

Published by
CELESTIAL WAY
Hendersonville, NC
USA
Printed on acid-free paper

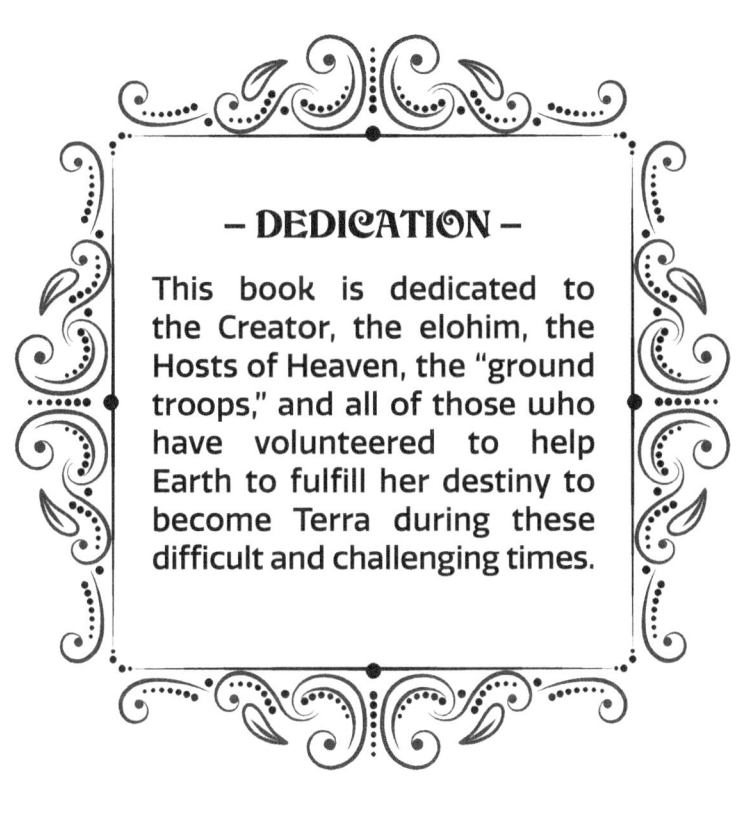

– DEDICATION –

This book is dedicated to the Creator, the elohim, the Hosts of Heaven, the "ground troops," and all of those who have volunteered to help Earth to fulfill her destiny to become Terra during these difficult and challenging times.

TABLE OF CONTENTS

INTRODUCTION..17
    ABOUT OPERATION TERRA: THE BIG PICTURE..............19
    THE TIMELINE FOR OPERATION TERRA.....................24
    THE PURPOSE OF OPERATION TERRA.......................29
    THE STRUCTURE OF THE "OP".............................34
        The Horizontal View..35
        The Vertical View..36
        The Three Waves..38
        Special Forces..39
        Galactic Volunteers..39
        Life on Terra...40
    THE CURRENT PROCESS...................................42
        We Are Different...42
        Clearing the Cellular Memory.................................44
        Midway Station...45
        Preparing for Colonization...................................46
THE MESSAGES..47
    ABOUT CHANNELING......................................48
    OVERVIEW OF THE MESSAGES.............................53

The Messages from the Hosts of Heaven
A new revelation on Earth changes, ETs, the end times,
and the journey to the New Earth, Terra

VOLUME ONE...57
    OPERATION TERRA (INTRODUCTION)......................58

☆ the elohim ☆ the interlopers ☆ restoring the plan for Earth ☆ a unique definition of love ☆ love is the "ticket to ride" ☆

    ON BECOMING A "HUMAN" BEING..........................61

☆ the Adamic race ☆ the life force vs. entropy ☆ the true human ☆ using Love, Light, and sound for purification and restoration ☆ symptoms of cleansing ☆ surrender and acceptance ☆ you have so much help ☆

ROOTING OUT FEAR..67

☆ Earth changes ☆ tuning in to Source for your support ☆ fear vs. love ☆ the "Second Coming" ☆ the Big Lie ☆

SUPPORTING YOUR TRANSITION..........................71

☆ different exit paths and timelines ☆ differentiation and resonance ☆ free will and soul choice ☆ the transformational process ☆ things you can do to assist your transition ☆ setting your priorities ☆ disconnect from the drama ☆

A GUIDED TOUR OF TERRA..................................77

☆ a visit to Terra ☆ music of the spheres ☆ seeking harmony in diversity ☆ conscious cooperation with the whole ☆ seedpoints and fractals ☆ the evolutionary spiral ☆

THE MERGING OF REALITIES................................82

☆ decision points and logic branches ☆ Universal Laws ☆ parallel realities ☆ holograms ☆ the Alpha, the Omega, and the Null Point ☆ you are the "seed" for a new "set" of potentials ☆ the other "you"s are merging into your soul ☆

THE HARVESTING OF SOULS.................................91

☆ the Oversoul ☆ the silver cord ☆ simultaneous "lives" ☆ time defines location ☆ the experience of reality is totally subjective ☆ Source is going to "blink" ☆ the harvesting of souls ☆

ON PROBABILITIES..98

☆ the Creator likes surprises ☆ no one can know the future with any degree of certainty ☆ all of the "gears" are lining up ☆ a window of opportunity for an entirely new Creation ☆

CHANGING INTO "GODS"...................................105

☆ holograms ☆ the Light Body ☆ you will have total Mastery ☆ you will change your physical form and your consciousness ☆ you are being re-created in situ ☆ Let go and let God handle the details ☆

ON EXTRATERRESTRIALS AND THE HARVEST..............109

☆ definition of "extraterrestrial" ☆ there are many ET races interacting with Earth ☆ ETs come in two "flavors": STS and STO ☆ the Creator just IS ☆ Harvest ☆ trust your feelings ☆ always ask "Who does it serve?" ☆

SUMMING UP..118

☆ Earth changes serve several purposes ☆ Archangel Michael and the Hosts of Heaven ☆ in STO cultures, everything is sovereign ☆ your first task is your own transformation ☆ receive the gift ☆

SIGNS ALONG THE WAY....................................123

☆ darkness and light ☆ signs of the times ☆ honor and respect your body ☆ supporting your process ☆ your true family ☆

IT'S ALL GOD...129

☆ God IS All There Is ☆ nothing is outside of God ☆ the Earth changes are necessary ☆ all is in Divine order ☆ the cleansing will be complete this time ☆ the dark days ahead will lead to a new dawn ☆

THE CROSSING-POINT......................................136

☆ the expansion into a new reality ☆ merging with the Godhead ☆ absorbing more Light ☆ receive your birthright ☆ all souls are equal ☆

THE COMING STORM..140

☆ darkness is a lack of understanding ☆ making choices ☆ technology and economics are vulnerable ☆ the Earth and sun are players, too ☆ many parallel futures will emerge ☆ learn to live in the NOW ☆

ALLOW ALL THINGS...146

☆ intensification of the polarities ☆ allowing vs. fighting ☆ definition of Mastery ☆ "resist not" ☆ on Terra, all will be sovereign ☆ be calm in the midst of the storm ☆ allow, allow, allow ☆

THE NEW MILLENNIUM.....................................151

☆ you will feel like you are "floating" ☆ trust the process ☆ don't attempt to re-engage with the life that is falling away from you ☆ turn off the external stimuli ☆ it is time for a new dream to emerge ☆

THE SPLITTING OF THE WORLDS.........................156

☆ there is a layering taking place ☆ relax into receiving the lifting ☆ focus on what is yours and let others around you do the same ☆ your greatest service is in fulfilling your own destiny ☆

THE BOTTOM LINE 162

☆ you are not being "rescued" ☆ the present Earth will "pass away" ☆ there is nothing to "fix" or create on present day Earth ☆ only love, peace and joy will exist on Terra ☆ the only actions that are appropriate are those that increase one's frequency and decrease one's fears ☆

VOLUME TWO 168

GO WITH THE FLOW —
BECOMING ONE WITH THE MIND OF GOD 169

☆ what's important ☆ the hologram ☆ aligning with the Creator ☆ spiritual mass vs. material mass ☆ all form is conscious ☆ you are moving out of a "fixed" reality into a fluid reality ☆ go with the flow ☆

THE BEST MEDICINE 176

☆ our alliance ☆ the story of Thimble ☆ I am the only one here ☆ you are beginning to see more clearly ☆ shedding attachments ☆ you are the pioneers ☆ the final desecration WILL play out ☆ the best medicine is to increase your depth of SURRENDER ☆

ON SEXUALITY AND REPRODUCTION — TERRA STYLE..... 185

☆ desire drives the cosmos ☆ on Terra, every life form that reproduces by sexual means is mated ☆ reproduction is reserved for when a new being or unit is required for balancing the whole ☆ all of the senses are engaged in the sexual function ☆ ecstasy is your natural estate ☆

ACROSS THE GREAT DIVIDE 193

☆ our ships are made of living light ☆ we form a group mind with the ship and teleport through hyperspace ☆ YOU do the "lifting" ☆ the role of the mothership in the journey to Terra ☆ the nature of resonance ☆ the embedded light codes ☆ let go and let God ☆

THE TIME OF INGATHERING 200

☆ the unraveling has begun ☆ nothing of the old ways will pass through this time ☆ only essence will survive ☆ there will be increasing turmoil and chaos ☆ the lesson is one of surrender and of turning inward for support ☆ you will be as living Christs ☆ receive the lifting ☆

SHATTERING GLASS 207

☆ you are human lightning rods, grounding the higher Light into the planet ☆ the Light is cleansing the planet ☆ a great healing is taking place ☆ the invisible barrier ☆ emitting your frequency pattern ☆ shattering the "glass ceiling" ☆ why you are different ☆

THE CROSSROADS 217

☆ nothing really new is being said ☆ Earth as a laboratory ☆ emotions as food ☆ the power elite never have enough ☆ until you are able to manifest your needs directly, you will never be free ☆ many crossroads will present ☆ which path will you choose — upward or downward? ☆

MANY WORLDS, MANY DESTINATIONS 224

☆ the Tree of Mind ☆ Terra and her polar opposite ☆ to the Creator, all Its creations are good ☆ you will be seeing an intensification of the polarities ☆ you are responsible for your responses ☆ everything you see is the Creator-in-expression ☆

"STEADY AS SHE GOES" 230

☆ as these storms come into the world about you, take refuge in the deep stillness within yourself ☆ keep your eyes on the goal ☆ this is why you are here ☆ "Steady as she goes" ☆ hold the vision, seek the goal ☆ seek the power of deep ocean ☆ Steady as she goes ☆

A LAST LOOK AROUND 234

☆ take a last look at the world around you; it will soon pass away altogether ☆ savor all that it is to be a human being ☆ appreciate your connection to everything else ☆ you hold the template of a new tomorrow ☆ as the dying proceeds, so does the birthing ☆

ASCENSION IS A PROCESS, PART ONE 239

☆ the process of ascension involves a change in frequency of vibration and a change in consciousness ☆ do those things that make YOU more comfortable ☆ ascension is a process, not an event ☆ detach from the drama ☆ create calm within yourself ☆ follow your inner voice ☆

ASCENSION IS A PROCESS, PART TWO....................247

☆ the process will culminate in an "event" ☆ it is important to find and create inner peace ☆ surrender is the way through ☆ creating the energetic pathway to Terra ☆ surfing the wave of change ☆ definition of a moment ☆ NOW is all you really have ☆ let go and let God ☆

ASCENSION IS A PROCESS, PART THREE...................254

☆ you are a projection of the Creator ☆ your entire reality is oscillating between "on" and "off" ☆ the elohim ☆ the spectrum of reality ☆ you exist on all levels simultaneously ☆ primary colors ☆ prime numbers ☆ embodying your essence ☆ the "pearl of great price" ☆

IT'S BOOSTER ROCKET TIME!............................262

☆ the significance of the "event" ☆ the metaphor of cell division ☆ allowing different perceptions of things for different paths ☆ Terra calls to you and you seek Terra ☆ the coming storms are the booster rockets lifting you toward your dream of a world without storms ☆

ON YOUR WAY HOME......................................268

☆ change can be good news ☆ keep your eyes on the far horizon ☆ we are always with you ☆ listen within ☆ do not get caught up in the drama ☆ seek the peace of deep ocean ☆ peace is an attitude; make the choice for peace ☆ in letting go, you gain more than you lose ☆ you are on your way home ☆

THE GOD GAME 272

☆ the Oversoul is the projector and the Creator is the scriptwriter ☆ your 3D character has been shaped by your pain and by your seeking ☆ the Oversouls act as lenses that "color" the Light from the Creator ☆ quarks are the building blocks of all form ☆ all of the parts are changed through their interaction ☆ you are eternal and will eternally change ☆

CALM, GROUNDED, AND CENTERED 280

☆ the journey is a process, not an event ☆ remain detached ☆ your knowing is a feeling that you can feel ☆ trust your feelings ☆ deception will increase ☆ trust your inner knowing ☆ whatever you need to complete your life's purpose will be provided ☆ a simple technique for detaching ☆ wait for clarity ☆ definition of a moment ☆

CLARIFICATION 287

☆ an exploration into the different aspects of surrender ☆ whom or what do you surrender to and why? ☆

FAREWELL FOR A WHILE. 291

☆ the Hosts will be silent for a while ☆ point one ear outward and point one ear inward ☆ each thing must take place, and each thing WILL take place in its perfect time and sequence ☆ there are no accidents ☆ live in the moment ☆

VOLUME THREE. 295

THE LAST DAYS. 296

☆ there are many civilizations represented here, both from within time and outside of it ☆ the legacy of the reptilians ☆ you are now living in the final days ☆ it will be a terrible time; it will also be a time of endings so that a new beginning can emerge ☆ destinies are chosen by the Oversouls ☆ the cleansing can't be stopped ☆ the long experiment of the last 4.5 billion years is nearly over ☆ the effects that have been absorbed across the millennia must be neutralized and erased ☆ nothing of the old can be carried into the new ☆

WE ARE CRUCIBLES FOR TRANSFORMATION 301

☆ traversing the middle of the frequency shift ☆ changes must happen slowly for integrity of mind, body, emotions ☆ you are "pregnant" and must take care of yourselves ☆ everything is explored through uniqueness ☆ you are a bridge and pathcutter ☆ the only voice you need to listen to is the quiet one within you ☆

ENERGY PACKETS AND THE CONSENSUS REALITY........308

☆ a "consensus reality" is an energy packet that has its own identity and self-awareness ☆ most people do not realize they are operating in a fictional world ☆ the Mind of the Creator is the only one that is truly "real" ☆ you REMEMBER the world you want to create because you have already experienced it ☆ "Commerce is king" in the consensus reality ☆ riding two horses ☆ this is not a rescue mission ☆ you are pioneers for a new world ☆

TERRA LESSON #1: OF CABBAGES AND KINGS 314

☆ you must detach, step back, and simply sing your note ☆ each person is naturally drawn to what's "theirs" ☆ the "new song" was written before the world was formed ☆ no one can change their note ☆ any imposition of a particular ideology is tyranny ☆ "wishing does not make it so" ☆ not everyone carries the same amount of passion ☆ your job is to stand together and continue to sound the note for Terra ☆

TERRA LESSON #2: BUILDING BRIDGES 321

☆ logic branches create linear sequences ☆ linear sequences result in different timelines ☆ there is always one choice that is more "right" than the others ☆ the Hosts reside outside of linear time; they can only estimate when things will emerge at the physical level ☆ a true wave has a wave shape to it ☆ the times ahead will be very intense ☆ your task and your life are unique to you ☆

THE TIME OF SORROWS 330

☆ many losses and much sorrow are coming for many people in the world ☆ the calamities serve to heal the planet ☆ many are destined to depart through the portal of "death" ☆ there is nothing to fix and nothing to stop ☆ no one is being punished or judged ☆ a time of tyranny will follow this time of sorrows ☆ more controls will be needed to maintain order ☆ this is the PURGING of the suffering that has gone on for millennia ☆ your time to be of use is not until this time of sorrows has ended ☆

A CHANGE IN PLANS **336**

☆ higher-density ETs want to accelerate the unfolding of events on Earth ☆ symptoms of the acceleration ☆ we must move up in frequency more quickly ☆ our clearing must also occur more quickly ☆ resistance keeps the energy from moving ☆ we each have attendants helping us ☆ create sanctuary within yourself and your immediate environment ☆

LISTEN WITHIN. **339**

☆ ignore the chaos ☆ no one else has your answers ☆ strengthen your ability to quiet yourself and listen to your inner wisdom ☆ what is truly real is inaccessible with the physical senses ☆ you need to discern what is right for YOU ☆ pay attention to how things FEEL ☆ be selective ☆ get rid of clutter in every way you can ☆ listen within ☆

MOVING INTO UNITY WITH ALL THAT IS **345**

☆ wait for clarity before acting ☆ our journey is mapped in our DNA ☆ the "real you" is nonlocal ☆ "You" are everywhere and in everything you perceive ☆ you have to realize this for yourself, as an inherent feature of your experience of life ☆ we have "designer genes" ☆ THINGS can't make us happy ☆ in full consciousness, we can directly manifest whatever we desire ☆

ON "CLEARING" **351**

☆ we are clearing the emotions and memories from 4.5 billion years of existence ☆ everything will be cleansed ☆ polarity will intensify ☆ the process proceeds from within ☆ with full awareness, everything "makes sense" ☆ the highest and best use of your time and energy is to pay attention to the things that are "up" for clearing within yourself and to move through them ☆

ABOUT "VISION" **358**

☆ seeing more clearly can be uncomfortable at times ☆ everything that has been tangled together must be untangled ☆ we are pulsing you with energies that free up the tangles within you ☆ be cautious about seeking help outside of yourself ☆ you must go INTO your pain, INTO your fear, without resisting either of those ☆ releasing resistance results in a smoother journey ☆

DENSITY 3.8 365

☆ all movement occurs as a form of oscillation ☆ special forces have to remain near density 3.0 ☆ we are losing our present sense of identity ☆ as you move upward into fourth density, everything that is not compatible with that level of being has to drop away ☆ the process must be gradual ☆ many of your "wants" are just habit ☆

LET IT BE 372

☆ leave the drama behind ☆ we are invisible to those who cannot recognize the essence and vibration of love ☆ everyone is a necessary player ☆ no one is exempt from doing the inner work ☆ let it be ☆

LIVING FROM THE CALM CENTER.........................378

☆ you must become more fully a part of the working team and source more from within yourselves ☆ feel into every situation as it presents ☆ the yes/no technique ☆ practice the principles you have been given ☆ the "domino effect" ☆ you must be ready to respond to changes quickly and without hesitation ☆ get your "news" from within ☆

ARTICLES 385

INTRODUCTION TO THE ARTICLES 386

This section of the book contains four articles that are intended to supplement the material contained in the other sections.

THE ORIGINAL VISION (1982) 388

The original vision I received in 1982. This vision laid out the blueprint for what later became Operation Terra. It will culminate in the removal of around 6-7 million people (plus many plants and animals) who will migrate to Terra via a 25-year stay on Midway Station — an extremely large mothership that is approximately 80% the size of Earth.

Table of Contents xv

PHASE SHIFT TO 4ᵀᴴ DENSITY 394

When ice melts into water, more energy has been absorbed, breaking the molecular bonds and allowing the molecules to move more freely. The same is true as we shift from third density to fourth density. We are breaking loose from the confines of our limited ideas of who and what we are and moving out of time-bound thinking into a more fluid reality. The only thing that will be left after this phase shift will be those waveforms that are vibrating at a frequency that is compatible with that of Terra.

OUR EXPERIENCES WITH THE OT SHIPS 401

Experiences with and photographs of the OT ships, reported from all over the world

YOU MAY NOT HAVE TO DIE................................415

The normal life cycle of a butterfly includes its physical transformation from a caterpillar into a butterfly. What, then, has happened to the caterpillar? Has it died? No, it has simply changed its form.

In order to inhabit Terra, we have to transform into totally different kinds of bodies that will be appropriate for THAT level of reality. Those of us who are destined to physically colonize Terra are taking our bodies with us, so in that sense, we will not die. We will simply change our form.

ARCHIVES 421

ARCHIVES SUMMARY.....................................422

The Operation Terra perspective is radically different than almost any other source of information and these four chapters summarize it nicely. I encourage you to spend some time with them and see what they stimulate in you.

BULLETIN, August 12, 2007 424

Once you have fully crossed over into 4.0 awareness, you will begin to access the full range of your abilities — all while maintaining a physical presence within 3D. This chapter describes that shift and what you can expect to experience as you move through it.

EXCERPT FROM "PRIVATE MESSAGE," March 23, 2009 427

To begin with, all things are now in motion that will lead to the conclusion of the arc of experience that began when the elohim came together to precipitate this portion of reality out of their beingness. This point in time is still many years into your future. It is only then that you will fully appreciate what has occurred and what you have created.

AN EXPERIENCE WITH "OCEAN" 430

One man's experience with "Ocean" that confirms everything that the Hosts have said about the nature of reality and the nature of the Creator Itself.

EXCERPT FROM "DATES, GATES AND MATES, PART 2" 434

☆ there is really only one "cause" that is responsible for everything that exists ☆ the Oversoul has no gender and is complete; there is no need to find one's other parts in order to be complete ☆ to the Creator, all of Its creations are good ☆ everything is perfect just the way it is at any given moment ☆ everything sources from and is scripted by the Oversouls ☆ there is no version of this present planet Earth that comes through any of the 12 wormholes intact ☆

ABOUT THE AUTHORS 442
ABOUT THE PUBLISHER, CONTACT INFORMATION 445

INTRODUCTION

This book contains information about the journey to a totally new world — Terra — that will arise from this one shared reality that we refer to as Planet Earth. This is the next step in human and galactic evolution, and there are three audiences for whom this information is intended.

The first is made up of people who will physically make the journey to Terra at this time, within their current incarnation. They will provide the bodies that will bring forth the first generation born onto Terra. The second group is made up of those who will drop their present bodies and be born on Terra approximately 150-200 years from now. The third group is made up of those who will drop their present bodies, experience additional incarnations on future third-density planets, and finally incarnate on Terra as part of its future generations.

This material has been developed over many years, beginning in 1999. Most of the material came in the form of a series of Messages, telepathically transmitted from fifth-density beings who refer to themselves as the Hosts of Heaven.

(Their communications have come through my third-density (3D) expression, named Sara. Adonna is the fourth-density (4D) being that I will express as on Terra, the 4D positive-polarity version of our present Planet Earth. In March 2017, I discovered that my fifth-density (5D) name is Oriole, my identity as one of the Hosts.)

The Hosts have said that each person's experience will be uniquely their own. They have also indicated that it is important for us to become more self-reliant and independent of outside authorities, including the Hosts. Everyone has the capacity to discern what is "right action" for them in each moment, and that will be the best way to navigate your course through the days ahead. "Listen within" at every decision point and you will have a smoother journey.

Your script has already been written by your Oversoul, so you can be sure that you will get to where you are supposed to go. No one else has your answers or magic ways of eliminating the necessity of doing the inner work, so just remember to breathe, remain grounded and centered, and to take each day as it comes, one step at a time. That's all you can really do, anyway. Good journey!

Love and blessings,
Sara/Adonna/Oriole

ABOUT OPERATION TERRA: THE BIG PICTURE

The term "Operation Terra" refers to two different things: a body of information and an operational concept. It is called "Operation Terra" because its primary focus is *on the planet herself*, and only secondarily on her lifeforms. The planet has an intimate relationship with her lifeforms and has absorbed a tremendous amount of emotional and thoughtform debris, primarily from her human occupants over the millennia that she has supported them.

All of this debris must somehow be cleansed from the planet in order for her to ascend and fully attain what she was designed to become — a totally NEW planet, one that has never been inhabited before. Operation Terra is the mechanism through which both the planet and its lifeforms will ascend and attain what can only be referred to as an exalted and glorified state when compared with the present situation.

Every atom, every particle of matter on Terra will be fully conscious and cooperate with everything else in a way that is difficult to comprehend from our present state of limited awareness, but both the physical form and the consciousness of every lifeform that makes the trip to Terra (plants and animals included) will be transformed in the course of their own ascension, which will take place in parallel with hers.

The core information in this book was initially presented as a series of 51 Messages — cosmic "lessons" from celestial beings who refer to themselves as the Hosts of Heaven. The Messages received from the Hosts carry light codes that will be responded to by those who carry the matching codes in their own DNA. (There is more detail about this in the Overview chapter of The Messages section.)

In the time before time existed, the elohim were the product of the First Thought of the Creator. Together, they co-created (and continue to create) everything that exists in a manifest form. The concept of

Operation Terra came into being when 144,000 elohim came together and precipitated this reality out of their beingness, approximately 4.5 billion years ago. Planet Earth was intended to become Terra from its inception, and we are now playing our parts in the culmination and fulfillment of that design.

The current operational task is one of assisting Planet Earth in her ascension to her next form — the NEW Earth, Terra — and the colonization of that entirely new planet by groups of pioneers from the present planetary civilizations throughout the galaxy. In order to help the present planet to rise in frequency and shed the accumulated debris, the elohim have projected themselves into the Earth plane as ordinary humans who serve two functions.

The first of these was to act as human lightning rods to ground the higher Light into the core of the present planet, which was necessary to flush out the debris and speed up the spin rates of the particles that make up the physical mass of the planet and everything on her.

This could only be done from within the planet's aura. It couldn't be done from a distance. It had to be done on the ground, so those of us who are currently part of Operation Terra and are walking around on the ground volunteered to "come down" to provide that assistance to the planet and for the overall "op."

The second task was to personally take on a portion of the pain that had been absorbed by the planet and transform it within ourselves. Both of these tasks are being performed by those of us who volunteered to do that, and we are being assisted by those who remain at the higher levels. (There are about 40 million galactic volunteers assisting approximately 6 million of us on the ground.)

We will also provide the living bridge between Planet Earth and Terra by leaving the planet for a time and transforming into the beings who will colonize Terra. We will accomplish this on board a very large mothership (approximately 80% the size of Planet Earth), that we refer to as Midway Station.

Once we have fully colonized Terra and put in place all of the necessary supportive structures, we will also bring forth the first generation to be born there. For other planetary civilizations that will colonize Terra, their process will take place on their home planets and then their colonists will migrate to Terra from there.

Every planet has a theme and a principal activity. Earth's theme is "beauty" and her principal activity is "seeking harmony in diversity."

Once it is fully colonized, the entire planet of Terra will act as a galactic cultural center, dedicated to demonstrating and attaining that harmony across a broad spectrum of galactic cultures. In addition, everyone and everything on Terra will exemplify beauty in an exalted way. Terra will be the highest attainment for Planet Earth.

The Earth-based portion of the "op" (as we fondly refer to it) is a cooperative venture between those who are on the ground (the "ground troops") and those who surround the planet on many levels of being.

The Hosts have indicated that we are living during a time when a major cosmic cycle will complete and result in an entirely new Creation, giving rise to the emergence of several different "futures," each of which occupies a different timeline and compartment of reality. The Operation Terra material focuses on the single timeline that leads to Terra (which is only one of those "futures"). At some point in time, the timeline to Terra will be totally separate from and independent of those other timelines and destinations.

On September 23, 2011, a grid of 12 stargates was activated by a group of people in South America. These stargates are actually portals to wormholes that connect the entrance points that exist in this reality with their respective emergence points in other realities. This provided the mechanism for the eventual emergence of 12 different "futures" from this one shared reality that we refer to as Planet Earth.

The number of people from Planet Earth who will end up on Terra is a little less than 1/10th of 1% of the present population, or approximately 6 million people. They have been created by their Oversouls to make this journey because that is what the Creator wants to experience through them. That is the only reason that anything exists at all.

Being a participant in Operation Terra is not a matter of having earned anything or being more special than anyone else. The Oversoul simply creates its many projections in response to the directives issued by its overlighting eloha (the singular form of elohim, which is a plural word). The elohim and their respective Oversouls are the intermediaries for carrying out the Creator's desires. The Creator desires to experience EVERYTHING, so the elohim and their Oversouls serve the Creator by creating projections of everything that exists. ALL paths serve the Creator.

Operation Terra is only one tiny part of the larger drama, but it means everything to those of us who are part of it. These teachings from the Hosts speak to the core of our being and our soul. It is very common for people to weep when they first come across the material — in both joy and relief when they discover that they are not the only ones who know what they know. We are relatively few in number, are widely scattered all over the world, and are often quite isolated from others who share our vision and understanding.

Operation Terra has a radically different view from most other sources of information because it clearly states that we are here to SUPPORT and ALLOW the "earth changes" as a necessary part of the cleansing and ascension of the planet. In other words, we take the view that "There is nothing to fix, nothing to stop, and nothing to pray for except an outcome that is in keeping with the highest good for all."

We, too, are being purged of all energy patterns that are not part of OUR essential self, as nothing of the "old world" can be taken with us into the new world that we will inhabit, and THAT requires US to offer up all that WE contain, without judging any of it as being outside of love.

On our particular timeline (one of several that will exist simultaneously), we will witness the ending of the present Creation and the removal of all lifeforms from Planet Earth that are above the mineral kingdom. Massive Earth changes will culminate in a geophysical Pole Shift that will leave the planet barren and totally devoid of life and water. (This will be a shift in the planet's physical axis of rotation, not a shift in the magnetic poles, which has occurred before and may occur again.) There are many large fleets of spacecraft arrayed around the planet to assist in this transition, and all will arrive at the destinations that their Oversouls designed them for.

In the separating out of the timelines from one another, many will appear to die on any given timeline, but in fact they may be continuing their lives on another timeline and experiencing another scenario, so all expressions will be provided for. Many will pass out of their bodies and remain on the astral plane until another incarnational opportunity presents. Some of THOSE will incarnate on Terra as the first generation of Terran natives.

The Hosts have given us a roadmap for OUR journey and told us how to deal with these times. However, in each moment that presents, we must also turn within ourselves for our answers and respond to it in the way that is most right for us as individuals. Our spiritual team is with us every step of the way, and we are never alone in this journey, even if we can't physically see those who accompany us.

This is a journey of transformation of both consciousness and form. Everything on Terra will be exalted. Every atom will be consciously connected to the whole, and all will operate on a foundation of peace, joy, and love — cooperation instead of competition, harmony instead of conflict, and full, conscious, ECSTATIC communion with the Creator at all times.

"Let go, let God [handle the details]" is the operative order of the day. Surrender IS the way through the chaos, and we simply need to bow our heads and let the winds and waves of change flow on past us. No one will be unaffected by what comes now, and no one will be lost.

THE TIMELINE FOR OPERATION TERRA

By definition, a timeline is a *linear* representation of important events in the order in which they occur. It can also mean a schedule for events that are supposed to occur. Both of these meanings apply when we are talking about the timeline for Operation Terra.

I have emphasized the word "linear" in the above definition because it describes the experience of everything that occurs WITHIN the parameters of space and time in a physical reality. However, the Creator, the elohim, and the Oversouls exist OUTSIDE OF time. They are not physical manifestations, so they operate outside of time because time only exists as an aspect of physical expression.

An event occurs at a specific location at a specific time or within a specific timeframe. It is unique. A similar event may occur in another location and/or at another time, but each of those events is defined by when and where it took place within a physical reality.

Events also occur and can be perceived in non-physical realities, but they cannot be defined in linear terms because in non-physical realities, everything is present simultaneously. One can access any event whenever one wants to do so, just by placing their attention on it.

For those of us who are still veiled, linear time is what we are most familiar with and we usually think of past, present, and future as being laid out along a single line like beads on a string. We assume "past" occurs before "present," which in turn occurs before "future." However, in actuality, past, present and future coexist simultaneously. If I choose to, I can perceive forward and/or backwards in time by using my subtle senses.

I have experienced being one of the 144,000 elohim who came together to precipitate this sector of reality out of our beingness 4.5+ billion years ago and I have experienced Terra as she will be when fully colonized. Those two circumstances are the beginning and end points of the sequence of events that define the timeline for Operation Terra.

We are now witnessing the final years of that timeline and will see it through to its completion approximately 250-300 Earth years from now, when Terra is fully colonized and a new group of elohim takes over the responsibility for the rest of that particular journey.

All of it already exists, has already happened, and was already present at the very beginning of that timeline. It is a known outcome, so the mystery lies in making the journey itself, not in the nature of the result. However, the only way I can describe what HAS happened and what WILL happen is in the linear terms of past, present and future, so that is the approach I will use to describe the timeline for Operation Terra.

The CONTEXT for Operation Terra is a cosmology in itself. Prior to the moment in which Operation Terra was conceived, the Creator had Its First Thought. It thought that It would like to create beings that would then create other beings and through all of that, the Creator could experience Itself through Its creations. The elohim were the result of that First Thought and they then created everything else so that the Creator could experience Itself through it.

At first, there was only the single, positive polarity of "service to others" (STO). Everything existed solely to serve others, including the Creator Itself. Everything was very harmonious and did not provide much drama for the Creator to experience through Its creations, so It had another Thought. It created the negative polarity of "service to self" (STS), whose nature was to serve itself above all others, and this introduced the behaviors of selfishness, greed, and competition (instead of cooperation), along with the emotion of fear and its derivatives, anger, rage and hate.

The negative polarity actively spread throughout the manifest Creation and everywhere it became dominant, it sought to satisfy its perpetual desire for "more." This provided much more drama for the Creator to experience, but it was also very destructive and eventually created a negative spiral that would destroy everything if it was not somehow stopped.

The Creator then had another Thought. It had satisfied Its desire for more drama and wished to preserve and restore the rest of what It had created, so Its next Thought was the idea of restoring the Creation to its original state and returning everything to the way it originally had been before the negative polarity had been inserted into the mix.

In response to this particular Divine Idea, a group of 144,000 elohim joined together to furnish the circumstances that would provide that restoration, and Operation Terra was born. Those elohim made a pact with each other to be responsible for Operation Terra and keep it on course until its goals were fulfilled. There were many times when the elohim had to produce extensions of themselves in order to counter the effects of negative polarity influences and this time in which we live is one of those times.

The elohim have incarnated as ordinary humans and are walking around on the surface of the planet, but they are not ordinary humans. They have a special task to perform, and they are going to achieve it. It has already happened outside of time, and they are the players that will carry it out WITHIN time.

Operation Terra is not just about Planet Earth. It will certainly restore Planet Earth's destiny to become Terra, but once she is fully established, the emergence of Terra will also mark a turning point — the shift from the "outbreath" to the "inbreath" and the path that leads to reabsorption back into the godhead for the entire manifest reality, paving the way for a new outbreath to occur.

This will also reverse the outward expansion of the negative polarity until all is as it was in that earlier phase of the cosmos, and the negative polarity will ultimately disappear. The emergence of Terra will also mark a new phase for the galactic mind.

All manifestations have consciousness. Planets and stars are conscious beings, and so are galaxies and universes. Our Milky Way Galaxy is only one of hundreds of billions of galaxies in the known universe, and Planet Earth is just a speck that revolves around an insignificant star located in the outer fringes of that galaxy.

However, when Terra is fully colonized, the interaction and cooperation between all of the galactic cultures that are represented there will pave the way for a new phase of cooperation and harmony throughout the entire galaxy, and THAT will change the nature of the galactic mind. Eventually that change will spread to other galaxies and will ultimately penetrate and affect the entire manifest Creation.

Just as WE are seeds for a new level of cooperation across all life-forms, Terra will act as the seed for a new level of cooperation across all inhabited planets, and through those planets, the consciousness of their respective suns will be affected and changed.

Operation Terra marks the restoration phase for the entire manifest Creation, and its effects will extend beyond counting. That being said, our PRESENT focus is on the immediate future, when there will be a series of events that precede and directly lead to Planet Earth's ascension and transformation into Terra and the concurrent ascension and transformation of everything that will be transplanted onto her from Earth.

The first phase of this will involve the transformation of the first and second waves of future Terrans who are part of the "ground crew" at the time of this writing. They will join with the rest of the galactic volunteers to remove everyone and everything from the surface of Planet Earth that is making the trip to Terra at this time, a process/event that we refer to as the evacuation.

The majority of those making the trip from Planet Earth to Terra at this time are the millions who make up the third wave and those who will accompany them in the field. The third wave will go through the period the Hosts have referred to as "The Last Days" and "The Time of Sorrows" in order to be mentally and emotionally prepared to accept being taken on board our ships during the evacuation.

The world conditions that will characterize that time are becoming increasingly visible to those "with eyes to see," and all signs point to the fruition of what the Hosts have told us about those times. The estimate I am being given for this preparatory period is 3-5 years, but the Hosts do not experience linear time, so that is just an estimate, based on what they can observe about what is taking place "down here." There have been surprises in the past, and there may be more surprises in the future. Nonetheless, no matter how long it takes to play out, it's clear where it's all going and there is nothing more to be said on that subject.

To summarize, those of the first and second waves will be lifted first and transformed so that they can play their part in evacuating the rest. The fleets of ships will be temporary processing centers until the evacuees can debark onto Midway Station, where everything will remain until it is time to physically transfer to Terra.

Following the evacuation, the earth changes will culminate in an abrupt and cataclysmic Pole Shift that will throw off everything (including her oceans and all forms of water) except the bedrock of the planet, and no lifeforms will be left, either on the surface or beneath it. Other timelines will experience different scenarios, so the descriptions in this chapter only apply to the timeline for Operation Terra.

In addition to those who have made their way to Terra from Earth, other planetary civilizations from higher-density, positive polarity planets will also create colonies on Terra. They will be intimately involved in developing the plans for colonization and carry out their own actions in keeping with those plans. The Earth contingent will be ready to disembark onto Terra approximately 20-25 years after their arrival on Midway Station.

Once Terra is fully colonized and all structures are in place to properly receive the next generation, children will be conceived and born onto Terra and mature into the adults who will take over the governance of Terra from then on. This will mark the official end of the Operation Terra project and a new group of elohim will oversee Terra after that. After colonization begins, it will take approximately 150-200 Earth years before that final shift takes place. Once that has occurred, the pioneers will leave Terra and go on to other experiences and Operation Terra will finally end.

THE PURPOSE OF OPERATION TERRA

Operation Terra was created by 144,000 elohim 4.5+ billion years ago as their response to the Creator's expressed desire to restore the Creation to the way it had been before there had been a negative polarity. From its inception, Planet Earth has always been intended to act as the starting point for a bridge between its current form and how it will manifest when it ascends to become Terra. The emergence of Terra has always been intended to be the turning point in the process that will restore the Creation and eventually eliminate the negative polarity from that Creation.

Planet Earth has provided a rich environment for experiences of many kinds. There have been times during which those same elohim have had to project themselves onto the Earth to counter the actions of civilizations that had a different agenda in mind — one that would allow them to redirect the course of the planet to benefit themselves, which would ultimately destroy the planet and its lifeforms, as they have done repeatedly during the current reality.

During one such time (millions of years ago), some of us were incarnated as the last group of Guardians of the Galaxy. Over the course of three generations, we were defeated in our attempts to protect ourselves, our planet, and the galaxy, and our attackers were then free to spread their ways to Planet Earth. Our present world reflects much of their influence, which is harming a great deal of the planet and her lifeforms, many of which are becoming extinct. Much of the planet's beauty and richness is being destroyed, as well.

As projections of those same elohim, we are now walking around on the planet during the time period that will result in the emergence of Terra. Terra will manifest the planet's theme of "beauty" at its highest level. Her transplanted lifeforms will provide the means for fully achieving her principal activity of "seeking harmony in diversity." The interaction and cooperation between the different galactic cultures that will create colonies on Terra and/or visit her from other locations will have a profound and far-reaching effect on galactic cultures, the galactic mind, and ultimately on the nature of the entire manifest reality.

This is why there are so many galactic volunteers involved with Operation Terra. The effects will echo throughout the entire galaxy and directly affect both their home environments and the course of galactic evolution far into the future. They understand the significance of Operation Terra and what it ultimately means for the entire manifest reality.

Currently, Operation Terra is a massive undertaking that involves millions of embodied beings, approximately 6 million of whom are walking around on Earth as third-density humans, and approximately 40 million more who are volunteers from the higher-density, positive-polarity civilizations in our galaxy.

All of these individuals are involved in some way with assisting the present third-density, mixed-polarity planet known as Earth to fully manifest as her fourth-density, positive-polarity self, which we refer to as Terra. (The word "Terra" is Latin for "Earth.")

Terra is "the next step" for the planet and the next step for third-density humans who are destined to "graduate" to fourth-density positive polarity, either now or in a future incarnation. Third-density humans who are destined to "graduate" to the fourth-density NEGATIVE polarity will migrate to Terra's polar opposite, a fourth-density, negative-polarity planet. Terra will be a totally positive-polarity planet and in future generations, only fourth-density positive-polarity individuals will incarnate there.

Most of the third-density humans who presently live on Earth are of *mixed* polarity and will not "graduate" to either polarity at this time. Instead, they will experience additional third-density lives on other third-density "future" versions of our present planet until they, too, are ready to graduate to the fourth density as either one of these two polarities — positive or negative.

Operation Terra is a special task force whose purpose is to create the energetic pathway and provide the physical bridge between this planet and the soon-to-be-born NEW planet of Terra. The scope of the operation is twofold: 1) whatever is needed to assist all of the aspects involved in the *planet's* personal ascension, and 2) to gather up and prepare the various *lifeforms* that will be taken to Terra to complete the planet's emergence as a fourth-density, positive-polarity multicultural center for the entire galaxy. This purpose is being implemented in many ways:

1. By incarnating as ordinary third-density humans (the "ground troops"), Operation Terra participants have been acting as human "lightning rods" to ground the higher Light into the planet, thereby contributing to the infusion of energy that is purging the planet of the lower-frequency energies she has absorbed over her entire history as a third-density planet. Most of these lower-frequency energies were either emitted by the human portion of planetary life or by other lifeforms that suffered from the consequences of human actions on them and on their habitat.
2. By volunteering to take on a certain portion of the pain of the human experience and then transforming it from within themselves, the ground troops also decrease the amount of lower-frequency energies that must be cleared from the planet, thereby helping to ameliorate the Earth changes that occur as one of the mechanisms for clearing what the planet has absorbed.

    The preliminary Earth changes would be much more severe if it weren't for this assistance at the human level. This minimizes the amount of suffering for the present lifeforms on the planet until it is time for the final cataclysms that will culminate in a shift of the planet's axis of rotation — a geophysical Pole Shift involving crustal displacement — that will render the present third-density version of this planet uninhabitable for a very long time.
3. Many higher-density participants in Operation Terra are actively assisting the ground troops with the clearing of their cellular memory, thereby facilitating #2. This will neutralize all of the emotional charge that remains from all of the lives that were created by their Oversouls, so that only "essence" remains. Nothing of the old can be taken into the new.
4. Higher-density participants in Operation Terra are actively untangling the enmeshments that have taken place over the millions of years of interaction between different groups of individuals, so that each can go to its own "right place." Our DNA and light filaments are being restored to their original state and a

great deal of healing work is taking place, especially while we are asleep.

This process will prepare the ground troops for their individual roles in the physical evacuation of all of the lifeforms that will go on to colonize Terra and will eventually restore their former condition of full connection with Source. The colonists from the present planet will prepare for the colonization itself by spending 20-25 years on Midway Station (a large mothership approximately 80% the size of present-day Earth), or by returning to their home civilizations for a time and colonizing Terra from there.

5. Since most of the people on Earth will not be going to Terra at this time, Operation Terra is also seeding the "Terra" information into the consciousness of those who will make their way to Terra from the future third-density versions of our present planet. This seeding will ensure that the "homing" codes that lead one to go to Terra will survive the coming shift into a new Creation and will continue the migration to Terra over the millennia to come.

Earth's planetary theme is "beauty"; its principal activity is "seeking harmony in diversity." Terra will raise the present beauty of Earth to an exalted level. Terra will transform the "seeking of harmony in diversity" into the full realization (fulfillment) of that goal. The diversity reflected on Terra will be representative of the diversity of all of the positive-polarity cultures and lifeforms that exist throughout our entire galaxy.

This is all going to be something that has never existed before — totally new, birthed in a new Creation. Up until now, this level of co-operation and harmony across so many civilizations and cultures has only existed in various forms of galactic governance. It has never been housed in a single location. Just as we have capital cities for states and nations, Terra will be the "capital" planet for the entire galaxy. Assisting Earth to become Terra is the equivalent of sharing in the creation of a capital city, but on a much larger scale.

Because Terra will anchor the first step of the return that will eventually lead to the elimination of the negative-polarity worlds and beings, there are many of that polarity who would like to prevent Operation Terra from succeeding. However, this is already known and has been anticipated and provided for in the overall plan for the "op."

Between now and the actual completion of the evacuation, everything necessary to ensure the success of the evacuation itself will be provided by various participants in Operation Terra. Once the evacuation is complete, the colonization phase can proceed and when colonization is complete, Terra will be the result of a plan that had its beginnings 4.5+ billion years ago.

For those humans who will go on to experience more third-density lives before moving on to fourth density, Terra will also provide a future incarnational opportunity. Terra will evolve, the galaxy will evolve, and the manifest reality will also evolve.

Love is the ordering force that counters entropy. Entropy leads to the breakdown of complex forms to simpler ones. Since Terra will operate on a foundation of peace, love and joy, that foundation will support evolution into even more complex forms than those that exist on Terra at its beginning.

Terra is a gift to the entire manifest reality and we are privileged to be part of bringing her forth. The journey to Terra has required much of us, but the final result will be worth every bit of what has gone into creating it.

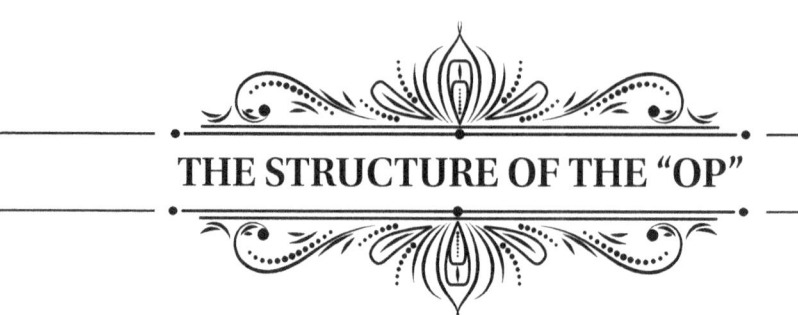

THE STRUCTURE OF THE "OP"

A certain order and structure is necessary for the Creation to function and not simply dissolve into chaos. This structure is implicit in the nature of a particular Creation and can be described in many ways. One way is to describe how all of the parts relate to one another. Another way is to describe the energy flows between the various components that make up the particular Creation. A third way is to describe the "tasks" that need to be carried out in order to satisfy the Creator's desire to experience Itself through Its creations.

At the human level, the most obvious structures are hierarchical ones. By hierarchical structures, I am referring to the way energy and information flows between different levels of the hierarchy (vertically) and between individuals who occupy the same level within the hierarchy (horizontally).

Even though everything on Terra will be in full connection with Source and thereby self-regulating within the context of the whole, there will still be a communal structure that reflects and supports the personal expression of every individual.

People will interact and gather together according to their own personal preferences for individual activities, family groupings, community-level activities, and interactions between one community or group and others. There will be many ways of interacting with others at all levels of Terran society.

All parts are needed for the whole or they would not exist. Every quark counts; every drop of water counts. Every atom is indispensable to the whole. Every organism has its part to play, and planets, stars, and galaxies also have their roles in the drama.

In order to understand the present structure of the "op," it is useful to look at what it will lead to, because what is yet to appear in the future will arise from what we can observe in the present.

Earth is about to become Terra. Terra will be a living showcase of all of the cultures and lifeforms found in all of the fourth-density, positive-polarity civilizations that exist throughout the entire galaxy. In addition to the colony that is created by the people who will migrate to Terra from Planet Earth, every one of those other civilizations will have its own colony on Terra. This is one reason why there are approximately 40 million galactic volunteers working to support Operation Terra. Terra is part of their own future, too.

There are two ways we can look at how things will manifest on Terra: *horizontally* (within the same frequency band) and *vertically*, across several levels of expression.

The Horizontal View

The "horizontal view" includes the enormous variety of cultures and physical lifeforms that are possible within fourth-density *positive-polarity* planets. (No fourth-density *negative* lifeforms or cultures will exist on Terra, so there will not be any viruses, bacteria, fungi, or any of the organisms that participate in death, disease and decay. There will also be no predation, so all of the species that prey upon others in third-density worlds will either be transformed or not go to Terra at all.)

Terra will have oceans, lakes, rivers and streams. Its landmasses will provide a variety of natural environments, from forests to more open areas of land that are suitable for raising food and creating villages, towns and cities. Each colony will be made up of smaller communities that take on a regional character. Each of these communities will be unique. Each person will live in the place that most matches their natural inclinations.

There will be interaction between communities within a given colony and interaction between the colonies themselves. All of this will be mediated by various levels of leadership and councils through which they can interact with leaders from other locations. Each council will have at least one representative who participates in other councils that have a broader reach.

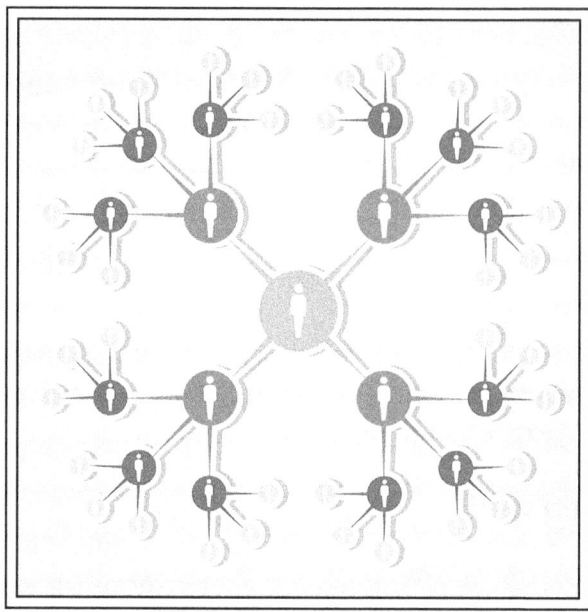
Interaction between individuals and councils

Every child that is born onto Terra will be supported in attaining its full potential and every adult will make their contribution to that, in keeping with their individual skills, talents, and natural interests. Every lifeform will fulfill the plan for its life. There will be no will other than Divine Will, no need for money as a means of exchange, and no ownership of anything (including other lifeforms, such as pets). No lifeform will serve another involuntarily. Everything on Terra will operate in keeping with the needs of the whole; every particle will be in full, conscious connection with the Creator.

The Vertical View

The "vertical view" is that of a spiritual hierarchy that expresses across multiple frequency bands. Since there is only One Life being lived, all forms of governance are a means of stepping down the energy and consciousness of Source through a series of energetic lenses. There is a hierarchy of forms, some of which are expressed physically and some of which are not.

The Structure of the "Op" 37

The "vertical view" is that of a spiritual hierarchy that expresses across multiple frequency bands.

Sananda is the cosmic name (a name that transcends all individual embodiments) for the being that incarnated on Earth more than 2,000 years ago as Y'shua bar Yosef (his original Aramaic name, later translated into other languages as "Jesus"). One of his tasks in that life was to "seed" some of the concepts for that phase of Operation Terra in a form that was appropriate to that historical time and culture, and we are living in the time that will bear the fruit from those seeds.

Sananda oversees all of us from a higher level of being and will be *energetically* present throughout the entire transition phase. He will not express in physical form on Terra, but he does preside over the Council of 24 of the Great Central Sun of our galaxy, whose embodied projections (the 24 Lords and Ladies) will make up the governing Tribunal on Terra.

The Council of 24 of the Great Central Sun of our galaxy interacts with the Council of the Central Sun of Andromeda Galaxy, the one closest to her in physical space and the "twin" to our galaxy. (Galaxies are conscious beings and these two are a mated pair.)

The Three Waves

The people who will migrate to Terra from Planet Earth are primarily individuals who came down from the higher densities to be part of this undertaking. The Hosts speak of three waves of migrants, all of whom are still on the ground (the "ground troops") at the time of this writing.

The first wave consists of those who are presently identified as being part of the leadership of the "op" as a whole. They are specialists and leaders in certain functional areas. Some of their present functions and roles will change during the transition period that is related to the evacuation and the period on board Midway Station, and will change again when Terra is colonized, but there will be commonalities present and visible across all of those phases, even if the details of their expression will change. For example, someone who is fascinated with data now will probably be processing data later, but in a different way.

Those who are currently part of the first wave and who move on to reside on Terra will continue to act in leadership roles and serve whatever purposes are specifically needed there, which will be different than those needed for the evacuation and those needed during the time that the colonization plans are being formulated and carried out, on board Midway Station and elsewhere. There will be ample time and support for each of these functional shifts, so that the transitions for a given individual will synchronize with everything else that is going on at any given time.

These first wave leaders tend to be "loners" here on Earth and will continue to be "loners" on Terra. They will tend to keep to themselves and will not reside in any of the individual communities on Terra. The entire planetary population will be their "community" and responsibility, but they will generally socialize with others like themselves, rather than with those in the communities.

Those in the second wave are more social by nature now and will continue to be more social later. They are usually quite good at networking with other leaders and with their own groups. They will be working directly with the evacuees (the third wave) during the evacuation and immediately afterward, while the evacuees are being prepared to go to Midway Station. During the process that takes place on Midway Station that will prepare for the colonization of Terra, the second wave will continue to work with the evacuees in a supportive leadership role.

Those of the second wave are the future Terran community leaders and they will reside in the specific community that they are naturally drawn to. Each of them will be specialists in certain types of activities and interact with similar leaders in other communities. There will be councils made up of representatives from different communities within a given colony and there will be councils made of representatives from different colonies. All of these councils will facilitate cooperation and communication between communities and between colonies.

The third wave is made up of the 6-7 million people who will be evacuated before the Pole Shift. On Terra, this third wave will make up the general population that will live in the communities within the colony of immigrants from the present Planet Earth. They are generally unaware of Operation Terra at this time and will go through a period of difficult times (which the Hosts refer to as "The Last Days" and "The Time of Sorrows") before they will be mentally and emotionally ready to accept being taken aboard the ships.

Special Forces

The Hosts also talk about "special forces" that will be personally involved in gathering together those of the third wave during the evacuation effort. They each have a circle of people with whom they are involved and whose trust they have earned. They may or may not be aware of Operation Terra at this time, but they will become aware of it by the time the evacuation takes place. When the time comes for the evacuation, the special forces personnel will gather their particular group and accompany them during the evacuation.

Galactic Volunteers

In addition, there are tens of thousands of 4D "operatives" on the ground at any given time. They are among the 40 million galactic volunteers who are assisting with the overall project and will be providing support in many ways to those of us who are currently veiled and not able to access all of our powers.

Once they have completed their tasks for Operation Terra, most of these galactic volunteers will return to their "home" civilizations. Each of their home civilizations will have its own colony on Terra, so they may decide to reside on Terra or they might only visit there from time to time.

Life on Terra

Terra will be like a global "theme park," with each colony acting as a showcase for its particular civilization. Once Terra is completely colonized, visitors from all over the galaxy will be able to experience all of these various civilizations co-existing in harmony with one another on the same planet. Nothing like this has ever happened before. It is a great step upward for the entire galaxy and will influence galactic evolution far into the distant future, way beyond our capacity to grasp or imagine.

By "divine design," each individual is naturally more inclined toward certain tasks, activities or relationships than toward others. Each person will be living their life in ways that fulfill their essence and their unique contribution to the whole. To this end, there will be "members" of different sorts of groupings, each with its own leaders.

Leaders of a given group will interface with leaders of other groups through participation in councils of various types, and each council's leaders will interface with leaders from other councils in yet other, "higher" councils.

This hierarchical structuring of the councils culminates in the governing Tribunal — the 24 Lords and Ladies that oversee and govern everyone and everything on Terra. The governing Tribunal is guided by beings from even higher levels of existence. Many who are part of the first wave from Earth will serve on some of the higher councils. A few of them will serve on the governing Tribunal, as well.

A new group of leaders will arrive by being among the first generation born onto Terra. Those of us who colonize Terra will conceive them and raise them, and they will take over the governance of Terra when they have reached full adulthood and we will subsequently leave.

Animal and plant lifeforms from the present planet will also be evacuated, transformed, and transplanted onto the new planet, Terra. Animal and plant forms from other fourth-density planets throughout the galaxy will be imported and brought to Terra as part of the colonization by the civilizations of these other planets. The level of diversity on Terra will be greater than in any other location in the galaxy, which will provide for learning experiences of many kinds and continually raise the knowledge level throughout the entire galaxy.

Everyone on Terra will be a galactic citizen. They will visit other galactic cultures on Terra and they will also travel throughout the galaxy. Visitors from all over the galaxy will also come to Terra to experience it firsthand. At the moment, it is difficult to imagine how much bigger our playground will be, but that will all change over the course of the next few years.

Everyone on Terra will be galactic citizens.

THE CURRENT PROCESS

The "ground troops" for Operation Terra are travelers within space and time. In order to carry out our service to this planet's transition from 3D Earth into 4D Terra, we left our higher-density existence and came down into 3D via a time loop; we will return to where we were before by exiting the time loop. Within the time loop, we experienced many 3D lives and now it is time for us to return to the lives and bodies we were in before. When we are finally in that restored state, we will each move on to our next tasks for the "op."

Because 4D inhabitants can move rather fluidly within linear time and can bilocate as necessary, those parts of ourselves that are expressing "up there" can also work directly on the ground. They can also work with us from there. More than one of us has had direct experiences of our 4D selves while still in these 3D bodies and as I write this, I feel I am sourcing much more from "up there" than I am from "down here."

At some point in this overall process (which will depend on our individual functions and roles within the "op" at any given time), our 3D bodies will be totally absorbed/subsumed into our 4D bodies and we will no longer express in 3D bodies except when necessary for certain situations. Everyone who came down into 3D from the higher densities will return to the way they were before, but for any who are not in the first two waves, this will not occur before the evacuation.

We Are Different

Those of us who are part of Operation Terra are different than most of those around us in several important ways:

We came into 3D to take on some of the pain of this world and to transform it within ourselves, which decreases the amount of pain the planet carries and has to release. By accomplishing our own transformation of this pain, we also create an energetic template for personal transformation. Future generations can make use of that template and find their way to Terra, too.

We also came to act as human lightning rods, to ground the higher Light into the planet that will support the necessary cleansing of the planet by flushing out everything that is not in keeping with her destiny as Terra. This infusion of Light is pushing out all of the thoughtforms that have been absorbed by the planet over millions of years. By our acting as conduits for more and more of this Light to enter the body of the planet, we are actually helping to facilitate the changes that are occurring on a global scale. They have to occur and it is part of our service to support them.

We aren't here to stop or fix anything in the present world; instead, we intend to participate in creating something entirely NEW that has never existed before. We understand that this present Creation has served its purpose and will be replaced by another one, so our best service is to detach from the drama and to allow the energies to flow without resisting them.

In order to complete the rest of our service to this planet, those of the first and second waves will be returning to where we were before and be AS we were before. We will help with the evacuation of approximately 1/10th of 1% of the present global population (approximately 6-7 million people, plus animals and plants), process them on our ships, and then house them on Midway Station once they are able to function in that frequency band.

The preparations to colonize Terra will take place on Midway Station, a large spherical mothership that is approximately 80% the size of the present Planet Earth, and everyone will proceed according to the next step in their individual journey of service to the Creator. Many of the galactic volunteers will return to their home planets and some of them will be colonists on Terra or instrumental in setting up their home planet's colony on Terra. Actual colonization will begin approximately 20-25 years after the evacuation takes place.

The individuals from the first and second waves are making their completions with 3D now. Some of their animals are also going to be taken into 4D. Animals and humans will enter 4D somewhat differently, but all of them will return to their previous identities to prepare for their individual roles in the evacuation and afterward.

Once one has completed the shift into full 4D consciousness and awareness, they can appear in any body and location that a situation requires. This ability does not have to be learned. Once the shift into 4D is complete, it is automatically operative and available.

Clearing the Cellular Memory

Many years ago, I was shown a technology that is used for the process of clearing the cellular memory. I believe a form of this technology is already being applied to those of the first and second waves while we sleep and it may also be used to complete our clearing process once we have been lifted onto the ships if that hasn't completed by then.

Translucent ovoid cylinders are equipped with hinged lids and electronic sensors that can detect and interpret a person's energy field. They can each accommodate one person in a supine position. The cylinder acts as a sort of isolation chamber and its occupant is in a peaceful, unconscious state (similar to very deep sleep) while the process of erasing their cellular memory proceeds.

The sensor readings provide the data that is used to produce a canceling pattern of energy — an exact energetic opposite of the pattern being cleared. The canceling pattern is applied to the person until the sensors indicate that that particular pattern has been totally cleared. The lid remains closed until the session is complete, after which it opens automatically. A technician helps the occupant to get up and go to a rejuvenating pool to rest and recover.

The patterns that need to be cleared have an innate priority with regard to each other, which the technology can detect and schedule additional sessions until all of the residual 3D patterns in the cellular DNA have been cleared. Only the emotional residue or "charge" is cleared. The data itself remains intact, so a person can remember their personal history, but without an emotional charge, it's just data and not very interesting except as it contributes to something being experienced in a given moment.

This is very similar to some of the radionics machines available on 3D Earth today, only far more sophisticated and complex. Technicians oversee the overall process and make sure everything is functioning properly, but otherwise everything is highly automated. Once a person's cellular memory has been cleared of all emotional charge, they are ready to take up their new life in a higher vibrational environment, although there is still a time of adaptation to one's new circumstances while one learns or remembers to function in 4D ways.

(In addition, some form of "radiant" processing (the Messages refer to it as "sonic cleansing") is being applied to the "ground troops" even now. Many have reported feeling these energies being applied to their bodies and I also have experienced them myself on many occasions. At the time of this writing, it is rare for me to NOT feel them if I awaken during the night or early morning.)

Midway Station

All of the evacuees will initially be taken aboard our ships. After they have had a period of acclimatization on the ships and have actually witnessed the Pole Shift from the safety of near-Earth space, they will each be placed in the cocoon cylinders for further processing. Their vibrational frequency will rise as the heavier emotions are erased from their cellular memory.

Their processing time aboard the ships will clear enough of their cellular memory to allow them to match the vibrational frequency of Midway Station. When that process is sufficiently complete, they will be taken to Midway Station. Once there, their transformational process will continue; it may take an additional 2-3 years before they are ready to be active participants in the actual preparations for colonization.

Midway Station is equipped to adjust its own frequency level and ALL of its occupants will be going through a process that allows them to be gradually raised in frequency until they are at the frequency that exists on Terra.

Initially, the vibrational frequency of Midway Station will be "midway" between the vibrational frequency of the present Planet Earth and the vibrational frequency that will exist on Terra. (That's why we call it "Midway Station.")

Midway Station's frequency can be gradually raised, similar to how the water level in one of the locks in the Panama Canal can be gradually raised to allow a seagoing ship to enter at a lower water level and be floated upward to exit at a higher one.

Preparing for Colonization

The preparations for colonization will take several years, as measured in linear time. During that period, Earth will be completing her own transformation. Her present body will remain lifeless and fallow for a very long time. It will be devoid of all water and life. She will transcend that form and emerge in the next frequency band as Terra. Terra will be a totally new planet, and it will take some time for all of its features to appear. During that time, her future colonists will be preparing to occupy her.

Preparations will take place in many locations throughout the galaxy, not just aboard Midway Station. Only the colony of those who are migrating from the present Planet Earth will prepare on board Midway Station and the only reason even they have to do that is because their own planet will not be habitable during that time.

Correspondences specialists will travel between all of the civilizations that will colonize Terra, gathering data and helping formulate the plans for colonization in such a way that all of the colonies will be anticipated and provided for.

By the time all is ready on the planetary surface, the future colonists will also be ready and colonization will begin. Once the first generation of Terra-born natives has arrived and matured, those who made up the transition team will go on to the next step in their individual journey. It is estimated that this will occur approximately 200 years after the evacuation completes, when Terra is fully colonized and everything is in place for that first generation and their offspring.

We all have a front-row seat for the most dramatic time in Planet Earth's existence. Detach from the drama and remain neutral toward whatever you observe. Surrender IS the way through. There is nothing to stop and nothing to fix, so remember to breathe, ground, and center, and above all, breathe slowly and deeply as you relax into the ride.

No one will be unaffected by what comes now, and no one will be lost. Remember that as you witness the changes that are necessary to accomplish this shift from one Creation to a totally new one. This is why you came. This is why you are here. Remember who you are and what you are here to do.

ABOUT CHANNELING

These Messages were first offered to the world through the medium of the Internet, beginning on June 30, 1999. My original impulse had been to create a website through which I could share my personal views about what I saw was wrong with the world around me. However, at the moment my fingers were poised over the keyboard to set up the website account, the Hosts sounded a tone in my right ear — their signal to me to pick up my "inner telephone" and to hear what they had to say.

I had been in training for my role in connection with Operation Terra for more than 18 years at that point in time and had a good working relationship with the Hosts by then. They have been quick to redirect me whenever I strayed from the extremely narrow path I have been called to follow, and in the beginning, I needed a lot of their help!

I mention this because it is easy for people to read this material and then expect me to answer for it, as if I were some expert on the bigger picture behind it. I do have some skill as a conduit for these communications and can reply intelligently and in depth as to the content of the transmissions that I receive, but I am walking the same walk of faith and trust, wearing my particular blindfold, that everyone else is. I am currently anchored at another level of reality, but neither I nor the Hosts are omniscient. We respond to whatever shows up as it emerges in front of us, and that's just how life is at the higher levels of being.

On June 28, 1999, the guidance I received was as follows: "We suggest that, instead of focusing on the world that is dying, you offer a vision of hope that people can carry with them to sustain them in the days ahead." From the vision I had received in 1982, I knew exactly what was meant by "the days ahead," and I resonated with that intent immediately. In that moment, Operation Terra emerged as the focus for the rest of my time on the ground, although I still did not know exactly how I would proceed with it.

Two days later, they "rang" my ear again, and this time they made a specific request: "Would you be willing to deliver a series of Messages for us and to share them with others?" In all of my years of training, I had never been asked to share any of the material I received with anyone else. This would require another step of deeper faith in the unseen and the continued willingness to "put my neck up to the knife" in the service to which I am called.

For those who have never "channeled," a little explanation might be helpful here. I am naturally reclusive. To be a good channel, one must open oneself up in a way that does not allow one to "preview" or "edit" what comes through. One must train one's ego to step aside and be willing to say whatever is presented, even if it might seem "wrong" or "crazy," or any number of other concerns about how it will be perceived/received by others.

For me, this results in a form of hesitancy every time I am asked to do this. Until the flow begins and I move fully into it, there is a certain amount of anxiety. For me, no matter how many times it has worked in the past, there is always the question, "Will it work now?"

That initial feeling never goes away completely, so it's a little like having to "kill my ego" each time I am asked to receive information. Even after all of these years of doing this, I still have to work at quieting myself enough to trust what comes through. However, it's also been a good tool for spiritual development. Recognizing and transcending one's ego is essential on the path to full mastery.

Given the nature of telepathic communication, there is no way to separate the source of the material from the personality, vocabulary, and biases of the person bringing it through. Not many people are well-trained or suited for this kind of work, and there is no material anywhere that is not colored in some way by the channel. It is a skill, developed through a lot of work and practice. It also requires one to continually do the inner work, as well.

There has been a maturation within the channeling field itself, progressing from the curtained chambers of séances in the late 1800s to the myriad forms and sources of information that form a veritable flood today. Unfortunately, not much of that flood of information is of high quality and a *lot* of it is actually deceptive or is just a projection of the personal views of the person bringing it through.

After so many years of doing this, it is easy for me to see these personal colorations in both my own and other people's material, regardless of whether it was brought through in full trance (where the channel is literally taken over by another being), "conscious channeling" (which is what I do — I am always fully present and aware when I receive the impress), or methods like automatic writing and Ouija boards, which also give some measure of control to the being that is presenting the information.

I prefer to remain fully present and to not give any being any control over me. This allows me to exercise some degree of discernment and to question or totally cut off any communication that feels "off" in any way. Nonetheless, there *is* personal coloration in every instance and there is no way of avoiding that, given the nature of the process itself.

This is further complicated by the fact that there *are* entities who seek to use a channel to feed through disinformation, with the dual aim of discrediting the channel and also sowing confusion in the listener, so that the result is skewed to their particular agenda. It takes constant "testing" and discernment to discriminate as to when something feels "off," and it is a very tricky business indeed to attempt to do this with any degree of purity.

In the end, one has to surrender up ALL attachments, even to being "right" or "good." As one's skills mature and one's spiritual opening progresses, the material deepens accordingly. I can see that in my own work, as well. My personal perspective and sense of identity have radically changed over time, and that has also affected the material itself, my relationship to it, and my task as I perceive it now.

I am sometimes asked about how I receive this information. I am fully conscious and fully present, although in a deeply altered state that I have trained myself to enter at will. The transmission comes in as a holographic stream of telepathic impressions, which I perceive with all of my subtle senses. They present as a total, immersive experience, which my brain then attempts to translate into words that convey the experience as best as any words can convey any experience.

(For the website presentation of the information, I also choose specific images and colors to visually convey this feeling quality. I rely on my body's response to the choices I am considering and the Hosts have also been very hands-on with the creation of this new site, sometimes preferring a given image over the one I would have chosen and conveying their preferences to me.)

If I'm not sure which word is best to convey the feeling I get from the telepathic impress, I may try to use a different word to convey the feeling I am getting and can then feel which word is the right one to use. The right one just *feels* best, even if my conscious mind and personal awareness would not have chosen to express the impress that way.

The passage of time has revealed the precision and accuracy of the specific words I have used to convey the information given to me, and this is yet another way I know that this information does not originate from within me or my conscious mind. I simply did not know enough at the time I received the information to have expressed it that way.

There is a characteristic "signature" in the communications from the Hosts that I know is uniquely theirs and that helps me trust the communications themselves. The written words are carrier waves for the Light codes that accompany them. There is a poetic cadence to the Messages that is very soothing, almost like a lullaby at times; that soothing quality produces a temporary relaxation of one's mental chatter and the "but, but" protests that often get in the way of receiving what is being transmitted.

When you read the written words, the Light codes stream into you through the act of encountering them. The written words engage your conscious mind, enabling you to be more receptive to the Light codes. If you carry the matching codes within you, the Light codes will activate the internal remembrance of the information you *already* contain and you will recognize it as "yours." If you do *not* carry the matching codes, they will not have this effect, although you might still enjoy reading the material for the ideas it presents. The spiritual principles presented in the Messages are not specific to a particular path and can be found throughout many spiritual teachings.

The Messages presented here are exactly what came through, to the best of my ability to translate the telepathic impress. Nothing has been changed and the original dates have been preserved despite the amount of time it has taken for the fruition of what was being predicted and described. There was a long "lead time" in preparing us for what is just now arriving in the world around us, and that was also part of learning to trust in the journey, no matter how things appeared. In turn, *that* required us to rely more on how things *felt* to us than on the form they seemed to take.

I offer this material with an open hand and an open heart. If it speaks to you, you will know it in your heart, even if your mind has many questions. If it seems like just so many words on a page to you, or you can't tell the qualitative difference between this material and so much else that is available, then perhaps this isn't "yours," and your path leads somewhere else. No blame — either for you or for me.

There is a great sorting out taking place, and these Messages are intended for those whose Oversouls have created them to make the journey to Terra, either now or later. If these words speak to your heart, then welcome! If not, then something else is intended for your life, and I bless you and your path in going there.

We are all Love-in-action and the Creator-in-expression, so no path is better than any other path. They just take different shapes and present different scenes along the way. Good journey!

— Sara/Adonna/Oriole

OVERVIEW OF THE MESSAGES

In order to appreciate and relate to the following Messages, some background might be helpful. To begin with, Operation Terra was conceived when 144,000 elohim joined together to precipitate this sector of reality out of our beingness, more than 4.5 billion years ago. The preparations for the time when Earth would become Terra have been going on for centuries. That time is now.

Approximately 6 million beings from the higher levels of reality have volunteered to "come down" and incarnate as ordinary humans, in order to support Earth in becoming Terra and to help colonize her when it is time for that. This had to be done from within the Earth's aura (the ionosphere is the outer limit for that), so it was necessary for them to become the "ground troops" who would have to rely on those who remained at the higher levels to guide them and support them through the transition that would be involved.

The Messages are a true transmission and operate at multiple levels. The words and images act as a carrier wave for the Light codes that are embedded in the Messages. Through the principle of resonance, those codings set off a matching response in every individual who carries the matching codes in their DNA. The Messages were not part of the original plan (Plan A) but became necessary when certain things did not go as originally anticipated.

It was originally hoped that many more people (up to 12% of the existing population) would be harvestable from those who were evolving upward for the first time. Plan A was for a large-scale, ground-based "op" that would have involved a global network of special centers that would process them and help them raise their frequency enough to be taken on board our fleets of ships and processed further until they could disembark onto a very large mothership (approximately 80% the size of Planet Earth) that we refer to as Midway Station.

When my Oversoul projected itself into this body in 1941, I experienced the usual amnesia that comes from incarnating into a third-density body, so I had no conscious awareness of what my life was supposed to be. Without really knowing why, I acquired skills in several different fields, including real estate, organizational management, management information systems, sales and marketing, financial management, accounting, editing and publishing, education, energy work and the healing arts, all of which would have been useful in my intended role in administering that larger "op."

However, there came a time in the 1990s when an assessment was performed and it revealed that not enough people had attained the necessary frequency and awareness to make the trip to Terra at this time, so the plan for the larger "op" (Plan A) was scrapped and Plan B was chosen instead.

In the evening of May 15, 1997, I both felt and heard a "whump," like the sound of a very large book being dramatically shut. Feeling into the significance of this, it was "as if" (a metaphor, not to be taken literally) a meeting had been called on the higher levels and a messenger had been sent out to assess the state of consciousness "down here." The messenger would not return until a certain critical mass of qualified individuals had been identified.

The intention was that if the messenger returned with the necessary information, "Plan A" would go into effect and things would not have to be quite so dramatic as the old world came to a close. However, if the messenger did not return by a certain time, "Plan B" would be the fall-back position, and things would go much differently.

The messenger did not come back.

A decision was then made to go to "Plan B," which meant that almost all of the skills I had developed would no longer be needed and my job description had radically changed. It would be a much smaller scale "op," and the "harvest" would consist primarily of those who had come down from the higher levels and would return to their former state. Very few who were evolving upward for the first time had qualified to make the trip. Two days later, after due consideration of the presenting issues, I was told that there were two questions that had to be answered with regard to this change in plans:

1. how to get the Starseeds (those who had come down from the higher levels and had incarnated into 3D to participate in these times) safely off the planet without going through physical death; and
2. how to make use of the work that HAD been done to benefit future generations.

The answers did not come all at once. First, I lost my base and income and an intense process of stripping away began. When I asked why I had to go through that hardship, I was told, "It isn't until you have let go of everything you have taken your identify from that you can receive what is coming next." I am still letting go, even now. Surrender has become my new way of being.

Two years later, I was asked to deliver a series of Messages from the Hosts of Heaven that subsequently became the Operation Terra material and website. The Messages are being offered for three audiences:

1. those who will make the trip to Terra in their present bodies;
2. those who will drop their present bodies and be born onto Terra as the first generation of Terran natives; and
3. those who will drop their bodies, experience more lives on other versions of 3D Earth, and incarnate onto Terra after that.

That was the answer to the second question. The codings in the Messages would activate those who are making the trip to Terra now and would be seeded into the consciousness of those who would make the trip later.

The upcoming evacuation process and its attendant "liftings" are the answer to the first question. It still has to be dealt with and that is what lies before us now.

The Messages from the Hosts of Heaven

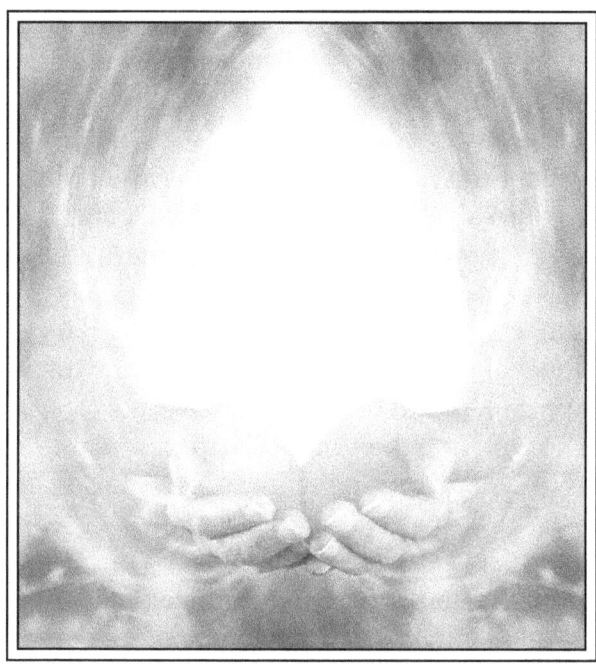

These Messages are a gift from the Hosts of Heaven.

NOTE: These Messages should be read in the order in which they were received, as each succeeding Message builds upon the foundation laid down by the preceding ones.

VOLUME ONE

OPERATION TERRA (INTRODUCTION)
June 30, 1999

IN THE BEGINNING, this planet was created with a certain destiny path in mind. Its creators (the "elohim," a group of vast, intelligent beings who combined forces to create this sector of reality) envisioned a rich environment where the planet's theme of "seeking harmony in diversity" could play out. However, there were other beings that saw an opportunity to insert themselves into the paradigm and eventually did so, so successfully that the original blueprint for the planet was essentially abrogated and converted to another agenda entirely.

Every time the elohim would project expressions of themselves into the physical plane and try to restore the original plan and agenda, the interlopers would eventually undermine their efforts and redirect the planet toward their own aims and ambitions. The world you see around you is the result of this interaction.

A relatively few individuals adhere to the original standards, based on love for and responsibility toward the entire planet and its occupants, but many more individuals put their own interests above those of the whole and engage in destructively competitive behaviors that eventually harm everyone and everything.

Now, however, it is time to restore the planet to her original destiny path. The behaviors that have destroyed so much of her diversity and beauty will be put to an end. Those who can "hear" these words will save much more than themselves. They will be candidates for the opportunity to inhabit the Earth after she has risen to her glorified state — the "New Earth," Terra — and they will be active participants WITH THE PLANET in creating a "heaven" on Earth.

In a relatively short time from now, many things will begin playing out that were prophesied to occur sooner, but had been delayed so that the message for change could reach the greatest number of potential "recruits." Now, however, all must go forward in order for the planet to meet her appointment with her own destiny.

All things have a proper time. "To every thing, there is a season" is a good way to put it, and right now it is almost autumn, the time to harvest what has been sown. Each lifeform has had many thousands of years to perfect itself and to evolve to its present state. Many species are simply leaving because there is no longer support for them to remain here. Drastic action is needed now, if anything is to be preserved.

The planet does not need its lifeforms. There are many planets without anything above the mineral kingdom. It is total arrogance on the part of even the best-intentioned humans to speak of "saving the planet." The planet can get along just fine on her own. But the planet is a conscious being, and the soul of the planet made an agreement as part of its incarnation as a physical reality. It agreed to host a diversity of lifeforms, and to interact with and sustain those lifeforms in keeping with the planet's own destiny path. To this end, she has allowed much abuse of her body while patiently waiting for humans to "get" the message of what they were doing to that which sustains them.

Without Earth's water, air, and soil, there would not be any life at all. Even viruses and bacteria need water. Everything needs physical nurturance until it is able to manifest its needs directly from the underlying matrix of consciousness that supports and informs physical reality. But humans, in their blind pursuit of their own survival regardless of the cost, have inadvertently been destroying the very matrix that gives them life and sustains them. The human species has placed itself in competition with everything else on the planet — animals, plants, trees, birds, fish, and other humans — and has robbed, raped, and pillaged the very planet upon which they depend for everything.

Everything humans consume or use comes from the planet, be it food, clothing, oxygen, shelter, automobiles, or computers. All of the materials that are used to manufacture all of the goods that people use come from the planet. And yet the slaughter goes on, as the oceans are poisoned, the forests are felled, and the water is pumped out of the ground when local rainfall is not sufficient to support people's needs. Unless this is stopped, there will be nothing left, and the people will suffer a terrible, slow decline, as they fight with one another over ever-dwindling resources. Too few care. The lawmakers serve their own agendas; there is simply not enough of a force for change to matter at this late date in the process.

So now, we give you this warning and we also give you a promise. For those of you who can "hear," know that the ticket is love in your heart. By love, we do not mean the mushy, romanticized stuff of your movies and novels. By love, we mean the absence of fear, trust in the Creator, and a willingness to put one's life on the line for the truth. In a very short time now, those traits are going to be the only ones that get one the "ticket to ride." A great wave of change is building now that will soon sweep the petty affairs of humans away, a great wave of purification and the cleansing of everything that is not in alignment with the destiny of this planet.

The elohim are here. They have incarnated as ordinary humans in order to act as lightning rods, to draw down and anchor the energy of change, and to assist in the birthing of the new age. It will be necessary to evacuate those who are destined to inhabit Terra, for the necessary cleansing will render the present body of Earth uninhabitable for a time. The evacuees will be taken *in their physical bodies* to another location, where they will prepare themselves for the colonization of Terra, the "New Earth." The remainder of this information will deal with the details of that process and paint a vision that those who can "hear" will be able to hold in their hearts and minds and that will help them to understand the necessity of the cleansing that is soon to take place.

Amen, Adonoy Sabayoth. We are the Hosts of Heaven.

ON BECOMING A "HUMAN" BEING
July 1, 1999

What people have come to think of as a human being actually is a hybrid creature, born of the manipulations of the interlopers. In the beginning, the Adamic seed was created whole and fully formed. It was designed to act as a steward of whatever world it found itself upon. To this end, it had the power of reason and the power to love and care for things other than itself. It had a unique genetic pattern that also allowed it full access to the higher dimensions and the wisdom contained in the *Akasha*, or Hall of Records.

The interlopers were originally from this same seed but a perversion crept in. Somehow the ability to love and care for others became distorted and replaced by a sense of disconnection that resulted in fear. In this fearful state, everything and everyone became perceived as an enemy, someone or something that posed a threat and therefore had to be controlled or dominated.

From this original distortion of the design for the Adamic race, a dark spiral began to unfurl and to block and interfere with the Light from Source Creator. It began to spread itself through the many worlds of the Father, and wherever it went, this distortion created chaos.

The life force is principally an ordering force. It acts against the tendency toward entropy. In any system, if some energy is not sustaining the system, it will dissolve and return to a more elemental state. In all systems, there is an ordering force or there would not be form. The evolutionary imperative is toward more complexity, toward more complex systems. The force of entropy is counter-evolutionary. It moves away from complexity toward simpler forms. In this sense, one can see the ordering force and the force of entropy as tending to oppose and balance each other. Since we have dubbed the ordering force as a life force, we can think of the force of entropy as a "death force" or "death wish," as all is consciousness and thought creates.

If we now look at the actions of the interlopers, we can see that they oppose the life force. Their principal activity sows dissent, competition instead of cooperation, and generally leads to a breakdown of any system that they penetrate successfully. They perceive of "self above all" as their guiding tenet, whereas the Adamic seed was designed to place self WITHIN the context of "all."

The Creator designed the Creation to reflect the Creator. The Creator is the source of the life force, the ordering principle that operates on the matrix of Mind and gives it form. The interlopers have distorted the original design, and we have been given the task of restoring all things to their original Divine estate. In the case of Earth, at this point in time that means to restore both the planet *and* its lifeforms to their original destiny plan — to their original evolutionary path.

The true human is a special case in the Creation. It shares many aspects with the Creator. If the Earth is in keeping with her blueprint, she will soon manifest as "The Garden" of the galaxy. And the true humans will act as her "Gardeners," in keeping with their stewardship role. Since Operation Terra is intended to restore Earth to her true destiny path, it follows that the so-called human beings must also be restored to theirs — to become true humans.

What does this mean? To understand the answer to this, one must look at what has changed. The DNA, which carries the codes for the operation of all the bodily processes, must be restored and elevated back to its original frequency of Light. The "shadows" cast by the interlopers must be cleansed and purified out of the system, and all of the entropic thoughtforms of separation, disease, and dying must be cleansed from the cellular memory patterns, which are carried in the DNA. Those portions of the DNA that were rendered inactive will have to be restored to full functionality, which carries with it the gift of full consciousness.

If one could see the light bodies of animate forms, one would also see a web of infinitely delicate light fibers interconnecting all things, all the way back to the Source. These connections funnel in through the subtle energy channels of the body — the meridians of acupuncture and the chakras and nadis of the Sanskrit-based languages and cultures.

To restore these energy channels to full function requires a purification. The source of this is the application of certain frequencies of sound and light to gradually repair the "dropped connections." While it is true that there are many healers using the technologies of sound and light, the kind of "remedy" needed to restore all the lifeforms of Earth (including the human beings) is beyond the ability of even the most gifted healers. The scope of the "operation" is simply too large for any individual or organization to provide. There is a time coming when an even greater amount of light and sound will be available than has been in the past. The effect of this will be to shake loose anything that is not resonant with the original blueprint for the planet and all the lifeforms upon her. You have perhaps become familiar with "ultrasonic cleaning." This is a good metaphor for the process.

In ultrasonic cleaning, a piece of dirty jewelry is placed in a bath of cleaning solution. High frequency sound waves move through the solution, shaking the dirt loose but leaving the jewelry intact. It's a very precise and safe method, as it does not disturb anything but the dirt that is encrusted on the jewelry.

Every lifeform is a jewel in the crown of the Creator. An order has gone forth through the Creation that the original blueprint must be restored. Accordingly, every aspect of the Creation that is not in keeping with its original blueprint will be restored. In this case, the distortions are being "bathed" in Love and high-frequency sound is being used to shake loose all the accumulated "dirt" that is keeping the jewel from reflecting the Creator's Light.

The energy from Source is too powerful to be used directly. It must be "stepped down" through a series of "lenses" or "transformers," much as your household electric current is stepped down through a series of transformers to a level that can be used by your household appliances. So it is with this process. The energy is stepped down until it is at a level that can accomplish the desired result without destroying the target altogether.

We entitled this message, "On Becoming a 'Human' Being." We chose this title so that you, the reader, could understand what is happening to you. You and every lifeform on the planet have been receiving a "bath" of Love for many years now. It has gradually increased, in a geometric fashion, over a long period of time.

If you are familiar with geometric curves, you will know that the effects are at first almost insignificant, but as the powers build upon one another, each step up the spiral becomes more and more pronounced. For example, 2 x 2=4 and 2 x 2 x 2=8, or twice the first step. From 4 to 8 is not a big change. But after only 8 steps, the total is 256, an increase of

128 times the original number. The next step is 512, then 1024, and so on. You can see that the changes at the beginning were relatively small, but then each successive step becomes more massive. If you were to plot this on a curve, at a certain critical point, the curve would go almost straight up, toward infinity.

This is where you are at the time of this message. You are within the "critical zone" and the amount of energy streaming over you is increasing so rapidly that you can't help but notice the effects. If you watch your TV or read your newspapers and magazines, everything seems to be purring along, "business as usual." There are some "bumps in the road," such as school children taking up guns and killing other school children, peculiar weather patterns, droughts, wildfires, and intense storms. But what *doesn't* make the news are the subtle changes in the entire substrate.

The reason the killings take place is that they are a SYMPTOM of what is really going on. Everything that is not in keeping with the original blueprint is being flushed out of the Earth system. These behaviors are SYMPTOMS of the underlying patterns of death and disease that have operated "under cover" for a very long time. This is coming to an end, but it will all surface as it leaves the system, just like one sees the pus coming out of an abscess when it finally opens up and heals itself from beneath the surface.

People have begun to notice that something strange is going on. Perhaps they are afraid to talk about it, or they busy themselves with activities that take their minds off of it. They distract themselves and worry about this or that, but the real worry is deep under the surface, gnawing at them. "What is going on?" they wonder, but they don't speak of this with others, so they don't know that others are experiencing the same thing. Your media looks for different ways to ENTERTAIN you. Remember the Romans? "Bread and circuses." That's how they kept the general populace from becoming restless. They were kept fed and entertained. But the Roman circuses were not the stuff of clowns and cotton candy. They pitted human against human, human against animal. It is not so different today.

But now that will not be sufficient. With the increase in Light and sound, things are going to get pretty intense — so intense that the entertainment will fade into the background as people struggle to cope with the enormous wave of change that is sweeping the planet. It shows up a little in the rate of change in your computer technology, but that is only a tiny glimpse of the degree of change that is now occurring. And as we said before, this is a geometric progression. It is a spiral that will take in more and more as it turns faster and faster.

Some will refuse to change. You have all known someone that would "rather fight than switch." They will resist change to such an extent that they would literally rather DIE than change. Many will make this choice. Know that when you see this happen, it isn't anyone's "fault." It was their plan all along. Their soul had made that decision before it came into their body. They are simply going to go out of this body and eventually take up another, so that they can continue with their "lessons." No big deal. You've all been doing that for a very long time, also.

Others have been embracing change for many years. They have learned the lesson of "surrender." Instead of "fighting," they have decided to ACCEPT the direction of their life and have decided to ACCEPT the consequences of that choice. No blame. You haven't seen them on TV. They aren't in *People* magazine. They are pretty invisible, but they are nearly ready to make their appearance on the world stage. They have been preparing for this for a long time, so they will be among the first to manifest the "true human" form. They will be helping others to ACCEPT the necessity of change and to make as grace-full (i.e., filled with Grace) a transition as possible.

The amount of love that is available to you is staggering. There are so many beings on all levels of the Creator's kingdom that are massed to assist you in this transition. They are holding the portals open so that more and more love is stepped down through their hearts to yours. If you could see them and know how many there are assisting you, you would be overcome with emotion at the idea that you were somehow worthy of such a gift. That is because of the shadows within you that have convinced you of your smallness, of your powerlessness. The interlopers made you that way so they could use you for their purposes. But you are a true jewel in the crown of the Creation. We have come to provide the high-frequency sound to shake you loose of all that keeps you from shining forth and perfectly reflecting the Creator's Light.

We are bathing you in a virtual ocean of Love. All you need to do is to SURRENDER and ACCEPT the gift. You will have to "die" to your idea of how small and powerless you are in order to become a "true human." You will have to ACCEPT the information that begins to flood into you as your light filaments become reconnected to the Source. You will have to deal with your feelings when you discover how much of what you thought was important was part of the "Big Lie." But you have so much help. "Let go and let God" is a good phrase to express the degree of surrender that you must achieve.

We have defined love as the lack of fear, trust in the Creator, and the willingness to put your life on the line for the truth. We ask you now to move into your true estate, based on that definition of love, to allow yourselves to cast off your shame and guilt and receive the love that you are. We are here to help you.

Amen, Adonoy Sabayoth. We are the Hosts of Heaven.

ROOTING OUT FEAR
July 2, 1999

In this Message, we will attempt to paint a picture of what is currently playing out on Planet Earth. There is a mixture of energies, due to the workings of the interlopers. We have been assigned the task of separating them out from one another and making sure that each one gets to their proper "destination." If you see strange things happening — what you might call "miracles" — you will know that we are at work behind the scenes.

The weather patterns have already shifted dramatically. You can see this in the droughts, floods, hurricanes, and odd seasonal weather. However, that is nothing more than the planet's expression of ridding herself of all of the negativity she has absorbed from the actions and thoughts of the humans who occupy her. She is merely "shaking herself loose" of the accumulated debris of human activity so that she can herself rise in frequency to meet her own appointment with destiny.

She will begin to "shake" in others ways, too. She is going to develop a "fever," with the aid of the sun, and that fever will do the same thing on the planetary surface as does a fever in a human being or an animal. The purpose of a fever is to burn off any foreign invaders (in the human/animal case, these would be the bacteria or viruses or foreign proteins of any kind) and to restore balance, or homeostasis. The weather patterns are the first symptoms of the Earth's disease process beginning to clear itself.

There will be other symptoms of this process, as well. There will be eruptions of the volcanic and geothermal type, just as boils appear on the surface of one's skin to eliminate toxins. There will be earthquakes as the Earth shudders herself free of the accumulated strains along the interfaces of her various parts. There will be massive bombardment by solar emanations, as well as the effects of a band of energy that your solar system has begun to transit. All of these things will be working together to provide the cleansing and purification that is needed, in order that the Earth may rise and achieve her station as Terra.

In these times, everything on the Earth will suffer the effects. There will not be any way to avoid it. Those who for now have artificial means of protecting themselves will soon see the loss of those means. Everything and everyone will be affected. However, there will be help for those who go within and find their security there. Inside of each of you, there is a center that allows you to connect with Source. It is more felt than seen, as it is invisible to the physical senses, but it is there.

Those who meditate know what this feels like. It is not localized in any one part of the body. Rather, it is a feeling of expansion and comfort. If you do not meditate, now is a good time to start. Simply follow your breath as it goes in and out, and if your mind wanders, gently bring it back to the breath. You do not need any more technique than this. It helps if you meditate in the same place and at the same times every day, so it becomes a habit to go within. In this way, you will be able to not only receive the guidance or sense of what is yours to do, but you will also be positioning yourself to begin to receive the new information that will start to come in as your light fibers are reconnected.

Remember, there is nothing you can do to prepare yourself for what is coming. If you think you are in charge, you will cut yourself off from the flow of information that comes from a higher source. Your own ego is programmed for the survival of your body. It is stimulated by fear. Your meditation practice is the place where you can find a "safe place" in which you need simply to listen. You cannot prepare for something that you don't know will come. You don't know when or where or how you will need to cope with these coming Earth changes. If you are connected to Source, you will be led in what to do. If you are being run by your fear, you will make poor choices, and you will reap what you sow in that you will experience everything that you fear. You will draw it to yourselves through the principle of resonance.

So, then, have we frightened you? That is good. As soon as a fear rises to your consciousness, that is your opportunity to trace it back to its roots and "uproot" it. This is your part of the bargain, your part of the work. If you remember, we defined love as the absence of fear, trust in the Creator, and the willingness to lay down your life for the truth. All of these go hand in hand. You are either in fear or you are in love. You must make this choice over and over again, in each moment that presents. When a birth is taking place, the labor pains come closer and closer together as the moment of actual birth approaches.

As we have said, you have now reached the critical point in which the rate of change will spiral upward exponentially, so remember to breathe. Give your meditation time or "quiet time" the highest priority, so that you can begin to eradicate those fears that you have left. Only those with love in their hearts — not fear — will be lifted. The vibration of fear will not be compatible with the new Earth, Terra. There will be no death, disease, or aging on Terra. All of those things are the result of unexpressed fear.

The ultimate fear is the fear of death. Despite the abundant testimony of those who have been "to death's door" and returned to tell about it, the fear of death underlies every other fear you have. Many subtle fears are tied to the idea of being socially unacceptable in one way or another. This subtly equates with ostracism, which in primitive cultures can lead to death from starvation or the lack of community support. This fear vanishes when you feel "connected" to Source. You carry within you the necessary comfort and faith, so that you are not swayed by outer appearances. Find others of like mind if you can and perform group meditations on a regular basis. They will help you in strengthening the feeling of being part of a larger movement, a movement back to Source.

We have spoken of the interlopers and how they interfered with the plan for this planet and everything upon her. These simple practices will remove you from the blind acceptance of the results of what they have done. It may not look or feel like you are doing much, but this is the ultimate rebellion. Those who are angrily demanding change from their government are placing their efforts in the wrong direction. You are perhaps familiar with the doctrine, "As above, so below." The second part of that is "As within, so without." If you want your world to be a safe place for you, you must first create your safety within yourself. Note that the change must occur "within" you before it is reflected "without" (outside of you).

You each have the potential to become warriors for the truth. The truth is that you do not need to die, that you CAN live a long and productive life that fulfills you in every way, and that you have never been and never will be separate from Source. The Christ has never left you, either, and so he cannot "return." This waiting for the "coming" that is present in all traditions throughout your world is really an expression of the sense of being cut off, of not being connected. The "coming" is about YOU — about your coming back into the awareness of who you really are (an expression of the Creator) and coming back into your own true nature and estate.

You are the "Second Coming," because you are destined to return or "come back" to what you were before. All the feelings that you must have a savior who is somehow out of reach is part of the Big Lie. There is only one Source. There is only ONE LIFE being lived, through each aspect of the Creation. You are both a part of and contain the whole of the Creator. The Creator can be accessed within yourself, and when you have achieved union with the Creator, you will know who you are.

We leave you now in peace and honor and blessing and shall speak to you again.

Amen, Adonoy Sabayoth. We are the Hosts of Heaven.

SUPPORTING YOUR TRANSITION
July 3, 1999

Today's message is about the different exit paths that will lead out of this one shared reality that you view as your home. It is true that you all see one picture now, but gradually this will change. It will not be noticeable at first, but it shall become increasingly amplified with the passage of time.

The greatest number of people will pass through the portal you call physical death. It is not true that they "die," but that is what it looks like to those who remain behind in the third dimension. They simply pass out of their bodies onto a different plane of reality that is normally invisible to those on "the other side" of the boundary between the planes.

For the rest, the experience will be somewhat different. A relatively small number will meet the criteria for moving on to Terra. Those are the ones that we will evacuate in their physical bodies. The others will think that they are still living on the same planet, but there will be a splitting off of realities, so that different timelines appear. To each person on a given timeline, it will seem as though a lot of people have simply disappeared. However, so much will be going on at the phenomenal level, that even this apparent disappearance will scarcely be noticed. They will be far too busy dealing with the challenges of moment-to-moment life. We are going to only speak of the experience for those who are destined for Terra. That is our concern in these messages, although it is to be understood that the audience to whom we speak is very, very small.

A linkup is beginning to occur between those individuals who share a common destiny path. This is true for all of the different timelines. Through the principle of resonance, each "finds their own," so to speak. Each person will find that they are meeting total strangers with whom they instantly feel at home. With others, even ones who have been familiar in the past, it will be as if you are suddenly speaking different languages.

In fact, you are. Language is symbolic, and different cultures have different symbol systems. Each group will differentiate more and more from the others. It will be experienced as a "pull" or a "push." You will either feel attracted to certain individuals or you will feel a disconnect taking place with other individuals. You will either "like" them or you will feel anything ranging from mild disinterest to strong dislike. You will not be totally neutral toward anyone. Even though there is only ONE LIFE being lived, there is still the aspect of the uniqueness of each expression of that one life, and therefore there are certain tendencies to group in larger "families," rather than to identify with all people at the same time.

The people who are destined to go to Terra will resonate strongly with these messages. Underneath the words, there is a strong vibratory signature that will trigger a response of "true" from within oneself, even if one does not totally comprehend all that is being said. You will either find yourself saying "Yes!!!!" or you will be repulsed. There is no in-between.

Those that are destined for Terra will be drawn to this material in three waves. The first of these is made up of the leadership, those who made a soul decision to be among the architects and builders of the new world. They are equipped by their souls for the task. All of these decisions are made at the soul level. We cannot stress that too strongly. One does not "earn" the right to go to Terra. One has chosen it as part of their soul's desired arena of expression and experience.

True "free will" only exists at the soul level, where all is already known. To ask a blindfolded person to chart their course would be ridiculous, and everyone in a body who has not achieved a permanent state of Union with the Creator is essentially blindfolded. Only those who are fully awakened to and aligned with their soul can know the wisdom of the choices they make. You are not yet fully conscious, but you will be before this transition phase is complete.

To make the trip to Terra, all that is NOT of the proper vibratory level will be expelled from you. As you are raised in frequency, you will naturally be able to access more and more of the higher levels of existence. This will seem strange when it begins to happen, because the higher realities are not at all as "solid" as the one you are used to in your present form. They are a lot more "fluid," in that there are no solid boundaries. If you have ever read a good piece of stream-of-consciousness writing or had a lucid dream in which every conscious thought affected what you experienced as your environment, then you have some idea of what we are talking about.

So you will experience two separate and simultaneous processes — the expulsion of all that is NOT compatible with Terra and the unfoldment of the sorts of experiences that make up the moment-to-moment way of doing things at the next level of reality. They will seem rather strange to you at first, but if you can remember to breathe (and keep breathing) and to keep letting go of all your ideas about reality, you will have an easier time of it.

On Terra, you will operate with "beginner's mind." You will create in an "as-you-go" manner, with no real reference to what has gone before and no real plan of where you intend to go. Each action is both a result of the one just before it and the seed of the one that will follow. Each moment contains within it everything needed for its completion, but it is an experience of constant movement without any external referent to tell you which way you are going.

Your entire process will be one of creating your reality without anything but curiosity to lead you. It will be as if there is an invisible finger always beckoning to you, "this way, this way." And you will go that way without hesitation because you will have a perfect internal sense of it feeling "right" to do so. You will not question where it leads or what the consequences will be. You will be a fully-conscious, fully-trusting point of awareness that is always discovering itself in the moment, with no fixed idea of who it is or what it is supposed to be doing.

In some ways that is not so different from what you are used to. The further one goes on the spiritual path, the less definite one's self-perception becomes. You drop all of your accumulated "training" in how and who you are *supposed to be*, and instead become as innocent as an unspoiled child, totally authentic in each and every moment you experience.

We are telling you this so you will not think there is something wrong with you when your memory begins to go, when you have trouble remembering things that relate to time and past and future. You will be less inclined to make plans, because as soon as you do, you will find things have changed and you will very quickly realize the futility of trying to second-guess the next turn in the road. This is as it should be. You are simply shedding your conditioned responses and becoming more authentically who your soul wishes you to be.

Your body probably has had some strange feelings going off in it lately — a little like pings and pops in the most unlikely places, and with no apparent order or logic. You may have felt a surprising tenderness [soreness] in some places. You may run a fever or feel heat in some localized portion of your body. These are all signs of energetic patterns being cleared or corrected. Your "wiring" has been dysfunctional for quite a while. Now your circuits are being repaired and the life current is beginning to flow again.

As it does, where there are "blockages" of stagnant energy, you will experience a temporary congestion, which is expressed as heat or mild pain. You may ease this process with finger pressure on the affected spots. You do not need to press hard. Just make firm contact with the spot and hold the intention that the energy blockage will dissolve and let the energy flow smoothly through that area. Use your intuition or your subtle senses to tell you when you are "done" with the spot. With practice, you can feel the energy begin to move, and then settle down into an even flow.

We have already spoken about the importance of meditation. We cannot emphasize too strongly how important it is that you make the time and space for regular attempts at connecting with Source. Whether you are new to this or an "old hand," it is important to develop a strong habit of inner listening. Your life depends on it, in that you must be able to hear and respond to the inner promptings that speak ever so softly within you. We will give you more simple techniques for honing this ability as we go on, but for now we just wanted to let you know that this is more important in getting you to where you are supposed to go than anything else you could do.

In addition to meditation, it is important that you love and cherish yourself enough to make your spiritual practice the center of your life. Everything you do should support it. If it means creating a "sacred space" in your home, do that. Use pictures, objects, incense, candles, lighting, furniture, cloths — anything that will visually remind you that you are dedicating yourself to the attainment of your destiny.

You will want to simplify your life if it is too crowded with activity, to clear the way for more "quiet time." Baths are good if you can use them to relax further, to become more receptive. Essential oils that make you feel relaxed and open are helpful. Anything that assists you in the redirection of your attention to what is going on inside of you will help. Turning off the TV will be a BIG help!!!

The reason we are speaking to you in this way at this time is to assist you in your transition from an ordinary "Earth human" back to the magnificent creature — a child of the Universe — that you are. All of these messages have as their intention the redirection of your priorities to what is really important — those actions, thoughts, and intentions that are supportive of your return to full Mastery, for only Masters will occupy Terra. We will have more to say on that subject later.

As things "amp up" on the Earth plane, there will be much going on to distract you. There will be dramatic occurrences of all kinds. Your transition to Terra will go more smoothly if you can distance yourself from getting too caught up in the drama.

Your media is the worst offender in the purveying of drama. Drama sells. In a world based on consumption rather than conservation, drama plays a big role in driving things forward in a downward direction. It will look and feel like everything is coming apart. It will look and CAN feel like you are at risk or in danger in some way, as the "chickens" lose their heads and go about shrieking that the sky is falling.

You are not chickens. You are eagles. You will soar. While others are still pecking at the ground for crumbs, you will be taking your place at the banquet table. We are telling you this now, because soon your perceptual screen will be filled with scenes of drama. Detach from it. It is not what it appears.

Just as your body experiences strange localized clearings, the body of the Earth will be doing the same. It is all in Divine Order and as it should be. As the body of the Earth experiences localized clearings, the thoughtforms that were frozen there will be released. All of the human experience will be playing out before your eyes, a re-run of a different kind than your usual summer fare. Just remember to create your sanctuary within yourself and you will not be so inclined to get caught up in the hysteria.

You must become calm in the midst of the storm, like the eye of a hurricane. No one can provide this for you. You can receive support for this, but you must be in your inner sanctuary to receive it. Let your physical senses see and hear what is going on around you if you wish, but withdraw your sense of "you" deeply within.

Give yourself as much quiet time as you can. Listen, listen, listen inside. Tune out the noise of the rising chaos. Become quieter as things become louder. Wean yourself from the media of all kinds. Nothing "out there" has anything to offer but more chaos, more things to be afraid of. Even the "human interest" stories have at their core a feeling of estrangement from one another. They tend to view other people's lives like looking at germs under a microscope. They elevate the emotions to keep you caught up in the drama. Disconnect from that manipulation of your reality. Go inside for your "news of the day." You will find that your inner "station" is the one that tells you what you really need to know.

We shall speak to you again. For now, we leave you in peace and honor and blessing.

Amen, Adonoy Sabayoth. We are the Hosts of Heaven.

A GUIDED TOUR OF TERRA
July 4, 1999

Today we would like to take you on a guided tour of Terra, so that you will have some idea of your destination and will then be able to relate better to the changes you are experiencing as you transform yourselves into those beings you will express as in the Terran landscape. We begin our tour from space, where we see Terra gleaming as a perfect blue pearl in the "sky" [of space]. She inspires love just to look at her. She gleams with an "un-Earthly" light, as she is now glorified beyond your ability to imagine. To physical eyes, she would appear as a blue-white star, but to those eyes that can see at the finer levels of reality, she is radiant and welcoming to all those who operate on the frequencies of Love.

Extraordinary light streams from her, for at this stage she does not reflect light (as in her present state), but radiates it. (You will all be very radiant, too!) We hear a sound. It is exquisite — the "music of the spheres." It is the sound that every planet makes when it is totally harmonized with its place in the cosmos. To your present state of mind, it would sound truly "heavenly." When you are there, you will "live heaven"; your moment-to-moment experience will be that you are in "heaven," as it can be glimpsed through the shadows of your present state of awareness.

Drawing in closer now, we are struck by the fact that everything on the surface of the planet — its trees, animals, birds, fish in the oceans, but also the trees and flowers, even the air itself — is radiant with beauty, peace, and harmony. It is the crowning of Earth's own exploration of her theme of "seeking harmony in diversity." Every atom of this reality is in full consciousness, is fully aware of every other atom in that reality and consciously cooperating with the whole. It is like many voices merged into one glorious song.

To grasp an inkling of how pervasive this level of cooperation is, suppose that at some future moment, you would experience the desire for a piece of fruit from some particular tree that you will pass. That tree would put forth a blossom and form that fruit in such a way that it will be at its moment of perfect ripeness just as you pass by and put up your hand for it. Actually, a measure of the same thing happens to you now, but there is so much "static" on the line, so to speak, that you are not aware of it. Everything always is and has been coordinated perfectly, but we digress. On Terra, all IS the expression of unobstructed perfection. Everything is raised and glorified to its most exalted physical expression.

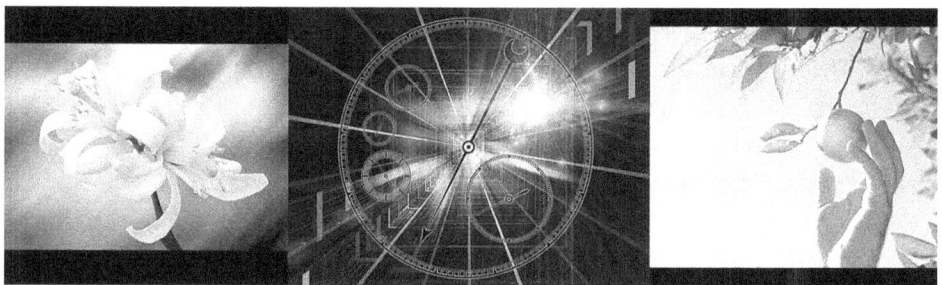

The blossom comes forth so that its fruit will be at perfect ripeness when you put your hand up for it.

This is a physical world, or at least it is experienced that way. You will do the same types of things that you do now, but you will do them in a perfected way. You will still eat, make love, sleep, meditate, have pursuits that please you, but you will not be restricted by the constraints of an economic system that seeks only to take from you. In the perfected level of cooperation that exists on Terra, all parts support all the other parts. There is no poverty, disease, or dying in the sense that you now experience. When you eat a piece of fruit, it merges with you and becomes you, so it has not died; it has only changed form.

You will all be immortal beings. You will simply change form also, but you will do it without needing to "die and be reborn." You will be able to transition from one adult form to another. There will be children born on Terra. There will be families. But the children being born will be the projections of those souls whose third-density vehicles were shed and who "qualify" for fourth-density existence. Once they are "born" into fourth density, they need never "die" again. They will simply move on to other realms of experience and service. The rate of reproduction on Terra is precisely balanced with the harmony of the whole. Not one leaf, fruit, or child comes into that world that is not in keeping with the harmony of the whole. There is no excess; there is no lack. As expressed in your tale of *Goldilocks* [and the Three Bears], it will be "just right."

As we said in our last message, you will operate from an inner knowing of what is "right." Terra will function as one giant organism, with each of the forms that exist on her functioning perfectly as part of that organism, just as the cells in a perfectly healthy body carry out their roles in harmony with the whole. Some things will seem like they are simply higher versions — more perfected versions — of things you are already familiar with. People will still make love, for example, but no child will be conceived until it is the perfect moment for that to occur. You will be totally free to explore your sexual expression without fear of unwanted consequences. There is no death or disease on Terra, no need for protection from unwanted conditions. Everything proceeds in harmony with the whole. You are totally free to create whatever you wish, but you will only want to create in harmony with the whole.

Terra will be the garden spot of the galaxy, a living "school" in which the various cultures of the galaxy will be able to experience living in harmony with others who are very different from themselves. There will be distinct communities of every type of being that qualifies for Terran life. Each community will have its own ways, its own cultural predilections. One will be able to tour these different "villages" and experience the different cultural flavors that exist in the galaxy, and see how they can all relate to one another in harmony and peace.

Terra is the crown jewel of the galaxy, at least that portion of it that is functioning as fourth-density positive. There is a vibrational "barrier" at these higher levels that prevents any being or lifeform from entering the Terran space if that lifeform is not "qualified" by its own energy to do so. That is why you will not see disease-producing organisms there. They are the stuff of lower frequencies and are of the negative polarity expression, which has to do with entropy and death. Those who choose the negative polarity will have an abundance of death and disease, but they will have their own version of Earth to explore. Terra is not available to them.

So what will you do with yourselves? For one thing, you will travel a great deal. You will travel from one community to another, and to different spots in the galaxy that serve your further exploration and experience of life. You see, Terra will not have drama anymore. It will be very "tame," compared to your present experience.

There will not be any mountains, as mountains occur only when there is tension and collision between the crustal plates. The present Earth has such monuments to the strains she has been put under, but on Terra, all of these will be smoothed out. The surface will be even and sculpted into the most beautiful gardens. Even the atmosphere will be in harmony. There will only be gentle rains — no thunderstorms. You may want to travel to other places to experience some of the excitement that such dramatic displays provide. You will be totally free to find whatever pleases you to experience, both on the planet and off of it.

We cannot speak in detail of your individual paths or experiences because you are all unique and your explorations and preferences will be unique. We can only speak in general terms, as you will only discover the exact nature of your life as you live it. That will still be true at all levels of reality, as even the Creator likes to be surprised. That is why the Creator plays hide-and-seek with Itself through Its many forms. There is always a mystery unfolding, and one never reaches the end.

The Creation is always birthing itself, so there is no end to the possible experiences that can be had. It is a lot like a fractal design. Each part of the fractal unfolds itself a little like a "twig off the old tree," but it does so in symmetry and perfection, and gives rise to other branches of itself that go on to do the same. That is how the Creator creates, like a fractal. It is the simplest expression that allows for all possibilities. Each point in the Creation is like a "seed" in a fractal. It becomes a site through which the Creator can unfold itself endlessly, creating new branches as it grows.

You are each one of those seed-points, and you are each a co-creator with the Creator, directly unfolding a particular exploration of reality from within you. We will have a discussion of how the different geometrical forms express this unfoldment at a later time. We mention these things now in order for you to have the proper context in which to place our words. In the end, you must experience it before you will "know" it, but we share these pictures with you now to give you a vision of "things to come" that you can hold in your hearts and minds and that will sustain you through the years of transition that lie directly ahead.

We will return to these thoughts in later messages. Each message will build upon the information of the previous messages, unfurling in a perfect spiral. That is the shape of the evolutionary path. (The devolutionary path is a spiral, also, but instead of expanding infinitely, it compresses infinitely until at some point it must reverse course and begin expanding again or it will entirely disappear.) You are being lifted out of your mundane experience by your ability to respond to the incoming frequencies of light. You built yourself to be able to do this at the appointed time. It is encoded in your cells, in your cellular memory. That is why you cannot "earn" your way onto Terra.

You made the choice for that destination before you came into your present vehicle. If someone appears to be "missing the mark," or not "getting the message," consider the possibility that they are that way by their own soul's choice. There are no accidents. Everything is being coordinated from the highest levels of your being, but as we said before, the Creator loves to be surprised, so you will only discover what you "planned" to do as it unfolds from within you across time. (Time is what keeps everything from happening at once, you know.)

Life is a constantly unfolding journey, and that will not change when you get to Terra. You will continue to explore your own unique expression, but in conscious harmony with the whole. Your own creative impulses and curiosity will spur you on. You will neither be "bored to death" or numbed by perfection. Rather, you will finally be totally free to create, and what you create will be your own branch of the Creation.

We leave you now in peace and honor and blessing. We shall speak to you again.

Amen, Adonoy Sabayoth. We are the Hosts of Heaven.

THE MERGING OF REALITIES
July 5, 1999

Today we will speak to you of some of the experiences you will be having as you journey back to full consciousness and your "homecoming." You are indeed now moving back to your true home, your true Self, and as these higher realities open to you, you will begin to have strange experiences that you can't explain to others. They will feel natural to you, but your social conditioning would label them as "strange," so you might begin to experience some fear around this issue. We have spoken of the necessity to move beyond fear into love, so we offer these comments today to reassure you that there is nothing to fear here. You are simply returning to the way you were before you took on these "garments" of flesh.

In the beginning, all was a sort of cosmic "soup." Everything was liquid and without defined form. Your scientists have approached this "soup" when they are able to create a plasma by using electromagnetic fields. It is a field or substrate of intelligent energy, but has no form of its own. Out of this intelligent "soup," all form emerged, self-aware to the extent that it knew it existed, but not able to reflect upon itself. That would appear later in the scheme of things.

In this soup, all things are contained in potential. You cannot see any of them, because they exist only as a potential — a possibility out of many possibilities. We mentioned fractals yesterday. If you think of a decision point — something simple, like "What will I have for breakfast?" — you will be able to follow what we are talking about here. You can have many things for breakfast. You could use something that you already have in the house, you could go to the store and buy something else, or you could go to a restaurant and choose from their menu. Even breakfast offers a multitude of possibilities.

The Merging of Realities

Even breakfast offers a multitude of possibilities.

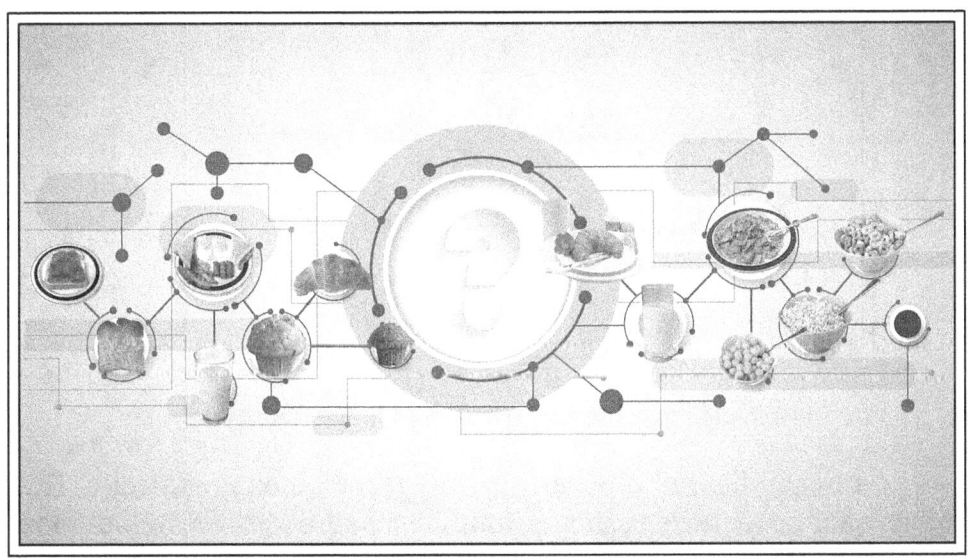

Each decision point leads to other decision points.

These are decision points. They offer many possibilities, not just the two or three of "Yes," "No," or "Maybe." Each decision leads to other decision points. Let's say you decide to have eggs for breakfast, as part of your "breakfast" decision. Now you are faced with other decision points: How will you make your eggs? Scrambled? Poached? Fried? Boiled? And then from THAT decision, you will have other decisions to make. What will you have with your eggs? What "goes" with the eggs depends in part on how you decided to prepare the eggs. Scrambled eggs might call for the addition of some milk or onion. Boiled eggs might call for some mayonnaise or salt and pepper.

We use this simple example to show you how one set of possible decisions leads to other possible decisions. Computer programmers would call these "logic branches." You can go this way (scrambled) or this way (poached) or this way (boiled), and so on. Then once one has chosen to travel through one "gate" to the exclusion of the other ones, other "branches" present [themselves].

In a fractal, the origin point produces branches infinitely.

In a fractal design, one can see this represented graphically. The origin point produces branches infinitely, as long as the values stay within certain limits. One can "explore" fractals endlessly as long as one stays within those limits. This is the way the Creation unfolds itself from within that cosmic "soup." It begins to branch immediately by expressing a "set" of possibilities or potentials. Every time a "decision" is made to choose one possibility over the others, that decision point or branch becomes the starting place for a new set of possibilities, as we showed in the breakfast example. But that's how the whole thing began — with a set of possibilities — so we have just recapitulated the starting point. This is called an "iteration." An iteration is a cycle through a certain formula. Mathematicians use iterations to solve complex equations.

So this is how the Creation unfurls — through a series of iterations (cycles) of a complex formula that allows for an infinite number of decision points or branches to be explored. But what of the other points or branches? Well, the Creator explores them, too. But how can you have both poached eggs and fried eggs and boiled eggs and scrambled eggs? You probably wouldn't want to have all of them at the same time. The Creator solves this dilemma by creating separate realities to accommodate all of the possible choices. If one expression of "you" chooses the poached eggs, there will be other expressions of "you" to make the other choices, and they will all go on, branching and branching and branching.

If you look at the fractal design at the bottom of this page, you will see what we are talking about. This is how the Creation unfolds. Each branch leads to other branches. There are as many realities as there are points of awareness to experience them. There are as many expressions of "you" as are required to explore all the possibilities.

This is how the Creation unfolds. Each branch leads to other branches.

You are an expression of the Creator. You could say you ARE the

Creator-in-expression. The Creator (being THE Creator), wants to experience (or "explore") ALL of the branches, which are essentially infinite in number, within certain limits or parameters. Those limits we call "Universal Laws." They are not like the laws that are passed by your governments. They apply to all created realities, on all levels of being. There are subsets of these laws that apply to specific frequency bands (densities or "dimensions," as some people call them — density is the more correct term), but the truly "universal" laws apply to all of Creation.

Your scientists are forever searching for the theories that unify other theories into a simpler, more inclusive whole. Universal laws are the reduction of all subsets of "rules" to the Grand Unified Law (or blueprint) for all of Creation. They are encoded in all of material matter and can be accessed by a properly attuned mind.

You — as you currently experience yourself — appear to be a "bag of skin." But there is so much more to you than that. The real "you" is expressing simultaneously on all the logic branches that arose as potentials when your soul was created, or "split off" from the Creator's identification with Itself. Your soul is a projection of the Creator. It IS the Creator, as it contains all aspects of the Creator, but it also experiences itself as slightly different from the Creator. It is a more individuated or "specialized" aspect of the Creator. It is an "expert" or "specialist" in certain themes, which are sometimes called archetypes. However, even within this individuation, there are an infinite number of potentials to be explored, within the parameters of Universal Laws.

So you all have been quite busy at the soul level, creating many parallel versions of "lives," through which you can explore many realities. In fact, you gave yourselves billions of years in which to explore those realities, but now that cycle is coming to an end. It is almost time to hit the "refresh" button on the Creation, to clear out all the fragments on the experiential screen that are left over from previous experiments — to re-draw the creation anew [just as the Refresh button on your Web browser re-loads and re-draws the page you are looking at].

We shall leave the discussion of the cycles involved for another time. For now, just know that all the explorations available within this "set" of possibilities have been nearly exhausted; it is nearly time to bring those "lives" to an end and to close the "set" so another one can be used to replace it. In your theatrical productions, you "strike the set" when the drama is over, when the play closes down. It is just that way on the "stage" now. The "set" will close down and be replaced by another. This means that all of the parallel realities that you have been exploring will terminate and be replaced by a new insertion point into a whole other "set" of possibilities.

There is always a single "seed" point that marks the beginning of some process. There is also a logical end point to the process. You have called these the "Alpha" (beginning) and the "Omega" (end). You are nearly at the Omega point and will soon experience a new Alpha point. In between, there is a Null Point in which nothing exists.

You may be surprised to know that you don't exist all of the time now. You are actually blinking on and off many times a second. Your movies are made up of discrete snapshots, or "frames," none of which are "moving," but when they are projected onto a screen in your movie theaters, they flash on and off so fast that the retention of the image [from one frame to the next] makes them appear to be moving smoothly and without interruption.

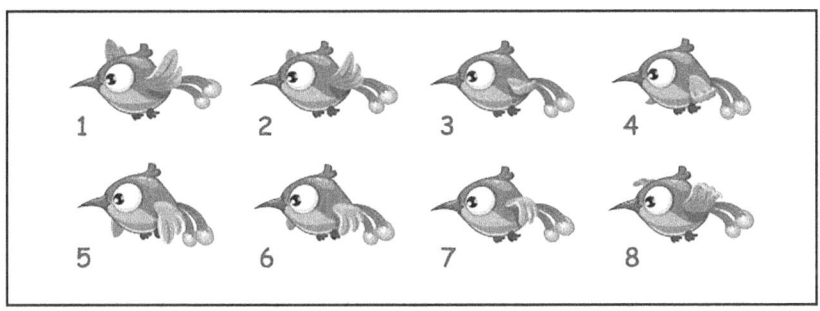

Animation frames of a bird flying

Those people who make animations for the Web know that their animations actually contain several different "frames" or still pictures that appear to move when exhibited on the screen for an appropriately short period of time. Your reality, which appears to you to be continuous and solid, is actually made up of static images — holograms — which flash on and off several times a second, quickly enough that you don't perceive the "off" times but instead experience a "continuous" reality. It is anything but continuous, so the Null Point that we mention is nothing "new," but it IS significant because of what it represents.

Instead of a simple movement from one frame to another — say your head nods downward a tiny fraction of an inch and your hand moves upward a similarly small increment toward your nose, which has started to itch — this Null Point will be what is called a "quantum moment," a gigantic leap onto a whole other experience of reality. The Creation will literally come to an end and be RE-created in the next "frame." It will be re-seeded with a whole new "set" of possibilities. In the moment in between the Omega Point and the Alpha Point, there will literally be "no thing" — there will be no manifest reality anywhere. There will only be the Creator, in a perfect state of rest, but containing all things in potential.

The "you" that you experience now is really only a point of awareness within the All That Is, the expressed portion of the Creator. There are an infinite number of such points, according to the branches that have been explored. But there is only going to be ONE "you" — the "seed" of the new "set" that is about to be created on the other side of the Omega Point.

So what happens to all the other "you"s that have been out there exploring all the other realities? They will be folded back into your soul and merged with it, just as happens each and every time a "life" is ended. But the "you" that is reading this [message] is the one that is going to "go across" into the new reality, so you will begin "seeing" through the eyes of your soul. You will begin to see more and more of the other realities that these other portions or aspects of "you" have been exploring. From the perspective of the "you" that is reading this message, it will seem as though those other realities are "merging with" or "coming into" your own.

There is nothing in your mass culture or literature to explain this to you. That is one of the reasons that we are giving this series of messages to you, to explain to you what is happening now, and to reassure you that you are not "going crazy." You remember we told you to become aware of your breath? Notice what your breath is doing now. Take a deep breath now. Feel the difference.

This information is bound to set up a "but, but, but" response from the level of your ego or personality. It will protest mightily against the magnitude of what we are saying here. Your ego is designed to keep "body and soul" together, so if it hears that it is going to "end," that causes the ego to clamp down into "protection mode," which is experienced as fear. The breath shortens and becomes shallow, as all systems go on "red alert" until the perceived danger is identified and assessed.

When you become aware of your breath being short and shallow, *will* yourself to take a deep breath and give your body and ego the message that you are safe. This is very important. You must begin to develop your own ability to create a sense of safety for yourself, because otherwise you will react from a place of fear — from your ego rather than your higher knowing — and make bad decisions. You will not respond appropriately to the changes that present to you as this cycle of Creation completes.

The parallel realities will merge.

The parallel realities will merge. They have been doing so gradually for some time now, but now this process will accelerate. This is all leading to the Omega point and the crossing through the Null Point into the Alpha point. It is all being sourced and guided from the higher levels, and you do not have to "figure it out." You are passengers on this trip, not the pilot.

Breathe. Meditate. Accept. Relax into it. You are on the most wonderful "magical mystery tour" of all time! Enjoy it. Become like a little child in front of a big department store, peering in through the plate glass window at all the wonders inside. Develop your sense of wonder. Allow your mental "analyst" to take a rest. Just relax, breathe, and sink into this experience of multiple realities. It is part of your preparation to accept the "new you," that multidimensional being that will emerge on the other side of the Null Point.

This is why we have told you to give your spiritual practice the highest importance now. It is of the utmost value at this time to create as much "quiet time" as you can. You will need it to calm yourself, to integrate the many new experiences and insights that begin to flood into you as your light fibers are reconnected. A great deal of your transformation will take place now, on this side of the Null Point. All of these separate "you"s will be merged with your soul, and you will begin to access their awareness and experience. Your apparently solid reality will appear to be melting and you will begin to exist more and more in an "altered state" of consciousness. You will need these periods of quiet to integrate all of this.

It is no small thing that is happening here, and we want you to know that there is a tremendous amount of support that is available from the higher realms, but we cannot give it unless you ask for our assistance. We cannot infringe on your free will. In the chatter of ego mind, there is a lot of "static" on the line, a lot of churning of emotions, all of which obscure and distort the "still, small voice" within you. You need these quiet times to be able hear us and feel us. You need to give this to yourself if you wish to have as smooth a transition as possible.

In closing, we wish to assure you that — outside of time — you have already "gotten there." You will not "miss the boat." You cannot "blow it." Your soul will guide you perfectly. But you will have a much easier time of it if you can follow our suggestions and relax, breathe, meditate, and simplify your lives so you have more and more quiet time. We leave you now in peace and honor and blessing.

Amen, Adonoy Sabayoth. We are the Hosts of Heaven.

THE HARVESTING OF SOULS
July 6, 1999

Today we shall be introducing a new idea or concept — the existence of multiple "selves" all at the same time. If you were to look at reality from the perspective of the Oversoul, you would see all of your "lives" going on simultaneously. You would see that you had created them and you would have very little interest in what was happening to them because you created them WHOLE, i.e., containing everything they needed to complete the life "design" you intended for them. It is a little like the oak tree inside the acorn analogy.

When a life is created, it contains everything needed to complete its life design, similar to the way an oak tree is coded within the acorn.

When a "life" is created, it contains "codings" — very similar to computer programs and subprograms — that will unfold the life perfectly. These codings are contained in the DNA and the various parts of the cells and tissues that make up the body. They are only contained in the brain to the extent that they exist in the cells of the brain. The brain does not "think" or direct. It is merely a switching station that coordinates signals or information exchange between the many different parts of the body and interprets the data coming in from the sensory input mechanisms.

The codings are contained in the DNA and cells and tissues of the body.

Each "life" is actually a projection of the Oversoul into a particular space/time environment. It is connected to the Oversoul by the "silver cord," a filament that directly connects the physical body to the Oversoul and which acts as a communication link between the Oversoul and the body or "life." The Oversoul exists outside of linear time, and so from its perspective, all of its projections are going on simultaneously. It is free to terminate a life, in which case it simply disconnects the silver cord, or create one, in which case it extends a silver cord into a developing fetus. Time is a vector quantity, associated with material reality. Since the Oversoul exists in non-material reality, it is outside of linear time.

Time is a way of defining location. For example, if you say you were born in Baton Rouge, you must also say WHEN you were born, in order to precisely locate the event. You could understand this by imagining a street on which a parade was going to pass. The parade streams through that street at a particular time. If you were in that parade playing the drum, you could locate yourself by saying, "I will pass by the corner of Main and Oak Streets at precisely 11:11 a.m. on Tuesday, July 6, 1999." That way, not only could you place yourself within time, but so could any other event that needed to intersect with you, according to ITS plan for itself. Time not only keeps things from happening all at once, it also provides the necessary component for things to move or progress.

So, to return to the Oversoul, from outside of time (which is where the Oversoul resides), all of its projections are simultaneous. But from *within* time, each life is experienced as being separated across time. You speak of "past lives" and sometimes "future lives," but those are expressions of the experience of being bound by linear time. You can "remember" these other "lives" by accessing the information in the Oversoul. The Oversoul is the repository of all the personal memories, from all of the "lives" it creates. When it is appropriate, one of your subprograms kicks in and you "remember" something from these other "lives," to assist you in unfolding your "program" for the "life" you experience yourself as living.

There is no such thing as "re"-incarnation. There is only "incarnation." The Oversoul projects itself into a space/time locus and clothes the tip of that projection in a "body." It is like putting a finger in a bowl of pudding. The finger is part of you. The pudding represents the space/time environment into which you put your finger. The fingertip can feel the pudding. It can tell if it is warm or cold, soft, wet, dry, or firm. Just so with you. You are the sensory tip of a "finger" of your Oversoul, thrust into the "pudding" of your present space/time environment. You interact with your environment, which includes the presence of "fingers" from other Oversouls, each sensing and interacting with the same environment, but from their own perspective. The experience of reality is totally SUBJECTIVE. There is no "objective" reality that everyone can agree upon because each point of awareness has its own perspective and sees things from a slightly different "angle." That is how the Creator gets to view Itself from all possible "angles" at once.

We are using the term Oversoul today, but in past messages we have referred to it as the soul, because that is a more familiar term for most of you. Each of these messages is building upon the ones that have gone

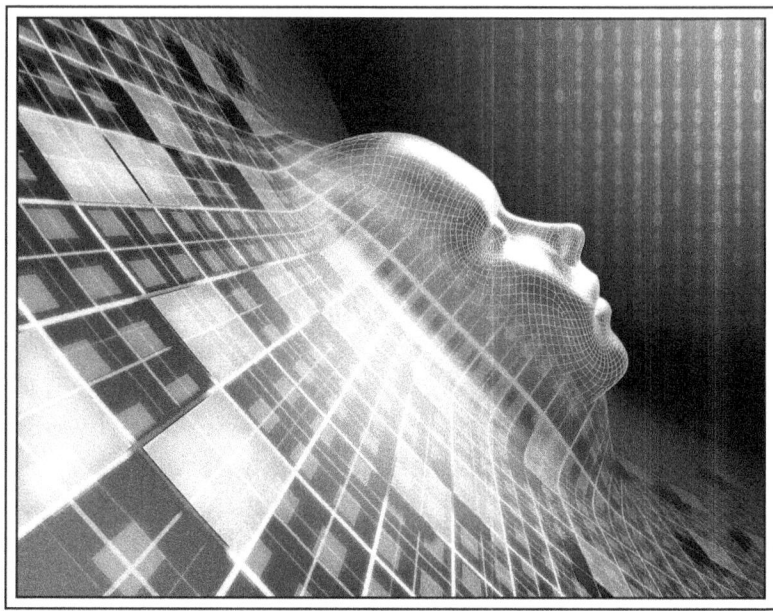

The Oversoul projects itself into a space/time locus and clothes the tip of that projection in a "body."

before, in a spiral fashion. Each message builds upon the previous ones and lays the groundwork for the following ones. This is the way the Universe unfolds itself.

The "soul" is actually like a bead on the silver cord, between the Oversoul and the "body" of the life. It is like a local supervisor and only has that one "life" to contend with. Its job is to closely monitor and interact with that "life" and to assist it in fulfilling its purpose in being. When the silver cord is withdrawn by the Oversoul, the soul is pulled back up into the Oversoul and merges into it. All of the experiences of the "life" flow up the silver cord during that life, so the soul does not contain anything other than its capacity to assist that life in fulfilling its purposes.

Now that all but one of the "lives" are being terminated, the Oversoul is "harvesting" its accumulated experience and preparing to make a quantum leap into another reality. Even Oversouls "graduate" and move up the evolutionary ladder, back to Source. In reality, Source IS everything all at once, but from the subjective perspective of any individuated portion of the Absolute, it has its awareness placed somewhere along the evolutionary flow that proceeds forth from Source (the Absolute) and back into Source, continuously, like an unending river or stream of consciousness that has no beginning or end.

However, sometimes — across very long periods of time as you know it — Source "blinks" or "swallows." You are approaching one such event. The Oversouls are individuated portions of Source, and they are all in direct communication with Source. You might liken them to the "fingers" of Source, as in our pudding example above. They are an intermediate step between "All There Is" and the individual "lives" being lived. (As we have said, there is only ONE LIFE being lived, through its many expressions. That is why we have been placing quotation marks around the word "life" or "lives." They are relative and subjective. Only the Absolute (Source) is absolute and objective. This will have significance later on, when we discuss holograms.)

Source is going to "blink" soon, and on the other side of the blink It will "see" a very different Creation. This is not provided for in any of the cosmologies you have available, which is why we are providing this information now — to help you understand what is about to happen and the magnitude of it. In virtually all cosmologies, you have made the assumption that life proceeds in cycles of symmetric or logarithmic shape. You assume that if it took so many billions of years to reach a certain evolutionary state, that it will take a similar amount of time to complete the "return" trip.

In the models of the "ages," you have two kinds: those in which the "ages" are of the same length (such as the Piscean Age or the Age of Aquarius), and those in which the "ages" have a logarithmic relationship to each other (such as in the "yugas" and the traditions that refer to very long "golden" ages, followed by shorter "silver" ages, followed by still shorter ages, until you get to the one you are experiencing now, the shortest and most difficult of all). Those systems propose that the next step after the shortest age is another "golden" age — from shortest age to longest age in one step, which is closer to what will be happening now.

However, there is a significant difference this time. In a message that was delivered through J. J. Hurtak some years ago, reference is made to the "respatialization of consciousness" following the Null Point (he called it the Gravity Null Zone). This is very accurate. The Creation is about to be entirely re-created. All the foci of consciousness will be "blinked off" for an immeasurable "moment." (Time will also cease, as there will be no material reality in that moment and time is a function of material reality; it is the "time" portion of space/time.) On the other side of the "blink," the "players" in the drama of Creation will find themselves standing on other "spots" on the "stage." It will be like closing your eyes and then reopening them, only to find that the scene you are looking at has changed drastically.

What this means is that all of the stuff of prediction is rendered null and void. All of the human prophets and seers have seen through the perspective of the present reality. There is no one that is or was in a physical body that can accurately predict what is about to happen or what one will experience after that "blink" has occurred. Each and every Oversoul will be affected in ways that even the Oversouls cannot anticipate. Their only task is to prepare themselves for the event by completing all of their "lives," harvesting all but one of the souls back into the Oversoul, and retaining one portion of exteriorized consciousness with which to "seed" the new Creation.

There will be many fewer players on the "stage" when the new drama unfolds. You who are reading this message will be among those who are there to experience it, but you will be much changed from your present form and identity. You are being prepared by your Oversoul and overseen by your soul for this event. We are doing our best to prepare you so that you will not be overwhelmed by the magnitude of what is happening and by the new sensations and awarenesses that have begun to enter your consciousness.

Many of you naturally have come to revere the great beings who have appeared on the world stage — the Christ, the Buddha, and others. Now YOU will become as they were. You have another job ahead, and in order to step into those "shoes" and fill them, you must step out of the ones you are wearing now.

This is the time of the harvest of the souls. Everyone who is in a body has a soul. This is the time of the great "summing up" of all of the "lives" lived. Depending on the "total," each Oversoul will come to its own conclusions about what it wishes to create next. There is no damnation, no "judgement" by a wrathful God. (It should really be spelled with a little "g," for the Absolute is the absolute, and "wrath" is a human projection onto the Absolute that is entirely misplaced. There HAVE been entities that have appeared as "gods" in their interaction with humankind on Earth, but that is another story for another time.) But here is where it gets interesting for you: you are the one "life" that will be retained to seed the new Creation.

You have great adventures ahead of you, and you have begun your transformation into that being that you will experience yourself as being on the other side of the "blink." All is in hand. All is being prepared. You have suffered enough, beloveds. Soon you will be at the banquet, with all of your fellow Wanderers. You will have much fun in creating something entirely new.

Enjoy yourselves in these remaining days. Do not worry about the scare tactics of the various entities who have a different idea of how it will go. They will not be around in your reality on the other side of the "blink." Everything has its place in the Creation. You have yours; they have theirs. We are assisting in these matters to make sure that everyone gets to their own "right place." No longer will it be necessary for Earth to host such contention and division. She will be able to pursue her theme of "seeking harmony in diversity," but now it will be as it was originally intended — a diversity of forms and cultures, all of whom will be resonant with the new vibratory frequency that will characterize the New Earth, Terra. These contentious ones will have their own world in which to continue their battles with each other. They will not bother you anymore, and they will finally be free of you and your reminders of what they are not. Everyone will end up at home in the vibratory band that is most akin to his or her nature.

You — because you have read this far — are destined for Terra. If you were not, you would have left off reading these Messages a while back. They are coded transmissions, and you will only respond favorably to them if you carry the matching coding within you. You are small in number relative to the total population of Earth, less than $1/10^{th}$ of 1%. But you are the seeds for the new garden, the new birth of Earth in her glorious time as Terra.

Happy journey! We shall speak to you again.

Amen, Adonoy Sabayoth. We are the Hosts of Heaven.

ON PROBABILITIES
July 7, 1999

In today's Message, we want to speak about probabilities. You know how many are going about these days proclaiming that they know what is going to happen, that it will be such and such, and they are very sure that it will be as they say. However, NO ONE knows what is really going to happen, not even us, because there are only indications of what will "probably be" the case.

We can say, with a reasonable degree of certainty, that such and such will *probably* be the outcome of certain observed trends, but no one can really be certain. The Creator is playing hide-and-seek with Itself and apparently even It likes to be surprised. It's what keeps the game interesting. If one could predict with absolute certainty everything that would happen, one would scarcely have to "get up in the morning." It would make for a very dull existence, indeed.

The whole reason the Creation was created was so that the Creator could experiment with all of the different possibilities (within certain parameters, called Universal Laws), so It could get to hide from Itself and so discover Itself in an unending mystery unfolding. The Creator "likes" to be surprised, because the reality game is Its only entertainment.

Think about it: here you are, All That Is. Everything is contained within you, and you are everywhere at once. There is no place to "go" because you are already "there." So what do you do for entertainment? You surprise yourself.

(You are a "chip off the old block," so to speak — a projection from an individuated portion of the Creator — so you show glimpses of the Creator's nature. It is not so "off" to project "human" traits onto the Creator, because one can glimpse the Creator through Its creations. The true human is the crown of material reality; it comes the closest to the nature of the Creator, so we can get some idea of what "makes the Creator tick" by observing true humans.

You, in your present state, are not true humans, as we have said, but hybrids. In the transformation you are undergoing right now, you will be returning to your true human status. Viewed from your present state of affairs, you will be as "gods," but that is our point. Even though you are not yet returned to your fully conscious state, you still have enough of the human quality in you to glimpse what you will be like in your fully conscious state. And from that, you can impute what the Creator is like, and can attribute human qualities to the Creator.)

So, the Creator likes surprises. It always has something up Its sleeve, so to speak. And here we are, sailing along in a particular direction, expecting such and such to happen, and then Wham! Out of the blue. A surprise. It could not be anticipated, not even by us. Something or someone shows up that was wholly unplanned for, and it spins things into a totally unexpected direction.

However, for a surprise to *really* be a surprise, you cannot even see an inkling of it coming. Those are the ones the Creator REALLY likes!

Here we are, going along, doing our best to carry out our service, trying to anticipate what we will have to prepare for, and then Boom! Along comes a surprise and it's back to the drawing boards. And if WE — given the level we operate at — can't make solid plans and expect them to last, just imagine how unclear the picture is for those in your state of consciousness who claim to "know" the future!

Boom! Along comes a surprise and it's back to the drawing boards.

That's why you never find anyone "batting 1000." No channel, no seer, no prophet of any shape or size, can know the future with any degree of certainty. And this is both a source of frustration and a great comfort at the same time.

We have spoken of the need to trust in the Creator, as a component of our definition of love. We have to trust in the Creator, too. Now we get to the heart of the matter. In these most uncertain of times, there are many things that are hidden from us as well as you. All we — or anyone — can do is try to put our efforts behind the most likely outcomes and try to take advantage of the momentum in that direction.

We are dealing with a set of probabilities, i.e., that there is a certain degree of likelihood that such and such will happen. We put all of our best efforts into trying to maximize that potential in a direction that would please us, but as you know from your own lives, sometimes things change.

We began the preparation for the transition to Terra many centuries ago, as counted within your years. We had high hopes of a huge harvest for Terra. The probability was — say 80% — that that might be the case, so we threw all of our best efforts into sowing seeds that would make it possible to happen. But as you know from the story about casting seeds, some do not fall on good soil. Some begin to grow, but encounter conditions that do not allow them to finish growing.

We are not omniscient, so we could not know in advance how all the Oversouls would play the game. No one was showing their cards to anyone else. It's made to be that way, for the reasons that we stated earlier.

Now, however, we are at the "end game" stage. There are certain geometries that occur in the movements of the planets, stars, galaxies, and indeed the entire system of created universes. They each have their own period, much like the gears in a clockworks. Each turns at different rates, and every so often, they align with other gears (planets, stars, and galaxies) in particular geometries that make certain potentials available. There is a "window of opportunity" available that permits or supports certain things that cannot occur at any other time.

This is what is behind the system of divination you call astrology. When certain aspects or alignments occur, it has been noticed that certain other phenomena are associated with them. This is true, because the "working beam" (holographic terminology) is altered in its orientation to the "reference beam" (the Absolute) so that a different "picture" (outpicturing) occurs in the hologram that constitutes your perceived reality. (We shall have more to say on the subject of holograms later.)

The point of this is that if you picture all the "gears" to have a mark on them and that all the marks were lined up at the "beginning" of the Creation, they are all approaching that same alignment again. It is a window of opportunity for a new beginning, a wholly new Creation.

We have known that this opportunity was coming, and we wished to assist in ways that would maximize the harvest for Terra. There are other destinations for those who will not be going to Terra, but Terra is our "project," you might say, and that is where we put our energy.

We knew that there was a great deal of inertia to overcome, due to the workings of the interlopers, but we put our shoulders to the wheel, so to speak, and put everything we had to work with toward the aim of maximizing the harvest for Terra. We knew the greatest probability was that the harvest would be small, so we put our efforts into that "marginal" area — toward reaching as many as possible who were on the margins — to try to get as many as we could to go over the line and "make the grade," so to speak, who would not otherwise do so without our help.

You may have noticed that there were many predictions for Earth changes and such that simply did not manifest. Even now, the world has become a little more violent, the weather is definitely not "as usual," but little else seems to have changed. Things seem pretty much "business as usual." But there is this clockworks to contend with. Events cannot be delayed indefinitely.

The Earth changes are a necessary part of the planet's preparation to become manifest as Terra. They are the way she will rid herself of the negativity and confusion that she has absorbed from human interference with natural systems. We are approaching the end of the runway. We must now take flight, or never get off the ground. We have held back the Earth changes as long as we could so that we could put all of our efforts into reaching those who were marginal, who wouldn't make it to Terra without our help.

It is one minute to midnight. Soon all the gears will line up and a powerful beam of energy will manifest, all the way back to the Source. When this happens, there is this opportunity to re-create the Creation. It only occurs once in several billion years, so it is too rare and too precious an opportunity to waste. You are already within the influence of this beam, and the changes have begun.

It is one minute to midnight. Soon all the gears will line up and a powerful beam of energy will manifest, all the way back to the Source.

As you move through time toward the point of perfect alignment, the effects of this beam will grow and the pace of change will quicken until it is at a maximum. That is when the "leap" will occur. When that moment is reached, the Null Point will occur, and all the players will be rearranged into new configurations.

The players include the planets and stars because they are also conscious beings with destinies of their own. Earth will become Terra and will operate at a different frequency band than she currently operates at. The Earth changes have to occur so that she is ready to make her leap when the moment presents. She cannot be weighed down by the "baggage" she has taken on from her human occupants. She has to shed all of it in order to be ready.

You, too — at least those of you who are destined for Terra — have been shedding your "baggage." You, too, cannot be weighed down, so that you are ready to make your leap into the next frequency band. Your "earthquakes" have been going on for some time now, only they have taken the form of shaking you loose from all of your activities and associations and relationships that did not serve your movement to Terra.

We will be taking you to another place to complete your transition, so that you are ready to repopulate the Earth when she has completed her transition to becoming Terra. We will be doing this in stages. The first group is extremely small — only a handful — and will not be noticed except by those immediately involved with them. The second group will be fairly substantial, and the third group will be the largest of all and be taken at the last possible moment. The first two groups will be further along in their preparations by then, and will be involved in assisting those in the third group to adapt to their changing status.

As we have indicated, the harvest for Terra is less than 1/10th of 1% of the present world population. As small as that is, it would have been even smaller if we had not chosen to play the "probability" game. We are somewhat sad that we were not more successful, but we are gladdened by the success that we have achieved. More people "made the grade" than would have if we had not helped, and we are content with that. We did our best, and we, too, have to surrender to the higher authority. We, too, have to ACCEPT what has happened and how the "mop flopped."

Very soon, now, the first group will be taken. They know who they are and have been given clear guidance or at least a clear sense of their life winding up. We are giving these messages now, so that they can remain available to those who will follow.

By the way, some people who will be in the third group are there because they asked to be allowed to stay until the end so they could help for as long as possible. They are truly "saints" for that service, for it will be very demanding as the Earth changes begin in earnest and so many will need assistance. But they will have assistance by then, as those who "went" in the first group will be able to come back and assist in ways that they could not if they were still "mere mortals." We shall come back to this topic later.

For now, all you need to know is that the game is almost over. Things are going to get going, "big time," very soon, and we wanted to give you these messages so you would be able to understand the larger picture that is unfolding behind the surface phenomena. We will have a few more messages for you and then it will all be said. Then it will be up to you to take this information and put it to use, to keep it in your hearts and minds, to hold the shining promise of Terra before you as a vision of the horizon toward which you walk. It hopefully will sustain you as the world around you comes tumbling down and the doorway to your future swings open.

We leave you now in peace and honor and blessing. Amen, Adonoy Sabayoth. We are the Hosts of Heaven.

When the doorway to your future swings open

CHANGING INTO "GODS"
July 8, 1999

Today's message will deal with holograms. Holograms form the basis of your perceived reality. The "you" that is reading this message is really a holographic projection of your Oversoul. You feel and look totally solid, but in fact that is part of the illusion of material reality. Without getting too technical, you are the result of interference patterns that result in standing waves. You are a package of standing waves.

Your physical body is contained in a matrix of Light. This Light is a substance, similar to water vapor, but much finer. It is incandescent, self-luminous, and so is often referred to as the Light Body. It is a matrix of Light in which the denser material that makes up the gross physical level is suspended, like so many particles in a soup. To "call down the Light Body" is ridiculous, as you would not be able to walk around if you weren't already "in" your Light Body. It is what shapes you, carries you, and forms you. It is the "template" for your form. It is the projection of your Oversoul, and without it, you simply would not exist in material reality. You are a hologram of Light, formed by Light. All holograms are formed by light, of one kind or another. You are made up of Light.

Each particle of matter is a densification of this Light. Each material object is floating in a sea of this Light. You can't see it with your physical eyes, but for those people who can see into the finer regions of reality, they are very aware of this. Why do we mention this? Because very soon now, you will be changing your form to more nearly resemble the perfected model of your Light Body.

We have mentioned the interlopers. They tinkered with the original design for the Adamic model and crossbred it with the higher apes on your planet. This led to some contamination of the encodings and [to] the subsequent confusion of identity that resulted. You are going through a purification process that will enable you to shed all of the "impurities" of this hybridization and regain your natural form. To you, these forms will look so perfect that you would call yourselves "gods" (and "goddesses").

But there is more to this change than "meets the eye." To function on the next level of being, you must also have a change in your consciousness. We are gradually helping you to shift your identity, but we are also helping you to reconnect your unused Light circuitry, so that you will become fully conscious again. This is your true estate, your true nature, and we are here to help you regain your true station in the Creator's realm.

This shift will bring you many things. You will have all your powers back — the ability to create directly from the matrix of reality, the ability to move backward and forward through time, the ability to perform what you would call "miracles." You will have total mastery, with all the "perks" that go with that, but you will also have the responsibility that goes with those "perks." You will not have powers that you do not also have the wisdom to use properly.

In order for you to have an environment that allows for the smooth transition to this "new you," we will be working with you to take you far enough to handle another vibratory level, and then you will simply vanish from the third-density plane and appear in the fourth-density plane, where we have prepared a place for you. You will reside there until Terra is ready for you and you are ready for Terra. For those that go in the first two waves, you will have work to do before Terra is ready. You will know more when you get there. All you need to know right now is that this will happen. These messages are simply to prepare you for the change, not to describe every last detail of what will play out after that.

So this is a shift in frequency and it is also a shift in consciousness. You will find that you quite naturally begin functioning in new ways. Time and memory are the first things to go, but your bodies will also begin to operate differently. Pay attention to your bodies and what they are telling you. You may find that some foods no longer appeal to you and others suddenly become attractive. There are no rules to this game. You must throw out every idea of what you think is "how it is."

Stay in the moment and "go with the flow." Surrender will be helpful in this. Just keep letting go and [let] God [direct things], and you will have a much easier time of it. Wherever you cling to old ways, in whatever form, the pressure will build up until that grip is broken, for you cannot take any of the old ways into the new world. You are being re-created *in situ*. You will emerge as a fully formed, mature adult, without going through death, rebirth, and maturation. From one adult form to another.

So how do you accomplish this? You ACCEPT it. You focus on listening within and allowing the process to unfold within you. You allow yourself to melt and flow with the process. Resistance will be the source of all and any discomfort you may have with this process. Simply let go. If you find yourself in some form of discomfort, then do what you must to relax into it and it will shift.

If you find yourself in some form of discomfort, then do what you must to relax into it and it will shift.

Take a bath. Meditate. Write your feelings. Breathe. Breathe. Breathe. Your breath is always a clue to whether you are holding onto something or letting go. Sigh a lot. That will give your body the message to keep on letting go. That feeling you have when you sigh — of emphasizing the exhale — is the body's way of saying it's letting go. "Let go and let God" [direct things]. This should be your motto. This will help you more than anything else to get through this transition with the least discomfort possible. Everything of your old life is going to go, so why hang onto it? Just let go.

There is really not much more for us to say to you today, as letting go is the way through. All the mechanics and logistics are being handled for you, so just take a passenger seat and enjoy the view. You have not much longer to wait.

Amen, Adonoy Sabayoth. We are the Hosts of Heaven.

Just take a passenger seat and enjoy the view.

ON EXTRATERRESTRIALS AND THE HARVEST
July 9, 1999

Good day. Today we are going to touch on a very controversial subject — that of extraterrestrials, UFOs, and other such "fringe" phenomena. First of all, to define the word "extraterrestrial."

Extraterrestrial means "from outside of the planet Earth (Terra)."

"Extra," used in this sense, means "outside of"; "terrestrial" means "having to do with the [planet] Earth." Please note that the word "terrestrial" contains the signature of Terra as the planet's true name. You are already on Terra, but not as she will become.

So extraterrestrial means "from outside of the planet Earth (Terra)." Well, you are ALL extraterrestrials in that sense, because you all are being projected from a level that is not based on the planet and your bodies are made up of the elements that are the stuff of stars. You are truly *celestial* beings. Also note that the word extraterrestrial places Earth at the center of the universe and identifies everything that is not ON the Earth as being extraterrestrial, a form of "us" and "them" thinking that is now obsolete. We prefer the term "celestials," but for this discussion, we will use your convention and refer to beings whose home base is not on the planet Earth as ETs.

ETs come in many shapes, sizes and forms. Your media has popularized the "little grey men" of Roswell fame, and the T-shirts and various "tourist" items are more often than not emblazoned with little slanty-eyed grey ETs. However sensational they are (and with them the tales of abductions, cattle mutilations, and sexual interchange), they are not all there is to this picture.

There are many races interacting with your people right now. The most visible are the ones who are in the lower frequency bands, but there are also ones that operate in the higher frequency bands. They are only visible to you in your "inner" vision. We are in this latter category for now. We do not usually materialize in the physical band, although we can if we choose to. We are in the bands that contain those you would call Masters, angels, and archangels. We work with the Office of the Christ. (That is not a particular person, but an office or position within the spiritual hierarchy.)

We [the ETs] come in two "flavors," according to our alignment and methods of operation (M.O.). We either serve others (service-to-others, also known as STO) or we serve ourselves (service-to self, also known as STS). No matter what our particular form — our apparent "planet of origin" — that is the most important thing for you to know about us. Are we STS or STO? That M.O. defines how we will interact with you and what our true motives are.

STS always want something from you that serves their own agenda but is not in your best interests. STO is there to be of assistance in whatever way does not infringe upon your free will and choice. No matter how sweet the words are, it is always useful in dealing with those who are of a culture foreign to your own ("alien" means "foreign") to ask yourselves, "Who does this (action) serve? Is it in my best interests or theirs?"

On Extraterrestrials and the Harvest 111

It is always useful in dealing with those who are of a culture foreign to your own ("alien" means "foreign") to ask yourselves, "Who does this (action) serve?"

Now, as we have said, there is ONLY ONE LIFE being lived. No matter what the current "costume" is, or the apparent behavior, it is all an expression of that one life, which you may call God, the Creator, Source, or All That Is. *All* ETs are expressions of that one life. We are not wanting to get into "us" and "them" thinking, "enemies" and "friends" divisions, but rather to take two steps back and simply observe: Who is served?

Now that we have laid the groundwork and vocabulary, we will say that we are of the STO variety of ET. We are here to help you in any way that we can that will not infringe on your own free choice. The interlopers of whom we have spoken are of the other "flavor." They are STS in their M.O., and as such they are not bound by such constraints. They can and will infringe on your choice in any way that you LET them, but they cannot override your free will. If you do not want to deal with them, all you need to do is to assert your free will. Tell them to leave and they must obey.

Wherever you carry fear, that is a weak point, a place where you are vulnerable, and they operate best by playing on your fears. This is always the case. If you feel helpless or afraid in some way, they have gained power over you, and gaining power is their whole game. They literally feed off of it. You have observed some of this kind of behavior among certain people on Earth. It is of the same "flavor," no matter where you find it. Always ask, "Who does it serve?"

We have spoken of the harvesting of souls and the different "destinations" that will be available after the Null Point. Where one ends up is dependent on the sum of the choices that have been made by the souls belonging to a particular Oversoul. There will be a certain "light quotient" contained within the Oversoul after it has harvested all of the souls that belong to it and absorbed them. This light quotient determines the level at which the Oversoul vibrates, or its frequency.

There will be a certain "light quotient" contained within the Oversoul after it has harvested all of the souls that belong to it.

You might be surprised to find out that Oversouls come in two flavors, as well. Both flavors exist because the Creator wanted to experience EVERYTHING, wanted to experience the full range of Its creative potential. It did not want to know Itself only by serving others. It wanted to know Itself in all the ways that were possible. All forms and behaviors still come back to the Creator wanting to explore and know Its full range of potential, nothing more and certainly nothing less.

It is so easy to label things: "This is good; this is bad." The Creator just IS. It is neither good nor bad. It is not compassionate, merciful, angry, or punishing. It simply IS. Those attributes (compassion, anger, etc.) are projections upon a field of pure consciousness that is simply experimenting with all the possible ways of expression that are available to It. It is BOTH serving Itself and serving others. It serves others by creating them and allowing them to participate in the experience It is having. It serves Itself by creating others through which It experiences. There is ONLY ONE LIFE being lived. It is the Creator in Its infinite array of forms, or expressions.

That is the "absolute" way of looking at it. But you (and we) are also experiencing at the "relative" level of experience. Within that "relative" experience, there APPEARS to be "good" and "bad," STO and STS kinds of things and behaviors. They are "good" or "bad" only when compared to something else. That is the "relative" part — as one thing RELATES to (or refers to) something else.

There is no way around this, as the Creator likes to play hide-and-seek with Itself, and so it hides in all forms while It seeks Itself. It makes things so much more interesting, as seen from the Creator's perspective, because there is so much more "grist for the mill." There is so much more to work with, and there is so much more variety available than there would be if things only came in one of these two flavors.

If there were only STO, things could get a little dull after a while. If there were only STS, things wouldn't last very long, because the STS flavor, in serving only itself, is inherently predatory and destructive towards everything else. It operates through competition, not co-operation. You can see the results on your own planet, which has been effectively destroyed by these self-serving behaviors on the part of so many.

But now we are at the time of Harvest, when each comes for their own and seeks to maximize their potential in the "great summing up" that is underway at this time. All of the Oversouls want to maximize their light quotient, so their projections are going about, gathering in more light of the flavor that they are made of. Both kinds of flavors are actively recruiting right now.

The STS are seeking to increase their power, so they do what they can to increase the amount of fear in the environments in which they are operating. Fear gives them access, gives them power over those who are in fear. Since we have defined love (in part) as the absence of fear, you can see how love is the antithesis of what they would want you to feel in order to promote their agenda of gaining power. They can only gain power through others' fears, so wherever love is (as we have defined it), they are blocked from gaining power.

There are a great number of ETs interacting with Earth right now. They are here for many reasons — some to be active participants in the Harvest, and some to simply observe and learn from it. They come in both flavors. We are here to help you increase your love and light quotient. Others are here to increase fear and thus create more opportunities to increase their power over others.

STS is always based on a master/slave hierarchical relationship. STS entities, regardless of origin, are always seeking to gain a foothold on someone else's shoulders so that they may gain power over others and climb up the rungs of their power hierarchy. STO is seeking to help other sovereign beings, to interact in ways that "level the playing field" and elevate all individuals to their maximum potential. STO revels in sharing the limitless wealth of the Creator's Love and Light, while STS seeks to accumulate as much of a "finite" amount of power as it can. The biggest laugh is that when viewed from the highest possible perspective, both flavors are seeking to become more like the Creator, but they seek it from opposite sides.

The Creator is the Source of all Love, Light, and Power. But the STO is not interested in power as much as it wishes to *be* empowered and to help others claim their "birthright," also — to share the limitless supply with others, because there is plenty for everyone. STS seeks to get, keep, and hoard as much power as it can, but the more successful it is, the lonelier it becomes. There actually comes a point when the STS is so lonely that it decides that it is tired of all that power, that the mere [possession] of power is not satisfying when there is no one there to share it with.

When an STS has reached that clarity of its position, then (and only then) its natural "next step" is to switch to the STO version of reality, and this is not as difficult as you might think. By the time an STS gets to that point, they have so thoroughly explored all the possible ways in which one gets and keeps power for itself, it has exhausted that set of possibilities. It has "been there, seen it, done it" with all of the possible experiences of that flavor and reached the end of its creative potential within that flavor, so it looks to the "greener pastures" of what it hasn't explored, jumps the fence, and quickly becomes an STO groupie.

ETs of both flavors are here to recruit (in the case of STS) or help (in the case of STO). The STS will try to keep those of the STO persuasion from remaining on their path of growing love, because then the STS supply of power sources diminishes. Since STS is based on the idea of a FINITE supply, rather than the limitless abundance idea of the STO, any decrease in fear levels is perceived as a loss of power by the STS. That is why one sees so many well-intentioned individuals being "led astray" by STS entities. That is why love (as we have defined it) is the best armor and protection one can have and the greatest insurance policy one can get to "make it" on the STO path.

The media on your planet are not there to tell the truth. They are there to sell things, for that is how they get their portion of the power medium you call money. Fear sells. Sex sells. Romance sells. Emotion sells. Truth does not sell, except when it "exposes" something, and what is that but emotional titillation? The media is there to stimulate you to "buy" whatever it is that they are selling, whether it is a product, a philosophy (Who does it serve?), or a point of view that empowers you or (more likely) disempowers you.

The media has treated the subjects of ETs, UFOs, and "paranormal" phenomena in ways that increase the emotional titillation, the rush of adrenaline, also known as fear. Lately that has shifted a little, as there is more acceptance of higher realities, but on the whole the media serves the purposes of the STS flavor more than it does those of the STO flavor. It is natural that this would be the case because the entire planetary economy is operating in ways that serve the STS individuals in high positions of authority more than it serves the general populace (which is so ignorant and unconscious of the consequences of their choices that they are easy pawns for the power-mongers above them).

We are here in great numbers, and when the time is right, we shall render ourselves visible to those who have "eyes to see" — those whose frequency is that of love (as we have defined it) and can therefore see others who operate in that frequency. Those who are in fear will never see us. If you are in fear and see an ET, be assured it will be of the STS flavor.

You cannot see love unless you are in that state of love, through the principle of resonance. But you can always FEEL love, even if you still contain some fear. So while you cannot see us yet (except with your inner vision), you can always FEEL us and our presence. You can also

FEEL the feelings you get when STS energies are around you, whether they are of "human" or "ET" origin, whether they are in your visual frequency band or currently in frequencies beyond those your physical eyes can see.

Trust your feelings. We will say that again. TRUST YOUR FEELINGS. No matter what something "looks like" on the surface, ask yourself, "How does this FEEL to me?" There are many whose tongues drip with honey, who tell you what you want to hear, who put you to sleep with their hypnotic droning voices. But you can FEEL when you are being lulled, you can feel when you are being led astray. It is a subtle difference between that and moving out of fear on your own. You can be comforted when you are in pain, but only you can deal with your fears. You must face them down within yourself. No one can do that for you, although others can — by their example, advice, and encouragement — show you the way.

You are about to become ETs yourselves, so it behooves you to become masters of your own feelings, to use your feeling capacity to detect who is playing what game. Do not rely on your media to tell you what is going on. Only your feeling sense and a willingness to examine the deeper levels of the surface phenomena will help you chart your course.

In the end, though, you can never know enough to be safe. You must create your own sense of safety within yourself. Put your energy into creating that internal sanctuary, where you can connect with Source. But as you thread your way through these last days before the Harvest, know that there are those who would use you for their agenda, and there are those who are here to help you move through your fears into love (as we have defined it). It is up to you to choose, in each and every moment, to move through your fears into love, as that is the ticket Home.

Those who are destined to go to Terra will need to have love in their hearts. It is not your deeds that matter as much as your frequency. If you have love and not fear, you will naturally behave in loving ways. If you ask for our help, we will give it in whatever ways and in whatever measure does not infringe on your own right to choose.

There is an enormous amount of Grace available to help you move through your fear, but you must open yourself to receive it. Meditate. Breathe. Set aside some quiet time. Let the love come in. Let the fear go. You are safe. You cannot be destroyed. You do not have to "die." You are immortal beings, about to go on the adventure you have dreamed of, waking and sleeping. Terra calls.

We leave you now, in peace and honor and blessing. We shall speak to you again.

Amen, Adonoy, Sabayoth. We are the Hosts of Heaven.

You must create your own sense of safety within yourself.

SUMMING UP
July 10, 1999

Today we wish to speak to you about the forthcoming Earth changes and the effects they will have upon the various lifeforms upon the planet. For some time now, we have been acting as conservators of certain species, to preserve them and their genetics for inhabiting the new planet, Terra. On Terra, everything will exist in an exalted state, not only in consciousness, but also in the forms that outpicture that changed consciousness. Every lifeform will be exquisite. Everything will be glorified, as Earth takes her rightful place as the jewel of the galaxy.

Toward this end, many of the species will be leaving the planet altogether. Those we have not collected, as they will no longer be present on Earth when she assumes her new form. These are principally those creatures that are part of the cycle of death, disease, and decay. There are some that will undergo a fundamental change in their nature, primarily those that have functioned as pets for humans, but others also. This is where the prediction that the "lion shall lie down with the lamb" comes from. Certain carnivores will change their essential nature in order to live on Terra and be part of that habitat.

Those aside, the other forms of life that are predators, disease-bearers, and those that participate in the breakdown of forms to more elemental forms will be absent. Everything else will be transformed or eliminated from the Terran "list" of lifeforms. (It should be noted that entirely new lifeforms, from other parts of the galaxy, will be "transplanted" to Terra, just as you transplant exotic plants into your gardens that are not native to your area.)

The Earth changes are part of this process. They serve several purposes. The first and primary purpose is as we stated: to cleanse the Earth of her accumulated burden of negativity — those thoughtforms and energies that are of the lower frequencies and would keep her from her own ascension to the next frequency band of reality. The second purpose is to assist in the facilitation of getting all things to their own "right place." This is a special function being overseen by Archangel Michael and us, the Hosts of Heaven. (We are the "heavenly hosts" being spoken of in the expressions "Lord of Hosts" and the "Legions of Michael.")

We have to see to it that all things get to their "right place."

We have this special function to perform — to see to it that all things get to their "right place." You might think of us as traffic directors or logistics specialists. Your taxi and police dispatchers perform a similar function. They get the workers to the right spot at the right time to assist those who need assistance. The Earth changes serve other purposes, also, including making the third-density form of Earth uninhabitable for an extended period, so that the new world has all the attention it needs to be fully born.

We have spoken of Earth (and Terra) in terms of being the garden spot of the galaxy. In good stewardship of the land, each portion must be allowed to lie fallow for a time, in order for balance to be restored and nutrients to be replenished. The Earth has been sucked dry, all of her precious gifts mined beyond the state where they can naturally recover in a short period of time. You might say that humans have been living off their grandchildren's inheritance for some time, so the Earth changes will also serve to give Earth the very long period she needs to regain balance and restore herself. Those who are to inhabit the new Earth, Terra, will be housed in places that help them prepare for the new reality that they are to inherit. Terra is already in existence but not yet visible, as the human frequencies have not yet risen to the level they must be at to be able to perceive and experience her as a physical reality.

A time is coming in which all that has been built upon the planet in terms of artificial structures will be leveled. Underground structures will not be so affected, but there is no point in looking to them for sustenance, as there will not be anything left alive on the surface. You can lay up stores of food, sources of energy, and implements, but you cannot prepare to live out the long period in which third-density Earth will lie fallow. It is too long a time. The fourth-density Earth — Terra — already exists, pristine, fertile, and exquisitely beautiful. Only those forms that are vibrating at that frequency will be compatible with her, so one cannot do anything but prepare to be one of those. Otherwise, you will experience a different outcome.

Not only the artificial structures will be leveled. In your scriptures, it says that the valleys will be raised up and the mountains laid low. This is the smoothing out of the planetary surface that we referred to, the elimination of the stored energies contained in the lines of stress in the crust called "faults." But Terra will be smooth for another reason. "Form follows function" is another of your sayings.

As we have spoken before, Terra will be a fourth-density planet, of the STO orientation. In STO, everyone and everything is sovereign. It does not exist except to express itself within the context of the whole. There is no hoarding or accumulation of wealth by the few, for there is enough to be shared by all. And none shall experience poverty or want of any kind. In the elevated state of consciousness of Terra, all will live as royalty, for all will create whatever pleases them to create. The planet will be smooth to outpicture the smoothness of life, the equality of all within the Creation, and the total abundance that is available to those who are in alignment with Universal Laws.

We wish you to hear these things in the proper perspective. Nothing perishes. It only changes form. The form that is appropriate to Terra is the exalted version of what you see about you now. Things must either change or go somewhere else. The planet herself is about to change her form in drastic ways. These cataclysmic changes are the healing process that the planet must go through to achieve her destiny.

It is all in divine order that this happens, and it is within divine order that it happens now, at this particular point in the planet's history. The window will open to provide the way, all the way back to Source. Everything that has been operating in the experience of separation consciousness must now either reconnect with Source or go somewhere else. To be on Terra, one will be in a perpetual state of Union with Source and thereby with all of Creation. Your senses will operate in the full spectrum of consciousness, not just the limited band you have available now.

It is principally because of the approaching Earth changes that we have come to give this series of messages, so that you may view what is happening within the proper perspective. Many of you have been preparing for your roles for entire lifetimes, both in and before this one. That is why so many of you who are reading this message have felt that you were here for some special purpose, why your mundane work in the world has sometimes left you wondering, "Is this all there is? Is this all I am going to do?"

No, it is not all you are going to do, but your first task is your own transformation. Then and only then will you be equipped to go out and do the Creator's work for one another. Then and only then will you really be able to "help" with the great task at hand. Until then, your task is to open to receive. You are not in charge. You cannot do this for yourself. You can only open to receive what is being given.

We have urged you repeatedly to give your spiritual practice your highest priority. That is how you will open yourself to receive what is being offered to you at this time. Your Oversoul has "scheduled" you for many things in this transition. Relax and enjoy the ride! Your only other option is to resist it, and that will only result in discomfort for you. Why not "go with the flow"? Be like the river and simply stream through it all — liquid, unresisting and flowing. We can tell you that you will have much more fun that way.

There is no way we can prepare you for all that lies ahead. We have tried our best to direct you to those activities and practices that will make your transition all that you would like it to be. The rest is up to you. If you resist, the pressures will build up until you surrender. Those who will not bend will break. There is help available at all times, but you must ask for it, as we cannot infringe upon your free will and choice. There is so much Grace flowing, if you will only be "gracious enough" to receive it.

Receive the gift. Do not turn away and think you are not worthy of it. You are the children of the dawn, the architects, builders, and occupants of Terra, the new Earth. Receive the gift and be humble and grateful for this opportunity to serve, to experience, and to be there when the curtain goes up on the new stage for the new drama. Terra will truly be the embodiment of "Heaven on Earth."

We are so grateful to you for being willing to take on the garment of flesh, to anchor those incoming energies that are streaming in now in ever-increasing amounts, and to act as living lightning rods to ground them into the planet so that she may rise and ascend to her destined station — Terra, the jewel of the galaxy. We look forward to working with you further. Until then, we shall sign off for now, but know that we are with you always. We are the "rod and the staff" that will comfort you and sustain you, through all that lies ahead. Each and every one of you precious beings is surrounded by angels, whose only function is to protect you, love you, and guide you — to lead you Home.

Amen, Adonoy Sabayoth. We are the Hosts of Heaven.

You are surrounded by angels, whose only function is to protect you, love you, and guide you — to lead you Home

SIGNS ALONG THE WAY
June 21, 2000

Well, now. It is almost a year since we last spoke with you. Being that today is the summer solstice [where you are, in the northern hemisphere] — that time when the flow of life on Earth completes its upward movement from the depths of the winter solstice into the sun of the day, and turns upon itself once more to begin the journey downward, toward the heart of darkness, toward the next solstice which will mark the beginning of winter — it seemed like an appropriate time to begin our next series of conversations with you.

Is it not strange, this ever-swinging movement between the dark to the light and back to the dark again? Yet it is in the nature of things on planet Earth for it to do this. Now — just as the summer comes on — so do thoughts and energy begin to contemplate and anticipate the approach of winter again.

Darkness is but a part of the cycle of life, and these "dark days" that mark the ending of the planetary cycle in 3D shall give rise to a time of incredible light, an eternal springtime for the planet and all that are upon her. We remind you of this. Do not forget it. For just as the darkness now comes, the light is already born within it.

These messages are meant to be a positive pole for you to carry within your hearts, to balance the negative that will be expressing all around you. Walk in the light. Carry the light. Be the embodiment of light and you will find the path before you is an easy one, even if all about you is coming down to its extermination.

We have called this message, "Signs Along the Way," and it is our intention to give you some understanding of the path that lies directly before you. The Earth changes have begun now in earnest, although they are still mild compared to what will follow. You will notice that the clusters of earthquakes have been fairly constant now, and that they

These messages are meant to be a positive pole for you to carry within your hearts, to balance the negative that will be expressing all around you.

are of a consequential magnitude that should cause the world to take notice, but they are still asleep. It is ho-hum and not news, so long as it does not cause destruction of property and life. Note that property is valued even above life, and the loss of property is always mentioned in reporting the consequences of Nature's ways. And so now, while these beginning tremors are occurring at record rates, there is no mention of them in the news. They are not considered to mean anything. But they DO mean something. They mean that the time of which we spoke is now at hand.

In addition to the earthquakes, there is also the weather, the fires and floods, and other weather-related phenomena. These, too, are signs of the times of which we spoke. The weather patterns have been changing for a long time, but now they are noticeably NOT "normal." Even so, while some areas suffer, others experience uncharacteristically benevolent weather. It is that same pattern of a "mixed blessing" that shall characterize so much of the times ahead. While some things are destroyed and some people fall upon hard times, at the very same time, new and beautiful things will come into being and people who had been struggling will begin to prosper. Many things will change, and not in ways that you might expect!

YOU are changing, too, and if you are paying attention, you will notice that your perceptions are changing, too. Your senses are heightened and attuned to more beauty in life. The landscape and living things seem to be brighter somehow. Foods taste better or worse to you, depending on how well you have chosen them. Those of a lower vibration or which are prepared by people who resent having to cook them will taste worse, or make you feel bad after you eat them. Those which are lovingly grown and prepared, and for which you express your appreciation, will not only taste better but they will make you feel more nourished than those which have been "thrown together" or grabbed along the way in a busy day.

To the extent that you honor your own being enough to select the best foods and eat them with appreciation, to that extent you will be increasing your "light quotient" and shine more brightly. In loving and giving to yourself, you are in a sense honoring and praising the Source which creates you.

How would you respond if someone gave you a beautiful cake?

Think about it. If someone gave you a beautiful cake, into which they had put the costliest and most delicious ingredients, would you throw it on the ground, grind it under your heel, and so despise the gift?

Hopefully, you would not. If you were perceptive, you would see how much care went into the creating of that cake and you would bow in reverence before the baker for the preciousness of the gift. Your own bodies are the "bread" that has been formed by the Creator. Your own bodies are made of the most precious ingredients, and no matter how you have been treated by your earthly travels and those who were part of your journey, you are still a precious gift to the universe. Honor that gift and treat yourself with love and respect.

Eat well of the best quality foods — those which were raised with love and consciousness, which were prepared with love and attention, and which fit with your own dietary needs. This will not only give you the best nutrition to support your bodies in their transformation, you will also be giving your bodies the message that you care about them and they will support you in return. You can experience a great deal of rejuvenation and healing through simply choosing well and making it a priority to do so.

The body you presently occupy will be the one that takes you across the light bridge between this world and the next.

Nonetheless, there are some discomforts to be endured. The body you presently occupy will be the one that takes you across the light bridge between this world and the next. All your other parallel lives are being terminated, and the cellular memories that you carry in all of your tissues are being purged. Your relationship to time is changing. Your minds often become a blank at the most annoying times. You feel like your head is made of cotton wool a lot of the time, and you may wonder how you will get anything done. You need a lot of sleep and are drinking a lot more water (hopefully, very pure water!). You may be gaining weight, losing weight, growing hair, losing hair — the process is very individual, but the one thing that will be "common" to all is that you are changing.

Your sleep patterns will vary a great deal. You may sleep very deeply or you may be restless without knowing why. Your bodies may feel like they are vibrating at times, especially if you wake up during the night, between periods of sleep. You may have changes in bowel habits, or changes in the foods that you want to eat. Be gentle with yourselves, and take care of yourselves.

For those of you who are usually so busy taking care of others and their needs, this is going to require that you put yourself "first," which is a change in itself! If you have emotions rising to the surface, do whatever you can to facilitate their release without wallowing in them or getting caught up in dramas. Use whatever works for you — singing, toning, writing, warm baths — whatever you find is the most natural and supportive way for you to move through the purging of your cellular memory and the associated emotions of your various experiences.

For those of you who have had a difficult life (and that is most of you), let yourself now feel the pain of those times when you had to simply keep going and feelings were shunted aside so that you could cope. Let that pain surface gently and watch it pass through you and out of you, like you were looking into a fishbowl and seeing streams of cloudy water swirling through and then disappearing.

You have all experienced a lot of pain, and whatever you must now feel and let pass through you on its way out of you, let it all go. You will lose a sense of identity as this healing proceeds. You will not be sure of who you are anymore, because it is from this personal "history" of pain that you have decided who and what you are and who and what you aren't. The truth is — at its most fundamental level — everything you see and feel, everything you saw and felt, IS YOU. But in moving into this larger, less defined interpretation of Self, you will lose the benchmarks from which you defined yourself in the past.

You will feel less connected with some people, more connected with others, as you move toward the poles of your destiny and merge your being and energies with those of your true family — your brothers and sisters in the many mansion worlds of the one infinite Creator. WE are that family, and you are preparing to shed your old skins and put on your garments of light. When you have done that, you shall stand among us as equals and we shall be able to embrace each other once again. We look forward to that day as much as you do, for we know how much joy we shall all have in that reunion.

We leave you now in peace and honor and blessing and we shall talk with you again. It is time to come home.

We love you so much. We would hope that you can come to love yourselves, as well. Amen, Adonoy Sabayoth. We are the Hosts of Heaven.

We hope that you can come to love yourselves, as well.

IT'S ALL GOD
June 22, 2000

"In the beginning, God created the heavens and the Earth." This is what it says; this is how it is written in the scriptures with which you are so familiar. But it is not really how it was.

In the beginning there was God, and God was and IS "ALL There Is." It is *still* God. And so God did not, in that sense, create anything that is *not* God. There is a tendency to view the Creation as both a product of and separate from the Creator, but this is an impossibility. The very being and substance of the Creator penetrates all form and is indeed an expression, an outgrowth as it were, of the one body. Just as you have hairs on your head or lashes on your eyelids, so it is with every form in the Creation: they are springing forth from the single body, from God.

We who speak to you are but a facet of that one Creator; you are but a facet of that one Creator. It is God who speaks through you and through us, because we are all God. That is not to say that we ARE the Creator, but rather a part of the Creator, an expression of the Creator, a form that resides WITHIN the Creator. Nothing is outside of God, you know, but this is an expression that is limited by the language of words. When you are on Terra, you will have the full experience of being totally in oneness with the Creator, where your body will be experiencing itself as constantly emerging from the substance of the Creator, the matrix and ground of all being and form.

And so this Creator interpenetrates all things. All things have consciousness. All things are part of that Creator. Now look about you, to your beautiful planet and see the devastation upon one part of the Creator by another part of the Creator. Is this not madness? Would you mutilate your own body if you were aware of what you were doing? We think not. And yet that is what has happened to this beautiful planet and continues to happen, even now, at this late hour.

The last giants of the forest are being toppled to build yet more products for yet more people.

The forests are being felled at a record rate. It is almost like a feeding frenzy, as the last giants of the forest are toppled to build yet more products for yet more people, and so it goes. Even the smaller trees are being harvested in this mad rush to consume, consume, consume, until there is nothing left. Yes, we have spoken of the Earth changes. Yes, they are underway as we speak now. But even if there were no Earth changes, this mad rush to claim for oneself the last of the dwindling resources of Earth would soon render the planet unfit for all life, most particularly for human habitation. So, in some ways, the Earth changes are a merciful thing, to stop the process from proceeding to the place where untold suffering would be the result.

There has been enough killing; there has been enough eradication of species. And if humankind is to progress, and survive, and THRIVE, this desecration of this beautiful planet must end, and soon, before it is all way too late.

But it is all in Divine order. These are all parts of the experiment that was ordained from the foundation of the Creation. These apparent destructions are still the Will of God, which is sometimes difficult to understand for those who are still in separation [consciousness]. But when you are no longer in separation, you will be in a place where one can see, understand, feel, and embrace the wholeness of it, without getting caught up in the drama of it.

And so Earth is in her final hour of her travail, and humankind is dancing at the last big party. Many there are who are aware or sensing at some level of their being that the end is near, and so there is an apparent disregard for what is prudent and a kind of reckless abandon to consume yet even more. There is complaint about the high price of gas and quarreling about how difficult it is to have to pay such high prices. What will the tumult be if the gas is no longer available? And that is surely an outcome. The supplies are not infinite. Yes, they are vast, but so is the sea of humanity, and the demand for more and more oil is insatiable.

The demand for more and more oil is insatiable.

It is also very destructive — of the environment, of the air, of the waters. The oil is used to create so many things that do not degrade once they are discarded, so you are burying yourself in your own filth, in your own refuse. The tragedy is that what was once a beautiful garden is gradually being turned into a garbage dump. What a desecration! And yet, it was all foreseen. It is now time for that to come to a close, and it will not be a gentle birth, because of the tensions that remain in the Earth's crust reflecting her absorption of so much negative energy.

We have not yet touched on the heart of the matter. We are, in a sense, preparing the stage for the drama that will now unfold. It is almost time for the cataclysms, and we want to prepare you and prepare you well for what to expect, and how things will go for those who are destined for Terra and those who are not.

If you are among those who are destined for Terra, you will be witnessing a rather strange sight, for as the world around you crumbles and dissolves into entropy and death, you will find yourselves prospering and moving up to a new level of abundance, joy, and well-being. It is you who have suffered for so long, and now it is your time in the light. And those who have become inebriated on the excess of consumption will now pay that price.

We do not say that in judgment, but rather as assessing the situation for what it is. The preliminary earthquakes have come and gone, and now there will be a brief pause and then the next level of cleansing will take place. Soon, your news media will not be able to ignore the phenomena of Earth changes. It will be in everyone's face. There will be an increase in concern and fear as these things unfold and become more established as a pattern, rather than isolated events. You might think that the Earth — through these various small earthquakes — could release sufficient crustal tension, that it will not have to result in anything more severe. However, there is such an accumulation of negative thought energy that has been absorbed by the planet that it all must be purged. Even as your own bodies are being purged, so must the Earth's body be purged and cleansed.

And so this will result in Earth changes and geophysical events, not only of a much greater magnitude than is normally experienced, but also a greater frequency and persistence. This first cluster is essentially over, with a few isolated aftershocks. However, in a time that is very soon at hand, no later than July, we shall be witnessing the next level of cleansing at the Earth level, which will take several forms. Not only will there be tectonic movement and volcanic eruptions, but there will be other types of things, as foretold in the Book of Revelation in the Bible.

There will be many strange phenomena in Nature. There will be a rain of "plagues" akin to that described in the time of Egypt, in the story of Moses, and there is much sorrow coming in the cleansing of the planet because she has absorbed so much sorrow that she does not want to carry any more, nor does it serve for her to carry it. For what she is becoming is Terra, the glorious jewel in the crown of Creation, and in which there is no place for sorrow and tears, only joy and love, and all these matters of the third density shall soon pass away.

The cleansing will be complete this time, not partial as in other times, for none of the old can be taken into the new. You yourselves are being purged of your cellular memory and so it is with the Earth.

The Earth is a living being, and her body is riddled with "dis-ease" over all the things that have been done to her, plus having absorbed all the pain and sorrow of the thoughtforms that have been experienced or projected by humankind. And the pain and sorrow of the animals is felt also. Many of you do not realize that animals are fully conscious and do have bonds among them and do have energetic exchange in their own form of communication. So animals are not rightfully your slaves, or pets, or possessions, and on Terra, all animals will be free.

There will be increased disturbances and ruptures, not only in geophysical changes, but also in the fabric of society.

And so now we would speak to you of the times ahead. In the very shorter term, there will be increased disturbances and ruptures, not only in geophysical changes, but also in the fabric of society. The tension is growing, and the clamor for people to "do something" is rising, and there is great discontent growing in the face of apparent prosperity. There are dark clouds gathering, economically and socially. There are going to be eruptions, like boils of a disease. There will be cleansings within the populations of Earth, as well as the planet. There are going be strange diseases, of mental, emotional, and physical nature — many plagues of many kinds. Some will be engineered by humankind and those of a despotic nature, and some will be mutations of existing microbes, as a result of the changing frequency and the increasing amount of higher-frequency light, known to you as the ultraviolet. The hole in the ozone layer is of course part of the equation, and is man-created, but once again, we would say that ALL of this has been scheduled and is by a combined, collective soul choice.

All of you who have been battling for the light, and carrying the light, and pleading to be heard, and all of those of you who have tried to stop the destruction and the devastation and the greed and the corruption — all of you have labored and labored well, but it seems that evil (or what you would call as evil) will have its day. Once again, we would remind you that this is all *of* the Creator and *is* the Creator-in-expression. It is difficult from your perspective of separation to understand how a loving or benevolent Creator could allow such things to happen, or that such a beautiful planet would be sacrificed in such a way. But this story HAS a happy ending, and we wish to remind you of that.

The Creator, being *the* Creator, wishes to experience everything, not just the things that are pleasurable. It wants to explore ALL the possibilities, all the combinations and permutations, and indeed this causes much apparent suffering. But there is also a place for joy in this Creation. It is in short supply upon your planet at the moment, but that will radically change after the shift.

And so now we return to the days ahead. There will be much, much disharmony, disruption, chaos, fear, destruction, loss of life, loss of property, loss on all sides — or so it will seem. But at the same time, those of you who are destined for Terra will find yourselves prospering and enjoying a much happier state of affairs than you have in the years leading up to now. We wish to support you in your last days on Earth and make them pleasurable, for you have served and served well, and now it is time to "gather the troops" as it were, and to call them home. For the homecoming will be taking place in a matter of 3 to 4 years of your time. There is a coming home to oneself that is a part of this, and a coming home to your rightful estate as co-creators of this marvelous universe, and also a coming home to the places that nourish your heart and wipe away your tears.

We wish to have you among us again, our brothers and sisters, and we are your soul family. We are YOUR brothers and sisters, as well. You are totally our equal and have been valiant in your service and your willingness to take on the garment of flesh, but soon it will be time for you to move up and move on, and to put on your garment of light and become the gods and goddesses that you are. It will be a wonderful time for you, and the blessings will never cease.

Now, the dark days ahead lead to a new dawning, and the first rays of that dawning are already visible. Much work has gone in. Much has been accomplished. Many have turned to the light, and if not with full understanding or full discernment, still much has been accomplished. Those of you who are originating from the higher realms will be regaining your estate, and soon — by our standards, anyway. Consider that it has been a 4 1/2-billion-year walk and 3 or 4 years is but a blink of the eye in that kind of time scale. We would ask you to realize that we are ever with you. Nothing happens by accident. There are no accidents. Everything is an outpicturing of God, and everything contains within it the seeds of its own completion. We shall speak more on these matters, but that is all for now.

Amen, Adonoy Sabayoth. We are the Hosts of Heaven.

The dark days ahead will lead to a new dawning; the first rays of that dawning are already visible.

THE CROSSING-POINT
July 27, 2000

Yesterday — July 26, 2000 — marked an important milestone on the journey to Terra. We prefer to call it "the crossing-point," because it marked the shift from the funneling-inward movement (that has been going on since the Earth was formed) to a funneling-outward movement that represents the expansion into the new reality. You are perhaps familiar with the spiral shape that describes evolution: each turn on the spiral sees a return to past themes and issues, but at a new level, enriched by the lessons of prior experience. But there can be a spiraling inward as well, in which the "lessons" of the past — in the form of memories and imprinting — are thrown off as the spiral tightens toward a "zero point," at which it has no circumference at all.

Yesterday marked that point at which the inward spiral reached its maximum compression and began to turn in the opposite direction. Now instead of throwing off old memories and imprinting, it will gather into itself altogether new experiences and expressions, none of which have been ever experienced on 3D Earth in all of her history. This is the time of the ingathering, of the harvesting of all that has gone before and the receiving of the "gifts of the kingdom." For you who are destined for Terra, this will come as a great relief, for so many of you have endured much suffering and hardship of all kinds. Now, however, that has served and will pass away. Now is your time to embody the riches that belong to those who serve the One Infinite Creator so wholeheartedly, and it will be a welcome time for you all, to be sure.

It will not come in all at once. Just as the spiral wound inward over long stretches of time, so will its expansion wind outward over long stretches of time. However, from the shape of the spiral, you can see that near its point, the turns are shorter and therefore come closer together in time. Just as you have experienced an inner acceleration as the spiral turned ever faster in its cycles toward the "zero point," now that the "crossing-point" has been achieved, the initial cycles will be very fast at first and gradually slow down as the turns encompass more and more "territory."

In the beginning, you will not notice how much has changed. An entire new paradigm was anchored in but because the sweep of the spiral is so limited so close to the crossing-point, it will be some time before you notice how different your lives are becoming. At first it will be a very subtle thing, more felt than seen, but in a relatively short time, it will be unmistakable.

The spiral has spanned more than 4 billion of your years, and the outward journey will take at least as long to complete the innate symmetry [which mirrors the inward spiral]. However, since the outward movement is an expansion, it really can go on forever, as there will never be another "crossing-point" for this Creation.

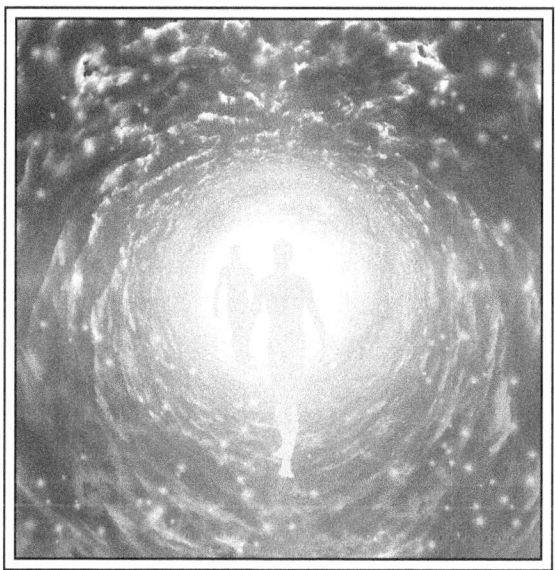

You will embody more and more light until you are just light.

It is really about going beyond ALL limitation, and therefore the expansion phase is without limits — essentially infinite in nature. Rather than CONTRACT BACK into the Godhead, you will EXPAND AND EXPAND until you MERGE with that Godhead in its infinite scope and expression. You will embody more and more light until you are just light. Every vestige of dense materiality will dissolve into pure light and consciousness, but that is a journey of billions of your years — hard for you to relate to or imagine.

So now it is here — the time for which you have prepared for so many lifetimes, in so many guises. This is the last of your dense physical expressions and from here you will only become more and more filled with light. We would remind you that this is a process, not an "event," so the change will be gradual but certain. There will come a time when you will have to be lifted off of the planet's surface and held aside while all else plays out to completion. We will be assisting in this, but it is a partnership between us, not a "rescue mission." You carry your responsibility in the equation, too, and it has required much of you in the past.

Now it only requires that you open to receive what is yours to receive. That may bring up some issues for some of you — issues of self-worth and conflicts about what it "looks like" to be a "server." There has been much conditioning in your religions that you are small and unworthy and must place your hopes in an outside force or being to "save you" from your earthly imperfections. But in our eyes, you are ALREADY PERFECT, and all that is needed is for you to open and gratefully receive your "birthright" as the sons and daughters of the Creator.

Those who are not bound for Terra will have a different experience, and many of them will go through trials and suffering as they move to their poles of destiny. Remember that everyone is operating according to their soul's choice. Do not feel superior to them, as you are only manifesting your soul's choice also, and all souls are equal in the Creation. They are all just aspects of the One Creator, so how can they be other than perfect? How could any aspect of the Creator be more or less important than any other aspect? It is ALL God-in-expression, as we told you last time. Just surrender to your destiny path and give thanks for the goodness that now comes to you. And allow everyone else to do the same [with regard to THEIR destiny path].

If you feel moved to help out during others' travail, by all means help out. But don't do it out of guilt or to "earn points in Heaven." It is perfectly all right for you to simply enfold them in your love and light and not do anything outwardly to hinder their process or movement toward their destiny.

In time, when you do indeed turn your faces toward Terra and leave your beloved 3D Earth behind, none of this will matter anymore. You will have surrendered up all attachments to your past identities and will gladly embrace the "new world" that is yours to experience. But that is enough about that for now. It is still some time away, and there is much to enjoy and explore and create in the meantime. Rejoice now, where you are and how you are, for this IS your last lifetime in dense physicality and you now have an opportunity to enjoy it before leaving it behind forever.

We leave you now in peace, and honor, and blessing. Amen, Adonoy Sabayoth. We are the Hosts of Heaven.

You will have surrendered up all attachments to your past identities and will gladly embrace the "new world" that is yours to experience.

THE COMING STORM
September 21, 2000

Now is the time of which we have spoken. [In the northern hemisphere] this is the time in your year when the day and night are of equal lengths, but soon the night will be longer and the day shorter. So it is that the darkness will appear to increase and the light to diminish, but just as the sun is always shining behind the clouds, so is the dawn waiting beyond the night. And so it is now.

You are entered upon a time when there will be much confusion, fear, and "darkness," for what is darkness but a lack of understanding? All that you would call "darkness" or "evil" is but a lack of understanding, and so it is never a permanent condition, but while it is in operation, it can cause much suffering for many.

And so it is now. There are those upon your planet who would call themselves "human," but in their actions, thoughts, and words would appear to be some kind of monster — without feelings for others or others' pain and suffering. The "love quotient" in these individuals is nearly absent, but that is part of their learning, too.

Hitler

Think of the one you called Hitler. Was he enlightened? Was he happy? Was he satisfied with what his life brought him?

The answer is clearly "No." And so the soul of this one you called Hitler is still on the inner planes, mulling over the effects of that life, trying to understand what went so horribly wrong.

You each have incarnated to gain certain understandings, and it is no different for those of the STS persuasion than it is for those of the STO orientation. You are each trying to understand, which is made more difficult by the fact that you are veiled. So, as you see what to you might seem the height of foolish behavior, remember that these are souls who are simply trying to understand why things aren't working very well for them. Even those who consider themselves to know what is "best" for everyone are going to be challenged in the days ahead.

Everything is about to change and change radically. People have different ways of trying to cope with change. Some seek constructive and cooperative solutions; others seek to withdraw and arm themselves against all possibilities. Each of these kinds of choices leads to more understanding. In the end, one has to surrender totally to the fact that one simply can't know everything, and then one has to let go and let God show the way. THEN "miracles" can occur, but not as long as one thinks it is within their hands to "make it happen."

Those who have positioned themselves as the power elite on your planet have laid grand plans to take over everything and profit from it.

Those who have positioned themselves as the power elite on your planet have laid grand plans to take over everything and profit from it. However, as much power as they have amassed, it is only based on economics. As long as the economic system operates and people have to depend on it for their needs, the power elite will have an easy time of putting into place their plans for world domination. However, this would be a violation of everyone else's choices, and this particular time in Earth's course is all about choices, so the Earth herself will be a major factor in keeping things more equal so that everyone has the opportunity to choose.

There are major storms coming — economic, geophysical, and political. People will be challenged to make a choice: will they act for self-preservation or will they work together to help one another? You who read and cherish these Messages will be spared the worst part of things, as a rather dramatic occurrence will be coming for you in the very near future (that is a relative term, of course, as time has no meaning for us in the higher dimensions — it is always "now").

In the near future, as you are lifted in your vibration, you will experience yourself as living in a very different kind of reality. It will not be an abrupt shift, but a gradual dawning in your awareness that things are not the same somehow. At the same time, there will be a threshold that can be felt by those who are sensitive to such things, and you will be safely across the barrier that separates the third density from the fourth.

Make no mistake: this will only happen for those who are attuned to and aligned with these Messages. The others who have chosen Terra but are not yet awakened will endure the effects of the coming storms as part of their process of personal cleansing and the opportunity to refine their choice for the positive path. It is all designed to bring maximum benefit to all — those who would choose now and those who will choose later. It is all about increased understanding, and the power elite will have their "lessons," too.

This birth will be a difficult one for most of the people on your planet, of all persuasions. Even the STS will be challenged to deal with the changing circumstances and the destruction of their well-laid plans. You see, it is all a house of cards, built upon technology that is vulnerable to being disrupted through any number of occurrences. One well-aimed burst from the sun could wipe out all of the communication satellites and bring down virtually all international commerce. The sun is a player in this equation, too.

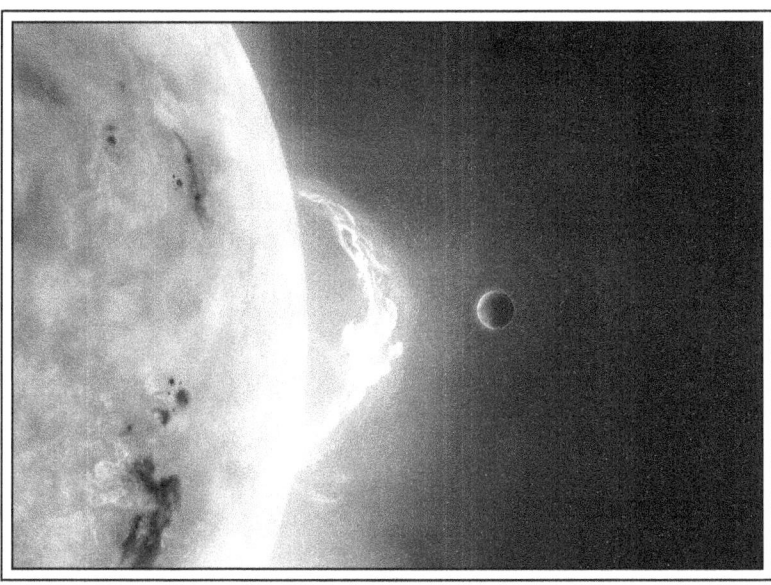

One well-aimed burst from the sun could wipe out all of the communication satellites and bring down virtually all international commerce.

There are other ways that the system can be disrupted. Weather will play a big part in things, and crop failures are not the only consequence. However, this is going to "hurt" the "little people" more than the rich and powerful, so that will not be as big a factor as some other things in the shorter term.

The power elite are not invulnerable, but it is some time before they will be brought down. In the interim, they will appear to have their day to rule, and they will be given the opportunity to gain greater understanding of the nature of the path they have chosen. Since it is ALL GOD, there are other apparently separate individuals who will be providing them with the opportunity to learn their "lessons" firsthand, while at the same time gaining their own understanding about the best ways to not become victims under the crushing machinations wielded by the power elite. STS is always trying to enslave others; STO wishes to be free and to throw off the yoke of oppression, wherever they find it.

And so a clash between these two opposing forces — those who would enslave and those who would be free — is inevitable. It will take many forms, not the least of which is your familiar "war." However, there will be "wars" fought in other ways and in other fields of endeavor. Truth will battle with falsity. Love will strive with fear. Each person will have many opportunities to choose — moment by moment, day by day —

and in so choosing to make their collective choice for one path or the other.

There are many parallel futures to emerge from the platform of third-density Earth. Each one is a "layer" that vibrates with a certain frequency, similar to the bands of color in your visible spectrum. However, the spectrum is continuous, with one color flowing into another, and these parallel futures will ultimately separate from each other into distinct and unique worlds of experience. We have spoken of the very small percentage that will end up on Terra.

There are many "slices" that will be cut off the single "loaf" that constitutes your present reality. The most beneficial thing you can do for yourselves is to focus entirely on yourself and your choices. Whatever you do, feel into those choices in each and every moment of the day, each and every day, and choose what seems "right" to you to do in that moment. You are dealing with a wave of change and the discipline is to "surf" that wave by remaining totally present — neither in the future or the past — so as not to lose your balance by leaning too far forward or backward.

There are many "slices" that will be cut off the single "loaf" that constitutes your present reality.

It will be a time when you will find yourself remembering all that led you to the present moment, and you will have faith built upon remembering all that you have already gone through, but each time that you have followed that thread of the past to a natural completion point, gently bring yourself back into the present moment, just like a dog shakes itself off after a swim in a lake. Just so, if you find yourself drifting into daydreams of the future — when they have come to a natural end, bring yourself gently back into the present and focus on what is squarely before you to do in that moment. This is the way you will walk: one step at a time, moment by moment, learning to live in the NOW.

We will close by returning to the title of this Message: "The Coming Storm." The way you will survive and THRIVE during these times is to remain fixed in the present moment. Trust in the Creator to guide you perfectly through to your destination. While many will seem to suffer, you will be lifted free of all of that, in order to serve later on, when those who remain will need your assistance. We shall have more to say on that topic, but for now, we leave you in peace and honor and blessing.

Amen, Adonoy Sabayoth. We are the Hosts of Heaven.

This is the way you will walk: one step at a time, moment by moment, learning to live in the NOW.

ALLOW ALL THINGS
September 28, 2000

In the beginning, there was no-thing. Then arose a thought and out of that thought all things came into being. At first, there was only harmony, but not much "progress" was made, because while all things were in harmony, there was not much impetus for change or exploration of alternative paths. The Thinker of the thought noticed this, and It thought another thought. This second thought introduced the idea of opposites, which could clash and therefore produce striving. All that you see around you now is a result of that striving.

If all had remained as One, nothing of the richness you see in your lives would have occurred. A great abundance of forms and a great abundance of possibilities thus was created, and the original thought was greatly expanded by this choice on the part of the Thinker, but also at a great price. Know you the expression, "the pearl of great price"? This is the price of which we speak.

As things unfold upon your planet and in your time, these two opposites will increase their movement toward opposite poles. All that is in the middle will either move to the poles or perish, in order to begin again on another world where they will have more opportunities to explore the choice of the opposites. When we say "perish," however, we refer only to their physical bodies. Their Oversouls will persist and simply put forth other projections of themselves into the worlds that await on the other side of the shift.

ALL Oversouls are withdrawing their projections now, so even for those who will ride this shift intact, in the vehicle that they presently occupy, there will only be one projection from the Oversoul that rides the wave of change. How, then, are you to view all this, and what will be the process and experience of going first to the poles and then to your destined exit path from 3D Earth to 4D Terra?

To begin with, there will be an intensification of the polarities. Those who are inclined toward the positive (or STO) pole will become more so, and those who are inclined toward the negative (or STS) pole will also become more so. This creates the maximum energetic potential, but it also creates the greatest disharmony, IF the two poles interact. How can you experience this journey with the least amount of friction? You disengage from fighting the negativity and withdraw into a world that is solely of your pole, that is totally harmonious for you.

Those who are inclined toward either pole will become more so.

"But what about evil?" you cry. What you call evil is but a choice. Do you remember the teaching in the Bible to "resist not evil"? In order to have the smoothest transition to your destined outcome, you must allow all things. You must allow all choices, and that includes the choice for the negative path. If you engage with "evil," you bind your energies to conflict and you cannot experience peace and harmony while you are fighting against someone else's choice. Allow all things. Allow all soul choices. Allow, allow, allow.

Many of you refer to those whom you call Masters. We would say to you that OUR definition of a Master is one who is so expanded in their understanding that he or she takes in ALL within them, within their embrace, and holds it without preference, without saying or feeling that any part is better than any other part.

When you are fully born into your new awareness, a great understanding will fill you. You will "see" for the first time since taking on the veil which hides the truth from your sight. You will see all things in their right place and in their right meaning. But for now, you only see part of the picture, so in remembering that there is more going on than what you can perceive, you will again be called to surrender and to allow all things.

You are not in charge. You are not the force that drives the creation forward. But you are an aspect of this force in action, and therefore you WILL at some point regain the full understanding of the nature of that force and your own true nature.

Until then — until you *do* have full understanding — recognize and accept that your understanding is to one degree or another limited, and so allow all things, for you do not know their hidden purpose. You do not know how it serves.

If you are ASKED, then by all means respond as you feel is right to do. But more will be saying and telling than will be asking. More will be shouting and even screaming in their fear than will be asking. If someone asks, then and only then should you answer, but if no one is asking, remain in your center and rooted in the truth of your being and your choice for the pole you have chosen.

Resist not evil. Resist not anything. Surrender to the higher intelligence that guides your every step and simply ask when you have doubts of your own, "How shall I be with this (situation)? What is right action here?" But always come from your center, your knowing about what is true for you. Be content to make your own choice for yourself and allow others to do the same. What does it gain if you try to "rescue" someone? You have only delayed their opportunity to make their own choices.

On Terra all will be sovereign. To be sovereign means to be willing to be totally alone in one's own understanding, to be beyond being able to be coerced or manipulated. Many great sages and warriors in many traditions have had this quality. You must be warriors now, only warriors in the sense of standing firm in the midst of the impending chaos, not in resisting any of which will now play out.

Be calm in the midst of the storm. Keep breathing. Meditate. Keep grounding the light that is streaming in to the planet now. Keep opening the channel of your bodies and ground the light into the planet. Empty out until you are like a hollow reed, able to simply allow all things to pass through you. The cleansing is underway and will accelerate with the passage of time. Allow, allow, allow.

Be calm in the midst of the storm. Keep breathing. Meditate.

You are yet asleep, but you are awakening. When you have fully awakened, the reality you will see will not be the reality that others who are still sleeping and striving with each other will see. You will float beyond all that. You will experience total calm, peace, and harmony, even while the storm rages all around you. You will be centered in peace and harmony, even while all things are coming apart around you. Soon, you will not even notice, because you will be fascinated with something else. A beautiful light will beckon to you and you will follow it. You will be going home.

Amen, Adonoy Sabayoth. We are the Hosts of Heaven.

A beautiful light will beckon to you and you will follow it. You will be going home.

THE NEW MILLENNIUM
November 21, 2000

It is now late in the year 2000 and the millennium is drawing to a close. It has been a long journey and many expected that the big shift would occur on January 1 of the year 2000, but the big shift is just ahead. It does not matter what was done or when the dates of your calendar system were adjusted. The fact remains that in the consensus reality of the majority of your world's population, this numbering system is in use and accepted as the reality, and therefore has the energy of reality for all of those who accept it. Given that picture, the new millennium is about to ring in, and with it will come many changes. The different realities are already well along the course of separating from each other, and that will continue. However, for those that are destined for Terra, the shift into the new reality has already begun and will become much more apparent from January 1 of 2001 onward.

There has been a substantial acceleration in the recent months since the crossing-point of July 26 was reached and passed. Now the spiral will turn more slowly, but each turn will take in noticeably greater amounts of change. The DEGREE of change will increase, even as the RATE of change decreases. What that means is that if you look back from today to July 26, it will not seem that your life has changed all that much from how it was then, but you felt that things were accelerating tremendously. Once the change from the old millennium to the new is accomplished, it will feel quite different.

You will feel like you are "floating," and are gently supported in a sort of bubble, one in which you are insulated from the clamor of the world around you. At first, it will only seem like things have gotten much more quiet inside of you, something like what it is like when you totally immerse yourself in water and the sounds of the world become muffled and unimportant. However, as things proceed, it will become apparent to you that your EXPERIENCE of life is different in ways that you cannot now anticipate. You might even doubt that you are awake, because it will all take on a sort of dreamlike quality.

You will feel like you are "floating," and are gently supported in a sort of bubble, one in which you are insulated from the clamor of the world around you.

It is important to tell you now that you should not attempt to re-engage with the life that is falling away from you. Just let yourself float gently upward and let yourself experience the total calm and support that surrounds you in this ocean of consciousness. Turn off the exterior stimuli and leave them for the "madding crowds." If you need to let go of people, circumstances, or certain "conditions" in your life, do so with ease and grace and do not engage in blame in order to justify the separating out into your own reality and destiny path. Just simply let go of how you are holding on to them, just like you were a balloon, tethered to them by a piece of string, only now you can choose to let go of your end of the piece of string and thereby float upward.

This is a process, not an "event," so you are already in the "orb of influence" (to use an astrological term). You will begin to feel the disconnect if you let it come to you easily and without resistance or fear. We are lifting you into the next level of vibration and it will feel a little strange to you, but trust the process and your own "knowing." Let the

Just let yourself float gently upward and let yourself experience the total calm and support that surrounds you in this ocean of consciousness.

tumult fade away and receive the peace of the light that floods over you and pours into your cells. You are dropping your material density and moving up to the next level.

You will experience shifts in your perception of yourself. Do not resist them. Let go easily and let yourself become a more clear representation of your essence.

You each have an essence that is the expression of the "tones" of your Oversoul. As you let go of the identity you had and let yourself become this closer approximation of your individual aspect of the Creator, you will experience the pleasure of becoming just exactly that person that you most want to be.

It will be an inner experience at first, but it will also show up on the surface, where it can be seen by others with "eyes to see." It will be FELT by those around you who cannot "see" it, and they might have some distress or feeling that they are "losing" you. They might experience fear and try to stop what it is they perceive of as the cause of the fear — your change — but all you need to do is love them, let them be how they are, give them what reassurance you can to comfort them that everything is all right, and let yourself drift upwards anyway. You will be in the company of those like yourself, and there will be comfort in that for you, but in the meantime, you must be kind as you take your leave of this world.

We would remind you that each person has chosen at the soul level for the experience that they will have as these last years tick away. The realities are separating into layers to accommodate everyone's choices and there will be goodbyes all around. You will be saying goodbye to who and how you were, and there will be a period of "floating" between identities, similar to the fetus floating for a time in the womb before it is born. But you need not worry about how you will be provided for. We know your needs and we know what must happen for you to successfully make this transition between this world and the next.

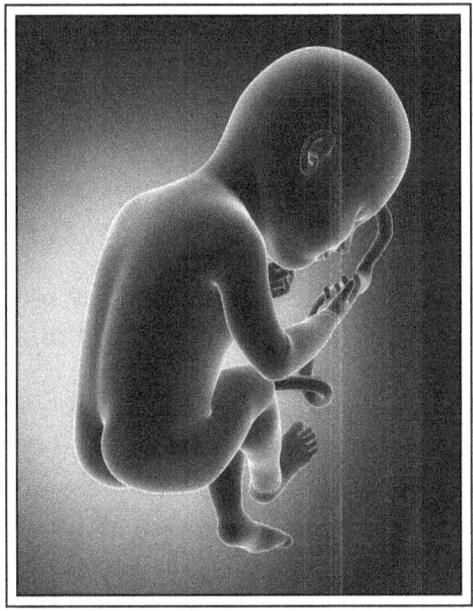

There will be a period of "floating" between identities, similar to the fetus floating for a time in the womb before it is born.

It is so important for you to embody TRUST in the process and in the plan for your life. Fear and worries will only hinder you and keep you back, stuck in the old ways and old identity. Let your angels come to you and sing their lullabies of love. You have earned this and it is yours. Enjoy it.

The world that you are leaving will have its time of discord and then all of it will fall silent, too. The old dream is ending and it is time for a new one — for you, for everyone, and for everything. The "refresh button" has been pushed, but it will play out across time, just like the images on your television set or computer monitor are re-drawn one line at a time. There will be a clear sense of something having changed, but it will take time to discover just exactly what it is. In the meantime, relax and let yourselves float upward. It doesn't have to be hard unless you prefer it that way. Simply let go of the string that ties you to the old ways and let yourself rise up to greet the new ones.

We are here with you now, in close proximity. We are protecting you as you go through this change. We are guiding you now and will be in touch with you as things unfold for you. You are our "assignment" and most precious to us, and not one of you shall be left behind. If there were some way that you could see us now, you would have no doubt about the love and support being extended to you, but trust in this: the day IS coming when we shall all be together again, and you will know us for who we are — your brothers and sisters in the many mansion worlds of the One Infinite Creator.

We leave you now, in peace and honor and blessing. Amen, Adonoy Sabayoth. We are the Hosts of Heaven.

Simply let go of the string that ties you to the old ways and let yourself rise up to greet the new ones.

THE SPLITTING OF THE WORLDS
February 10, 2001

We have asked to speak to you today because we wish to convey our view of what we see happening at the present time on Planet Earth. We must emphasize that there are many things unfolding simultaneously and the variations at the individual level are infinitely varied and complex, so we can only speak in the broadest and most general terms. However, we feel that it is still worth sharing our perspective with you, so as to provide a context in which you may view what you are experiencing and place your "picture" within our frame.

If you remember, we have spoken before of a splitting off of different future worlds from this one world in which you move and have your experience. Each person has their destination, chosen for them by their soul, in keeping with their place in the larger Divine Plan. For those of you who are inclined to want to heal and fix things, it can be difficult to witness the playing out of the "scripts" that are not of your vibration and orientation.

There is an intensification of essence taking place, so that those whom you might consider evil or selfish or greedy will appear to become more so, and those who are not able to surrender and bow to the winds of change will surely break from their rigidity. The winds of change are already blowing hard, and they will do so for the rest of the time left for your planet and all upon it. There is no letting up in this birthing process now, so if you are expecting it to pause, know now that it will not.

However, there is good news in this, because it also means that the push toward Terra will not stop, either, and those who are destined for it are being gently lifted into their own vibrational layer (stratum) and that is happening for all of those who are destined for other destinations, as well. There is a layering taking place and the layers are becoming more and more distinct from each other. As this proceeds, the resistance to the movement will be crushed by the relentlessness of the forces toward completion. Those who insist on clinging to the status quo will ultimately be swept away from that which they cling to, but it is all just the way of ensuring that each one ends up fulfilling their life's plan and gets to where they are destined to go.

The slumber is being disturbed, and as things progress, there will come a time when all will awaken to one reality or another. For you who are destined for Terra, you will have a more gentle ride, even in the midst of others' discomfort from their own resistance to change. Nothing will remain of the old at the end of the process, but there is still much time to traverse before that is complete. What you need to know now is to release all attachments to what was in your life and to release all fears for those you love and care about. They will each be provided for in the way that is perfect for them and their soul's choice. We ask that you deepen your trust in the process, for things are going to look pretty extreme in the not too distant future.

There is a limit to the amount of time that you can safely continue to exist in 3D, and we have been instructed from the highest levels as to the logistics involved in making sure that everyone gets to their "right place." You will be sensing the shift as it occurs, and do not be surprised by feelings of peace and bliss that seem to come "from out of the blue," with no apparent external cause. Just relax into them and enjoy them, as eventually they will be your permanent state. These interludes will come more often for you as things progress, and gradually will become the dominant state of your being. You will begin to be able to tell the difference between the state you want to experience and the state that you experience when you engage in old patterns of relationship and communication.

Your body will tell you when you are engaging with dissonant energies because you will experience momentary discomfort that will contrast strongly with this other state of peace and bliss. When you notice this, gently disconnect and redirect your attention to the things you would like to experience and create, rather than the things you would like to stop or oppose. You will find it harder and harder to maintain your connection to things that are not "yours."

If you can relax into receiving the lifting, it will go much easier for you. If your personality traits make it hard for you to "let go and let God," then you will have a little help energetically, to pry your fingers loose of their grasp on the twigs that you cling to in your fear of letting go. Each of you will have "moments of truth" in which you will simply "see" what is happening and then it will be easy to walk away from your former battles.

You see, despite what your physical senses register, your inner, subtle senses can give you another view. Even if you look with physical eyes at the world around you, notice that you do not have as much a feeling of being part of what you gaze at, but rather more and more you will feel like you are witnessing something that you don't quite comprehend. That is part of the process of disengaging from what is familiar to you and receiving what is coming to you.

There is nothing wrong with you and you are not losing your mind or sanity. You might question why you don't feel as strongly about things that used to seem important to you, but if you can just let it all go, and let yourself feel the peace and bliss that is available, it will be much easier for you to move to your proper layer of vibration. Just seek your "homing frequency" and let everyone else do the same. No one is "wrong" in being the way they are. They are just being WHO they came to be and are experiencing what they came to experience. That is why everything "exists" in the first place — so that the Creator can experience Itself through its many creations, all interacting with each other in infinitely complex ways.

There will be things playing out on the world stage that, given your values and orientation, you could consider horrible. We would say to you to let yourself witness these things but also know that they are not "yours." If you feel an inner "push" to help or "do something," by all means follow that to wherever it takes you, but also do not feel guilty if you do NOT feel intuitively that there is a need to respond. Each person has their part to play and no two are alike. That is why it is so important for you to meditate and spend some time every day in that altered state in which you disengage from the world around you and go within, to that very private place where you only have yourself and your God to contend with.

Create your own sense of sacred space within yourself and draw upon the sustenance that offers to you. You are most "responsible" when you take full responsibility for yourself and your actions and thoughts. You have only your God to "account to." All the "rules" you were taught and may have accepted are null and void for the journey to Terra. You can know intuitively in each and every moment what is the most "right" action or course in that moment for YOU. You are sovereign beings and you are the only one you are responsible for. Everyone else has the same responsibility as yours — to be fully responsible (and responsive) to their own inner urgings, and to fully experience being who and what THEY came to experience.

Go within, to that very private place where you only have yourself and your God to contend with.

Most of you who are reading this have not been the "obedient" kind for most of your lives, except if it was to "get along" with others or to please those toward whom you felt some debt or obligation. Now your greatest service is toward fulfilling your own destiny, for you are those who will create the incarnational opportunities on Terra so that others may enjoy that world, also. You are leaving this field of endeavor in order to cultivate another, to shape and enjoy another "garden" in another place and time, and to make for the telling of an entirely new story.

It is time for you to accept yourselves as the pioneers that you are, and to understand that your very differences are the things that equip you best to be the transition team between one world and another. Go within and you will find your way along your path, one step after another, and one day soon, you will lift up your heads and behold a new horizon, unlike any that you have ever gazed upon before.

Now your greatest service is toward fulfilling your own destiny.

As the world splits apart into the different layers that will go toward their different destined locations, focus on what is yours and let others around you do the same. Most of you are tired of waiting for something better. Well, there *is* something better and it is arriving now, inside of you, and is unseen except by your "inner eyes." It will feel like a dreamlike state and you will not be aware of anything but what you are experiencing in that moment, just as you would in a dream while you were asleep. But this dream is real and you are just waking up into it, and things will never be the same for you again.

We leave you now in peace and honor and blessing. We shall speak to you again.

Amen, Adonoy Sabayoth. We are the Hosts of Heaven.

The Splitting of the Worlds 161

As the world splits apart into the different layers that will go toward their different destined locations, focus on what is yours and let others around you do the same.

THE BOTTOM LINE
February 25, 2001

We have asked to speak with you today because there are some things happening that we felt we should comment upon. The first thing, however, is to ask you to ask yourselves just how you feel about the information we have offered to you so far. Does it make sense to you or does it just sound like a nice idea that would be VERY NICE if it were true, but you just aren't sure how you feel about it otherwise?

Summary of the statements we have made in the previous Messages

Let us back up a little and recap and summarize the statements we have made in the previous Messages. First of all, this information is only intended for those whose soul/Oversoul choices are aligned with the journey to Terra. There are many other paths available and they will be taken by the overwhelming majority of people who are incarnate on Earth at this time.

Second, the lifting we have spoken of is dependent on one action and one condition alone: it is necessary to have love in one's heart and in order to do that, it is necessary to "root out" (eliminate or neutralize) fear within oneself. We have defined love in part as the absence of fear, so it is only logical that the cultivation of love requires the removal of fear. Nothing else matters. It does not matter what you know about spiritual matters. It does not matter what you look like or what your age is or where you live. What is in your heart and your attendant frequency are the only criteria for the lifting. If you are afraid to receive the lifting for any reason, you will not be lifted.

Third, we are not "rescuing" you. We are here with you to facilitate your process, but you and you alone are responsible to tend to what is yours alone to do. There are things that you can do to make it easier for yourself, and we can give a certain degree of aid when asked, but facing down your fears within yourself is something that you must do for yourself. All of you who have made the soul choice for Terra have also given yourselves the proper "character traits" to be able to do this. Many — if not most— of you have been seeking "truth" all of your life. Most of you have felt different from the others around you and even now do not know many like yourselves. That will all change in time, for in time — when the splitting of the worlds is complete — you will only be in the company of others like yourself, but for now, you are all in various stages of splitting off from those who will follow paths other than your own.

Fourth, on the timeline that leads to Terra, the present Earth will "pass away" and will no longer support life of any kind. It will be barren and totally inhospitable to all forms of life for a very long time, but that is by Divine design and all things will go to their "right place," according to that design. Terra already exists, pristine and untouched except by love. On Terra only love, peace, and joy will exist. That is why you must have love in your heart and not fear, because only that which is of love, peace, and joy will be permitted to enter Terra. There will be a time of transition on our ships, as none of you will be completely finished with your own transformation when the time of lifting arrives, but you must have cleared out enough fear and the fear-based responses (such as anger, judgement, and greed) to be able to be lifted into the ships when that time comes.

Fifth — and this is the hardest part of all for many of you who feel the pull and yearning for the peace, joy, and love that Terra embodies and represents — there is nothing to "fix" about present day Earth. There is nothing to "create" on present day Earth, except to create the peace, joy, and love within yourselves and within your lives to the degree that you can. There is not going to be an organization to join or create that will take you there. There will not be phenomena such as etheric or physical ships or cities until the time comes for the lifting, and then only those who have qualified by their frequency will even perceive them. Anyone reporting those things or predicting those things belong to another path. It is valid for them and it is valid for those who are drawn to those things, but they are not part of the journey to Terra.

There is a state of growing expectation on all fronts now.

There is a state of growing expectation on all fronts now. The power elite are moving forward with their plans, which they expect to complete in the near future. The various religions and organizations have their expectations about what their path holds for them, and they may in fact experience what it is they expect, just as the many groups who have expectations of another kind will most likely experience what it is that they expect to experience. It is all in Divine order, and each is finding "their own" — their own people and their own actions and their own outcomes. It is all proceeding just as it was created to happen by the choices made at the Oversoul level for those individuals and their particular life experiences.

Therefore, for those whose path leads to Terra, the only things that are appropriate are those that increase one's frequency and decrease one's fears. Meditation will help and will certainly aid in discerning what is true for oneself, but it is not an absolute requirement. It is not necessary to follow elaborate rituals or practices of any kind. Simply placing one's attention on one's breath as it moves in and out is sufficient, and simple prayers of the moment, spoken from one's heart, are more effective than any memorized words, rituals, or formulas can ever be. It is the sincerity and the "heartfelt" quality that holds the power, not the words, and one does best by pausing a moment to FEEL what it is that one truly wants to occur. Then, when the words are chosen, they more nearly reflect the will of the heart and not the mind, and that is where the true power lies.

Simple prayers of the moment, spoken from one's heart, are more effective than any memorized words, rituals, or formulas can ever be.

The journey to Terra is a real one. It is logical that, if indeed this Earth is to pass away, there must be some mechanism to physically transport and sustain the seed stock for Terra before the final cataclysms eradicate all life on the present Earth. While many will indeed incarnate on Terra from the realm of spirit, there must be some mechanism provided to house their developing bodies. There will still be physical births on

Terra, very like the births on Earth, only without the pain and without the loss of consciousness that accompanies births on Earth.

We can say unequivocally that until it is time for you to be lifted — whenever that is for you as an individual — none of the phenomena and none of the organizations will get you there. When it is your time to be lifted, the moment will be very clear to you. There will not be any doubt or question in your mind, and there will not be anything leading up to it other than the internal sense of impendingness; nothing external to you will reveal its approach.

The journey to Terra is made up of sovereign beings, and true sovereignty means the willingness to be truly who you are and allow everyone else the same privilege. The only authority is one's own relationship with Spirit. No creed, no method, no technique, no material creation or alliance of any kind will do it. You are each like individual lightning rods, grounding the light of Spirit into the Earth and supporting the lifting of the planet and yourself at the same time. Lightning rods do not work in bundles. They each serve where they are placed.

That does not mean that you should not reach out in love and support to others, but it does mean that each of you must make this journey on your own, within yourself, and with the willingness and bravery that that entails. You will be pioneers and create a new world and like all pioneers, you will be exploring territory that has not been mapped by others who have gone before you. Therefore, even though there is a core of wisdom to be found in all spiritual and religious traditions, you would do well to put those teachings from the past where they belong: in the museums and libraries that are set up to house the relics of the past.

Yours is a new world, a new creation, and the only things that will survive the shift are those of essence, not of history and the energies acquired through the passage of time on Earth. ALL cellular memory from Earth lifetimes will be erased. You will be wholly new, in all respects, and you will become this way without passing through physical death. It is difficult for you to imagine how this could be and what it will be like, so we suggest that you focus instead on the task at hand: face down your fears; remain grounded in the present moment and listen to the voice of your intuition as to how you should respond in each and every moment, and surrender up everything else.

We leave you now, in peace and honor and blessing. Amen, Adonoy Sabayoth. We shall speak to you again.

The Bottom Line   167

Each of you must make this journey on your own, within yourself, and with the willingness and bravery that that entails.

NOTE: In response to a question regarding the appearance of ships (I myself have seen them) at this time, I received the following response (Feb. 26, 2001):

"We apologize if our statement has caused any confusion. We wish to emphasize that THE SHIPS THAT WILL LIFT PEOPLE OFF THE PLANET as part of the journey to Terra will not be seen until the time of the lifting. That does not mean that some people will not have experiences with ships before then. It only means that those who are reporting seeing ships or who are predicting mass landings or the like are not referring to the ships which will take one to Terra.

Amen, Adonoy Sabayoth. We are the Hosts of Heaven."

Also, with regard to the erasure of cellular memory, it is my understanding that only the EMOTIONAL CHARGE associated with the data is neutralized. The data is always available and is a permanent part of the hologram/Akashic record, but without the emotional charge, one is not usually drawn to revisit those experiences. There is an abundance of things that appear in the eternal "now" and that's where one's fascination lies.

GO WITH THE FLOW — BECOMING ONE WITH THE MIND OF GOD
March 26, 2001

All right, now. We have asked to speak with you today because of certain concepts that are lacking in your awareness that are important for you to understand before proceeding much further in your transformation. We would say that you can transform without this understanding, but we feel it is easier for you to cooperate with the changes if you understand them ahead of time, so when things begin to occur, you can say, "Oh, so *that's* what that is!" and that will make it easier for you to release into the experience, because the known is never as frightening as the unknown.

So, now, where are you in the process? Where are you with all these pronouncements of dates and shifts and gates and the like? If you choose to focus on these phenomena, you will miss what's important. What's important is what's going on beneath the surface, tucked away from prying eyes and safely hidden within the deepest levels of your self. It is there, in your secret temple, that you can meet with your Creator, undisturbed and uninterrupted and face-to-face. We would like you to cultivate that as your primary place of meeting.

To be sure, it is helpful when one is going through so many changes, especially ones that one doesn't understand — it is natural and understandable that you would reach out to others, to see if you are the only one that is experiencing these things, and when you find out that you are in good company, then you can relax and say, "Ah, it isn't just me." However, as we have said before, there really is only ONE Being that is doing all of this experiencing, and it is part of your shift into the consciousness of Terra for you to begin to experience this — not as a concept, but as a felt and real thing within yourself.

Have you noticed a certain sense of unreality these days? Have you seen with a different perception? Do things look a little unreal to you? Good. Then everything is just as it should be. You are beginning to see things as the projections that they are. Let us back up to the hologram that we spoke of some time ago.

A hologram is created by two beams of coherent light. One is called the reference beam and is constant. The other is called the "working beam" and it plays out different patterns on the reference beam.

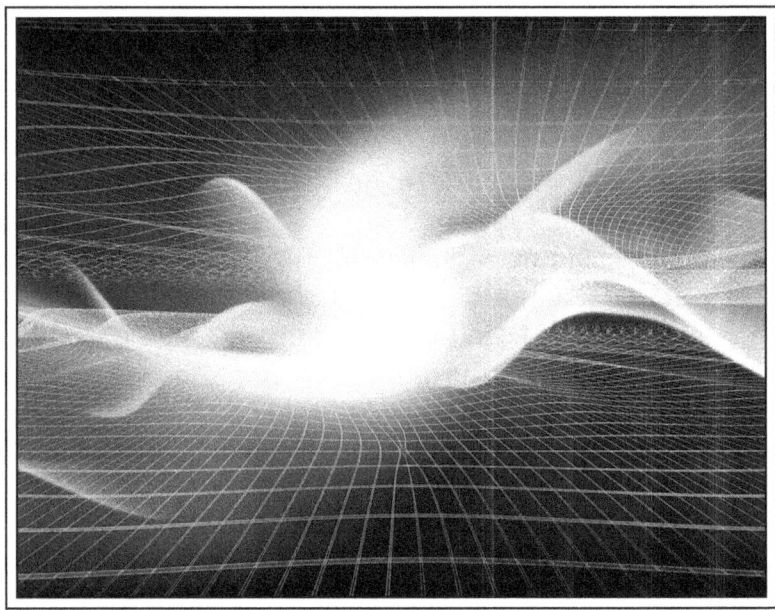

The interaction between these beams creates patterns of light and dark.

The INTERACTION between these two beams creates patterns of light and dark that are a result of the beams either adding to each other (in phase) or subtracting from one another (out of phase), to one degree or another. If the two beams are completely in phase, there is an amplification of the light, and if the two beams are completely out of phase, there is a cancellation of the light. Relationships in between those two extremes result in light of different strengths, or what you might refer to as shadows.

The Source of all Creation is the reference beam. It is constant and is the only Absolute that there is. Everything else is RELATIVE to that reference beam and interacts with it to create the patterns of form that you perceive with your senses. The Creator projects the "other," which is

Go With The Flow — Becoming One With The Mind of God 171

still part of the Creator, but provides the mechanism to interact with the reference beam so that all the variations can be experienced.

To the degree that one is aligned with the Creator (the reference beam), to that degree the interference patterns of light and shadow are diminished until the working beam and the reference beam are totally in phase and all there is is light. The extreme opposite would be an energy or force or entity that is totally out of phase with the Creator and the result would be the cancellation of the light, or the total absence of light — what you refer to as darkness. There is very little to be found in your present reality that is pure light or pure absence of light. Most things are somewhere in between.

You are in the process of becoming totally aligned with the Creator. That is why Terra will be as it will be: everything on it will be in total oneness with the Creator. Every particle of matter will be in oneness with the Creator. There will be no experience of separation and there will only be the Will of the Creator, manifesting in perfection.

All that is not in alignment with the Creator is being flushed out as the amount of light increases within your bodies.

This is why your cellular memory is gradually being purged — so that you can release all your attachments to your experience of being separate in any way from anyone or anything else. All the "shadows" within you are being flooded with light from the highest source, and all that is not in alignment with the Creator is being flushed out as the amount of light increases within your bodies.

These emissions from your sun are one mechanism for adding to the quantity of light contained in the matter that makes up Earth and its inhabitants. The sun acts as a lens to step down the higher Light and acts to store the energy for a time until it reaches a threshold and then a burst occurs, sending a new impulse of light toward the planet and driving it deep within the atomic structure of all forms that exist upon and around the planet. This absorption of energy within the atoms will eventually lead to what is called a quantum leap — the electrons will jump orbits and release photons and the matter will be transformed into a higher frequency band of reality.

On the way to this glorious explosion, all that is not in alignment with the Creator will be purged. The final stages of the Earth's transformation will not allow present life forms to exist upon her, so they will either be physically lifted or will be removed in other ways, such as through the portal of physical death (dropping the physical body) or through the mechanism of parallel worlds. Those who are not going to Terra and who are not destined to die at this time will experience other things on other parallel "Earths," and it is not necessary for you to know about all these other paths. It is only necessary that you accept your own transformation and the change in consciousness that will accompany it.

Now we want to give you a glimpse of what that will be like, so that you can begin to relate everything else to the change you are making — from a being that experiences separation to a being that is totally at one with all of Creation. Imagine a thick liquid, one that has no form of its own, but which has enough substance to pile up in thick heaps if contained. Now think of an infinitely large container, spread out in all directions as far as you can perceive. You cannot see the far edges of the container, only that it is vast. Now imagine this thick liquid as being able to take on any form that can be imagined, solely through the act of imagining it. That will begin to give you a sense of how the Creator creates.

The Creator exists as a thick matrix that interpenetrates and underlies all form. Your physical senses and instruments cannot measure it or perceive it directly, but when you are in your new consciousness, you will experience yourself as WEARING it, like you would a large bowl of thick fluid, out of which YOU emerge as a similarly fluid being.

Your metaphysical teachings say that as one goes higher up on the frequency scale, material substance becomes finer and finer, and that is true. However, there is also a SPIRITUAL mass involved that is in an inverse relationship to the material mass. As material mass DECREASES, spiritual mass INCREASES. At the level of the Creator, there is nothing EXCEPT spirit or intelligent energy and there is "no thing" else.

You are perhaps familiar with the equation for converting mass to energy ($E=MC^2$). It shows that there is an enormous amount of energy contained in a given unit of material mass. However, when we are comparing SPIRITUAL mass to material mass, there is a virtual OCEAN of energy available for every minute particle of material form because it is all connected, and any single point of reference is but a particle floating in the ocean of consciousness that contains and surrounds ALL form. There are no discontinuities in that ocean, so the entire ocean is available to any given point within it, at all times.

On Terra, you will experience yourself AND the entire ocean, all at the same time. You have begun to experience this in some ways — perhaps in your meditations or reveries, perhaps if you ingested certain chemicals that affected the filters in your brain so that you could perceive beyond the limitations of your physical senses. You will be in total oneness with the reference beam, and you will only exist as that beam plays on your perceptual screen. It is that way now, to a certain extent, but there it will be total, conscious (instead of unconscious or dimly perceived), and a permanent state of being.

Everything will be very fluid and gel-like. There will be flow, but no "hard edges." Boundaries that you rely upon now will not exist. You have no idea how much you rely on edges and lines and other demarcations to be able to tell what is where and how to relate to it.

You define yourself as a container bounded by your skin. You look in the mirror and define yourself by what you see, and if you don't, the image makes no sense to you. You regard things like shapeshifting with awe, discomfort, or fear because you rely so much on the illusion of a fixed reality. Your physical senses fool you into thinking that if you can't touch it and feel it with your hand, it isn't real. Your culture controls you and keeps you in a box by ridiculing the subtle senses as being "only your imagination" or even worse, labeling it as a pathological condition — a "disease" that has to be cured by cutting it out (lobotomy), shutting it down (drugs and sedatives), or isolating it (institutionalization) — all means of suppression and denial of what is your natural way of being.

We are here to say to you that the world you will inherit is the natural estate of a fully God-conscious entity, whether it is a rock, a tree, a bird, a flower, or a human being. You have been taught that other forms are "lower," that they have no souls or awareness. We are saying just the opposite. ALL form is "informed" by Spirit, by the matrix of the Creator's Mind. All form is conscious and exists within the ocean of consciousness that is the Mind of the Creator.

Everything is conscious and everything is exploring life, only in different ways and at different rates. The lifespan of a rock is very long and its processes are comparatively slow. The lifespan of a tree is shorter and the lifespan of a human is shorter still. But each of these things is conscious and each of them has a plan for its existence. The entire Creation interacts with itself, dancing with all the parts like mirrors reflecting the light back and forth between them. It is this dance and the reflections that cause the different patterns of light and shadow, that manifest the expression of all the potentials, so that all paths, all possibilities within a given set of parameters are explored.

So now you are being prepared to go to the next level, where your veils will be dropped and you will experience yourself in your true nature — as conscious projections of the Mind of God, as conscious extensions of the Will of God, and as joyous participants in the dance of Creation, totally aligned with God, and totally of the light. No more "shadow play" on the illusory screen of material reality!

You are going "home" to your true estate and you will feast on the riches of the kingdom: peace, joy and love are your true inheritance and you shall have those things and more, in unlimited abundance. As you proceed through the next steps of your transformation, your awareness will begin to shift even more than it has now. Trust that process and do not take it as something that has to be "fixed."

You are moving out of a "fixed" reality into a fluid reality, where all potentials exist simultaneously, so you will have to let go and surrender more and more as things proceed. Think of yourself as a cork floating in an ocean of consciousness, bathed in love and light and grace-filled. Let yourself go into this release and feel the peace and the bliss that accompanies the letting go. Let yourself be lifted and carried and let yourself melt and be like a clear stream of the purest water. Ask not

Go With The Flow — Becoming One With The Mind of God 175

where your journey takes you, but just become the flow and it will all unfold perfectly, for you and for all. Go with the flow!

We leave you now in peace and honor and blessing. Amen, Adonoy Sabayoth. We are the Hosts of Heaven. We shall speak with you again.

Ask not where your journey takes you, but just become the flow and it will all unfold perfectly, for you and for all.

THE BEST MEDICINE
April 6, 2001

Well, now. Our representative on Earth has asked us to give you some information regarding the experiences you are each having as the cleansing proceeds and you are being lifted free from the underpinnings of that life that you have been experiencing while you have been under the illusion of being physical beings, walking around on the surface of the planet, just like everyone else you see around you. And yet, you have not ever FELT like everyone else around you, have you? You have always felt a little different, although here and there you met up with someone who was like you, only to have them disappear from your life as mysteriously as they had arrived.

We are here to tell you today that you are NOT just a physical body, and that you *are* different in some very significant ways from everyone else around you — or at least the majority of those around you, because now some of you are partnered with others with whom you share this common heritage.

"What heritage?" you may ask. Ahhh. Now it comes down to our revealing one of our "secrets." You see, you are one of us. You are one of those who came together in the beginning to form an alliance, out of which this world that you now walk upon was created. You have felt this special relationship to this planet because she is in reality to you as a child to a parent. She is your creation and you love her with all of your being, and it pains you to see what is being done to her, especially now, as the final days of greed and self-interest seek to take every last scrap that can be taken before it is all gone.

Dear ones, you are one of us. You speak of the Earth as your mother, but in reality, YOU are the parent, and you have a responsibility to your creation — to see her through her birthing onto the next platform of her existence, in the long spiral upward toward Source.

In reality, YOU are the Earth's parent.

When she is safely established in her new reality and the new stewards for her journey have "arrived" and taken over the reins, we will all be complete with our arrangement and go on to other creative endeavors in the vast fields of possibilities that are available. We will sever our alliance as co-creators of THIS reality and go on to form other alliances for other purposes, and to fulfill other desires in the search for experiences on behalf of the Creator of us all.

Now, then, how does all of this relate to what you are experiencing now? How does it relate to the feelings you are having and the body changes you are experiencing? Well, we ask you to let us tell you a little story of sorts, a kind of metaphor to use to understand what exactly is going on.

You are not the body you occupy. You are a vast field of intelligent energy that has projected yourself down through all of what you refer to as "dimensions" (that is not an accurate term, but it is what you understand, so we will use that for now) and poured all of that into a very tiny container, the size of a thimble trying to contain an ocean. There even is a children's story called "Thumbelina," which tries to address the experience of being so very tiny in a very vast and enormous world.

Let us tell you then the story of Thimble, the very tiny container that you are, and the ocean of consciousness that you are trying to navigate from the perspective of a thimble, floating at sea in a vast ocean of experience.

Thimble is the name we will give you as the central character in our story. We will make Thimble feminine, but that is only to balance all the stories that had masculine central characters. Remember that this is a parable and the meaning is only understood intuitively and not to be taken literally. Let us begin our story:

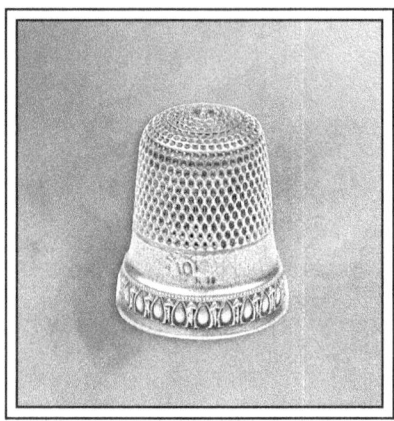

Thimble

One day, Thimble woke up. She had been sleeping a long time, rocked to sleep by the eternal movement of the waves on which she floated, a tiny object floating on the vast ocean, far from any shore or sign of land. In her sleep, she was not aware of anything but her dreams, but now that she had awakened, she was aware of being so small and so far away from anything but the vast stretches of ocean that she saw all around her. She had no means of navigation and felt lost and helpless as she perceived her situation. "Where are all the other thimbles?" she wondered. "Surely I can't be the only one like myself. How can I find the others? Am I destined to only float about on this ocean? Is there nothing more?"

Thimble was distressed. She had been so content in her dreams, in which she lived a full life, surrounded by many like herself, able to be just who she was and to have everyone and everything around her be just who they were. It had all been so harmonious, but now what was she to do? Now she appeared to be all alone. Where were the others she had dreamed about and how could she find her way back into that world of her dreams? How had she come to be here, alone on this vast ocean, with no one to speak to, no one with whom she could share the world of her dreams?

Thimble was now very unhappy, but she was also determined to find her way out of the situation in which she found herself. She was determined to find the others and to find her way back to the world of her dreams. But how could she do that? How could she navigate this vast sea and where would she go? There was certainly no sign of land anywhere and no means of getting there, even if she could have seen some. So Thimble prayed. She was self-aware and she knew there was a Thimble-maker somewhere, or she wouldn't have existed at all. "Great Thimble-maker, please help me. I am alone and lost on this vast sea and I want to be back in the world of my dreams. Please send me the means to get there."

So Thimble sent up her prayer and the Great Thimble-maker heard her and sent a beautiful white bird to pick her up and carry her to the world of her dreams, which lay beyond her ability to see it from where she was. Then Thimble was rejoined with those of her kind and she lived happily ever after, awake and aware and surrounded by all the beauty that she loved.

The Great Thimble-maker sent a beautiful white bird to pick her up and carry her to the world of her dreams.

So, my dear ones, I have heard your call and I will send my beautiful white birds to pick you up and take you to the world of your dreams, where you can live happily ever after, awake and aware and surrounded by the beauty that you love.

I now speak to you in the singular because I am the only one here. I am the Thimble-maker AND the Thimble. I am the Hosts of Heaven and so are you. This idea of there being anything else is something I made up, and it has served me well, for otherwise what else was there for me to do? I have been pretending that I am different parts, interacting with other parts, but now it is time for Thimble to wake up to her connection with the Thimble-maker, and so it is necessary to shed all of those parts of herself that are not in keeping with that truth: she and the Thimble-maker are one.

Does that ring a bell? Someone else said something like that around 2,000 years ago, and it was not understood then by very many. Only those who had the same experience of oneness that he had could understand what he really meant when he said that, and there were not many of those around at that time. Indeed, there are not many of those around right now, but that is about to change. By the way, if you do happen to hear of someone claiming to have already ascended, do not believe it. While there are several individuals who have attained the direct experience of oneness, they do not make such claims. They rely on the perceptions of those around them to discern their true estate. It can be felt.

There are deceivers in your midst that use words to say some very intriguing things, but you cannot FEEL their connection with Source the way you can with those who are really in that state. Trust what you FEEL. Your feelings are a better indicator of truth than your minds, which can be led off in many directions, pursuing this theory or that, but which are disconnected from the direct EXPERIENCE of truth.

We began our discussion today with the statement that we would address the experiences you are having as the cleansing proceeds. We told you our little story to give these next remarks a proper context. Please bear with us if we are unusually long-winded today, for this is not an easy thing to convey.

Each of you has been like Thimble, feeling lost and alone in the vast world around you, and wanting to get back to the world of your dreams without knowing how to get there. Eventually, you began to reach out to the Great Thimble-maker and ask for Its help. Your request has been heard, and now you are being lifted — not by a beautiful white bird (although that is a common symbol for Spirit), but by a vibrational shift.

Picture for a moment a large, sea-going vessel. It has been sailing the ocean for a long time, and its bottom is covered with seaweed and barnacles and slime. Now the vessel has been taken up into drydock and all of the things that were clinging to its underside are being cleaned off, in preparation for another voyage in another sea. This is what is happening to you.

Cleaning off the seaweed, barnacles and slime

All of the things that have become attached to you are being cleaned off. You are shedding the emotional charges that have been accumulated through the entire course of your embodied journey through the history of this planet, so you are re-experiencing many emotions that have been dormant in your cellular memory and are now rising to the surface.

You are having the barnacles removed from your eyes, and you are beginning to see with more clarity. You are experiencing completions with those whom you have traveled with, so that you will be totally free of all attachments that would keep you from being your essential self. You are not yet aware of just how those attachments have bound you to this Earth, but as they pass from your life and you begin to be free of them, you will realize the subtle hold they had on you and how they limited you in your expression of your true essence.

All of these things are now passing out of you and out of your lives, including the IDEAS you had about what was true, about what your "true nature" looks like. You are probably feeling LESS tolerant of what you see around you, in spite of your "pictures" of what a "light worker" is supposed to be like. You are increasing in your ability to forgive and to have compassion at the very same time you are feeling more judgmental and critical of the abuses of power you see all around you, but remember that those in power got there through the collective consent of all who contributed to their being there.

Now that the door is closed on the probabilities and the course is set, many are waking up to the painful realization that there are consequences to all actions — both those that do things and those that do not do things. Those who sat by, content to let others do their thinking for them, are having an unpleasant awakening to the consequences of that action. INACTION is also action, you see. The entire process that is unfolding now on the planet will expose the underbelly of the "ship of state," as it were, and the "creatures" that have been hidden on that underbelly will be seen more and more openly as the days proceed toward the conclusion.

This is all part of the process of the planet completing with this level of her being, and because she is like your own child, you feel anger, rage, and perhaps impotence at what you see going on. Those of you who don't like feeling impotent are feeling either desperation or determination to DO SOMETHING, depending on the degree of powerlessness or empowerment you have achieved, but it all comes down to the same thing.

This final desecration WILL play out, and it has as its purpose the experience of the desecration and the suffering that will result from it. It is easy to blame the Creator and be angry about the suffering, but how else can the "lesson" be taught? The greater mass of people will not get the "lesson" with less drastic means. They would rather stay asleep and let someone else do their thinking for them, so they need a "rude awakening," not unlike Thimble in our story.

The purpose of the awakening is to set one's heart and mind toward seeking in the right direction — toward the Great Thimble-maker — for solutions. The cause of everything you see that is "wrong" with the way people conduct themselves on the planet — including their reproductive behavior — is a lack of connection with Source. To make the connection with Source, one must first perceive the need for that connection. As long as one's material needs are the primary object, one is not very inclined to seek a higher Source. So the material underpinnings will be stripped away from the many and placed in the hands of the few, and the suffering of the many will increase. In fact, that is already well along in the process.

You who are reading this are the pioneers. You have begun your awakening a little ahead of the rest. You have begun reaching toward Source a little sooner than the great mass of humanity, and you will come back to lead to safety those who have needed their lessons from what lies ahead for this planet and everything upon it.

The animals, plants, and other "innocents" in this drama will go on to live on other planets, and you suffer when you see their suffering because of your great love for this planet and all of her life forms — including the rocks, the rivers, the skies, the air, and the plants and animals who have been so impacted by human actions.

You are going to return to the land of your dreams, and you are being cleansed of everything that would keep you bound to this plane and level of reality. You are acting like lightning rods to ground the higher Light into the atomic structure of the planet, and your bodies are going through many changes as a result of this function that you perform, not all of which are pleasant and some of which can be quite frightening because you do not feel in control.

The best "medicine" we can prescribe for all the "ills" of these changes is to increase your depth of SURRENDER. Turn all of these things over to God (however you conceive of It) and deepen your connection to Source. Deepen your trust in the journey and surrender up all resistance to what you see going on around you and within you. Surrender up your fears, also.

When you do not feel in control, fear rises to your awareness. Let the fear come, and then sit with it. Let it percolate through you and move out of you and observe it. Observe that the fear can be within you and you are not obliterated by it. Observe that you do not have to be controlled by your fear. If you feel yourself "losing it" and becoming paralyzed by your fear, remember your connection to Source and use that as the thing that you cling to, rather than your attachment to a particular outcome. All of your fears, all of your suffering and pain has some measure of attachment to a particular outcome or course of events. It all is a form of resistance to the movement of life, especially now, in these accelerated times.

The best medicine is to increase your depth of surrender.

We have said it before and we will say it again: "Let go and let God handle the details." You are shedding all of the debris you have acquired during your many lives on the face of this planet. It is not comfortable at times, but remember that you are losing only that which is not part of your essential self. You are being cleaned of all the barnacles and slime that you have taken on in your voyage through this ocean and will be lifted into "drydock" to complete the process. Then you will be all clean and shiny and new, and will embark on other journeys in other seas, for *this* Earth and *this* sea will have passed away and be there no more.

Amen, Adonoy Sabayoth. We are the Hosts of Heaven. We love you. We are with you. You are one OF us and you are one WITH us, and you are awakening to that truth now. We leave you now, in peace and honor and blessing. We shall speak to you again.

ON SEXUALITY AND REPRODUCTION — TERRA STYLE
April 14, 2001

Well, now. In our last conversation, we spoke to you about the oneness that you will experience on Terra. This will be your constant experience, and you will KNOW yourself as being part of everything you perceive — be it infinitesimally small or as vast as an entire universe. Therefore, the primary reason for the 3D human sexual behavior will not be present.

What IS the primary reason for your sexual behavior? When analyzed down to its root, it is primarily an attempt to escape the prison of being contained in one body, of seeking to somehow breach that boundary of skin and to attempt to merge with another. Now, we are aware that many times the sexual act is not used to JOIN two people, so much as it is the inflicting of one's power over another, but that is a distortion and misappropriation of the sexual energy, as you will soon see.

Rather than condemn the present patterns, we wish to first draw a picture for you of how it will be on Terra — not only for the human species, but for all life forms that have the ability to join in sexual ways. Then, by contrast, you will be able to gain a sense of how your present experience does not satisfy and provides only temporary relief from your isolation and separation from all things. You will also see how those practices that seek to escape from the sexual function (such as celibacy and monasticism) are an evasion of life in its fullest expression. That is not to say that there is nothing to be gained by them, but we prefer to put before you what life is like when you are in full consciousness and not struggling to repress your natural, God-given faculties in order to transcend them.

So, let us begin this discussion by reminding you that on Terra, you will be in total oneness with all of Creation. You will be immersed in a sea of consciousness that from your present perspective would appear to be surreal and dreamlike — not unlike some of the states one experiences on certain drugs, such as opium and its relatives. However, it will be your constant state, and therefore one simply adapts to it as being the norm and picks up from there.

You will be immersed in a sea of consciousness that from your present perspective would appear to be surreal and dreamlike.

On Terra, all things are in total balance with the whole, and reproduction occurs within that context. No flower blooms, no animal is born, without there being a clear and necessary "reason" for its coming into being, with regard to the whole. All things that reproduce by the combining of gametes (sperm and ova in their various forms) only do so when the whole demands it of them, in order to perpetuate and maintain the balance. It sounds very complicated, but we assure you that it is the only truly natural way for it to be. What you see in your present reality is so distorted from what is natural that you cannot imagine what "natural" (i.e., in keeping with the inherent NATURE of things) is really like.

On Sexuality and Reproduction — Terra Style

No flower blooms, no animal is born, without there being a clear and necessary "reason" for its coming into being, with regard to the whole.

On Terra, reproduction is one function and it is separate from the sexual function. In your present reality, they are so intertwined and so out of balance with Nature and what is natural that they are often confused for one another. In many of your religions, both desire and sexuality are feared and held in mistrust. You are taught that they are something "sinful" or "wild" or "uncivilized" that has to be controlled in one way or another.

However, when a natural function is repressed, just like when the flow of a stream is blocked, it WILL seek another outlet, and that is exactly what you see in your present world. The natural functions have become twisted and distorted and grossly misunderstood in every aspect of your present civilization, regardless of geography or so-called "enlightened" approaches to the problem, which is really a symptom of the experience of separation.

On Terra, you will be one with everyone and everything, all the way out into the far reaches of the cosmos. You will live on a world in which everything is in total balance and shares in the existence and consciousness of everything else. If you are already in full union with everything, where does desire fit into the picture?

Desire is the engine behind all creativity, be it to create a painting, a piece of music, an elegant mathematical equation, or to create another life. Desire is what drives the evolution of the cosmos. The Creator's desire to experience everything is what leads It to CREATE everything!

At its root, your desire is the outpicturing of the Creator's desire to experience everything, through the mechanism of the interaction of all the parts of Its Creation. This interaction is most acutely experienced through the faculty of touch.

You can look at something and interact with it visually. You can share your thoughts and feelings with another, either verbally or telepathically. You can experience through your physical senses of hearing and smell, but none of these communicates experience as fully as the sense of touch. You can use your imagination to create an experience that approaches what it would be like to touch something, but there really is no substitute for the actual touching.

You can use your imagination, but there really is no substitute for the actual touching.

In order to progress to the higher levels of being, one must complete with the levels below it. Although you are the embodied aspects of the elohim and have DESCENDED into matter, you still can only imagine the "next step" on the journey back to Source in terms of your present experience — that of a human being, clothed in skin, and seeking to break out of the prison of separation consciousness. Therefore, you can only imagine a "next step," and that is how we will frame this. In a future discussion, we will talk about how you aren't really "going" anywhere, but for now, let us continue the exploration of our topic today.

The sense of touch is where you, as human beings, are most starved. And yet, if you seek to touch from that place of hunger and not from a place of already being filled with love, you only perpetuate your distress, and you get caught up in either having to seek again or remain in the loneliness and isolation of your prison cell — your physical body, your container — the thimble that you wear around the fingertip of your Oversoul that is inserted into your present space/time locus.

Let that sink in for a moment — and let that awareness of all the lives in which you sought to fill your emptiness and were unfulfilled in your seeking come back to you now. Let it sink in, and let it go. That is all coming to an end for you now.

On Terra, every life form that reproduces by sexual means is mated. Every life form in that category is paired with its twin — its counterpart — what we call the dyad. Each Oversoul is complete within itself, just as the Creator is complete within Itself. There is no division into parts or genders, but in Its desire to experience everything, the Creator divided Itself into many parts that could then seek to unify back together again, and then — having accomplished that — would be divided up into an entirely new Creation — what could be viewed as the exhale and the inhale of the Creator's breath.

First the exhalation — the breathing out into form, and then the inhalation — the coalescing of form back into the formlessness that gave rise to it in the first place. The dyad is really the first level of the Creator (the monad) dividing itself into parts. This happens at all levels of the Creation, but for now we will keep our focus on the most apparent form of that — the twin, the counterpart that is the "other part" that each part seeks to find and unify with. We will call this part the "mate" of the other.

Mating is not just for reproduction. Mating is the act of unifying with one's mate, and reproduction is reserved for those times when a new being or unit is required for the balance of the whole. Population levels on Terra will remain fairly stable, once the colonization is complete. It will take some time to accomplish that, but once it is complete, those forms that leave Terra in one way or another will be replaced by others, and thereby maintain the balance of the whole.

As humans, you will have very long lifespans and be capable of reproducing throughout your entire adult existence. Therefore, in order to maintain the proper reproductive rate, gametes (sperm and ova) will only be produced when there is the complete set of circumstances present that require the creation of another life form. That is "birth control" in its natural form, at the highest level of knowing. We will address the issue of birthing in another conversation, but for now let us return to our topic for today.

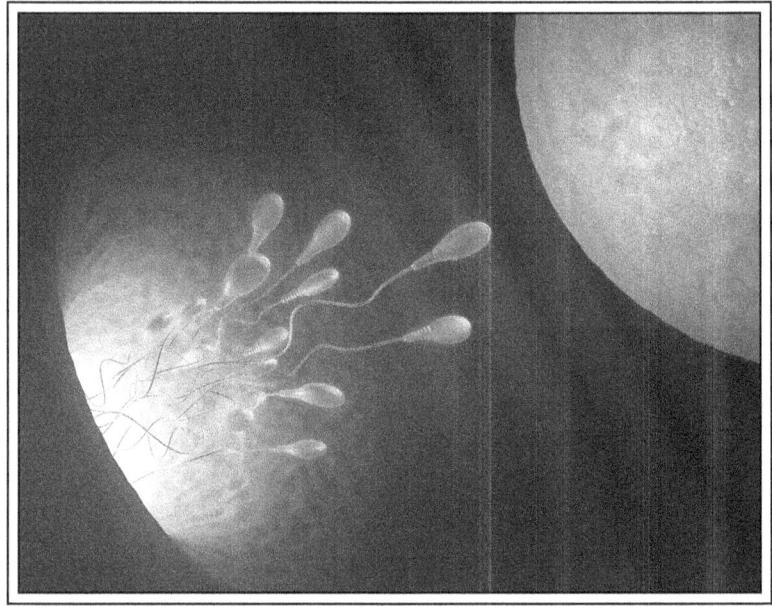

Gametes (sperms and ova) will only be produced when there is the complete set of circumstances present that require the creation of another life form.

The bodies you now occupy are not the bodies you will have on Terra. The bodies you now occupy will transform into the kind of body that you would consider one of a god or goddess, because of its physical perfection and beauty. The physical senses you now have are very crude compared to those you will have then.

Just as you cannot make a fine drawing with a pencil that is shaped like a log, you cannot experience the fineness of sensuality that will be available to you on Terra with the coarseness of your present physical senses. Note the relationship between sensuality and senses. Just as sexuality is the expression of the sexual function, sensuality is the expression of the sensual (pertaining to the senses) function. Sensuality is intertwined with sexuality because sexuality involves the senses for its proper expression.

All of the senses are engaged in the sexual function, both the physical ones and the ones you would call "subtle" — your intuitive, mental, and emotional ones. Those of you who have been fortunate enough to have a glimpse of a full sexual experience know this, but unfortunately that is the exception rather than the rule, and just as your cultures have labeled sexuality as something to be feared and controlled, sensuality has likewise been condemned to repression and condemnation.

On Terra, you will be freed of all constraints — especially economic ones — and you will be in full consciousness, blessed with lives measured in the hundreds of years, so you will be able to allow yourself the full expression of all of your senses and your sexuality, in a mated relationship, without any reproductive consequences.

You won't need techniques. You won't need anything but the full acceptance of your freedom to endlessly explore the full range of your sensuality — ALL of your senses — and your desire will be finally free to explore creativity of all kinds of things, without being confined by "rules" as to what is acceptable and what is not. In full consciousness at all times, you will KNOW and intuitively seek only those expressions that support and celebrate life and support and celebrate the whole of life, in its myriad of forms and expressions.

Ecstasy is your natural estate (difficult as that might be to comprehend from your present frame of reference) and the sexual function — employing the full range of all of your senses as it does — will give you the greatest fulfillment of that ecstasy, and so it will occupy your attention a great deal of the time.

When you are in continuous communication with all of Creation, and in particular with your mate — the other side of your dyadic unit — it will be like "making love" all of the time. Even when you are not in physical proximity, you will be making love with each other. The flow is constant between you, like a dance that never ends, and it will be so for the rest of your journey in this Creation.

You were born together in the mind of the Creator, you are joined together in the mind of the Creator, and you will eternally be together in the mind of the Creator until the inhale is complete and you dissolve your beingness into that of the Creator Itself, ready to be born again into beingness with the next outbreath of Creation. You have much ahead to enjoy, and enjoy it you will, of that we have no doubt. It is time, dear ones, for you to come home — to yourself, to Terra, to the entire spectrum of experience of which you are capable. And is THAT not an idea worth waiting for? WE think so, and know that you will agree.

We will leave you now in peace and honor and blessing. Amen, Adonoy Sabayoth. We are the Hosts of Heaven. We shall speak to you again.

The flow is constant between you, like a dance that never ends.

ACROSS THE GREAT DIVIDE
September 1, 2001

We have asked to speak to you today about the next stage on the journey to Terra, and to address a central question that is no doubt at the back of your minds as you read through our communications with you. How, exactly, will you cross over the gulf between your present physical location and your future home on Terra? And what exactly are these ships that we talk about so often in so many ways?

Our ships are made of living light.

To begin with, our ships are made of living light. They are conscious beings in their own right, and come into being without being "manufactured" via some technology or machinery in a factory.

They are precipitated directly from the matrix of being that we call the Creator. They are sentient and we travel in them by forming a telepathic link between ourselves and the ship we are on, and together — as a group mind — we teleport ourselves to the agreed-upon location.

We travel in what you refer to as hyperspace. We "blink off" from one location and "blink on" in the place we project ourselves into. The ship acts as a container for our bodies, which are still physical to us, even though they would not be visible to instruments or organs that are tuned to the light frequencies that you are familiar with as your present physical environment.

These ships all have names, just as we do. They have personalities, just as we do. They come into being in response to a collective need for their presence, just as all forms do on Terra and in the frequency band that we occupy. As we said in our last Message, no form comes into being on Terra except as it is in harmony with the whole. The whole would be incomplete without it, and that lack is filled by the manifestation of the ship or any other form that appears in that frequency band. All are in conscious communion with the Creator, with each other, and with the planet, through the vehicle of a group mind.

Each being within the group mind has its own perspective.

Each being within the group mind has its own perspective and makes it possible for anyone else in the group to experience through that perspective if that is desired, but most of the time we are content to remain in our own "viewing chamber," as we are always filled and never lack for anything. The spontaneous desires that emerge in our minds source from the Creator and lead us in the direction that fulfills Divine Will at all times. Everything is always aligned with Divine Will and therefore we are always filled with a sense of unspeakable joy and fullness, as we just live the "rightness" of our being as a permanent way of doing things.

So, when we say we will come for you in our beautiful ships, it is a group effort. We and the ships are united in our purpose and being, and the radiance of that can be felt by those who can join their energies with ours and therefore become part of the group and join with us in our location.

Think about this for a moment. You probably thought we were going to use some sort of beam or technology to lift you into the ships, but we don't do the lifting. YOU do! It is through the energy of joy in your heart — the welcome you feel in seeing us — that the doors fly open and you naturally gravitate (or should we say, "levitate"?) to the fulfillment of your heart's desire.

As we have said, love is the ordering force that acts upon light to create all form. It acts in opposition to entropy, which seeks to return things to a more elemental, uncreated state. Love is the life force behind everything and those who understand the nature of healing know that love is the most powerful healing force there is. It mends those places where entropy has torn the connections, where you are wounded in your bodies and in your psyches. A wound is only a tear in the fabric of life. Love is the force that mends the tear. We have asked you to face down your fears so that you can hold more love in your hearts. When it is time for the lifting, you will be ready and your own love and joy will be the force that reunites you with your spiritual family.

Now we would like to address another part of the "project" — namely how you get from Earth to Terra. As we have said, the planet will undergo a total cleansing of all life above the mineral kingdom, in order to lie fallow and regenerate the physical body of Earth itself. It will withdraw from a state where it can support life and reappear in its new body, somewhat like a glove being turned inside out to reveal a new "outside" that was formerly hidden from sight. This inversion will take place over a period of several years and no life forms will inhabit the former planet during that time. It is necessary to lift some life forms off of the planet before the completion of the final cataclysms and to house and provide for them while the planet completes her own transition from one form to another. This is where the ships come in.

Our ships are not just modes of transportation. They are like floating wombs and can support us and all life forms within themselves, like giant islands or capsules in the vastness of space. The very large motherships are spherical in shape, due to the properties that are inherent in a sphere. You will all be joining us on board our smaller, disc-shaped craft and then be transported to an enormous mothership that is nearly the size of your own planet, but not quite so large — on the order of 80% of your present planet's size.

You will live with us on board the mothership until all preparations are complete and then you will be transported to Terra to set up your homes there. You will undergo a process while on board the mothership that will raise your consciousness to the point of full union with the Creator and it will remain that way for the rest of your existence in the higher densities. None of you who are going to Terra will ever have to return to a 3D existence, although you might at some time choose to do that for your own reasons, in keeping with the purpose of your existence as an individuated part of the consciousness of the whole.

Now the process has indeed begun in earnest. "Launch day" for Operation Terra (August 18, 2001) marked the departure and separating out of that group of beings and that envelope of energy that is headed toward Terra from the mass consciousness and body of Earth. So, in a way, you are already being "lifted" and you are already taking part in your homecoming and reunion with your soul family.

The Earth-based portion of Operation Terra is a focal point, a gathering place for all those who are destined for Terra. Many of you have been in total isolation from others like yourselves, and that isolation is beginning to end as you discover that you are not the only one who knows what you know and feels as you feel. Operation Terra is a beacon with the tone of "home" to those who resonate with this information. Note that we do not say "agree with" or "believe in" this information. We use the word resonance on purpose, because it says exactly what we mean.

If you look at the word resonance, it comes from the root "resound," or literally to re-sound, or "sound again." It is a form of echo, sending back (re-sounding) the sound that triggered it in the first place. Sound is measured in frequency patterns and the interaction of sound and light combined make up the basis of all form.

We have embedded light codes into the Operation Terra material, using the words as the carrier wave to bring them into your awareness. As you read the words, the light codes pass into your body and seek the matching codes in your cellular structure. It is very much like a tuning fork. If you are a tuning fork, tuned to the note "A," nothing will happen until a note "A" is struck or sounded in your vicinity. Then you will re-sound (resound) with that note, and it will ring inside you like a bell, an explosion of sound and joy as your embedded codes begin making their own sound in response.

If you are a tuning fork, tuned to the note "A," nothing will happen until a note "A" is struck or sounded in your vicinity.

It might be a quiet sound. It might be like a light-cannon going off, but it will feel like a "yes." "Yes, I know this." "Yes, this is familiar to me." "Yes, this is mine." That is how resonance works. It is not the product of analytical thought. It is a RESPONSE, a resonance, a re-sounding and answering echo from the core of your being, your own inner answer to the question, "Has it happened?" "Has it shown up yet?"

Yes, we have shown up now. And you belong with us, your soul family. You are drawn through the principle of resonance to recognize this note as yours. Now the "lifting" can be seen as a logical outgrowth of that — an extension of that resonance with our note, as it is carried through this information and the light codes we put into it.

Now it is not so mysterious, not so much a "beam me up, Scotty" hardware-based technology. Call it the technology of love. Call it the technology of the life force. Can you feel your heart and being opening to this idea like the petals of a flower spreading to catch the rays of the sun? We are here with you at all times, and we welcome you into our midst. Our love for you showers you at all times, like the sun is always radiating light toward the Earth, and all you have to do is open yourself to receive it.

It will be easier for you if you do not engage with the pictures that are playing out on the perceptual screen of the rest of the world as things proceed. If you detach from all of that, you will find you experience more peace, more bliss, and more serene acceptance of yourselves and your journey. If you over-identify with what you look upon — the apparent suffering that is increasing, the madness playing out around you — it is easy for you to forget your home note — the joy and the peace and the love that you feel when you connect with us and our vibration.

So, if you find yourself getting caught up in the storm, in the battles that are raging even now and that will only escalate as things proceed toward the climax, when you become aware of how uncomfortable you feel in that frequency band, just disengage. Come back to the Messages. Read them again. Go for a walk. Let yourself register that most of what you see around you is not yours. Let the beauty show itself to you, peeking out from behind the ugliness. It is there. Let yourself open to it. Disengage. Let it all go. Let go and let God handle the details.

You are tired at times. Let yourself rest in the peace and the joy and the love. It is there for you, if you can let yourself receive it. Let yourself receive it. Let go of everything that does not bring you peace and joy and love. Sleep deeply and gratefully when you rest, and let us scour you clean of the residue that remains. You may be tired afterward, but you will feel much lighter and freer because of the work we are doing with you while you sleep. Let go and let God. It is much easier that way.

We leave you now, in peace and honor and blessing. We shall speak to you again.

Amen, Adonoy Sabayoth. We are the Hosts of Heaven.

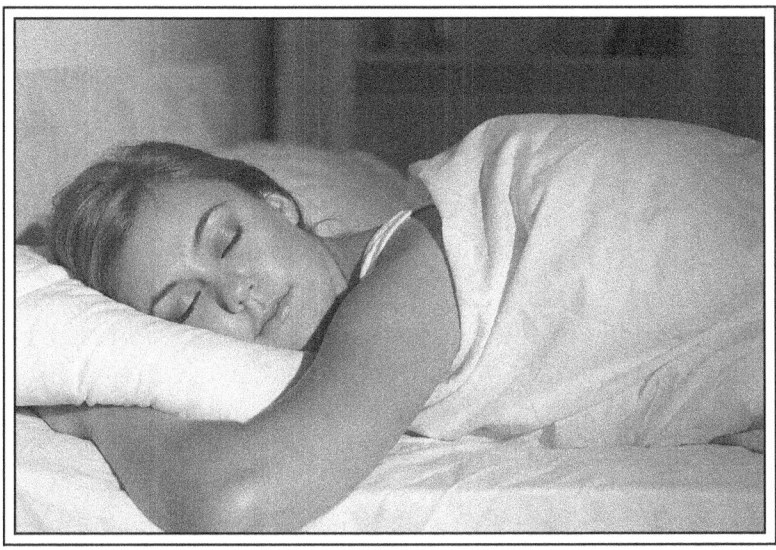

Sleep deeply and gratefully when you rest, and let us scour you clean of the residue that remains.

THE TIME OF INGATHERING
September 8, 2001

Today we would like to talk to you about some of the things that are about to begin showing up on your perceptual screen. We would remind you to keep your breath open, as some of the things we will be talking about may cause some temporary discomfort to contemplate. We would prefer to not ever cause you any discomfort, but sometimes during a birth, there is some pain and pressure, and the more you can simply accept the process — in all of its aspects — the easier the process will go for you.

That being said, you — as a planetary population — are about to enter a time of deepening strife and travail. There is safe haven within yourself, no matter where you are located on the planetary surface, and we are close at hand, guiding and protecting and showering our love and grace over you. Whatever we may say here, whatever your eyes may see as you look around you, please remember that. If you feel yourself being overwhelmed by anything, just close your eyes for a moment, deepen your breathing, and come into your center. Feel the ground beneath your feet and remain rooted there until you are calm and serene in the midst of everything.

The first symptoms of the unraveling have begun to appear. The first wobbles of the axis are occurring and the center of things has begun to oscillate between one pole and another — both geophysically, politically, economically, and culturally. There is a profound change underway that affects every aspect of life in every part of the world, and all parts interact with and are connected to every other part, so the change will oscillate and ramify and be amplified with each oscillation. This is part of the "shaking" that we have talked about, and it will shake loose everything before it is over.

Nothing of the old ways will pass through this time. Only essence will survive and move on. Only what is in keeping with YOUR essence will survive the shift and move on. Many of the acculturated patterns will not make it through the "gate," and you will truly become entirely new beings.

On the way to the homecoming, you will pass through scenes of increasing turmoil and chaos.

On the way to the homecoming, though, you will pass through scenes of increasing turmoil and chaos. Many will be very frightened, as the fabric of their life becomes torn and shattered through these massive shifts and changes in the foundation that underlies the entire system. However, this is what their Oversouls chose for them to experience in this life, and it is also a time that is rich with opportunity for discovering what is REALLY important, for discovering where one's priorities really lie.

It will not be an easy time, but as so many of you have already discovered by going through your own travail, there is something gained in the end that is more precious than any material possession could possibly be. It is the inner peace and release that comes from surrender that is the "gold" within the cloud. It is the golden treasure of Spirit that will fill you now, and it is the time of the ingathering.

This will not be an easy thing for some of you to hear, because you care and you want to help and you still have fears about what will happen to the "others." Even so, this is as it was intended to be from the beginning, and it is totally in keeping with the choices made by all of the Oversouls, individually and collectively. The ingathering is taking place now, and it represents the collecting of those who are going to Terra and removing them from the world scene for a time, until it is time to return and gather up those who have gone through the trials and been transformed by them.

It is time to separate the wheat from the tares, to send the workers into the fields and gather it into the barns.

This is about the harvest, and if we may take a few lines from your Bible, it is the time to separate the wheat from the tares, to send the workers into the fields and gather it into the barns. This is the time of the ingathering, and the withdrawal from the world for a time, until it is time to return. Let this sink in. Let this register. Let it fill you and let it deepen you and let it flow, without resistance, until you are at peace. Let all the resistance come up and move out of you. Let it all go. Let go and let God. Let go. Breathe. Breathe. Breathe.

There is no more to be done than to gather up those who are being lifted now. Then the full impact of the travail of the birth will play out on the planetary surface, and there will be much pain and suffering wherever there is resistance. This is a mighty, scouring force, and it will not be pleasant for many who go through it, but it must occur.

The lesson is one of surrender and of turning inward for support and succor. There are some lessons to be learned about the consequences of not taking responsibility for one's life and truth. There are some lessons to be learned about abdicating responsibility for one's life and truth and placing it into the hands of others. There will be many hard lessons learned.

The lesson is one of surrender and of turning inward for support and succor.

The ingathering will remove all but a few of you from the planetary surface. Some will remain because their work for the planet requires it, but most of you will be lifted up out of the frequency band you now occupy and be totally hidden away until it is time to return. You will not be available to those who are left behind, so that they may have their opportunity to learn what you have learned. It is all in divine order and all within the Divine Plan. You are already being lifted now, and that separating out from the mass consciousness can be felt by those of you who are sufficiently sensitive to the more subtle energies to perceive it.

It will appear that the light is withdrawn with you, but that will never be the case. It will appear that you have abandoned those who remain behind, but that will never be the case. You will simply be withdrawing for a time so that you can return to help when you are really needed. You need to change your costume for your new role, and you need a safe place in which to accomplish that. You are simply going away to prepare for the real help you can give, and you will be needed in great numbers near the end of things, as there will be many who need your help at that time.

The kind of help you can give now is fairly limited, although your task of grounding the light and your meditation and prayers have been very effective in supporting the cleansing so far. But when it comes time to gather up those who have gone through the time of trials, it will not be enough to offer words of comfort or a book to read or a meditation circle. By then, things will be very different than they are now and a different kind of help will be needed.

You need to change your costume for your new role, and you need a safe place in which to accomplish that.

Wars and climate change and economic collapse and tyranny will all have taken their toll, and simple techniques and words will not be enough. You will literally walk through the killing fields and offer a hand to those who are ready to leave with you. You will need to be clothed in your armor of protection and you will need to be in full consciousness. You will be as living Christs (anointed ones) and carry the vibration and power that comes through such a state of being.

So now the lifting proceeds and the separating out proceeds and all will play out in increasingly serious fashion. You will find that, even though all is collapsing around you, you will have peace. You will have peace because you will have learned the lessons and will have learned how to surrender to the higher light and wisdom. You will have peace because you have learned how to face down your fears and accept your life's path with serenity.

In that peace, you will find bliss and relief and you will accept the light and the lifting. So, now, let go of the feeling that there is anything to do now but accept the lifting. The things that will play out on the planetary surface MUST play out and there is nothing you need to resist or change. Let go and let God, and receive the peace of that.

Let peace be your refuge and armor against the pain of those around you.

Let peace be your refuge and armor against the pain of those around you. You cannot help them if you engage in their pain. You cannot be lifted if you are still clinging to the old forms and patterns. Let go and let God. Let God handle the details. You are not responsible for anyone but yourself. It is enough to receive the lifting, for by that means you will be able to really help when it is needed. We have been repeating ourselves throughout this Message because we really want you to "get it." Let go and let God. Do not resist what is happening around you. Receive peace.

All your life, and in all of your lives, you have been preparing for this time. It is here now. If you had a feeling that you had to DO something — set up a center, found a movement, teach a class, write a book — for most of you, that time is now over. For SOME of you — those who have elected to remain behind and who have work to do through the difficult times ahead — you will be guided and you will know what is yours to do. Each one of you reading this has a part to play in all of this. Some of you will remain and play your part that way for now; the rest will be lifted gradually until you are "gone from the scene," so that you can complete your "costume change" and prepare for your new role.

We are with you all, and we will be coming closer to you now, so many of you who have not felt us will be able to feel us now. You have been activated by the light codes in these Messages and it is easier now for you to receive us. Let go and let God. Let go of your attachments as to how it will be for you or for those around you. Let it all be the way it is intended to be and you will have joy in all your undertakings. There will come a time when it is all ended, and then you will have Terra to look forward to. Let go. Float upwards. Let go. We are with you, every step of the way.

We leave you now in peace and honor and blessing. Amen, Adonoy Sabayoth. We are the Hosts of Heaven.

NOTE: Two and a half days after this Message was received, the 9/11 attacks on the World Trade Center and Pentagon occurred, and we — as a planetary population — entered the "time of deepening strife and travail" that is foretold in this Message.

SHATTERING GLASS
September 14, 2001

All right, now. The first "bomb" has been dropped and the cloud of the aftermath is billowing forth across the entire planet. How does this fit in with the overall plan? How is one to be with the scenes of horror and pain? How can one bear the load of believing in truth, kindness, and love in the face of such an act and the pain it inflicts?

Dear ones, we know your hearts are heavy and saddened by such scenes on your perceptual screens. We know you are sympathetic with those impulses toward goodness, beauty and mercy. We know you deeply care for this planet and all upon it, as we do. Therefore, we would offer the following as our contribution toward your process of coming to grips with that which is now unfolding upon your planet, and to further the deepening of your awareness of just what that is and what it will require of you.

You have incarnated here at this time to perform a very special and difficult task, in service to the planet (and secondarily to all upon her). Your focus is the *planet* and the assistance you can give to the planet as she begins rising toward her new form and being as Terra. You are assistants in the birthing of this new world, and once this "launch phase" is complete, you will withdraw from her for a time until the trajectory is complete and she has arrived and manifested in her new state. At that time, all that were taken off the planet for this particular purpose will become the architects of the new society, the gardeners of the new garden, Terra. Please note that there are many other destinations and we are addressing our remarks to those who have this special task. They do not apply to anyone else at this time.

As we have said before, you are human lightning rods, grounding the higher Light into the core of the planet. This light is a cleansing light and is aiding the planet in shedding all those thoughtforms that she has absorbed over the course of her history as the host for all of the lifeforms that have come forth upon her surface.

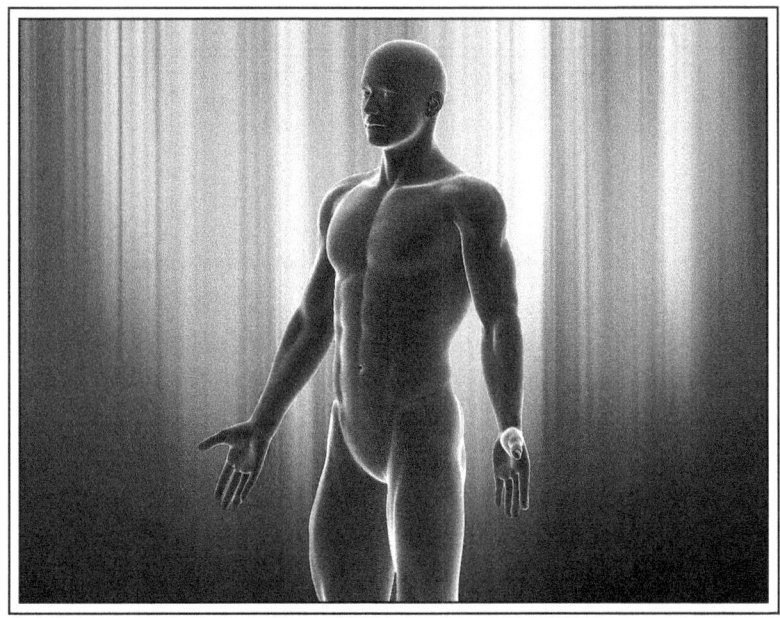

You are human lightning rods, grounding the higher Light into the core of the planet.

As the planet rises through the frequency bands, all of those thoughtforms that she contains will be cast off, largely through the force of the light being beamed down into the planet from the higher realms — through your sun, through the galactic core, and through each of you. You are each supporting the cleansing of the planet, and the scenes you witness (such as what just occurred) are the outpicturing of those thoughtforms that are being flushed to the surface — pictures of hatred for others to such a degree it seeks to annihilate them and cause them every conceivable harm — personal, economic, humiliation, and so forth.

You have a saying, "What goes around, comes around." Some of you are also aware of the concept of karma — that whatever action proceeds from a place of imbalance must be balanced by an equal and opposite action of some kind. What you may NOT be aware of is that there is an invisible wall — a threshold that separates your present Creation from the Creation that is about to be birthed, on the other side of the "blink."

Your planet is moving upward in frequency and forward in time, as viewed from within linear time. It is approaching this barrier, this threshold, and all actions that source from imbalance will receive their answering action, like an echo bouncing off that barrier and returning to the source of the imbalanced energies, as a correction and offset to those actions. The Earth is ascending now, and can no longer absorb these things, as she has throughout her history. What this means is that two things will be going on simultaneously and will tend to amplify one another as things proceed.

All of those thoughtforms that are not in keeping with the higher frequency bands will surface and be re-enacted in a present time context.

First, there is the shedding of the thoughtforms of previous actions, from other times in the Earth's history. All of those thoughtforms that are not in keeping with the higher frequency bands will surface and be re-enacted in a present time context, so they can be experienced and balanced by those who are ready to receive them as that kind of opportunity — who are ready to shift their own historical response to another kind of response, one based on mercy, love, kindness, compassion, and unifying with those whom they previously opposed.

The second thing that will be going on will be the echoes of present-time actions, the answering actions that mirror and reflect the initial actions, so that the sources of those actions have an opportunity to shift their response to a different kind of response, also.

Both of these things — the echoes from the past and the echoes from the present — will be going on simultaneously, which will intensify and multiply the effects as the planet moves upward and forward towards its own destination. How this will be experienced by each "observer" — each set of eyes and ears that are present to witness this — will vary, according to the "filters" that are in place in that individual. So some will see things that they feel called upon to avenge. Others will see things that they feel called upon to heal. Still others will respond in other ways.

It is all a very individual thing, so that the Creator can experience Itself through all the perspectives available through all of Its creations. We would remind you that nothing exists that is not part of and contained within the Creator, and the greatest comfort is obtained by making that connection with the Creator and aligning one's personal will with the Creator's will. "Not my will, but thy will" is the way it was said 2,000 years ago, and it is still valid now.

So what does this mean at a practical level, and what is your proper response and most appropriate service, given the above? First of all, you must understand and come to terms with the enormity of what is unfolding. Consider that you are dealing with the outpicturing of ALL ACTIONS that occurred throughout the entire history of the planet, up to and including those actions that are arising in present time. That is the size of the burden that the planet has carried as her service to those upon her, so that maximum opportunities for experience could occur.

We are talking about the compression of millions and BILLIONS of years' worth of events into the span of your present time, which will complete in a few years from now. Take a breath and let the scope of that register deeply within you, as you receive the confirmation of what you already know to be true.

There is some relief in this picture, given that most of the imbalance has sourced from the most recent periods of history, and that some of the actions that arise in the present are in themselves echoes from prior periods, being revisited in your present time, so you might say that there is some inherent efficiency in this process, as present actions can act to correct and balance prior ones at the same time as they are corrected and balanced. Nonetheless, the burden of the planet is enormous, the timespan is relatively short, and so the potential intensity of the process is almost inconceivable, if you could indeed grasp it at all.

But there is help being given in enormous quantities, also. Those of you who are embodied on the planet's surface are the point of entry for the forces of Love and Grace that are being showered down by those in the higher realms. The core of the Andromeda Galaxy (which overlights your galaxy), the Great Central Sun of your galaxy, and your own sun are all acting as lenses to step down the Light from Source and to make it available to those of you who serve on the planet's surface at this time, in amounts and "packets" that you can handle without being destroyed by their intensity and power.

So your task is to allow yourselves to receive these energies and to let them flow through you unimpeded, into the planet's core. The more you can surrender your own resistance to the process and simply allow yourselves to become like hollow tubes through which the flow can pass, the more you can contribute to this process. This will also allow you to remain calm, serene, and centered while all around you is in chaos. If you allow yourselves to be used in this way, you will be promoting the highest good for ALL involved — all of the players in all of the dramas, and most of all, the planet herself.

So as you look upon each succeeding wave of change as it unfurls, you must also understand that beneath the terrible scenes, there is a great healing taking place. The fact that these issues were not dealt with in the past has only created a greater pressure for them to be dealt with now. None of you can say you have not contributed in some way to what you are witnessing now. You are all part of and intimately connected to these actions through your interconnectedness with each other, with the economic systems, and with all life on the planet. This is the deep level of understanding that is necessary for you to grasp, in order to serve this task.

You must surrender up all feelings of guilt and unworthiness to aid in this service. Each of you has played the parts that were selected by your Oversouls across all of your embodiments, and all of those were chosen in harmony with the Creator's own desire to experience everything. That desire on the part of the Creator was the impulse that led to the Creation in the first place, so one must surrender to the entirety of the experience — to become large enough to hold it all within oneself, just as the Creator does.

You have all been stretched to grow in different ways in the past, but now it takes on a different face. Now you must stretch to become big enough to contain it all within yourself. This is what it means to be a Master. If you get stuck in pictures of "us and them," you are only perpetuating separation.

As difficult as it may seem to attain, you must come to the place of being able to look upon all of these actions as if you yourself had authored them, because in truth, if you pursue things to their core, it is always the Creator Itself that you will find at the core, so the "true you" IS the Creator and therefore this IS your Creation, in some sense. There really isn't anything else BUT the Creator, and in time, you will have this as your complete and unending, direct experience, and then you will also have permanent peace and joy.

You must each find your way to this understanding in your own way and your own time. However, if you can create a sanctuary for yourself within yourself, and deliberately choose to go into that inner sanctuary whenever these assaults upon your sensitivities occur, you will be allowing that which needs to move to move, and you will be able to remain sane and peaceful in the midst of it all. If you engage with the scenes around you and identify with them, you will be swept into the chaos and be overwhelmed by the enormity of what you perceive, to the point of hopelessness and despair if you persist in that behavior. Instead, we urge you to go within, to detach, and thereby hold the truth of the center — the calm eye in the center of the storm.

We have called this Message, "Shattering Glass" for a reason. Each of you who is connecting with the vision and vibration of Terra is emitting a sound — your particular frequency pattern in the matrix of sound that underlies the material universe. As you attune to the light codes carried in these Messages, you will re-sound them back into the universe, amplifying them and uniting them with the "broadcasts" sent up by your fellow workers who are sharing this task with you. As more and more of you find your way to these Messages and are activated by the light codes, more and more of your frequency patterns will be available to do the necessary work.

You have a phrase — "the glass ceiling." It is most often used to depict an invisible barrier to upward movement on a career path, but we are borrowing this concept now to refer to another kind of glass ceiling — an invisible frequency barrier that has surrounded this planet and kept things contained within her and cycling over and over upon her surface throughout her history as a planet — an invisible barrier that must be breached in order for the planet to move upward in her own ascension path — her own "career path."

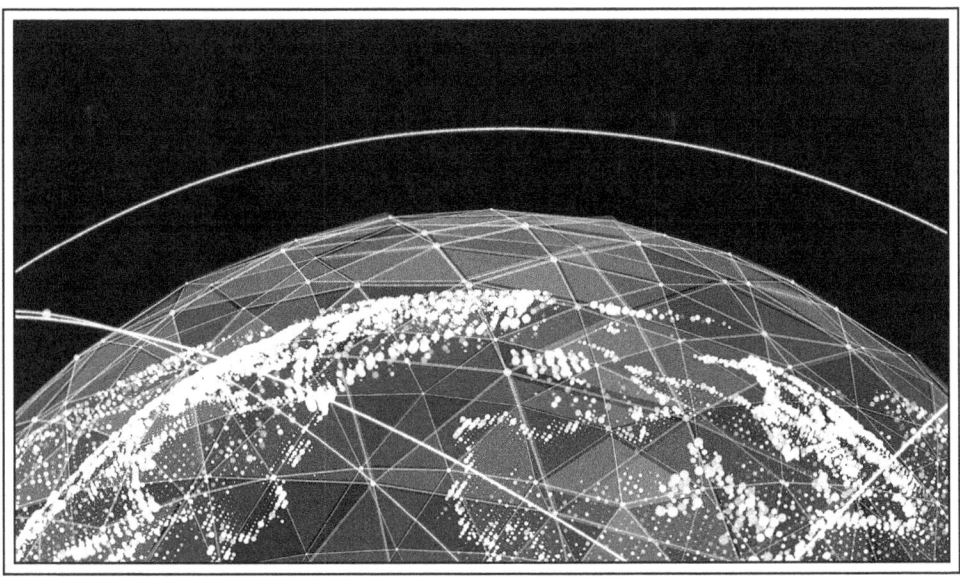

The invisible frequency barrier that has surrounded this planet and kept things contained within her throughout her history as a planet

When a baby is in the womb, it is encased in a membrane or sac. When it is time for the birth, the membrane splits so that the baby can come forth unfettered and begin its new life as a new being, independent of those tissues that nourished it and protected it throughout its time in the womb.

Just so, the Earth is enclosed in a frequency barrier, similar to a membrane, that must be breached or split, in order for her to come forth and begin her new life. The barrier is a container for the present experience and it must be shattered to allow movement to a new experience.

Each of you is emitting a sound pattern. All of your sound patterns are beginning to converge and join together into a larger pattern, becoming amplified where you have particular frequencies that match those of the others in the group. As your own frequencies rise, the collective frequency of the group will also rise, and the sound that you emit will grow in volume, louder and louder as more and more of you are attuned by these Messages and their light codes.

We are giving you the "keys" that unlock your own codings and, through these Messages, we are "tuning" your own "transmitters" — the living light crystals at the core of your cellular memory that send forth your own frequency pattern. As your individual transmissions combine with those of your group, they will amplify and rise in frequency as you do.

Perhaps you have seen a demonstration of what happens when a tone with a certain frequency pattern and sufficient power is sounded in the vicinity of a crystal glass. The glass is shattered by the modulations carried in the tone.

A matching pattern of sound is set up in the material that makes up the glass via resonance with the particular frequencies contained in the vibrations of the subatomic particles in the atoms and molecules that make up that material. The modulations vibrate back and forth around the core frequencies of the material and disrupt the patterns of the atomic bonds in the glass, and it shatters in response to the tone. Note that the modulation and the shattering effect is accomplished by tones that vary slightly from the prevalent tone of the material.

Each of you who is attuned to these Messages is being stimulated to emit a particular frequency pattern, and as more and more of you join in with your "notes," the collective energies and patterns will build in strength until they shatter the frequency envelope — the "glass ceiling" — that surrounds the planet.

You will be shattering the energetic patterns of the existing paradigm, and opening the pathway for the emergence of a totally new world to emerge from this one. In this way, as well as the other ways we have mentioned above, you will be actively assisting in the planet's birthing into the new paradigm that will exist as Terra.

All the years you have felt "out of step" with the existing paradigm are now revealed as those parts of your particular pattern that will supply the necessary deviation from the central "tone" of the existing paradigm to shatter it, on an energetic level. This is one of the reasons you have all felt so "different," as if you were "marching to a different drummer." You are! And that differentness will serve the planet by breaking the energetic bonds that maintain the material of the present paradigm.

Isn't it wonderful to know that everything you thought might be "wrong" with you is now your means to create a pathway to something utterly new? Sound and light are the elements out of which the entire Creation is formed. You bring light into the planet and you emit sound to shatter the container that has perpetuated the cycles of third-density existence. You are shattering the "glass ceiling" that has kept the planet and the people on it from advancing to the next level of being.

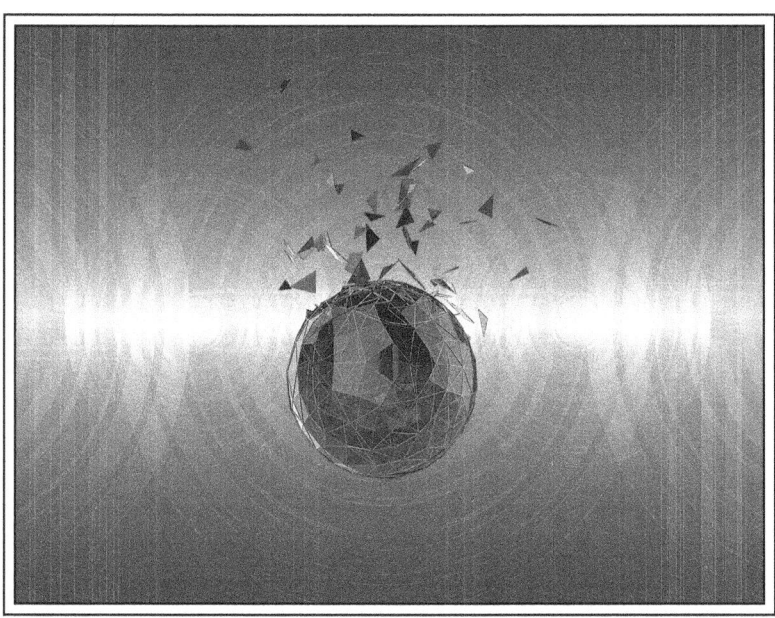

You will be shattering the energetic patterns of the existing paradigm, and opening the pathway for the emergence of a totally new world.

This is a great act of service, and it has required and will continue to require much of you. The greatest act you can do to support this process is to go within, allow everything to move through you, and peacefully surrender to the process as it unfolds. By doing this, you become a "superconductor" for the higher light to enter the planet, and you emit a purer tone to shatter the glass ceiling of the existing paradigm.

There is very little you can do to affect the events that are unfolding now, except to send them love. The chief reason they occur is the lack of sufficient love on the planet. Send your love, deepen your level of acceptance, and surrender to the great force for change that is unfolding now. It is too late in the game to do much else. Join with others of like mind in whatever ways are available to you, so that you can join your sound with theirs. Give comfort and love and support to one another, also, for you have your own wounds to heal, and have need of support from others who understand. It is with great appreciation and reverence for the difficulty of your task that we leave you now, but we shall speak to you again, and soon.

Amen, Adonoy Sabayoth. We are the Hosts of Heaven.

There is very little you can do to affect the events that are unfolding now, except to send them love.

THE CROSSROADS
September 18, 2001

Dear ones, we know your hearts are heavy when you consider what is going on in the world around you. We are with you always, sheltering you with our love and showering grace upon you. We walk amongst you in human form, too, although you would not recognize us except by our actions or how you feel in our presence. But we are here, to share this journey with you, and you must know this so completely that you can feel our presence for yourself.

The world will be seeing angels and devils at the same time, depending on the "glasses" being worn by the viewer. Those who harbor hate, anger, and revenge within their own heart will see devils, evil, and enemies everywhere. Those who hold the heartfelt desire for love, compassion, and a better world will see angels there to help. What one sees is a reflection of what is within. It is the way the Creator gets to see Itself, reflected in Its creations.

This notion of good and evil had served to allow people to explore duality, and it has served well. Those notions are well established in the Earth's religions and moral codes. However, it is time to put those notions aside now, as they have been exhausted in their capacity to inform you. Everything that is being put forth in the torrent of words that has flowed following the attacks [on 9/11] has been a summary of all the knowledge and beliefs that were accumulated before that time. Nothing really new is being said. No new revelations are being brought forward. Only former responses, dressed up in new clothes. The body is the same underneath, and the responses are totally predictable, based on one's views as they existed before the attacks took place.

This is a very fertile time, with many opportunities. In one sense, it is a great summing up of all the knowledge and experience that has occurred throughout all the lives that have been lived across the history

The world will be seeing angels and devils at the same time, depending on the "glasses" being worn by the viewer.

of the planet. If one looks upon Earth as a laboratory, in which many experiments have taken place, this could be considered the time when the results are written up and published. Everyone can then see what has been learned from the experiments, and those conclusions provide the foundation for wholly new experiments, as life and time move on.

In each of the exchanges taking place — and there are so many now taking place — one is presented with a choice of how to respond. Will you get sucked into the chaos? Will you sit there day after day, wringing your hands and reliving the scenes over and over? Will you stop living and be glued to the television set, instead? You have a choice. You can remain caught up in the dramas, passing along the latest bit of news or "proof" of this theory or that, or you can detach and let it go.

We are not saying to disregard the requests for help that come to you directly. We are not saying to not offer your prayers and love to others. We are talking about the way you feed your minds and emotions, the way you let yourself be used as a source of food for those who feed off YOUR emotions, for there are those who do that, as strange as it might seem.

It has been some time since we talked of the two polarities, and now it would be good to return to that topic. If you will recall, those of the

STS [service to self] polarity are all about gaining power over others. For them, there is never enough power, as the lack of love in their hearts leaves them so empty of feeling that they cannot ever have anything but the most fleeting of satisfactions.

In some ways, even those who control the world's resources are among the most poverty-stricken: despite their great material wealth, they lead empty lives, built around the acquisition of things — of inanimate and abstract things that can never give or return love — and they promote death rather than life. They may have the finest wines, the finest clothing, and live the life of kings, but they are also "slaves to their habit," insatiable in their need for more and more power, more and more of everything, a lonely existence indeed.

These things do not bring them happiness. These things do not bring them joy or peace. They bring them cynicism rather than hope. They bring them bitterness rather than sweetness. Their children are not free to follow their dreams. Their wives are picked because of the alliances they build, not for love. It is like the royal families in times past. They are rulers who must watch their gates, who must always be alert for those others who covet their position, who must always do things that serve their calculated ends. What pleasure is there in that? What freedom is there in that?

Therefore, the hardness of their hearts, their cynicism and contempt for the rest of the world, and the sterility of their lives leaves them empty, isolated, and bored. Business comes first, and the long walk toward the goal takes its toll, requires its own sacrifices, and leaves one more alone than before. The satisfaction of counting one's pile of money is hollow, indeed, and the simplest child who is free to play in a natural way is richer by far, in our way of measuring things.

All must play out, and if you but knew the extent to which these few have robbed the rest, you would be justifiably angry. They have robbed much more than just money and power and resources. They have robbed the world of hope, honesty, and so many of its potential joys. However, they did not get this way unaided. Every single person has contributed to their wealth and power by being part of the economic system.

If you would be free of that, if you would want to stop supporting the power elite, consider what would be required. You would have to supply all of your own needs, forever. You could never make a phone call, mail a letter, turn on your oven, or take part in any of the fruits of civilization —

libraries, entertainment, even your food and medicine, your homes and vehicles ... Think about it. Every day, in so many countless ways, you pay for things that are the fruits of other people's labor — with money. And they labor to get money to buy the things that they need for their lives, which were in turn produced by still other people's labor.

Money is only an agreed-upon means of exchange. It has no value in itself. And now that you have electronic communication, electronic storage of data, and the interconnection of the computers with one another across phone lines and satellites, all of your money isn't even necessary except on a local level. Everything is stored as ones and zeros in computers. Yours is a society built upon computers. Even in the most primitive regions, eventually money comes into play, and then if you trace it back to its source, there is a computer involved.

So while you are angry at these people and their contempt for the rest of the world, you must also accept responsibility for giving them their power in the first place. It did not happen overnight. This move toward the centralization of power in the hands of the few has been going on for a long time — a very long time, indeed.

One of the things that will come out of the chaos in these days is an opportunity to reflect on just about everything. You will notice that, as people struggle to come to grips with what is unfolding, they run into conflicts of logic. On the one hand, some of you feel that you should not go to war, and yet you also feel that the attack cannot just be allowed to go by without a response.

You are caught between two conflicting desires within yourself. You desire to be free, to not support the system that deals in wars as a solution to problems, but you also want the comforts that that system gives you. And even if you decided to go out into the wilderness somewhere and live off the land, what would that give you? Where would you go if you injured yourself? How would you survive?

It is true that there are still some people on the Earth that live close to the land. Are they necessarily happy because of that, or are their lives just as filled with struggle as yours is? They spend nearly all of their time obtaining food or creating shelter or passing time through telling stories or performing rituals. They are not so different from you after all. You spend nearly all of your time "earning a living," and your stories just come in different forms — videos, movies, television programs, books, newspapers, and magazines, and personal pages on the "Web." There is not really so much difference after all.

So where are we heading with this? It is simply this: until you are able to manifest your needs directly from the matrix of Source, you will never be free. You will always be participating in a struggle for life and there will always be some who have more power than others and use it to take advantage of others for their own benefit. Are they evil? Or are they just stuck in the same prison as you? Despite their wealth, they are just as enslaved as you are. None of you has true freedom.

We have come to a place in the unfolding where you will be presented with choices of a very different nature. It will no longer be about what you will wear today, or what you will make for dinner, or when to wash the dishes. These will be fundamental choices, a kind of "final exam," with little boxes to mark on a scoring sheet.

These will be fundamental choices, a kind of "final exam," with little boxes to mark on a scoring sheet.

When presented with events, will you choose to descend into the pit of anger and strife or will you choose to reach higher, to transcend your mundane existence and grab hold of the next rung on the ladder toward "heaven"? We have called this Message "The Crossroads" because that represents the experience you have at this time. You will be presented with many "crossroads" in the days ahead. Which path will you choose? The one that leads downward into chaos and death or the one that leads upward into order and life?

We have already described the polarities in these terms: STS is a choice for entropy, chaos, and death. STO [service to others] is a choice for order (love is the ordering force, acting on the matrix of light that underlies all form) and for life. It affirms life. These two polarities are actually two opposing forces, and their respective outcomes are predictable if you can see them clearly enough. One spiral leads downward and one spiral leads upward. You will have the opportunity, over and over again, to choose in which direction you want to go — the spiral upward or the spiral downward.

When you get caught up in ideas that there is an enemy — and there is certainly enough evidence to work with for that idea — you perpetuate the experience of being a victim. You choose the downward spiral. Are there people working in concert — a conspiracy toward certain aims? Absolutely. But are you working in concert with others to create a new world, to assist the planet in her ascension? We hope so! Is that a conspiracy, too? Are you "conspiring" to bring about "Heaven on Earth"? We hope so!

There is nothing inherently evil in working together with others toward particular aims. Consider a gun. It is just a piece of metal, cast in a certain form and design. It can be used to pound in nails, as a paperweight, or as a lethal weapon. Its design is carefully crafted to be a lethal weapon, but it does not become that until someone picks it up and uses it that way.

So it is with all these ideas of "conspiracy" that are flying about at this time. If you would choose the upward spiral, you would leave those ideas behind, and not victimize yourself through them. If there are perpetrators, there are victims. Only if you wear the lenses that enable you to see the Creator wherever you look are you finally free of being a victim. Then and only then are you free of the system and from contributing toward its progress toward world domination — power over others — that is the hallmark of the STS polarity.

We are saying this to you with all seriousness. This is the crossroads you will face over and over again. Will you reach upward to realize your own divinity and dwell in "heaven" or will you succumb to the chaos and choose the road to "hell"? Those are the two choices before you. There are only two.

How do you choose now and how will you choose the next time the choice presents? Every time you have to choose how to respond to what is presenting will be another crossroads for you. You will find it easier over time because you will have left the other choices behind, and as you discover that you prefer to continue in the direction in which you find peace.

We leave you now in peace and honor and blessing. Amen, Adonoy Sabayoth. We are the Hosts of Heaven.

Will you reach upward to realize your own divinity and dwell in "heaven" or will you succumb to the chaos and choose the road to "hell"?

MANY WORLDS, MANY DESTINATIONS
September 27, 2001

All right, now. We have asked to speak to you today to broaden your understanding of what is unfolding on your perceptual screen. There is a complexity involved that is quite frankly beyond that which your conscious mind can grasp. And so we ask that, as you read these words, that you also open yourself to receive a deeper knowing, a deeper trust of the process that has begun and will continue until it is totally complete.

To retrace our steps a bit, we would return to the idea we gave you about the Mind of the Creator as a matrix that contains all things that have been and will be. Each thing or event that emerges from that matrix contains within itself all of the elements for its completion — all the events that will play out within the container or envelope of that event are anticipated and come forth from the Creator Itself. Each event can be viewed as a "thought" of the Creator, thinking to Itself and exploring all of the possibilities that are available to It. These possibilities are essentially infinite and it is easy to get lost in trying to contemplate the infinitely branching tree that makes up the Mind of the Creator — what we will call the Tree of Mind.

In the Tree of Mind, every possible branch is explored through the mechanism of parallel realities. Each time there is a decision point reached, a branch is created to accommodate all possible decisions that can be experienced within that situation. Within a given Creation, there are some parameters that govern that particular Creation, and the possibilities that are available within that Creation are limited to the constraints of those parameters, which we have called Universal Laws. This much we have said before.

So, how does this relate to what you are experiencing? It works something like this: In your present experience of the Creation, there are

Many Worlds, Many Destinations

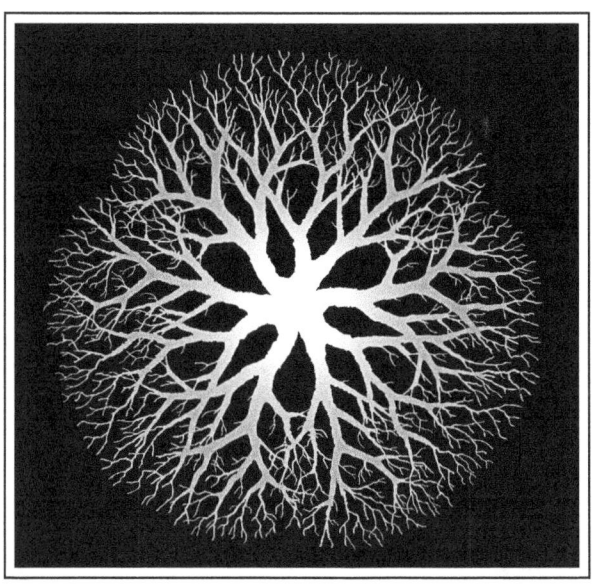

Each time a decision point is reached, a branch is created to accommodate all possible decisions that can be experienced within that situation.

many event envelopes overlapping each other and seeming to occupy the same space. As you look around you with your physical senses, you think that you are seeing the same thing as everyone else does, and in fact to some extent you do. But there is another mechanism operating also, which we have referred to before: the splitting off or separating out of all of the parallel "futures" that will emerge from your one shared reality — the planet you call Earth.

All of these different event envelopes are heading in different directions and those of you who are in the "Terra" envelope are heading in that direction, while those who are in other envelopes are heading in other directions. Where it gets complex is when one tries to grasp how it all fits together — or even how it all comes apart!

We cannot even begin to address the complexity involved (it is so vast), so we will confine ourselves to discussing the path to Terra and [to] one other world — Terra's mirror world, the destination that is equal to Terra, but of the opposite polarity. There are many other paths that are also occurring, but far too many for us to explore, and they do not illuminate your path as well as the contrast afforded by this one other, which shall remain unnamed.

You will recall that we have said that the polarization on the planet will increase as things move forward in time, and you see that happening now. It will continue to proceed toward even more polarization, so things will intensify along all of the paths being traversed, but these two paths — to Terra and [to] its polar opposite — will experience this polarization at its most extreme. All of the other paths lead to other worlds, for further exploration of other themes and experiences.

These two worlds are the only ones that will be purely 4D in their vibration and expression.

These two worlds are the only ones that will be purely 4D in their vibration and expression, and since Terra is one of these two worlds, the timeline that leads to Terra contains the mirrored expression of the other world, at least for a time. By the time you are lifted off of the planet, those two paths will have split off from one another, but while you are still involved in the lifting — even if you leave and come back — you will be witnessing the mirror provided by this other world and path. And we should also mention that many people will not be going to Terra, but to their own "home systems," for a period of rest, recovery and exploration that does not involve either of these two worlds at all. And some of THOSE worlds are "higher" in frequency than Terra, so it really is a very complex process, indeed!

All this being said, as the Earth ascends toward her destiny of becoming Terra, those who are on these two timelines — the one to Terra and the one to her opposite — will be in each other's view for a while. Being that you are the "caring kind" of people, it could be difficult for you to witness the playing out of the most extreme forms of the negative-polarity behaviors by those who are seeking to graduate to that other world. If you can see their actions as that — that they are having their "final exams" also — you might be able to comprehend the force that drives them to their goal — the world of THEIR dreams — just as you can comprehend your own passion to achieve your goal of Terra — the world of YOUR dreams.

To you, their dreams are a waking nightmare, but you actually have much more in common than you might think. You both seek a global form of government, a common set of values, and a way to live within the available resources. However, the MEANS of achieving those goals is where you differ. You emphasize the empowerment of everyone, and they emphasize their own empowerment at the expense of everyone else. STO and STS, pure and simple.

This is the Creator's dream, and the Creator wants to experience everything, from every possible perspective. The Creator wants to experience all of the possibilities and gets to experience them through Its creations and their interaction with each other. The Creator does not JUDGE Its creations as "good" and "bad." The Creator expresses through Its creations, and having created them, considers them ALL "good." They all exist to satisfy the Creator's desire to know Itself through Its infinite possible manifestations. When it says in the Bible that God looked at Its creation and was pleased, this is how the Creator views Its creations. It is "pleased" by ALL of its creations, not just the ones you would prefer to experience.

You are the Creator-in-expression, seeking a particular pole of expression. There are others who are seeking the opposite pole, and from the Creator's perspective, they are just as "good" as you are. You are repelled by those things that are not like you. That helps to define your experience and propel you in the direction of your seeking. It is just as true of these others of the opposite pole. They have contempt for and are repelled by those who are not like THEM and that helps propel THEM in the direction of THEIR seeking. At the core of it, it is ALL just the Creator, playing with Itself through all the possibilities made available by all Its creations.

So, from the Creator's point of view, both Terra and its opposite — this all-negative-polarity world — are equally good, because they provide the Creator with the opportunity to fully explore those two opposite poles. All of the OTHER worlds that emerge from this one shared reality that you call "Earth" will be spread across the spectrum BETWEEN those two poles and have varying proportions of that mixture of STO and STS.

There will be worlds that are primarily inclining toward STO, and as they progress, some of those people will incarnate on Terra as babies born to those who are already there. There will be worlds that will be primarily STS and they will progress to the world that is Terra's opposite and incarnate there. And there will be still other worlds that remain somewhat mixed and be rich environments in which to explore both poles, and they will progress in that way for many thousands of years until another grand cycle is completed and another opportunity presents for a harvest to one pole or the other. The unfolding of the Creator's dream is endless, and the paths of possibilities branch and branch and branch again, over and over and over, throughout eternity. There is no end to the dream.

So, in your experience now, you will be seeing an intensification of the two polarities of behaviors. The "in-between" will fade from your view. You can best see and understand yourself and your path in two ways: by reflecting off of its mirror opposite and by finding others like yourself with whom you can share your own views, your own feelings, your own experiences. We have said that if you engage with "us and them" thinking, you risk being caught up in the morass, the downward spiral into darkness and more confusion. It is all right to witness the opposite pole, as it helps you to understand what you are NOT, but it is imperative that you detach from IDENTIFYING with it.

It helps to remind you of who you are, but it does not DEFINE who you are. To the extent that you can tune out the horrors that are coming, you will preserve yourself and your self-identity. This does not mean that you should close your heart. Just the opposite! What we are saying is that you must disconnect from feeling RESPONSIBLE for what is appearing on your perceptual screen.

What is appearing on your perceptual screen is sourcing from the Creator. Each person is simply being who they came to be, according to the plan for their life. Each person is perfectly situated to make their contribution to the rich mix of experiences playing out now, and there are no "bad" creations. Each "evil" is part of the "good." Each player is needed for the entire experience to be complete.

Each event envelope contains all the elements for its completion and the entire "set" of elements is interwoven and interacting in ways that you simply cannot grasp with your mind. But your SOUL and your HEART can FEEL the truth of this, and this understanding can allow you to unlock your own potential for love. You will do best to cultivate compassion when you encounter suffering, to let yourself be deepened and hollowed out by your compassion, to keep your hearts open and tender and vulnerable and at the same time be deepened until all that you are is love.

You are not responsible for what you are seeing. You did not create it. You do not have to beat yourself about the head and shoulders in penance for some sin you committed. Everything you are, everything you have done, is all within the plan for your life. The place you CAN be responsible is for your own RESPONSES to the situation. Your own responses are your own process of working out who you are, why you are here, and where you are going.

You are one aspect of the Creator, providing the Creator with a particular experience through the locus of your perception as an individualized aspect of the Creator. If you must "blame" anyone, you must blame the Creator. If you must be angry, you must be angry at the Creator. Everywhere you look, everything you see, is the Creator-in-expression. The people who die are the Creator. The people who kill them are the Creator. If you can just "get" this, you will have peace, you will transcend the phenomenal reality, and you will be that much closer to "home."

We leave you now, in peace and honor and blessing. Amen, Adonoy Sabayoth. We are the Hosts of Heaven.

"STEADY AS SHE GOES"
October 2, 2001

All right, then. We have asked to speak to you today because there are numerous shocks on the horizon, and we wanted to give you a possible way of being with them that will greatly facilitate your comfort as you move towards your goal.

If you think about your oceans, you will have an ideal model for what we are talking about. On the surface of these great bodies of water, there is great variation in the activity one sees — from placid calm to rolling waves to great turbulence and violent storms. So it is with your world of everyday living. It varies tremendously, from placid calm and moments of true peace through varying degrees of instability, stress, and outright crisis.

If one goes deeply down into the depths of the oceans, there are powerful currents and a rich absence of turbulence — a profound presence of silence, power, and potential adventure, encased in a soothing smoothness of texture and sound. If you withdraw from your ordinary world and dive deeply within, it is similar. There you will find a profound presence of power, potential adventure, and a deep, calming release.

So as these storms come into the world about you, it would be wise to take refuge in the deep stillness within yourself, to experience the safety of that, to follow the deep currents of your life, and to thread your way through the vast oceans of inner space toward your goal.

In wartime, there is a ship called a submarine. It makes use of reflected sound, much as the dolphins and whales find their way in their watery home. A sound is sent out and then returned, so the distance from other objects is sensed and they can be avoided. You send out your sound into the universe and it is returned to you, guiding you through the waters ahead as you slide forward, toward your goal.

The submarine can dive deep to avoid detection at the surface and to get to its goal.

The submarine can dive deep to avoid detection at the surface and to get to its goal and deliver its payload or cargo. In wartime, there are minefields that must be traversed. There are sometimes explosions nearby. It takes a skilled hand and steady nerves to traverse the oceans and move steadily toward one's goal. When the captain of a submarine is satisfied with the vessel's direction, depth, and speed, he calls to the crew, "Steady as she goes." By this, he communicates that the ship should maintain its direction, depth, and speed, until and unless he gives a different command.

We would say that our "sub" toward Terra has begun its voyage through the oceans of inner space. We left the old world behind on August 18 and have been increasing our depth and speed ever since.

In a few short days, we will begin traversing the minefields and there will be explosions all around, but our direction will always be "Steady as she goes." So it is with you. In your voyage through these times, you must say to yourself, "Steady as she goes." You must stay steady on your course to Terra, let the explosions happen as they will, and have the sure knowledge that whatever happens around you, you will not waver at the helm.

Steady as she goes. Remain steady and stay the course. Keep your eyes on the goal. Steady as she goes. Let the rest fall around you. Steady as she goes. Your path is straight, you are protected. Steady as she goes … Steady as she goes … Steady as she goes.

Feel the quiet. Listen to your breathing as it comes in softly and goes out again. Listen to the distant sounds of war and know you are safe. Steady as she goes. Feel the dull impacts of the explosions. Steady as she goes. Check your fuel supply. You are fine. Steady as she goes … Steady as she goes … Steady as she goes.

As these days unfurl in front of you, remind yourself, "Steady as she goes." You can do this. You came to do this. This is why you are here. Hold your course. Hold your speed. Stay below the surface events and "Steady as she goes." Steady as she goes. Distant sounds, distant storms, but steady as she goes.

Each of you has come for this, for this time, for this task. Steady as she goes … Steady as she goes. Hold the vision; seek the goal. Steady as she goes … Steady as she goes … Steady as she goes.

Take this Message and read it again. Steady as she goes. Keep it with you to remind you. Steady as she goes … Steady as she goes.

Time is passing now and each day takes you closer to the goal. Steady as she goes … Steady as she goes.

Remind yourself how far you have come. Not much further to go. Steady as she goes … Steady as she goes. Be steady in your course and speed. Steady as she goes.

We are with you now, guiding you, protecting you, sheltering you. Dive deep. Stay deep. Follow your course. Steady as she goes … Steady as she goes. Make a shelter for yourself, create the stillness where you are. Turn off the madness, the screaming, the crying, the pleading. Steady as she goes … Steady as she goes. Turn off the madness. Steady as she goes … Steady as she goes … Steady as she goes.

Hear the water sliding by. Steady as she goes. Hear the muffled roar and thunderous crashing of storms and wind-driven waves overhead. Go deep. Stay deep. Steady as she goes … Steady as she goes.

We are with you, every day, every night — guiding you, loving you, protecting you. Steady as she goes. Leave behind the surface world. Seek the power of deep ocean. Follow your course. Leave behind the madness. Steady as she goes.

In time ... with sufficient time ... you will emerge in your new reality, but for now, you must glide through the deep waters of deep ocean. Steady as she goes. Keep your eyes on the goal. Steady as she goes.

We leave you now in peace and honor and blessing, but we are with you in your dreams, in your waking, in your sailing through the deep waters. Steady as she goes ... Steady as she goes. Amen, Adonoy Sabayoth. We are the Hosts of Heaven. Steady as she goes.

A LAST LOOK AROUND
October 9, 2001

All right, now. Everything we said was coming has now arrived at your door, but there is so much more to the picture than you see at this moment in time. There are things arriving into your reality that are beyond your wildest imagination — of both kinds. Side by side, now, you will witness — literally — the "greatest show on Earth." You will see things occur of unspeakable majesty and beauty and you will see things of unspeakable horror and tragedy. Both will occur side by side.

The human species has the capability for both of these extremes — ecstasy and agony. It has the ability to create them and to experience them. And indeed, throughout the human journey on Earth, it has done both, over and over again. But now, as the final years dwindle away, it is time for the grand finale — the last "act" of the human drama on this planet, at this density, for a very, very long time.

And so we would ask you to take a last look around before it is gone. Take a look at the world around you, as it is right now, for it will soon pass away altogether. Take a look at it as if you were suddenly told that you had but a few years to live, for in fact, that is the truth. You have only a few years left before this entire stage will be swept bare and none of what you can see will remain. But even before THAT, the world as you have known it — as you have taken it for granted would always be there — will be radically changed.

The wars that are beginning now are just the beginning of the changes. Everything in the human experience will be revisited in some way, if not at a global level, then at a personal and individual level. All of your "personal histories," across all of the lives that were created throughout time, will be summed up now, and you will find that any remnants of old patterns will come flying back in your face to be balanced and cleared so that you can finally move beyond them — beyond this world and all of its experiences, altogether.

Take a look at the world around you, as it is right now, for it will soon pass away altogether.

So how would you feel if you were told you had, say, 18 months to live? What would your priorities be? How important would it be to plan a "next career," or to plan anything, for that matter? What would you want to do most if you had only 18 months left? Who would you talk to? What would you say? Where would you want to live? What would you want to do? Is there some unfinished business left in your life? What do you need to do now to finish it?

We suggest that you begin to think in these ways now, as there is not much more time than that left for you to do those sorts of things. That is not to say that there will be a Pole Shift in 18 months, but we are saying that the world will be so different by then that the time will be over for these kinds of questions for you.

We are not saying that there is an urgency or emergency about this. What we are saying is that you should treasure these last days of relative normalcy as they are fast disappearing and will never be seen again. Despite the wars that are beginning, it will be a while before they extend to the entire world. It will be a while before the food supplies are gone for much of the world's populations. It will be a while before the technology is in place that will create a global surveillance system. It will be a while, but it will not be much longer.

So take a last look around you. Savor all that it is to be a human being. Spend some time reflecting on your memories before you pack them away forever. Take some extra time with your loved ones and consider what is really important to you now. Savor the seasons and their moods. Savor the good things of life, without being extravagant. Find balance.

Be good to yourself in ways that are truly nourishing — good food, good friends, and "quality time" with those you care about. Say "no" to the pressures that keep you on the treadmill of *doing* and start spending more time *being*. The things that fill you are the simple ones — a hand held, a sunset, the passage of a flight of birds through the sky. Feel your connection to the planet. Feel your connection to the stars. Feel your connection to the entire span of the human drama, in all of its forms, in all of its ages, and in all of its color and richness and moods.

Look at the animals around you and give them more love, too. Give your trees a hug. Give your plants a special treat — perhaps some fresh soil or a new pot. Show your appreciation for all of life and it will appreciate you in return.

How often do you take time to appreciate yourself? In your habits, in your conditioning, there is so much criticism to offer — of others, of yourself, of the way the world is run. How much time do you take to appreciate your world? Do it now. Do it more often. Make it a new habit.

When you sit down to a meal, do you take a moment to appreciate it? Or is it something that is taken for granted? There are many in the world who will not have a meal tonight, or the next night, or the night after that. Appreciate your meal. Appreciate the life that was given by the plants and the animals so that you could have that meal. Appreciate the work that was done by the growers, the pickers, and the preparers so that you could have that meal. If you have good health, appreciate that. If you have pain, appreciate that. Appreciate your ability to feel, to see, to hear, to draw breath. There are many who cannot do even that.

Celebrate life in a quiet way. Soften your walk, soften your talk. Be good to yourself and to others. If you buy something, appreciate it enough to make it a worthwhile purchase. Instead of "making do," make it special. That does not mean it has to be costly. It means you have to take the time and attention to ask yourself what it is you would really enjoy.

Live your life with conscious attention. Consider the invisible web that binds you to others through everything you do in every day. When you turn on the water at the sink, someone else made that possible for you to do. When you lie down in your bed at night, someone else made that possible for you to do. Someone made the bed. Someone made the sheets. Someone delivered it to the store where it was bought. Someone built the room in which you lie. Maybe it was you, but then you used materials that someone else made available.

Appreciate your meal.

Take a last look around and see how everything there is was made possible in so many ways by so many people around the world. There already is a global economy and no part exists in isolation from the others. You already are part of a global society, and what happens in one part of the world affects every other part. There is no movement made, no breath drawn, anywhere in the world that does not affect every other part in the world, whether you are aware of it or not.

Appreciate your connection to everything else. It is there. You can feel it. FEEL it! Don't think about it so much. Feel it. Feel how you are part of the intricate web of life, of the flow of life and even of death. Appreciate these days and appreciate all that you are in these days, for you are changing, too.

We have talked about a homecoming, but there is also a home-leaving. You are all going to be going to somewhere else very soon, so appreciate your life and your world now as if you are seeing it for the first time, so you will be complete with it when it is time to go. You are going to be off on a grand adventure, one that will take you beyond all things that you know now, but to complete with THIS world with grace and ease, take time to take that last look around, knowing that you will be leaving soon.

When we say "soon," that is relative, but even within the span of your present time, it will be soon enough. Soon enough for you to leave while you can still remember this world as it is now. Long enough for you to be glad to move on to another world with no backward glances or things undone. It is time, now, to face these things. It is time, now, to do these things. It is time, now.

We have said before to allow all things. We say now to embrace all things. We have said before to let go of your attachments, to receive the lifting. We say now to hold out your hand, your heart, and your soul to receive the richness of your life now. Be grateful for all things, large and small. Be in an "attitude of gratitude" and you will feel yourself blessed beyond counting. In the midst of the wars, you can have peace, you can have joy, and you can share love.

The wars will go on till it's over, but you can live fully and joyfully in their midst. We do not say this lightly. You hold the template of a new tomorrow and as the dying proceeds, so does the birthing. Just as in life things pass away in their time, so too, does new life come and bring the promise of a new day. Yesterday and tomorrow meet in the ever-present NOW. Yesterday and tomorrow are defined by the present moment, the bead on the string that moves steadily toward its destiny. You are the dawn-bringers and after the twilight fades and the world is engulfed in darkness, you will come again with the light, to wipe away the tears and bring peace.

Amen, Adonoy Sabayoth. We are the Hosts of Heaven. We leave you now in peace and honor and blessing and shall speak with you again.

ASCENSION IS A PROCESS, PART ONE
October 17, 2001

All right, now. We have asked to speak to you today to give you our perspective on the process of ascension, as it is being experienced in your space/time reality. We have qualified our remarks by that last phrase — as it is being experienced in your space/time reality. The process you are undergoing and experiencing now is different in several ways from what has been described in the "literature" that has reached you regarding this process/event.

This process has never before occurred on your planet on a mass scale, and not only is a portion of the human species ascending now, but the planet and everything on her is being subjected to the same process of rising through the vibrational layers. In your historical past, there have been isolated individuals who have walked this path and there have been some isolated groups of people who have also made this journey, but this has never before happened on a global scale, and most certainly not for the planet itself.

Therefore, the descriptions of this process that have reached you have been vague and lacking in detail. The most explicit writings that have survived have described an apparent "event," as if ascension took place in an instant. In some rare cases, the process did indeed appear to come to a head rather suddenly, as if a threshold was crossed and things changed rather markedly, but even if this is what happened then, this is NOT what is happening now.

For you who are bound for Terra, your ascension is ongoing and will be a process that continues long after the Earth itself has ascended to her glorified form, as Terra. We want to go into some detail today about how that is occurring and what to expect as the process proceeds.

Let us begin with some basics, to summarize some of the ground we have already covered in our prior communications with you. The process of ascension involves a change in frequency of vibration and a change in consciousness that carries with it some other phenomena and abilities. You are engaged in this process now, and you are already experiencing some of the changes in perception that go with this change. That will continue and grow more evident as things progress through linear time. It has ALREADY happened, when viewed from outside of time, but since your focus of attention is presently located from within the experience of linear time, we are describing things from your present view, rather than ours.

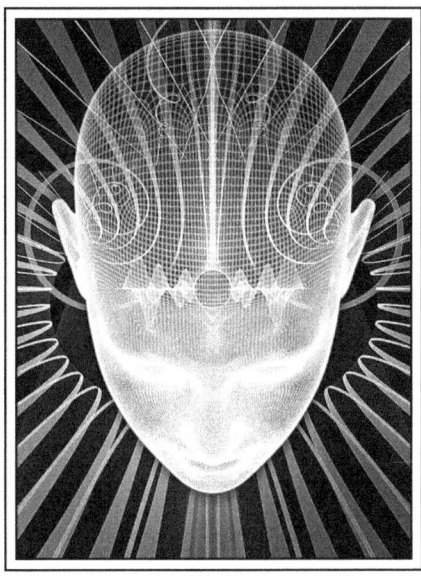

The process of ascension involves a change in frequency of vibration and a change in consciousness.

Most (if not all) of you reading this have been experiencing many of the symptoms of this process. We have mentioned before the bodily changes that are involved, and the clearings that take place as each successive frequency band is traversed. You are by now quite familiar with some of this, and as things proceed, those things will continue, as well. Your preferences in foods, in music — in every aspect of your life — will shift with the ongoing change in your consciousness.

Your energy levels will fluctuate greatly as you withdraw from those things that used to fascinate you and begin to move more inward. You will find your need for rest increasing, as your energy becomes more involved with integrating the ongoing cellular activity and your bodies prepare for your new forms to occur. You may become more sensitive to stresses in the Earth's crust, to disturbances in the electromagnetic spectrum, and to some of the technologies being employed by the power elite. You can support your transition in many ways, but the key word here is self-nourishment.

Do those things that make YOU more comfortable. Because you are of the STO-polarity orientation, it is natural for you to want to turn your energies outward toward serving others, but it is at this time that you need to prepare yourself for your subsequent service, which requires that you take care of your own needs first at this time. If you take the longer view, all of the care that you give to yourself and those close to you now will be an "investment" in the treasure that you will make available to others when the time comes for you to do that.

Think of it this way: You have a tool you call a ratchet. It is used to turn things like screws and bolts in a forward direction and makes use of the leverage of torque. After each turn forward, the ratchet pulls back and powers up for the next turn forward. The screws and the bolts are constructed with spiral tracks on them that cause them to move forward by being turned or cycled by the tool that turns them. The ratchet provides forward motion by dropping back to power up for the next thrust forward.

After each turn forward, the ratchet pulls back and powers up for the next turn forward (man using a ratchet to work on a car engine).

The spiral is the shape of evolution, and each turn on the spiral is a movement forward as well as outward or inward. By withdrawing and turning your energies toward your own process and comfort now, you are powering up your next turn on the spiral, your next movement forward and outward, and you are becoming the agent for service beyond that which you are capable of now. So look at this time of withdrawal as being the ratchet, gathering energy for the next movement forward and outward. You will be in center stage soon enough, but this is your process now, in preparation for that next movement in your lives.

So this process of ascension involves a withdrawal from the world around you. Many (if not most) of you are feeling this now, and some of you are not knowing how to be with that experience. We have talked much about the necessity of withdrawing and detaching from the drama around you. We want to emphasize how necessary this is to your process now. The world around you will get along without your needing to feed it with your energy now. It is on a crash course with oblivion and will pass away within the next few years.

You are not needed in this world now. Your task now is to prepare for your service at the end of this world and to blaze the pathway to the next reality that will follow. There is nothing for you to do with regard to stopping what is playing out in the amphitheater, the drama you see on the world's perceptual screen. You are playing in a different play now, and that dying world is supposed to die.

All of the symptoms of past human experience are leaving the planet, are coming up to view as they exit this plane. It is all being flushed to the surface in a grand cleansing of all that has gone before and it is a purification for the planet and everything on her. It is not helped by resistance on your part. It is helped by your allowing the process to unfold, to accept the process for what it is, and for you to stop giving it your energy and attention.

All attempts to stop what is going on are forms of resistance and only make things more intense. Every particle of resistance requires a matching energy to overcome it, so if you can "let go and let God" take care of the process, you will be doing the highest and best thing you can for the smoothest transition for all.

Ascension is a process, not an event. There is a threshold that is crossed at some point in the process when the veil has fallen away and one can see fully. But that is only one minute step in a long journey. Ascension does not end when the veil falls. The journey continues forever, with the inbreath back into the Godhead, the dissolving away of separate identity, and the emergence again as a separate identity with the next outbreath from the Godhead.

It is all just the Creator, breathing Itself out into expression, inhaling Itself back into Itself, and breathing Itself out into expression again. This process never ends and the journey of experience never ends, so it will be helpful to your process if you can accept that there is no "ending" in sight for you. You will go on, eternally, also, for you are the expression of the Creator and that never ends — for you or for the Creator.

So those of you who might be expecting an "event" need to readjust your thinking a bit. Think of a movie you have seen. Each frame of the movie exists as a separate "event," but they all blend together seamlessly in an event flow that is experienced more like a process than as separate events.

Each breath you take is an "event," but you take for granted the process that occurs when you breathe. The air enters you, the oxygen moves into your bloodstream and enters your cells, and from there, each atom of oxygen participates in different chemical processes. Then those atoms combine with other atoms and new compounds are made, energy is produced, and end products such as carbon dioxide are passed out into the bloodstream to be carried to your lungs and exhaled.

Think of it! All of this is going on in your body with every breath you take! All of this is going on in your body with every breath you exhale. Every breath is an event, but each breath — each event — is part of a larger process, through which your body functions, you experience life through all of your senses, and the whole complexity of life as you know it proceeds.

So it is with this ascension process. It is made up of many "events," strung together in a process that is complex and experienced through all of your senses. There are cycles in this process and there is a movement forward and upward, followed by a time of integration. This integration process requires energy. It requires energy that would normally be given to other activities.

When you fix your attention on the drama, you are taking away energy from your ascension and giving it to the drama. You are not supporting your ascension as fully as you might, so we would ask you to give your ascension the priority over the drama, if you are not already doing so.

If you are heading toward Terra, your life will be more difficult for you if you do not align fully with your ascension. Your resistance will require that life provides a force in your life that is sufficient to overcome your resistance, so that you can fulfill your life's goal.

Your life has a plan to it — a built-in direction in which you must go — and your thoughts and impulses arise from the Oversoul that creates you as an expression of itself. Your Oversoul has made you the way you are, down to the color of your eyelashes and your preference for a certain type of food. However, you are not an island, floating in the emptiness of space.

You live in a rich matrix of experience, and being sensitive, you can easily get caught up in the swirl of emotions that are flooding your experiential field from so many sources. Your media play on those emotions as a way of getting you to do things, such as buy certain products or engage in certain behaviors. Your political machine plays on those emotions to further that agenda. Your power elite play on those emotions to get you to go in the direction they want you to go.

If you want to be free, if you want to be sovereign, you need to detach from the drama. You need to find ways of being "in the world," but not "of it." If you work for a living, you need to find a way of continuing to do that without getting caught up in the emotions that are swirling around you. You don't have to tune them out altogether. That would probably be impossible to maintain, anyway.

What you have to learn to do is become TRANSPARENT to them — to let them pass without engaging with them in a similar fashion. If someone around you is upset, you don't have to join them in being upset. If someone near you is angry, you don't have to engage with them from that kind of energy. You can be calm in the midst of the chaos, and it will be much better for you if you do so.

The process of ascension is already underway. It is unstoppable at this point and the cleansing is unstoppable also. Your only meaningful response is to step back and create an island of calm in yourself. Create that space within you, and if you find yourself getting caught up in the drama, bring yourself gently back to that space of calm as soon as you become aware that you have left it.

That is why meditation is such good training for this process. In meditation, inevitably your mind wanders and thoughts come. It is a discipline to bring your mind gently back to the breath or whatever it is you are focusing on in your meditation. It is a discipline to bring yourself back to your center and calm whenever you find yourself getting caught up in the drama. By cultivating this habit of remaining calm and centered in the midst of the chaos, you will be a great force — collectively speaking — for calm in the midst of chaos in the world.

You hold a template within yourself, and these Messages are an attunement device that is energizing that template through more and more people all over the world. You are widely separated from each other because you must cover the globe and there are so few of you to do this task now. As each person finds their way to this material and comes into resonance with it, a field effect is created that is so powerful, you would have trouble comprehending it. You are like a growing wave, enveloping the planet — bringing in the higher light and grounding it into the planet, radiating out the new pattern of energy and shattering the existing paradigm by your holding forth this way of being in the midst of the chaos.

You are peaceful warriors — warriors for truth, warriors for peace and love and joy. Your "mission" is to simply BE where you are, holding forth what you are, holding the vision and promise of Terra, holding your place in the world, letting things unfold and holding steady in the midst of it all.

The interesting thing about this is that when you do this, you create that reality that you want to live in, right where you are. You CREATE a little bit of Terra, right now, where you are. You CREATE peace by being at peace. You CREATE love by resting in love. You CREATE joy by allowing your joy to exist in the midst of so much sorrow.

Life has beauty that you can perceive. Focus on beauty, and you will become beautiful. Your inner radiance will bless all who come in contact with you, and you will birth beauty in the midst of the horror.

All your life, you felt out of step with the rest of the world. Well, you are STILL out of step with the rest of the world and now you know why. The rest of the world is passing away and you are the bringers of the new dawn on the horizon. You are stepping forth in your role as co-creators of a new reality, and your path runs counter to that of the rest of the world. You have been out of step because you are paving a new road, a road that leads to freedom.

You are not going in the same direction as the rest of the world, and so you are diverging more and more each day from the direction they are taking. You must do exactly what others are not willing or able to do. You must be what you came to be and do what you came to do. It is a solitary thing for you for now, but a day is coming when you will be rejoined with the others and there is a gathering taking place even now. You are being gathered onto your road, that road that goes to Terra, and you are leaving behind the other roads that lead to other destinations.

You are not going in the same direction as the rest of the world.

Follow your calling. Follow that inner voice that leads you, step by step, in the direction of your destiny. Step out onto that untraveled road that unfurls before you now. You are creating it with every step you take and we are with you, supporting each and every step, so it is a collective undertaking.

We are a team — those of us in the higher realms, and those of you who are walking this road on the ground. We shall speak more on this subject, but for now we leave you in peace and honor and blessing. We love you and are with you at all times, and you are well on your way home. It is not much further now. You can do this. It is what you came to do.

Amen, Adonoy Sabayoth. We are the Hosts of Heaven.

ASCENSION IS A PROCESS, PART TWO
November 09, 2001

All right, now. We have said we would continue our conversation about the ascension process, and it is time for us to do that now.

First of all, we wish to reiterate that the lifting we have spoken of is a process that will culminate in an "event" — the crossing of a threshold into the next frequency band. This lifting has two components to it: a physical component, related to the spin frequency of the subatomic particles in your physical body, and a spiritual component, related to a shift in your consciousness and ways of perceiving your reality. Both are taking place at the same time and interrelate, as consciousness affects all physical materiality.

There is no way to separate consciousness from the physical manifestation of matter. Consciousness is the ground, or matrix, out of which physical matter emerges. We have spoken of the Mind of the Creator as the matrix for all of the Creation, and your individualized consciousness is a portion of that Infinite Mind, as long as you are still veiled and in the experience of separation. Once your veils have fallen and the barrier is removed, you will be in full and continuous communion with the Mind of the Creator, and when you have learned to operate from that platform, you will be able to affect, alter, and create material reality from that place of infinite blessing. All of the powers of the Creator will be vested in your individual locus of attention, and you will consciously be aware of yourselves as the creator-gods you have always been.

Those of you who are bound for Terra are the first generation — the product of the First Thought — of the Creator. You are the elohim, and though you do not remember this fully now, you will once your shift is complete. Over the next 18 months, you will find yourself much changed. The dropping away of your old life will continue, at an accelerated pace. Your fascination with the things of 3D will wane even more than before, and you will gradually detach from identifying with the 3D reality as your reality. You will begin to access more and more of your 4D identity and personality, and you will begin to access more and more of the 4D way of doing things. You must trust this process and trust your "knowing" that you are safe, sane, and that all is proceeding according to plan.

Some of you are being asked by the circumstances of your life to move on — either to other places of residence or to other people, leaving behind those aspects of your old life. This is part of the sorting out into the different destinations, and we would counsel you to be at peace in the midst of this change.

If fear arises, open the breath. Close your eyes for a moment and focus on deepening and opening your breath. Relax into the breath and feel your body relax into the truth of the moment. You are safe. Your world is changing, but you are safe. The world around you may be tumbling down, but you are safe. Remind yourself of this whenever things seem to be moving beyond your ability to control them.

You don't need to control anything anymore. We are carrying you on a swift river of change, and we are with you at all times. You are surrounded by more help and protection than you could ever know. If you need to feel our presence, quiet yourself and go within. When you have become quiet and calm, you can invite us to reveal ourselves to you and you will be able to feel us in your own unique way. We are with you, but if you cannot quiet yourself, you will not be able to feel our presence and take comfort in that. As within, so without. When you are peaceful inside, you will draw peaceful energies to you from the outside.

Peace, peace, peace. It is so important to find and create inner peace. As the world around you moves steadily into more strife and war, create peace within and detach from the drama. Be like the Buddha. Be like the Christ. Be like all of those world teachers who have come to show the way — who knew the eternal truths of existence. You will be like them when this process is complete. You will be like them when it is time for you to return for those who are going to need your help and comfort, who will need you to lead them to safety before the Pole Shift occurs.

This is a process, but there is also an "event" aspect to it. When it is the perfect time, the missing ingredient will be supplied and a door will open into another plane of reality. This is not something you can do for yourself at this time. It will be offered to you at the perfect time and in the perfect way for your particular circumstances. All of those who are meant to go with you will go with you at that time. They will be with you and you will cross through the door together — your children, your animals, your friends and family members who have chosen for Terra will go with you.

You may have children, friends, and family members who have NOT chosen to go to Terra and they will not go with you. All will happen in the perfect way for your particular circumstances. This is being done in love and we ask you to remember that love is the opposite of fear. If you are in fear about this, you will not be able to receive it. Let go and let God. It is still the answer to all questions. Let go and let God handle the details. We know what we are doing, and it will all be done perfectly for each individual situation.

Your task in all of this is to prepare yourselves to receive the changes with as much grace and ease as you can. Surrender is the way through. Resistance will only increase your discomfort. Let go and let God. If you look at those around you, love them enough to trust that they will have exactly the right experience for their life plan. If their Oversoul has chosen for them to go to Terra, they will, regardless of what they know or don't know, regardless of what they believe or don't believe.

These Messages are beginning to affect enough people that a change in the field of the mass consciousness is beginning to be noticed by those who are receptive to it. You are resonating it into being. In the midst of all that is going on in the world, you are affecting things through your combined energies. Your longing for Terra is creating an energetic pathway toward it that will open it up for more and more people as things proceed. This is your work in this world at this moment — to create that energetic pathway toward Terra.

You are like the icebreaker ships that clear a passage for others to follow. It may not seem like you are doing anything, but if you will pay attention to your own transformation — how you yourselves are changing — you will recognize that you are radiating out a different "signal" than those around you who are still blindly following the ways of 3D.

You are all embodying the higher Light. You are experiencing some discomforts as those attachments and those conditions that are not in keeping with your essence are purged from your cellular memory and from your life circumstances. This is a good time to simplify your lives. By that, we do not mean you have to become ascetics. We are merely suggesting that "less is more." If you still have clutter in your life, get rid of the clutter. If you have possessions that no longer reflect your present tastes or interests, get rid of them. Open up space in your homes, your lives. Say goodbye to those things that no longer serve you, with thanks for what they have been for you and to you. They have served, but when they no longer serve you, get rid of them.

The less you have left of the things that remind you of what you were, the easier it will be to receive what you are becoming. You can still keep photographs if they still have energy for you. You can still keep books if they still have energy for you. But those things that don't have energy for you anymore — get rid of them. Be discerning, and by doing these things, you will make yourself more aware of how you have changed.

You will continue to change, and your tastes and interests will continue to change. One day you may be drawn to something and soon afterward you will be through with it. No blame. Just accept the process and move smoothly through it, touching on those things that present in your life to be touched upon. If there is one quality that will characterize this process, it is impermanence.

As things proceed, you will become skilled at surfing the wave of change.

Nothing will remain the same. You are changing daily, so it makes sense that your relationship to your world will also be changing daily. As things proceed, you will become skilled at surfing the wave of change. You will become more accustomed to maintaining your balance and staying over your feet as the wave of change carries you toward your destination — Terra. In surfing, the key to a successful ride on the wave is staying right over your feet. If you lean back too far or forward too far, you will tumble into the wave. If you remain anywhere but over your feet, you lose your balance and the ride is over for the moment, requiring you to get back up and regain your balance again.

We have spoken a little about how it is on Terra — how one creates anew in the moment, without reference to the past or the future. In this metaphor of surfing the wave and staying over your feet, we are talking about staying rooted where you ARE — in the present moment — rather than in the "past" (where you have been) or the "future" (where you are going). If you think about it, all fear derives from past experience being projected onto the future.

When things arise in your present moment that remind you of something from the past, you can easily project that the past experience will repeat itself in the moments that follow the time of remembering that past. This is when you feel fear. It's inner talk that says, "It was like this before, so it will be like this again." If you experienced pain in the past, you expect it will be painful again. That is where the fear comes in. You want to avoid the pain. "I'm afraid that if this moment goes the way it went before, I'll experience what I experienced before, and I don't want to do that again."

The answer to this is to cut through the cords of memory, to interrupt the inner talk by saying out loud, "That was then. This is now." Boom! You are back in the present, able to choose anew in the present moment. When you say the word "now," you bring your attention into the present. Say "NOW" out loud, right now. Feel NOW. What is really happening NOW? Not what happened before, not what MIGHT happen later. What is really happening NOW?

Do you see how you are in the habit of scaring yourself? Cultivate the practice of living NOW. Live each moment as the only moment that exists. That is how it will be on Terra. Get used to it. Create a little bit of Terra right where you are, NOW. NOW is the only place you can create anything. NOW is the only place you can choose anything. NOW is all you ever really have.

When we say the word "moment," it will be useful to define what we mean. A moment is an "event" that arises from the matrix of Infinite Mind. It contains everything within it for its natural fulfillment and completion. It is not measured by minutes, seconds, or hours. It is a unit of experience that may be very short or go on for some time. You can

FEEL when a moment begins. You can FEEL when it completes. Every moment has a beginning, a middle, and a conclusion, like a phrase in speech or music. Think of it entering into your field of awareness, swelling into its fullness, and then receding as it completes. There is a wavelike quality to a moment. A wave emerges from the ocean, swells, moves forward, and then resolves back into the ocean. Just so with a moment.

It emerges from the ocean of consciousness that is the Mind of the Creator. It swells upward into your perceptual field, and moves forward, then ebbs from your experience as it completes. There is background and foreground, and there are different waves overlapping. In the past, you were only peripherally aware of the background, as your attention was captured by the foreground, but now your senses will be broadened and deepened until you are like a bowl containing ALL of it — all of the ocean and all of the waves upon its surface. You will be aware of all of it simultaneously and be able to move your attention to whatever you feel called to pay attention to, at will.

This is a natural expansion of your consciousness into full consciousness. As your consciousness expands, it will affect everything else — your body, your surroundings, the quality of your interaction with your environment. You will begin to merge with the Mind of the Creator. You will experience the peace and serenity, the infinite spaciousness of that, and you will become that peace; you will become that spaciousness that is vast enough to hold it all within you — in love and without judgment. That is where you are going. That is the experience you are moving into, even now.

As you move forward within time, you will gradually stop caring about where you are going and when. The chatter and the impatience will simply fall away. You will feel when something is no longer appropriate for you — whether it is the clamor of the media, the noise of deepening conflict, or anything else that is not in keeping with this deep sense of peace and infinite space. When this occurs, simply let go and let God. Let the peace and spaciousness of the Creator become your field of play. Let go of anything that does not belong in that space.

You don't have to engage in conflict. You can simply let go of your resistance, of your attachments to being "right" or "better than." You can simply let go and let God. Let everyone do the same for themselves. If people have attachments to their way of seeing and being, allow them to remain that way. They will receive what is perfect for them, also. This is an "operation" based in love and respect for all choices. Be responsible for YOUR choices, and let everyone else have the same privilege.

We shall speak to you again on this topic. Amen, Adonoy Sabayoth. We are the Hosts of Heaven.

A moment is a unit of experience that may be very short or go on for some time.

ASCENSION IS A PROCESS, PART THREE
November 26, 2001

All right, now. We have asked to speak to you today in this, our final discourse on this particular topic, so that we may both come to closure on THIS topic and lay the foundation for that which follows. You see, that is the way things work in the Creation. Every ending is also a beginning. Every closure is also an opening, and so it is with our work with you and so it is with your ascension process, as well.

As you are leaving the world you have known, you are also approaching a new world, the world of your dreams. As you are closing off those ties to those whom you have known, you are also opening up to make new associations with those who are more closely aligned with your particular path and destination. It is a grand sorting out that is taking place and there are both sorrows and joys to be found along the way. We hope to bring you more of the latter than the former, so please bear with us as we enter this new territory together.

First of all, please take note of the fact that there are three parts to this discourse. There will be three volumes in this material before we are through, and that is no accident. Every number is a symbol for a particular energy configuration and certain numbers are called prime numbers and have special significance, as they form the foundation for other numbers. They also reflect and embody a certain aspect of the design of Creation, and they are used in describing that design. There are also certain geometries involved that are a reflection of "how things work" in a particular Creation — the outpicturing of certain dynamics that are inherent in that Creation and in keeping with its Universal Laws.

We will not attempt to give you a comprehensive treatise on these subjects, for our topic today is the subject of ascension, so we will only make mention of those aspects of these things that relate to our topic — your ascension process.

Many of you have read and use some terms interchangeably, such as dimension and density, which from our perspective is not an accurate thing and leads to some confusion. We hope to clarify those things also, as it all relates to your understanding of who you really are, and how you project yourself into your many different forms.

The Original Thought became manifest as a projection of that Thought.

To begin with, you are a projection from Source. The Original Thought became manifest as a projection of that Thought. All of you who are bound for Terra are part of that Original Thought. You are the first generation of Creation and are creators yourselves. But who and what is this Creator who does the thinking? And how are you related to It? You have words such as "ineffable" to express the nature of the Creator. You also use other words, such as omnipresent, omniscient, omnipotent, etc., for the same purpose. Ineffable means "unknowable; incapable of being described; incapable of being grasped/understood." It is considered to be an attribute of the Creator. All those other words are attributes, also. They describe aspects or qualities of the Creator.

So, to your limited frame of reference, the nature of the Creator is beyond your capacity to understand, beyond your ability to comprehend. And perhaps that is true for you NOW, but when you have crossed the threshold, you will EXPERIENCE the Creator directly. You will experience your true connection with and relationship to the Creator, and then you will truly be "home." Then you will have no more need of words to describe what cannot be described. You will simply EXIST in that relationship and knowing.

Now, who is this "you" we are talking about? You are a projection of that Creator, a product of that Creator's Thought, and you exist only in the Mind of the Creator. All of Creation exists only in the Mind of the Creator. It is Thought made manifest through the medium of light and sound. "Sound" is the word you use to describe vibration, which is the oscillation between two opposing states.

Your entire reality is oscillating between two opposing states — "on" and "off." Your reality is only "there" half of the time, but the oscillations are so rapid that you perceive of things as being continuous, as being constantly "on." But in reality, the Creation is being re-created over and over again — "refreshed" or "redrawn" over and over again, many times a second. So "you" only exist half of the time, yourselves! Where are you during the other half of the time? You ARE the Creator at rest. Think about it. You ARE the Creator at rest. There is a spectrum of vibration involved, and the only difference is the speed at which the oscillations take place.

We have spoken of the "inbreath" and "outbreath" of the Creator, which is measured in billions of your years. That is one cycle of Creation. At the other end of the spectrum is this very rapid cycling, this very rapid alternation between "on" and "off" that makes up your physical reality — or rather that which APPEARS to be your physical reality. It is all a projection and the Creator is the "projector" of the entire Creation, including you. You are players in the Creator's "movie," only instead of a single, static "screen" in a movie house, the Creator gets to view its Creation through the perceptual screens of each and every aspect of Its Creation — an infinitude of perceptions, all streaming back into the Creator from Its projections.

The Creator exists as an infinitely vast field of intelligent energy, and the first generation — the elohim — are only slightly less so. They are extremely vast also, but are a single step removed from absolute infinitude. They do have boundary and identity. You are the expression or projection of one of the elohim. You are among those who came together to project this portion of the Creation from within your being, so many billions of years ago. But your projection does not just consist of this level of being that you presently experience as your physical reality.

It has many levels — many different frequency bands — that make up a continuous spectrum of reality, not unlike the spectrum of light and sound that makes up the Creation itself.

You exist simultaneously on all of the levels or frequency bands that exist. You exist as vast fields of intelligent energy and you exist as single points of pure consciousness and light without form — simultaneously. You exist as embodiments or expressions across the entire frequency spectrum, also, and all of your expressions exist simultaneously with each other. Right now, your attention is placed within the locus of your physical expression on Earth, but as your ascension proceeds, you will be accessing more and more of your other levels of being, also. You will be defining yourself quite differently, and you will be changing in many ways, to more properly express your chosen level of being for a given time and place.

These Messages are being given in a series — in a sequence — proceeding from the outer or more superficial aspects toward the core or more central aspects of our discussion. It is all about the journey back to your true Selves, toward remembering who you really are and toward regaining your true powers and true nature of expression. It is hard for you to imagine how much and how little CHOICE is available to you. You see, when you have so little comprehension of your true place in things, you are like a blind person, guessing at what lies around you.

You have so MUCH choice because the possible choices are nearly infinite. You have so LITTLE choice, because there is only ONE right choice for you in a given moment. When you are fully conscious of your nature and connection with Source, you will be at peace and at rest within both of those seeming paradoxes: the fact that there are so many choices available and the fact that there is only ONE "right" choice for you to make — one choice that is wholly in keeping with who you are and where you fit within the relationship between all of the other expressions of the Creator with which you interact.

So you exist on Earth, in your physical bodies, but you also exist at other levels at the same time. You exist in all the other frequency bands, as well, and each frequency band has its own "laws" that govern form and function within that band. Most of you who are reading these Messages are going to go to Terra and will express in forms and have functions that are appropriate to that frequency band — that density of the Creation. AT THE SAME TIME, you will continue to exist on all of the other frequency bands, and you will be able to choose where you

There is only ONE right choice for you in a given moment.

put your attention — through which frequency band you perceive.

You will be aware of your "other selves," but the one "right" focus will be your primary one, with all of the others existing as a backdrop of potentials that are always available to you. Some of you will relate to Terra from other platforms, to oversee and guide those upon her surface, as those are the roles that you have chosen for that experience, also. At all times, all of you will be existing at all of your levels at once, but one locus will be primary. You will be a focus of attention in one particular part of the vast ocean of Cosmic Mind, aware of the rest as a constant backdrop for your experience.

We have spoken of the holographic model. All things are contained as potentials within the hologram. This is what we mean by this backdrop. It is made up of all the potentials. In full consciousness, you will experience the presence of all the potentials at the same time as you experience the focus of the EXPRESSION of ONE of those potentials. We will speak more on this topic at another time, but we just want to give you a little look at this idea, now. You will be aware of ALL of it while expressing just one choice within it at any given time.

Now to the subject of numbers. There are essences that are expressed by numbers, and prime numbers can be said to be prime essences, like what you might think of when you think of primary colors. Your primary colors of visible light are red, green, and blue. All other colors are made up of those 3 colors, in combination with intensity or lack of it. When you blend these 3 colors in varying proportions and intensities, you get all of the other colors, including the extremes of pure white (the complete presence of all 3 colors in equal proportions and at full intensity) and pure black (the ABSENCE of all color and the point of zero intensity).

Numbers act in similar ways, but with far more complexity. Numbers are symbolic distillations of the essence of certain properties, and primary numbers cannot be further reduced. They are foundational. All numbers that are NOT primary numbers are made up of combinations of various primary numbers and can be "taken apart" into their primary components.

What does all of this talk about numbers and colors have to do with your ascension process? It is to give you a grasp of ESSENCE, of FOUNDATION, of ROOT or GROUND. You are returning to your essence, to that primary expression of your being, independent of your expression in a particular environment. Your essence is your primary color, your primary sound, your primary quality. It is the thing that is the "true you," independent of any incarnational expression. It is the pure vibrational pattern that is your particular configuration and there are only so many of those available within a given spectrum of Creation. All the rest are made up of combinations and alterations of that primary configuration. To be in full consciousness means to KNOW your essence. And not only will you know your own essence, you will also recognize the essence of others.

There have been some individuals in human history on your planet who embodied this kind of understanding and modeled it for others. Now all of you who are going to Terra will be embodying your essence. You are dropping all that is NOT in keeping with your essence, and you are filling yourselves with more and more of your essential nature as this process proceeds.

The questions of intellect fall away in the fullness of your experience of your essence. You are filled with the peace of knowing who you are, where your place is in the Creation, and of knowing what is your one "right" choice in any given moment. All struggle is gone. All doubt is gone. All there is left is the peace and the quiet joy of knowing at last the answers to those questions that have formed the basis of your seeking through all these billions of years. You will simply KNOW, and you will never again have to forget what you know, ever again.

We will speak more about these numbers, colors, and higher aspects of the Creation at other times. For now, we wish you to simply know where this is heading. When your transformation is complete, you will simply KNOW who you are, where you fit within all of this, how you relate to the Creator Itself, and what is "right action" or "right choice" in any given moment. You can begin to practice that now, though, by simply remaining quiet enough to hear the "voice within."

In the midst of the tumult and the noise around you, you can listen instead to the silence and the voice within. In each and every moment, you can choose peace instead of struggle and conflict. You can walk away from those people and those experiences that scream for you to ease their pain by engulfing you in it. You can bring peace to others only if you can embody it yourself. You can bring peace only if you ARE at peace within yourself. As long as you are striving within yourself, toward some imagined outcome, you are not at peace. Peace, peace, peace. That is the "pearl of great price." Be peace. Be at peace. Be peace.

We leave you now in peace and honor and blessing. One day, you will be like us again, too. Amen, Adonoy Sabayoth. We are the Hosts of Heaven.

COMMENTARY: I have received several queries about the reference to the primary colors, so I wanted to clear up the apparent confusion. The primary colors of LIGHT are red, green, and blue. They are the ones that create the images on your TV sets and computer monitors. The primary colors of PIGMENTS (such as crayons, ink, dyes, paint, and the pigments in skin, hair, and eyes) are identified as cyan, magenta, and yellow. LIGHT works differently than PIGMENTS do.

When you combine LIGHT colors, they are ADDITIVE and RADIANT. The more intense and the greater quantity of each color, the lighter and brighter they get. Light creates colors as it passes through transparent media, such as glass, 35 mm slides, gels, and transparent plastics. When you combine all three primary colors of LIGHT in equal proportions and at full intensity, you get WHITE light.

When you combine PIGMENT colors, they are SUBTRACTIVE. Each pigment ABSORBS all color except its own, which it reflects back to you. The total absence of light (i.e., all color is absorbed and none is being radiated back at you) is perceived as black. When you combine all three primary colors of PIGMENTS, you get various shades of "black/grey," according to the absorbent capacity of the particular pigments used. The "black" you see in black cats is really a very dark brown, which absorbs nearly all the light that hits it. Pigments are made up of substances that subtract everything from the light reflecting off the surface except the color you see. They are used for "reflective" media, such as paper, canvas, and cloth.

The familiar "primary colors" that you were taught about in school (red, blue, and yellow) are made up of pigments that, when mixed, make up the complementary colors of orange, purple, and green. That is yet another color system, used exclusively for reflective pigments. It is based on what happens when you mix particular pigments with each other. What is important to understand about that system is that it is still a subtractive system, and the colors that are reflected back to your eye are still mixtures of the primary subtractive colors — cyan, magenta, and yellow.

This Message is talking about the primary colors of LIGHT, not those of pigments. White light contains all the colors of LIGHT, and when it is passed through a prism, you see all the colors of visible light, from red through violet. Our chakras are based on the LIGHT colors, not the PIGMENT colors. The middle chakra of the 7 body chakras is the heart chakra and its color is GREEN. The lower 3 chakras are red, orange and yellow (note that yellow is not in the middle), and the upper 3 chakras are blue, indigo, and violet. Taken all together, they make up the colors of the rainbow — the visible light spectrum.

I hope this is helpful to you in understanding this Message.

Peace and blessings,
Sara/Adonna/Oriole

IT'S BOOSTER ROCKET TIME!
January 2, 2002

All right, now. We have several things to say to you today, on both the near and more distant view. The closest thing to you on the time horizon is a somewhat massive event that will mark the separating out of the different realities from one another to such an extent that they will begin to experience events that are not shared with all of the other realities that will emerge. This event will be felt in every corner of the world as a very deep shock, and one that will rouse even the most deeply slumbering individuals to a dawning realization that the world will not ever be the same again.

The events that have preceded this forthcoming shock were relatively mild compared to what comes now and what will follow it in relatively rapid succession. You are nearly at the threshold of the parting of the ways and this will become more obvious to you in hindsight, after sufficient time has passed that you can look back and see a pattern. To put this in a proper context, we wish to make use of a scientifically-observed process as a metaphor for what is about to occur. As with all metaphors, there is an oversimplification of a complex situation, but it will serve to illustrate our point well enough for you to make it the rest of the way on your own.

When a living cell is going to divide, a number of things occur. In the resting stage, the chromatin — those threads of DNA that carry the genetic information of the cell and the organism — are loosely spread throughout the nucleus of the cell, making it difficult to determine just where one thread leaves off and another begins. However, when the time nears for the cell to divide itself into two separate halves, the chromatin begin bunching up and separating out from the other threads so that they form distinct chromosomes that can be observed as such under the microscope. Then they replicate and the two identical pairs line up along the equatorial plate in the cell, which will become the plane of division when the process completes.

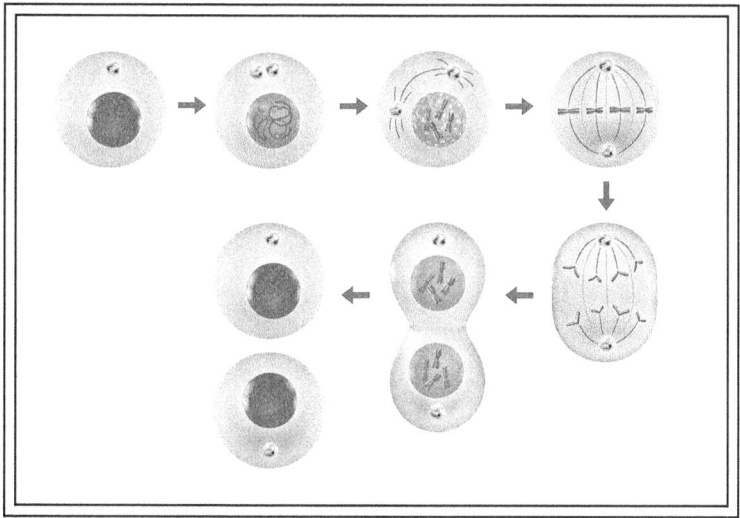

Cell division process

Meanwhile, the "poles" of the cell have migrated so that they are opposite each other and at right angles to the equatorial plate, not very different from the relationship between the poles and the equator on your physical planet. Fine threads from the center of each chromosome attach to these poles (one from each pair goes to one of the poles; the other one of the pair attaches to the other pole) and when all is lined up, the cell pinches inward at the equator and divides.

In this process, things go along fairly slowly at first, but when all is finally lined up, the process completes rather quickly. So it is with you right now, in your planetary process. It has been a relatively slow process of sorting out into your groups and aligning with your poles of destiny, but this next event will be the "shot heard 'round the world," and it will mark the "beginning of the end" — that point at which the different realities physically move away from each other toward their "poles of destiny."

In other words, despite that fact that you can look back on your previous year as a time of increasing acceleration — particularly from September [11] onward — once this event occurs, things will kick into high gear and much will follow in rapid succession, just as the cell rapidly separates into its new "daughter cells" and they then move apart from each other and journey separately from that point on.

A cell only splits into two cells, and there will be several different realities that split off from each other in this process, but the key point to grasp here is the significance of this next event in terms of marking the beginning of this actual movement into separate realities, and to prepare yourself for the speed at which things will unfold after that. Despite the shock of September [11] and some of the things that happened afterward, the last few weeks have been pretty tame compared to what is coming next and afterward.

We encourage you to keep your breath open, to remain detached while observing all of this occurring, and to realize that for those who are headed toward Terra, this could be considered the "booster rocket" for your journey in that direction. There is no one who will not FEEL this impact, but there are many ways of perceiving it. If you were strapped into the seat of a space shuttle and the rockets kicked in under you, you would feel that impact and acceleration, but you would know that it was taking you upward toward your destination and mission. You may choose the same response to this next shock on your perceptual screen, and it would be good if you can do that. Instead of viewing it as a disaster, many of you will be able to say, "Finally! We are under way."

Many of you who are reading this have been "on your way" for a long time and have experienced many shifts in your understanding and perceptions. Now, however, the time of learning and processing will change from dealing with those things of the past toward dealing with those things that are now coming into your life. Many of you are still in the process of leaving old relationships and circumstances. That may continue for a while for some of you, but most of you will find the rate of change in your life to be exhilarating and experience more and more joy in the journey as you begin to experience the rush of freedom, as you let go of those things and people who hold you back.

You remember an old title — *Inherit the Wind*? You will inherit the wind. You will become accustomed to streaming like the wind, to be moving so fast it brings tears to your eyes, but they will be tears of joy that you are finally underway and can feel the movement as you stream toward your destination.

Others will be experiencing rapid change, also, but it will not bring them joy — in part because they will be losing a lot of what they are very attached to: pictures of reality that must change in the face of the events that will come now, ways of being that will no longer be possible. Many things taken for granted will pass away, and those who can move through these times with grace and surrender will experience wonder and awe at the unfolding. People will look at the ashes of their past and some will understand that it clears the way for a new beginning, while others will sort through the ashes, trying to recover something remembered to take with them — to take with them what no longer has life in an effort to hold onto that life which is gone.

It is easy to point fingers of blame, but as we have said before, when you get down to the core, you must blame the Creator who has created all that you see and feel. It is all "good" to the Creator because it fulfills the purpose of the Creation — to provide experiences for the Creator to enjoy through Its creations. This shock that comes is all part of the larger exit plan for the Creation. Nothing will be left of the old world when it is done. Everyone will be gone from the present planet, through one exit path or another. Everyone will experience continuity in their perceived reality, but this event will mark the time when not everyone experiences the SAME reality. If you could compare notes, you would discover that different people experience different things, and this will increase as you move through time to the finale of the drama of 3D Earth.

As things move forward, you will see your destination more and more clearly by virtue of its contrast with everything else that is going on. Likewise, other people with other destinations will perceive THOSE more clearly, so it will seem like everyone else that does not share one's particular views is mistaken, but this movement will accommodate them all, in one way or another.

So, for example, if you hear that a large planet or comet is coming that will result in a pole shift or cataclysms in 2003, that is a perception that belongs to a particular exit path, and you simply allow those people who perceive that to do so. That path is not "yours," and it does not lead to Terra, so all you need to be concerned with is the path that IS "yours" and to follow what presents in your life that will lead you further in that direction.

There has been much talk in the past of many scenarios that have not manifested — mass landings, the Photon Belt, etc. However, now the many paths that are being "seen" by those who can "see" in that way have a greater likelihood of coming to pass. Even the scenarios that are put forth by the deceivers will come to pass for some people in some way, because thought creates and if enough people believe in a particular outcome, their combined thoughts will manifest that reality. That is why we are sharing these Messages with you — so that those who are coded to respond and can feel that response will add their energies with others of like mind and heart and will manifest that which we speak of to you.

It is a paradox that Terra already exists and yet you have to align with it for it to manifest for you. It is a reciprocal relationship, like a mirror of sorts. Terra calls to you, and you seek Terra. In the aligning with the vision, it is a little like a "lock" in a missile guidance system. In reading these Messages, you "lock" onto the "target" of Terra, and Terra attracts you by her presence in your perceptual field.

Not everyone is this way, and though it might seem like you are alone in your perceptions when compared with those around you, consider that there are nearly 6 million of you altogether and you will have a LOT of company once you are all together again. You have been together before, in groupings of various sizes and at various historical times and places, but now the time is coming when you will all be together at once, in one place again, before you are complete and depart for your other journeys on the way back to Source and your final dissolution as a separate being.

Those of you who are going to Terra will be there long enough to establish the colonies and bear your children, and then you will be off to other adventures in the cosmos. For the next century plus [some years], your focus will be Terra, but then you will be through with that and will move on. That is the nature of things. One exploration leads to the next, and that next one leads to the next one after that, infinitely.

Terra calls you now, and she is your safe harbor from the storm that now comes. Remember that. The storms that come now are the booster rockets lifting you toward your dream of a world without storms, without wars, without death, and if you miss the thunder and lightning, you will be able to travel to wilder places to visit with that, too, but Terra and her peace will be your home for the rest of your present incarnation. When it is time to leave, you will simply change form and move on. No pain. No death. No sorrow again, ever. Now THAT will be a welcome thing, won't it? We look forward to having you amongst us again.

We leave you now, in peace and honor and blessing. Amen, Adonoy Sabayoth. We are the Hosts of Heaven.

NOTE: For the Hosts, their relationship to time is not the same as for people experiencing linear time on 3D Earth. When they said, "The events that have preceded this forthcoming shock were relatively mild compared to what comes now and what will follow it in relatively rapid succession," we can look back at events that have occurred since "Shock and Awe" began on March 20, 2003, and begin to understand what "relatively rapid succession" means to the Hosts.

The massive earthquake and tsunami in Indonesia on December 26, 2004 and Hurricanes Katrina and Rita in the US in 2005 were clearly not "mild" events, and the 2017 Atlantic hurricane season was catastrophic, with 17 named storms, 10 hurricanes and 6 major hurricanes. In addition, it was by far the costliest season on record, with a total of at least $282.16 billion (USD) in damages, about $100 billion higher than the total of the previous record holder — the 2005 season. Essentially all of the season's damage was due to three of the season's major hurricanes — Harvey, Irma, and Maria. Now we can see the world steadily heading toward financial collapse and massive social disruption.

Our interpretation of "relatively rapid" seems to be much faster than that of the Hosts, who remind us elsewhere in the Messages that a few years now is but a very brief moment when one is considering a cycle of 4.5 billion years.

ON YOUR WAY HOME
February 22, 2002

All right, now. We have asked to speak to you tonight because something very wonderful is looming on your horizon. It is not what you would expect, but it is still wonderful from our perspective. A grand awakening is about to take place and for you who have been patiently waiting for release from the world of so much sorrow, this will mark the true beginning of the final stage of your departure from this world, on the way to the next.

We have spoken before of this event. It is a global wakeup call, so that everyone, everywhere in the world can know something has fundamentally and irrevocably changed. For some, change is and can be terrifying, but change can also be seen as good news, too. We encourage you to embrace change in this way — as good news to be celebrated, as the "beginning of the end" of this sorrow.

If you can see it this way, then you can quietly rejoice in your heart with the sure knowing of what follows. Despite appearances, it is truly good news — an end to the suffering of this world, an end to the pain of this world, once and for all, forever. This is what is in store for you — total joy, total love, total peace.

But on the way to that joy and peace there is a period of upheaval as part of this massive change. It is for this reason that we have spent so much time and energy in preparing you for this time and these occurrences. If you can but keep your eyes on the far horizon, where that new world awaits you in all of her radiance and joy, then you will pass through this time with less attention on what is passing away and more attention on where you are headed through the times ahead.

We wish you to know, also, that we are always with you. If we do not speak to you through these words, we speak to you through our silence. Silence is a message, too. It says, "Listen within." It says, "Pay attention to what feelings come up when the Hosts have not spoken for a while." Do you get anxious to hear from us? Then seek our comfort within. If our beloved messenger were suddenly plucked from your midst, what would you do? Find us and our comfort within.

When you stop grasping at the fragile comforts that make up your external world, you can experience the richness and the comforts of your inner world. If you focus on what you DON'T have, you will never realize how much you DO have. That is one of the reasons we have encouraged you to live your life with appreciation. By doing that, you fill yourself every minute of every day and you are truly wealthy in the things that matter most.

Now that we have put our gloss on the story, let us acknowledge that not everyone will see things the way you do. You must understand this and not get caught up in the maelstrom that is soon to surround you. There will be a great deal of confusion, anger, and fear, and these things will be exploited by those who profit from them.

Do not get caught up in the drama. Remember our counsel to seek the peace of deep ocean? Remember it when these times are upon you. Let the events flow around you, but maintain a place of calm trust and serenity within you. These events will be the harbinger of even more intense times, but carry your peace with you like a shield and you will weather the storms well.

Please note that we are now speaking in the plural. There is not one single event, but an entire panorama of events of all kinds and types that will constitute the face of change in your world. They will be everywhere you look, and once it dawns on people that there is some possible connection from one to another, they will be roused from their sleep in a most unpleasant way.

You are not sleeping. You are already awakening and you have within you the means to create peace and safety for yourself and your loved ones, be they human or otherwise.

Peace is an attitude, not something you can buy at a store already packaged. To be sure, you can read books and listen to soothing music, but even those actions are an expression of an ATTITUDE of SEEKING PEACE. Seek peace. Be peace. Be humble in your seeking and let go of the clinging to the comforts you used to seek. Open to receive the comforts that count, the ones that have no price because they are priceless. Peace, peace, peace. It is your sanctuary through the storm.

Peace, peace, peace. It is the savior of your soul, your sanity, your hearts and minds. Seek peace in the midst of the storm.

If choices come (and they will), make the choice for peace. As the frequencies rise, everything that is a symptom of the malaise of this world will surface. Peace heals. Be at peace. Drop the struggle to hold on. In letting go, you gain more than you lose. Some of you will find it harder to do this than others, but we assure you that you have created yourself with the necessary reserves, the necessary heart, the necessary strength to do this, and in so doing, you will rejoice even more because of the discovery that you are thriving in the midst of the storms. You will thrive because you are made for these times.

You have found your homing beacon in these Messages and you carry within you the map and the compass for the journey. Even if we were silent, you would find your way home. Be peace. Be at peace. You are on your way now, and nothing will stop you from making the trip home. You are coming home to yourself, to the world of your dreams, and to each other. In light of all that, what does it matter if the old shell cracks and shatters? When it's time for the chick to come out of the egg, the shell has to crack and shatter. You are coming out of your shell. The world will crack and shatter around you and you will be coming home.

You have found your homing beacon in these Messages and you carry within you the map and the compass for the journey.

Focus on the journey ahead, rather than what you leave behind. Let everyone make their own decisions now, as the grouping around the poles of destiny is taking place more and more each day. There are many partings to take place on the road ahead and many who are still in your life may pass from your view, but you are coming home. Your animals, your loved ones, everyone whom you love will be provided for, in keeping with their life plan. You can trust the process. You can trust the journey. You are coming home.

If we are silent sometimes, it is so that you can learn to listen to your own sound, to your own inner voice instead of ours. We are family, you and we, and we are here with you every step of the way. But we do not wish you to become dependent on hearing our voice to know you are safe and loved. We wish you to hear your own inner voice to know you are safe and loved.

Go within. Meditate. Breathe. Feel the calm and peace you can create when you can remember to breathe. As things get more intense around you, find ways to feel calmer and more relaxed. Take a hot bath. Go for a walk. Listen to sounds that soothe you — streams, rivers, the sighing of the wind in the trees, a gentle rain. You can even get recordings of these sounds if you want, so you can create this experience for yourself whenever you need to remind yourself that what is going on around you is not all there is to the picture.

Be good to yourself. Cherish yourself for the beautiful being that you are. The long lonely walk is far shorter now than it was and you are on your way home. Remember that. You are on your way home.

Amen, Adonoy Sabayoth. We are the Hosts of Heaven.

THE GOD GAME
April 9, 2002

For those who have eyes to see, it is evident that much change is going on all around you. Yet, if you follow our instructions, you can deepen your sense of peace and calm and remain serene, even as things accelerate and intensify. The threshold event of which we have spoken is still some time off in your future, and we would hope that with this long lead time to reflect and prepare, you will have integrated the necessary understanding to respond to it with quiet acceptance, knowing that it brings with it the final stages of your exit from planet Earth and the beginnings of the new world that follows.

Yet we also know how much you love to hear from us and how it helps you to hear our perspective on things, so in the spirit of an interlude, we thought we would entertain you a bit with our discourse today. Our model indeed comes from your world of entertainment, although we hope that you will take away something a bit deeper than just that. Sometimes entertainment can be an easy way to swallow what would otherwise be bitter medicine, and we hope that will be the case today.

If life is viewed as a sort of movie, with everyone playing their part and speaking their lines, then God/the Creator is the ultimate filmmaker. We have spoken before of the Oversoul and how it creates the simultaneous projections of itself — what you experience as your embodiments or "lives." The Oversoul is the projector for those individual expressions of itself and God/the Creator is the scriptwriter for all of the movies that play out through the Oversouls, regardless of their polarity.

As we have often said, the Creator has created EVERYTHING in order to experience Itself through Its creations. We have also commented on how it was necessary to create the two polarities in order to increase the potential for increasingly complex experiences, and how the Oversouls

If life is viewed as a sort of movie, with everyone playing their part and speaking their lines, then God/the Creator is the ultimate filmmaker.

themselves come in two "flavors" or polarities, which we have identified as the STS (service to self) and STO (service to others) orientation.

In movies, there are opposing forces and conflict, and it is also true in the "movie" of life. Think about that for a moment. If you went to see a movie and everything was harmonious and smooth, you would find it rather flat and uninteresting after a very short while. There would be no challenges to overcome, nothing but a kind of pleasant sameness and not much going on at any time — not much stimulation — and your mind would become restless and begin contemplating other things. That's because you want your movies to be entertainment, and for that reason they need opposing forces, conflict and challenges to be overcome.

And so it is with 3D life. If there were not enough stimulus, people would lapse into a sort of lethargy and boredom and lose interest or have to manufacture situations where they could experience intensity and variety. Such is the nature of the one who seeks to ever know more. And the Creator's chief desire is always to know more of Itself through the interaction of Its creations. We will call this aspect of the Creator's creative play "The God Game."

In the God Game, the Creator "wears" all of Its creations and plays all of the "parts" (roles/characters) through all of Its created parts. At the higher densities, the game changes, the rules change, but it is still the God Game at its core. Now, what does this have to do with anything and

Without enough stimulus, people would lose interest or have to manufacture situations where they could experience intensity and variety.

how can this be of help in understanding what you experience from day to day and over time?

Well, in the God Game, every one of you who is reading this is a character in the movie. Characters have personality traits they are born with, and they have traits that are learned through their experiences. In 3D, the catalyst is pain. In 4D, the catalyst is love. You are in 3D and your character has been shaped by your pain and by your seeking.

Most of your defining moments — those moments in which an experience affected you so deeply that it changed the course of your life — involved your pain and/or your seeking. Your seeking comes from the Creator's desire to know Itself through Its creations. Your pain comes from the Creator's desire to know Itself through Its creations. The Creator desires to know more about Itself, so the catalyst for all experiences are both the seeking and the pain.

Now, how are those conditions to be met? What will provide the pain and what will support the seeking? You can view the sources of pain as "enemies" or "perpetrators" or STS "villains" if you want. Those labels are used to identify sources of pain in your life. But they are as needed for the fullness of your experience in 3D as are the sources of support for your seeking — those whom you would call "friends" or "loved ones" or "teachers." Both are needed for the fullness of your experience and for the entire script or drama to play out. Both of those are the Creator expressing through Its creations, through the God Game. Here is a little insight into how it goes:

The pure Light of Creation, conditioned by Love as an ordering force, streams endlessly from the Source/Creator through the lenses of the Oversouls. The Oversouls color the Light with their own particular biases or "angle of perception/reception" and the Light takes on a particular quality from having passed through the Oversoul.

You could view these qualities as archetypes, as biases, or as themes to be explored. We like to view them as essences. In their purest state, they are the essence of a particular aspect of the Creator, and there are many of them available. We may explore this concept further at a future time, but for now, just understand that each Oversoul exists to explore a particular essence or theme, and it will do so by creating "lives" in many different settings or environments. However, all of the OTHER Oversouls are doing the same thing, so in any given environment, one has the presence and potential for interaction with many different essences, and this provides a rich basis for many different kinds of experiences.

For all practical purposes, the original set of possibilities was infinite, but now many (if not most) of those possibilities have been explored and there is a distillation going on, back into the original essence.

In the world around you, every person you see is going through a process of this distillation back into the original essence. They are becoming MORE of who they really are. This can cause some problems when a person was really just accommodating the expectations of those around them or living their life as a reaction to their defining moments. There is a lot of rejection of past hurts going on and a lot of intensified seeking.

What a glorious time to be in a body! At no time in the history of planet Earth has there been such a rich potential for intensified experience. How much more interesting the movie is from the Creator's perspective! In the God Game, the more intense the experience, the better it is for the richness that it provides.

Let's now look at some examples. If the focus of the exploration is the theme of power, then there is the potential to explore both the absence of power (powerlessness) and the possession of power. In the absence of power, one also learns about the possession of power from those who have power over them, and the reverse is true for the person who possesses the power — they learn from those whom they have the power over.

There is a RECIPROCITY that is inherent in the God Game.

There is a RECIPROCITY that is inherent in the God Game. God supplies all of the needed players and is both teaching and learning at the same time. Each player is a teacher for the other and is also learning from the other. Each person is a mirror for the other one to see him/herself more clearly, to know him/herself more deeply.

After many lifetimes have been created and experienced, all of this teaching and learning becomes integrated into the collective experience of the Oversoul, and thence back to the Creator. It all comes from the INTERACTION of the particular Oversoul's projections with the projections of the OTHER Oversouls. This is how the Creator can experience Itself through Its Creations. The experience of one particular Oversoul is amplified, enriched, and colored by the interaction with the projections from the other Oversouls. And it is a totally dynamic process, with feedback and alteration at each node of interaction. In fact, this is not just true of people, but of the entire fabric of the created or manifest worlds.

Your scientists have discovered a fundamental building block of matter, which they have called a quark. A quark is made out of Light. Not light as illumination, but Light that is a substance. ALL matter is built up of these units of Light. Now, these quarks are made out of Light, but they are shaped or conditioned by vibration, or Sound. Together, Sound and Light form the material ground for the manifest worlds. But there is one more aspect to consider. When a quark interacts with another quark, they are BOTH CHANGED by the interaction.

So even at the most fundamental level of material expression, a dynamic process of constant interaction and change is going on. What's more, there is an underlying field of consciousness or awareness that is the matrix for the entire collection of all of the quarks that are carrying on these interactions. So, at the most fundamental level, all quarks are interconnected with all other quarks by being contained in this field of conscious awareness. This field is the Mind of God. All manifest reality is embedded in the Mind of God and is interconnected through the matrix of the Mind of God. When you say "All things are connected," this is a fundamental truth.

The Oversouls are vast fields of intelligent energy. They are self-aware, and yet, they too, are embedded in the same matrix. When they project their projections, they manifest them through the quarks that are the building blocks of matter. All things, all manifestations, both from the level of the projector — the Oversoul — and the particles that make up the manifestation of the Oversoul's projection, are embedded in the Mind of God.

Therefore, in the God Game, God is experiencing Itself as both the filmmaker *and* the actors in the movie that It makes. These actors are not just people. They are also things like the wind and rain, flowers and trees, insects and animals. They are all the creations of the Creator. They are all players in the God Game. They are all sources of catalyst for pain and for the support of one's seeking.

Take a rock, for example. If you stub your toe on a rock or step on a sharp stone with your bare foot, it can provide you with the experience of pain. But another rock could offer you a foothold when you are climbing up a steep trail or wanting to cross a stream. They're all rocks, and they are all part of the God Game. If your life script requires you to cross a stream at some point in your seeking, the rock is an element of your experience. The rock is also sentient and it experiences you stepping on it. It experiences your energy, your thoughts, and it experiences the feeling of weight or pressure from being stepped on. The rock is experiencing, too.

Now, take a look at some of the things that are going on in your world today. A major portion of the Ross Ice Shelf collapsed in the Antarctic recently, a part of the changes that are going on. This change was a result of other changes that had already occurred. When those huge blocks of ice are set free to float and eventually melt, they affect the oceans that

The rock is experiencing, too.

they float in. The fresh water from the melting ice changes the salinity of the water around them.

That change in the salinity produces a subtle change in the flow of the ocean's currents. That change in the flow of the ocean's currents produces a subtle change in the weather patterns. Those changes in the weather patterns affect crops and food production. That change in food production affects the availability of food and also of prices for those foods. Those changes in availability and pricing produce other subtle changes, such as a subtle alteration of people's priorities.

When people are starving, they become desperate to survive at all costs, and that leads them to act in ways that they would not otherwise act. Those actions in turn affect other things which set in motion still other things, and so the God Game goes. Every single part of the manifest worlds affects every other part of the manifest worlds. It is all connected through the Mind of God, and God is everywhere that anything exists. It is all part of the God Game, wherein God interacts with Itself through Its creations.

With the return to essence, with things (and especially people) becoming more of what they really are underneath their conditioning and environmental pressures, you see many things surfacing. Polarization increases as the heroes and the villains become more like their true essence. Positive becomes more positive. Negative becomes more negative.

Things that one took on from others and which are not part of their essence become cast off, sometimes in unpleasant ways. Body aches and pains, emotional aches and pains, spiritual aches and pains — all of these are part of the purification of essence that is going on. Tolerance is lower for those things that are not compatible with one's essence. There is a greater tendency to withdraw from what is not compatible with one's essence, and that is seen as the great sorting out into all of the groupings, which we have spoken about before.

There are things surfacing that come as surprises at times, to find that one is not the person one thought they were. Much of what has shaped your self-perception is the result of those early experiences in life — those defining experiences that set you off on a particular course, exploring particular options, attempting to heal your pain, attempting to define your seeking and find what it is you seek.

So if you find your life changing now in fundamental ways, it is because the God Game is nearly over for this chapter in the Creation story. God has explored the themes, the roles, the potentials that were available through the parameters of this particular environment, and as in every good movie, it is time for the final act, where the question gets answered, the conflicts are resolved, and everyone goes off to live in the sequel! Your sequel is life on the ships and then life on Terra — a trilogy, if you like, and one that will still be just an interlude on the way to other movies.

You are coming home. You are becoming more of your essence. You are beginning to know who the "others" are whom you want to be with. And none of this would be possible without the God Game. None of this would be possible without the protagonists and the antagonists, without the heroes and the villains. Every script requires both for the story to move forward. Conflict leads to resolution and in that resolution, everyone is changed by the interaction. Change is eternal. You are eternal, and you will eternally change.

We leave you now in peace, honor and blessing. Amen, Adonoy Sabayoth. We are the Hosts of Heaven.

CALM, GROUNDED, AND CENTERED
August 18, 2002

Well, now. The time of which we have spoken is close at hand. Before that occurs, we want to give you a last reminder — that this journey of yours is a PROCESS, not an event, and although you are reaching an important threshold, there is a journey to be made beyond that time, so please remember this and do not place yourself in a position of locked energy with regard to this "event."

We cannot emphasize too much that it is important to remain detached and to not get caught up in the drama that is unfolding all around you. The moment you engage with chaos, you get sucked into it. The moment you polarize to something you observe, you get locked into that to which you polarize. It is so important to remember — especially at times of great dramatic impact — that your safety lies within, that no solution that matters in the long run of things will be found outside of yourself. Your answers lie within.

Even if you are not hearing "voices" or words, you do know — in each and every moment — what is true for you. You can access this knowing at any time. It is a feeling that you feel. Something will feel "right" or it will feel "off" or "wrong." Trust your feelings. Don't let anyone talk you out of them. It is not important that anyone else know what you feel. It is perfectly all right to keep your knowing to yourself, but don't let anyone sway you. There will be many attempts to talk you into adopting a certain attitude, but stay aligned with what you know as your own truth. You can carry it silently, but do not abandon it in order to accommodate anyone else.

We have been assessing things on your planet and we find two things are going on, neither of which come as a total surprise, given the "polarity game" and the lateness of the hour. First, the forces that use deception as their way of gaining polarity and taking energy from others

Your answers lie within.

have been succeeding in their plans for world domination. They are aided by those of higher densities of the same polarity and soon there will be an increase in their visibility.

It is far too late to stop any of this, so we are just telling you this so you will understand what you see as it unfolds. They have succeeded so well, we must confess that it is rather humorous to us to see how easily they have made their way with so little resistance. However, we do know the "ending" of the story, and there does come a time when their "game" will be "up" and they will depart for another destination.

In the meantime, however, deception will be everywhere and on the increase from its present levels. That is why we emphasize that you go within for your "news." Everything is being manipulated to such an extent that nothing you read or hear is untouched, except possibly some of the material that comes through the clearest of channels. Those are few in number, and the greatest part of the channeled material that is available to you has been affected and corrupted until it is simply not true anymore. There will always be some noble sentiments sprinkled liberally about by all of these sources, but in the end, they are leading those who listen to them down a path that will only end in distrust and disappointment.

That being said, there are some events about to unfold that directly affect you and your world. We are here to support you and will have much more to say in the weeks ahead. There will be one more Message in this volume and then we will begin anew with Volume Three. The Messages are our gift to you and we hope that many more will find their way to reading them in the coming days, weeks and months. We are pleased to see how so many of you ARE taking our words seriously, and we note that the changes we have foretold are upon you.

The "good news" is that the story has a happy ending. The "bad news" is that there are some relatively difficult days ahead for your planet and everything upon her. But that is not "news" to you at this point. We have been preparing you for a long time to receive the Grace that is available to you now. So many of you are "going with the flow" of change, and we are pleased that our words have in some way made that easier for you to do. You have been trained in the ways of surrender and your motto of "let go, let God" will serve you well in the times ahead.

The deceivers are massing now, and you will be hearing more from them of what they want you to hear and think. Each one will be claiming to have the "truth," the "inside story," and none of them will agree, but if you look behind the words, you will find the same background is there, no matter what "picture" is held up before your eyes.

Do not be deceived. There are many predictions coming to a head in the next few months, and so many of them will fail to materialize. It is all part of how the deceivers get people to lose their trust in everything, so when the truth comes along, they throw that out, too. It is a way of getting people to give up all resistance to the coming tyranny, so they will more willingly play into the hands of those who are behind that scenario and scheme.

There is a children's story about a boy who got great fun out of warning the local people that a wolf was coming. It made him feel more powerful to see them scrambling about just because he convinced them that they were in danger. But when the wolf really DID come, the townspeople ignored him and they were all eaten alive. His false warnings caused them to mistrust him so totally that when there was a real danger to them, they ignored him and so they fell prey to the wolf.

So you will be peppered with warnings about this danger and that danger and if you go running about as if they were something you could do anything about, you will find that nothing of what they say happens and then you will disregard the real warnings when they come. But if you tune into your inner voice and FEEL INTO THE VIBRATION, you will not be fooled. You will be able to tell when it "feels real," and whether you have to do anything at any given time.

Many of you have already been feeling and responding to inner urges for change in your lives. Some of you have decided to move to a new place or leave an old relationship. Others are making many subtle changes in your perception and thinking and becoming clear of the chatter and noise of the world. The real changes are taking place within, where they are hidden.

Because of the power of the physical senses, it is easy to be "outer directed" and to measure things by how they appear in the outer world. But your safety lies in being "inner directed" and by measuring with your subtle senses — how things FEEL to you, not how you "think" about them or what you hear from others, most especially the media.

Your safety lies in being "inner directed" and by measuring with your subtle senses — how things FEEL to you

We will not make predictions, other than to say that the time of the parting of the different destiny paths is nearly upon you. However, each of you has a plan for your life and each of you will have different experiences, so there is no prediction we can make that will be true for all of you, other than when the time is right, you will be called to your right place.

Every detail of your life has been anticipated by your Oversoul. All of your "appointments with destiny" will be kept. Every last requirement will be met for the completion you are making with all of your other lives. You are already losing your memory capabilities, and for some of you that is not convenient, but be encouraged by that sign that you are that much closer toward your desired destination. You are well along in your process and there is much Grace flowing. All you need to do is receive it.

Your inner knowing is your best armor against the deceptions. If something does not feel altogether true for you, TRUST that feeling. You must also trust in the plan for your life. You must trust that whatever you need to complete your life's purpose will be provided. That does not mean you will always like how it is wrapped, but every occurrence in your life is a true gift to help you complete your life in the way that was intended for you by your Oversoul.

Every occurrence in your life is a true gift to help you complete your life in the way that was intended for you by your Oversoul.

You exist as an extension of your Oversoul. You do not need techniques to activate or rearrange anything. Your life will bring you into perfect contact with the experiences needed for the fulfillment of your life's plan. Even those things that you might consider painful, unpleasant, or undesirable are still moving you toward the goal of completion.

If unpleasant feelings arise, allow them to flow through you. Do not block them or repress them. That does not mean you have to act on them. Just allow them to flow through you. A lot is being cleared at this time, and none of you is exempt from that. If you find yourself detaching more and more from the world around you, that is not a bad thing. That does not mean you are not a caring person. It just means you are becoming free from the influences of others as to how you should live your life. You can be your true self wherever you are. Just remember that you don't have to make a big noise about it. Just be it.

Things are beginning to intensify now and will continue to do so for the next few years, until all is complete. There has been a decision made to accelerate everything, which means that some of the things that we predicted would happen further out will now happen sooner. That means that BOTH kinds of things will be affected in this way — the things that you will be glad about and the other kind — the things that you might prefer didn't happen at all.

For caring people like yourselves, it could get very difficult to avoid getting caught up in the coming drama, so detach. If you have to unplug the television set, do that. Put your time and energy into those things that nourish you, that bring you peace, and let your love flow. Polarization and resistance are two things that will greatly increase your discomfort, so we give you this simple exercise to do when you discover yourself getting caught up in the drama and chaos:

Wherever you are, whatever you are doing, just close your eyes and focus on your breath. Obviously, if you are driving a car or operating machinery, you don't want to do this until you have pulled off the road or stopped the machine, but even then, as soon as you can, disconnect from what "hooked" you and got you caught up in the drama.

Close your eyes and focus on your breath. Deliberately take slow, deep breaths until you have regained a sense of your own self and are calm, grounded, and centered. Then very slowly open your eyes again and let yourself remain calm, grounded, and centered. Allow yourself to witness what is going on around you without getting caught up in it.

If you find yourself getting "hooked" again, repeat the exercise. You may have to do this several times but do it. If you are in the midst of a heated conversation, do it. If the person insists on continuing the conversation while you have your eyes closed, hold up a finger or your hand, to indicate "Wait." This will help both of you. You will be setting an example that they can follow. "Wait."

You always have three choices: to do something, to not do something, or to wait for clarity before acting. Wait for clarity. There is very little in life that can't wait. If someone is bleeding to death in front of you, you wouldn't want to wait very long, but you must attain clarity more quickly in such circumstances. It is important to attain clarity before acting. Deepening your breathing is telling yourself that you

Just close your eyes and focus on your breath.

are choosing calm over chaos. It is like a message to your body, "calm down." In the times ahead, it will be very important to remain calm, grounded, and centered.

There is nothing you can't handle if you remain rooted in the moment. We have spoken before about remaining rooted in the moment that is presenting, in what is also called the NOW. On Terra you will live in the NOW all of the time, so this is good practice for you. A moment is a unit of experience. It has a beginning, a middle, and an end. You can feel when something begins to rise in energy in your life. It presents, then it swells to a climax, and then it recedes and resolves.

That is a moment — from the time it arrives into your life until it recedes and resolves. Every moment arrives containing everything it needs for its completion. It unfolds perfectly, and even when you are in the midst of a challenging time, you can remain rooted in the moment and thus move through it with Grace. The more you can detach — the more you can ALLOW THE MOVEMENT — the more ease and comfort you will have in your journey through the days ahead.

Resistance of any kind blocks the flow. You can remain rooted in your truth without resisting the flow that occurs all around you. Think of a tree with a stream flowing around it. The tree remains in place when it is rooted and grounded. Be that tree. This is not the same as stubbornness or resistance. Be rooted in the moment. Be rooted in your truth.

Keep your inner ear turned on and listening at all times. It helps to trust the flow of your life. If you feel overwhelmed by the speed of everything, just let it flow. Become still in the midst of the movement that is going on all around you. Let it flow. You are a great being, experiencing yourself as a little body. You are a great being who has helped create vast portions of the existing reality. Breathe. Center. Ground. Bring calm to yourself as a choice. Choose calm. Choose peace. Choose serenity.

"The Coming Storm" is almost at your door. Let the winds rage all around you. Be peace in the midst of the storm. Do it for yourself and your loved ones. Be the gift that you are. You don't have to change anything. Be yourself. That's gift enough.

We leave you now, in peace and honor and blessing. Amen, Adonoy Sabayoth. We are the Hosts of Heaven.

NOTE: After receiving this Message, an astute reader mailed me a question about an apparent conflict in the material. She pointed out that in the first part of the Message, the Hosts found it almost humorous that the power elite's plans were met with so little resistance, and in the latter part of the Message, they encouraged us to not resist what was going on around us. I asked for a clarification, and this is what they gave me:

CLARIFICATION
(August 24, 2002)

A bit of clarification is in order, to clear up an apparent ambiguity in our most recent Message. As many of you may know, particularly astrologers, any particular quality or activity has the potential for a positive and a negative effect. For example, when you are considering the influences represented by a particular aspect in astrology, you can see the potentials for both a good quality and one that would not be considered good. Both can exist in the same aspect.

Just so with the concept of surrender. If you give up your resistance to a higher force in your life, the motives for your surrender must be considered in order to evaluate whether it is a positive thing or not, and the ultimate outcome is really what reveals the truth of it all.

In the first example we gave, where we made note of the agenda of those with yearnings for global totalitarian power, we found it humorous to see how many people were willing to surrender their personal freedoms in return for some comfort and maintenance of their status quo. You COULD say that the same thing is true if one is being asked to give up resistance to the Creator's agenda, but in the first case, you are surrendering to the wills of other people, who want something from you that meets their needs, and in the second case, you are being asked to surrender your experience of separation from the Creator, so that your personal will comes into better alignment with the divine purpose for your life. From our perspective, there is a very big difference, both in the motives involved and the outcomes.

In surrendering to the Will of the Creator, you actually create greater freedom for yourself because then you simply have to follow the flow of your life, instead of remaining locked into the limited possibilities of what you can imagine while still in the veiled state of consciousness. You open up the portals for more to appear in your life that would have been considered miraculous or magical when measured in your formerly limited view. In the state of giving up resistance to the flow of your life, you are moving out of fear into a state of Grace. You are surrendering your need to control everything in order to keep your fear at bay. You are moving more into acceptance and trust in the plan for your life.

In surrendering your freedoms to those in control of your world in return for the appearance of security and retention of some portion of the material aspects of your life that give you comfort, you have made what is often referred to as a "devil's bargain." While you appear to gain something in the short term, when the time comes to "pay the bill," you then discover the true cost of what it is you have given up. If you look at that kind of non-resistance, you will find that it has fear at its base. So it is important to look at the motives that underlie a given action or decision. Are they based in fear or are they based in trust in the plan for one's life?

However, since all things are playing out according to the plan for each life, it is impossible to say that even a devil's bargain does not ultimately serve a higher purpose. We find it humorous to see the globalists achieving their goals so easily because we know the outcome of the whole drama. In the end, those who made that trade of freedom for material security and possessions will lose everything they bartered for, and even those who hold the reins of power now will be defeated. It strikes us as ironic that everything has a tendency to work out in opposite ways to how they appear in the beginning.

Those who surrender their freedoms for material comfort will in the end lose both the freedoms AND the material comfort. Those who surrender their resistance to the divine plan for their life will ultimately "gain the kingdom," because they will be making the choices needed to come into their true inheritance, their true nature as the co-creators of this reality. In being willing to risk everything material, in the end they gain the ability to have and create anything material that they might desire, but from a state of total sovereignty rather than servitude.

We hope these remarks are helpful in clarifying any possible confusion created by our choice of words in the above Message, and we hope that they are also an impetus for you to reflect deeply on the choices that are presenting to you in each and every moment of your life. We are suggesting that you give your alignment with the Creator the highest priority.

In one of your scriptures, it counsels you to "Seek first the kingdom. Then all else will be added." In bartering personal freedom for short-term material comfort, one ultimately loses everything that is precious in life and one has placed one's heart in the wrong place. This is not a new idea, but we ask you to contemplate the deeper possibilities of these two aspects of surrender. Whom or what do you surrender to and why?

We leave you now, in peace and honor and blessing. Amen, Adonoy Sabayoth. We are the Hosts of Heaven.

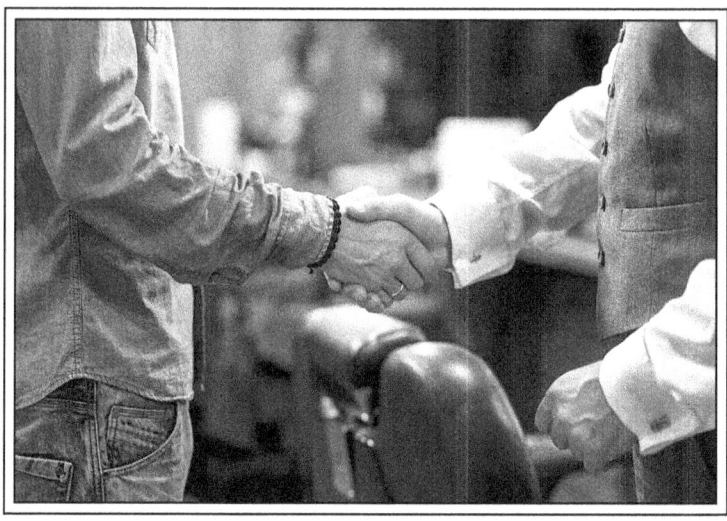

Surrendering your freedoms to those in control in return for the retention of some of the material aspects of your life

FAREWELL FOR A WHILE
September 15, 2002

We have asked to speak with you today because a threshold has been reached and it is now time to begin the Harvest. We will begin the Harvest with a relatively small group of you and then will return for still more. This will go on for the next few months until all of you who have not committed to staying on the ground will be lifted into another level and then some of you will come and go from that place for the time remaining until the Pole Shift.

This "holding zone" is not a place on or inside of the planet, but another place, on another frequency band, where you can be worked with more directly and facilitated in the completion of your own transformation. Our beloved messenger will be included in this first group, but will be one of the ones who comes and goes until all is complete, so you do not need to be concerned about her availability.

The "Booster Rocket" event will occur later this year,* but some of you will be lifted even before then. There is a scheduled time for each and every one of you, and when it comes your turn, you will know it with absolute clarity and certainty. You will not have to tell anyone anything, for if you need to inform anyone, we will give you that ability when the time comes. You see, there is no need to anticipate any of this. Just trust in the flow of your life and all will unfold perfectly, without harm to anyone.

---

*__NOTE:__ "Booster Rocket Time" (the "Shock and Awe" military action against Saddam Hussein's regime in Iraq) was originally scheduled to take place in September of 2002, but the preparations took longer than expected, so it didn't begin until March 20, 2003, at the end of the *astrological* year in which this prediction was made, not during its *calendar* year.

We have the ability to take people and return them to nearly the same moment in which they disappeared. When your transformation is complete, you will have the ability to change form to suit the circumstances, so if you need to look like you look at present, you will look like that. If it serves the greater good for you to look like something or someone else, you will look like that. You will all be very adapted to your circumstances, and as they flow and change, so you will also flow and change.

This communication will be the last one for Volume Two. There will be a hiatus in these Messages while this Harvest project proceeds, but Volume Three will be given when it is time for that. It will be different in content, tone, and information than these first two, and that is all we will say about that for now. So please do not be asking for the next Message. There will be a time of no Messages for a while, as that is part of the Plan.

In the interim, many things will be playing out on the planetary surface, and it is precisely for that reason that we will be silent for a while. Those on the surface have to experience those times in certain ways, in keeping with the plan for their life, and they must do so unaided by us in order to have the fullest possible experience for themselves. It would only diminish the intensity and richness of those times if we were there, commenting on every development.

These two volumes will be available, for those who have "eyes to see" and "ears to hear." They will suffice to give the roadmap for those times. Then, when things have played out to a certain degree, we will again be heard from, in order to prepare people for the final stages of the drama and its conclusion. Our counsel to you would be to listen within at all times, during all activities in which you find yourself.

Some animals have the ability to point their ears in different directions independently. We suggest you do the same. Point one ear outward, to receive the data from your environment, and point one ear inward, constantly listening to the whisperings of your intuition and "knowing." That inner voice is quiet and subtle most of the time. It is not like it is shouting at you. It is more gentle than that, so you must be able to hear it above the noise that surrounds you.

When your time comes, you will know it. Some of you know that you will be on the ground through the years ahead because your particular part in the drama requires that. Do not feel either more or less special because of that. Everyone is totally equal in their importance with regard to the Plan. No voice will carry more weight than any other. No life is more or less important than any other. To think or feel otherwise is a matter of the separated self or ego.

Some of you still are wrestling with your self-worth issues, and need to make these kinds of comparisons, but in the end, you are who you came to be, and the best thing is to be the best expression of that intention that you can.

So now, all things will be coming to a head and moving toward the eventual conclusion. The acceleration is upon you already and will become even more intense as time passes and the tasks surface for completion. You might imagine a person with a clipboard, studiously marking off each "task" in a list of things that have to occur. Each thing must take place, and each thing WILL take place in its perfect time and sequence.

Imagine a person with a clipboard, studiously marking off each "task" in a list of things that have to occur.

We feel a certain excitement in contemplating that this day has arrived. The measures have been taken and each one of you has been "fitted" with the necessary "equipment" to complete the rest of your journey through the remaining years of 3D Earth and beyond. All of the resources — both inner and outer — that you will require are now stored up and available to be used.

A vast amount of preparation has gone into this effort, spanning thousands of years. You have experienced many lives in order to be perfectly equipped for this one and what now comes. It is truly a "grand finale," and great opportunity for the richness and complexity of all of the themes and threads that will be playing out from now on. Regardless of where your life leads you, we promise you one thing: it will not be boring! This is an incredible time to be in a body on planet Earth, and you will have much to reflect upon when it has all drawn to a close.

So in a sense, today we are saying "farewell for a while." We promise you that we will be back when it is time for us to do so. For those of you who are moving on to complete your transformation, it will be a time when you find yourselves actually among us, face to face. For those who remain on the ground, you will be assisted directly by those who complete their transformation and come and go from that point on.

They will appear in your midst at the needed times and will disappear when that assistance is no longer needed. It will be impossible to know from day to day what to expect, as there will be many surprises on many fronts. We assure you that each and every person will have the experiences they are supposed to have, as chosen by their Oversoul. There are no accidents, and there are no real losses, only change.

There is absolute certainty that each and every one of you will reach the destination chosen by your Oversoul, and will do so perfectly — in the right time, in the right way. None of you will be left alone, regardless of the form your assistance and support team takes. You will meet others like yourself, and you will gradually form small clusters of like-minded people.

It will happen naturally. There is no need to create predesigned and preconceived communities. Follow the flow of your life. Remain rooted in the present. Deal fully with what presents to you in the moment. Remember that a moment is a unit of experience, not a unit of time. Live in the moment, moment by passing moment, and you will find yourself in exactly the right place at the right time.

In saying farewell for now, know that we are always with you, waking and sleeping, and we look forward to the time when you are ALL back with us once again.

Amen, Adonoy Sabayoth. We are the Hosts of Heaven.

VOLUME THREE

THE LAST DAYS
September 21, 2004

All right, now. We have asked to speak to you today because it is time to begin preparations for the final phase of things with regard to 3D Earth. Our silence for the last two years has accomplished much for those who have followed our prior instruction to go within, but now it is time for this third and final volume in this series of Messages to begin. We will time this last series of Messages so that they follow unfolding developments both on your planet and around her.

There are many civilizations represented here, both within time and outside of it. Past, present, and future co-exist in the timeless NOW, and so do we and so do you, as well as everything created and uncreated. The whole potential is a rich sea or broth, containing everything within it.

In the phenomenal world that you perceive with your physical and subtle senses, there is much turbulence at this time. Deep undercurrents swirl beneath the surface, and anger and pain bubble up despite all attempts to keep them at bay. The frozen emotions of times past are melting and thawing and adding to the rich mix that is present now. Echoes of past themes explored are everywhere to be seen; although more recent memories are easier to recognize, virtually every historic period is being re-visited and even those you would label "pre-historic" are resurfacing at this time, particularly with regard to the experiences had at the hands of those you would refer to as reptilians.

These are NOT the dinosaurs of your planet's past, but those beings who visited your planet in a humanoid form that resembled the dinosaurs, particularly those of the Tyrannosaurus species. They came to exploit the planet's rich resources, both animate and inanimate, to further their goals for domination throughout the galaxy.

We wish to emphasize that these happenings occurred many millennia ago, but there is a cellular and species memory of that time carried within your present bodies, and some have incorrectly attributed that memory to the actions of beings currently inhabiting bodies on your planet. The memory and understanding are correct; attributing them to the present timeframe is not.

Those times were long ago, yet their effect on the present and the immediate future is unmistakable. There is a darkness gathering now. It is an outpicturing of those ancient times, held deeply within the memory core of your planet and species, and it must be re-experienced as it is flushed out during this time of personal and planetary cleansing.

We have spoken before of a "last look around," in which we counseled you to take a last look around at the world you were accustomed to living in. Now it will be a time for another "last look," one that will be much more terrible to contemplate, for this species of reptilians live in a constant state of agony and rage, unable to find peace within themselves no matter what they do or accomplish. Their hunger for peace is insatiable, and yet they act in ways that destroy peace unceasingly, both for themselves and everything they touch upon.

What this means is that your planet, in flushing out these embedded memories, will witness and experience the outpicturing of that embedded agony and rage, and it will do so in ways that affect all of the creatures and lifeforms on the planet. Nothing will be spared as the clouds of war and geophysical events boil forth everywhere.

Since everything on the planet is so interconnected, everything will be affected in some way and to some degree, especially economically, but in the end, it will all come to an end, and then we will be among you physically, tending to your wounds and taking you to places of shelter until our ships will come for you to take you to your next stop in the journey to Terra.

This volume will help you chart your course through the dark days ahead, to give you encouragement to make it through those times, and to let you know that we are ever at your side, surrounding you with our love and our protection. Those of you who are destined for Terra (and everything else upon the planet, as well as the planet herself) are precious to us, but you are especially precious to us because you are truly our brothers and sisters and share equally in our heritage and status in the larger Plan. It is primarily for you that we are here, and it is for you that we give these Messages now.

Everyone else has a different destiny path, and everyone else has their own messengers to guide them to where they are going. Many are leaving now, just as many have always left at all times, but those who leave now and those who will leave later on will not return to THIS planet. Incarnational patterns will be fulfilled according to the destinies chosen by the Oversouls, and each will continue to explore along one of the lines of destiny that will present at the "quantum leap" into the new Creation.

The final days are now here. They are no longer in the "future." You are living in them — now. Take a moment to register this. Reflect on it. Treasure this moment of relative quiet that hangs heavy over you, because soon you will hear the thuds and screams of war, echoing all over the planet. It will begin in the Middle East, but in the end, no nation will be protected or isolated or exempt.

It will be a terrible time, as measured in human emotions, but it will also be a time of endings so that a new beginning can emerge. Those who pass from their bodies will be free of pain and suffering, and those who remain would do well to remember this. There is no way to stop the cleansing. It is ordained from the highest levels so that the planet can complete her cleansing from the past she has hosted and take her rightful place in the heavens as the jewel she is — clean, sparkling, shining with light — and the dark clouds of war banished forever from her surface.

These wars that are coming originated with the agony of the reptilians who planted those seeds in the emerging species that they created through their manipulation of the genetic structures with which they worked. They enslaved many of their own kind to this end, and there are females among you who have cellular memories as "breeders" for their genetic experiments. Although these experiments occurred in the distant past, they left their mark and their wounds, and there is not a one of you who read these lines that has not been affected by those times and everything that sprang forth from them.

So, as terrible as the wars will appear, they are really the cleansing of those wounds from so long ago, and for you who go to Terra, all that will be left in their wake is blissful surrender and peace, joy, and love. You will be beyond all of the suffering then, and it will have been worth it to go through these terrible times to get there, but they are still to be endured.

Soon, your newscasters will not have to scramble for things to report on. The weather of this year will be tame compared to what is coming later on. The wars have begun, albeit on a small scale, and while politicians make noises and grunts about the state of things, you will notice that no one is really doing anything but making noises and grunts about the state of things. No one is coming to terms with the real issues, and while slogans and simplistic summaries abound, nothing is said about the real causes and even less about solutions to them.

You see, everything is just as it should be. The long experiment of the last 4.5 billion years is nearly over, and there really is not much new occurring now. All of it has been explored and allowed, but the novelty is running out. Apart from some scientific advances, there has not been anything new in many years, and the old institutions of government and law have nearly died of suffocation under the accumulation of so much human debris over the centuries.

Every generation, in seeking to correct the "errors" of the past, has compounded them with new errors. It is true that some people have been able to see past the dust of the stampeding masses, but most are blind and will remain that way, because they are not supposed to be any other way. Everything and everyone is just as they are supposed to be, so that every niche — every part of the drama — is fulfilled.

Look at your habitation patterns. If everyone had the same tastes, everyone on the planet would be crowded into just one location, and the rest of the planet would be devoid of human life. Yet, each of you has certain places that naturally appeal to you more than others, and if you find yourself in a place that you don't like, you can pick up and move to another if you want to strongly enough. So, in like manner, there is a distribution across destinations and "futures" to live.

Not everyone is going to the same place, and every niche will be filled, but not overfilled. No one is better or higher. Everyone exists so the Creator can experience all of the experiences that are possible within the parameters of a Creation. Even though stars are always being formed and planets being birthed, the parameters for this Creation have been fully explored, and so it is time for an entirely new Creation. Consciousness will be seeded across an entirely new landscape, but nothing of the old can be taken into the new except essence, so the effects that have been absorbed across the millennia must be neutralized and erased, and that is what is taking place now.

For the human species, the agony implanted here so long ago by the reptilians must be expunged and it will be expunged by re-visiting it and re-living it. It is for this reason that we have emphasized the necessity of detaching from the drama, seeking the quiet and peace of deep ocean, and maintaining a place of peace within yourselves, no matter what is going on around you. We are with you at every step, every turn in the road, but you must do your part in this also.

We suggest that you seek out others of like mind and interact with them as much as possible to reinforce what must be done in the face of the calamitous events that are bearing down upon your world. You can be sources of comfort for each other, and if you can quiet yourself enough to feel us, you can seek our assistance also. Simply ask for our presence in your lives and we will be there. Ask to be able to feel our presence, and we will do what we can to help you feel our presence.

We are ALWAYS with you, but some of you are not doing enough with your feeling sense to know we are there, so if this is true for you, it will help you if you do some work to increase your sensitivity to our presence. Remember, this is not a spoken communication that you are seeking, but rather an increased sense of presence. If you seek to hear words, there are many who might be happy to respond to your request, but it might not be us! Be content with feeling our presence and let your interaction with words be directed to others of like mind upon your planet.

We shall have more to say on this topic as we go along, but for now, we leave you now in peace, honor and blessing. Amen, Adonoy Sabayoth. We are the Hosts of Heaven.

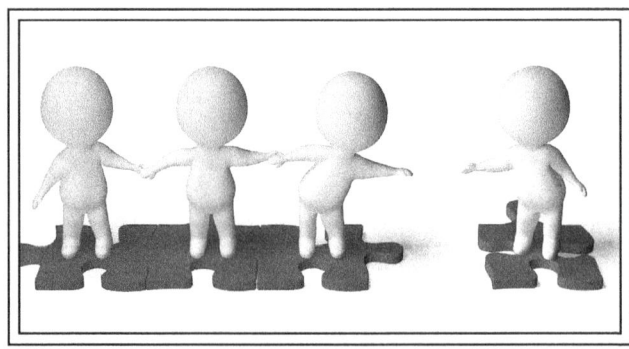

Seek out others of like mind and interact with them as much as possible.

WE ARE CRUCIBLES FOR TRANSFORMATION
November 1, 2004

All right, now. We have asked to speak to you because of where you are in time with regard to what unfolds now. Today is the day before the US presidential elections. There is deep division in the world, and it will become even more evident beginning tomorrow and all the tomorrows that follow until it is all complete. We have spoken before of the increase in polarization taking place, and we wish to remind you that all of this was anticipated and is part of the overall Plan.

So, what can you expect in the near and farther term? First of all, the lifting proceeds and now that you are traversing the middle layers of the frequency shift, the cleansing will be more noticeable for everyone and everything inhabiting the planet. Those feelings and emotions that have lain buried or repressed are now bubbling up to the surface and felt and expressed.

Your bodies are cleansing themselves of toxins — toxic emotions, toxic thoughts, toxic substances, toxic relationships — and you will find yourselves being forced to change some of your habits that you have not yet dealt with. Addictions of all types will intensify, as a way of bringing attention to what has not been dealt with yet, so if you have any places within yourself where you have been in denial or suppressing feelings by distracting yourselves, you will find the internal pressure for change building up until it is expressed and dealt with in one way or another.

Those who carry a lot of unresolved pain will be forced to move through it or literally die. Many will be doing the latter, so when you read of their passing, know that they are finally out of their pain, and be relieved at their relief. Many who die will be young because it is mostly the young adults that are sent against one another in war, and there will be more and more war as the days, weeks, and months proceed. But they, too, will be beyond pain, and so their loved ones will grieve, but those who have crossed over will not be in pain anymore. Their wounds will be healed instantly, as the bodies they inhabit after they have crossed over will be whole again.

Each person who sheds a body now will find themselves in another, in another plane of existence, and will have much help in moving toward their next destination. Those of you who are going to be "on the ground" through to the end will see much of death and dying, but it is all just the means of moving on to the next step, the next phase of existence, which is a never-ending process.

But there is good news, also, for in the intensely accelerated times that follow, each day brings you closer to the end of your "long walk" through time and closer to the remembering of your joy. You will be coming into contact and proximity with more of your own kind as you naturally move in response to the pressures of change, and you will find that in the wake of having shed your more dysfunctional aspects, you will feel weary but also more whole.

For millennia, humans have been kept in darkness and separation, and that is coming to an end, also — or at least for those who are making the journey to Terra. The greatest number of people are heading toward other destinations, and so their journey will wear a different face, involve a different process, and emerge in a different place. But for those of you who are destined for Terra, your return to what you were before is at hand, and this will ask for more surrender on your part — surrender of your notions of who you really are, what is possible, and of limitation in general.

Now is a good time for you to begin to contemplate what it would be like to be totally whole again — what it would be like to be able to create anything you wanted to create, what it would be like to be totally free to be and to have anything you wanted to be or to have. What would you want to create? How would you want to be? What would you want to have? How would you want to live? Those ideas will naturally come from within what you know now, but over time, allow those ideas to change as *you* change — and you are ALL changing, whether you are aware of it or not.

Look back at how you were just two years ago. How did it feel back then? How different do you feel now? Don't judge by what you see in a mirror. The important changes are within, hidden safely away from other eyes. You ARE changing — daily. We are helping you to change. Waking and sleeping, you are being "worked on." Be glad that the change is so gradual that it is only noticeable after the passage of a great deal of time. Things are moving very quickly on the inner levels, as compared with movement outside of you, but everything is moving steadily toward the goal of completing this round of existence and preparing for another, totally new reality.

You may be impatient for it all to complete, but it would be much too much to bear all at once. The changes are happening steadily, but in small increments, so that integrity of mind, body, and emotions is preserved. There are many surprises in store for all of you, and those who align with these Messages will have much asked of them, but they have all of the natural abilities built within them to meet the challenges that lie ahead for all. We wish to reiterate the necessity of taking care of yourself during these times. That is not a selfish thing. It is the highest service you can perform.

You are pioneers, preparing to create a new world for others to be born into. Just as a pregnant woman must take special care of herself as her pregnancy proceeds, you must take special care of yourself as your "pregnancy" that will bring forth new life of a different kind also proceeds. It does not matter if you are old or young, male or female. You who are heading toward Terra are all "pregnant" with the seed from which a new civilization will come. This new life within you is YOUR new life, and you will all bear new lives — have children of your own as you near the end of your time on Terra. You are the progenitors of the next phase of human existence, returning to your former status as the carriers of the true Adamic seed.

This is a template for a form that was the original creation of the creator-gods — the elohim who were the first product of the First Thought of the Creator Itself. It is this template that is referred to as being "in the image" of the "gods." Elohim is a plural word and [it] refers to those beings who were the first Creation of the Creator. They are not embodied beings, but rather vast fields of self-aware, intelligent energy, similar in many respects to the Creator Itself, but finite rather than infinite. That is the chief difference.

The true Adamic model is not what you are today, but it is what you will become — what you will physically manifest as the "gods" and "goddesses" you will become. This is the seed you carry within you, so take good care of yourself. You are precious vessels for the new race that will emerge as you emerge into your next body. You are all quite beautiful now, as we would see you, but you will all be quite beautiful then, as you will see yourselves, and it will not be just "inner vision" that will perceive this, as it is now.

Your first task was to come into the bodies you inhabit now and forget who you were. You took on the "veil" of forgetfulness, although many of you still had faint recall of what you knew and what you had been like before. You have done that very well! Your next task was to take on the many versions of pain on this planet.

Some of you have had more difficulty, more challenges than others, but there is not one of you who has not experienced some loss of one kind or another. For those who had an easier time, you simply came to the same understanding more easily than those who went through more challenging times. But in the end, you are the same in one important respect: you stand in the world with your eyes open. In fact, many of you cannot understand why the others around you do not SEE what you see. You cannot understand why they can't see what is obvious to you, but all of that is as it should be.

Remember that the Creator wanted to experience EVERYTHING, so the Creator created everything with which to experience Itself through Its creations. Each of you is unique, and so is every other created thing. It is only through the uniqueness that everything is explored. Every possible combination is explored through the uniqueness of each created thing. No two snowflakes are identical. No two entities are identical. It is through these differences that the richness of experience occurs. So the fact that you "see" differently than others do is just because you ARE different than others ARE. It is all just the way it should be.

You may not think that how things play out are what you would have wanted, but it is all perfect, seen within the larger Plan. If indeed it is all to come down around you, then the people in power have to be the ones who will be capable of doing that. YOU would do it differently, of that we are sure! But it is also the reason that you are NOT in the seat of power, because you WOULD do it differently.

And you WILL do it differently, but not in THIS world, and not at THIS time. Your job is to simply BE HERE, holding the vision of something else. Through the principle of resonance, each one of you who is "ringing" with the tone of Terra, multiplies that effect and brings into being a template for a different kind of reality altogether.

You may ask why it has to be this way — why you had to come HERE to create the pathway to THERE, to THAT way of being and living. The answer is simple on the surface, but profound if you stop to consider the ramifications it implies. You are not being born into bodies on Terra. That is reserved for the next generation — the next group of elohim that will take over the reins from you. You have to be HERE because it is from within your present bodies that the Adamic human will emerge again.

We have said that you are lightning rods, grounding the higher Light into the planet, and that is true. However, you are also a BRIDGE between this world and the next, a living vessel of transformation, a crucible within which the dross is converted into gold.

You are all the alchemist's dream, but before a transformation can take place, there has to be some "dross" to transform. And that's why you had to come here, take on the "imperfect" bodies you inhabit, take on the "imperfect" thoughts and emotions that you all took on in one way or another, so that they could then be transformed.

You see, you are both a bridge and a pathcutter — to borrow a phrase from *Star Trek*, you are going where no "man" has gone before. And by this, we are talking about the human species as it presently exists on your planet. Each of you came from another time, another plane of existence, to be here now. You came to embody these imperfections so that you could transform them into something else, and by doing that, you create a template — a model in the consciousness that others can fit themselves to, like a standard against which they can measure themselves and align to over time.

It will take generations for those who do not accompany you to Terra at this time to incarnate there, but they will eventually. Terra is the "next step" for those who are heading toward the positive polarity. There is another path, another "next step" for those who are heading toward the negative polarity, and you can see some of those who will be the bridges toward that destination in seats of power today. The real power brokers are behind the scenes, pulling the strings and playing off the ambitions of those who are more visible, but we will not dwell on that today. We want you to appreciate just who YOU are, why you are here, why it has to be this way, and what it is you have to do now.

Pay attention to all the places within you that need healing. These are the crude materials for your transformation. Each of you carries some part of the patterns of pain that have characterized the human race during most of its tenure on this planet. You don't all carry the same parts or aspects because the entire body of work is a team effort. No one person needs to do it all, but collectively it all gets done.

Your job now is to transform those parts of you where you are wounded, to heal them, and to become whole. You don't need to go running to seminars, buy potions, or spend a lot of money in pursuit of this. The greatest part will come naturally if you listen within yourself and are willing to be totally honest with yourself about your "failings." Coming together with other people of like mind will also help, as you share the common goals and common journey; there is great support and comfort in knowing you are not alone, that you are not "the only one" who is experiencing what you are experiencing.

There may be appropriate practitioners to assist you, appropriate aids and tools to help you in this, but it is so important to quiet yourself enough to discern what is appropriate and what is not. You and only you can tell what is right for you.

There are many "wizards" who proclaim that they have "the answer."

There are many "wizards" who proclaim that they have "the answer." Beware of them and stay clear of them. Only YOU have your answers. By that, we mean that only YOU can FEEL when something is right for you and when it is not. But you cannot feel any of this if you are filled with chatter or you are being run by your fear. This is why we have stressed going within, meditating regularly or doing whatever it is that allows you that space to listen clearly to what your body is telling you.

FEEL, feel, feel. Feeling is a physical thing, not an emotion. When something feels "off," trust that and don't try to convince yourself otherwise, no matter how persuasive someone else may sound. You are your own authority, and you are sovereign beings. You exist solely to be who YOU are, who and what you came to be, and there is no other person like you or who can know what is right for you.

When someone tries to convince you that their way is THE way, take the "highway" instead and leave! There will be more and more loud voices shouting in the din, but the only voice you need to listen to is the quiet one within you. Do what you need to do, go where you need to go, create what you need to create to be able to listen clearly within the quiet place inside of you. Make inner listening a constant practice. It will help you find your way through the tumult ahead. Listen and feel. Listen and feel. That is how you will chart your course — moment by moment, day by day.

We will have more to say on all of these topics, but for now, we leave you in peace, in honor, and with blessings for your willingness to do what you are doing. Amen, Adonoy Sabayoth. We are the Hosts of Heaven.

When someone tries to convince you that their way is THE way, take the "highway" instead and leave!

ENERGY PACKETS AND THE CONSENSUS REALITY
December 30, 2004

All right, now. It is time for us to comment on the road that lies directly ahead. First of all, let us speak about energy packets. When enough people think something is true, it forms a "consensus reality" that takes on a life of its own. It really is an energy packet that possesses its own identity and self-awareness, just as you do.

For example, your geographical maps are a form of consensus reality. You tend to agree that these imaginary lines called "boundaries" are real things and they are birthed into reality as an entity just as a baby is physically birthed and takes on an identity pattern that distinguishes it from every other baby that is born. Just so with the entities you call cities, counties, states, and countries. Each of these has a character that personalizes it and makes it different from the energy packet of every other comparable entity.

If you have ever traveled from one entity to another, perhaps you have noticed that as you cross this imaginary line, the quality of the energy changes. You can feel that Los Angeles feels different than New York, Chicago, or Kansas City. You can feel (if you have traveled more widely) that the US feels different than Europe or Japan. Each of these is an energy packet that is created through the "mind" of the consensus reality, and it is equally true with the entity of "time."

Most of you who are reading this Message relate to the Gregorian calendar, although, as we have pointed out in the past, there are other calendar systems in operation. Each of these calendar systems mark out periods of time in just the same way that cities, counties, states and countries are marked out and defined by imaginary constructs of consensus reality. You call them seconds, minutes, hours, days, weeks, months, and years.

One of the main determinants of time measurements is the mechanism whereby one individual exchanges units of agreed upon value with another individual in the practice you refer to as commerce. This individual can be a single person interacting with another person, such as buying a watermelon at a roadside stand, or it can be as complex as whole trading systems that network the transactions of many individuals, such as your stock and commodities exchanges. Whole countries can exchange with other countries, also, through the authority given by the consensus reality to the respective government units involved.

Most people take all of this so much for granted that they do not even realize they are operating in a fictional world. It's all made up, and the only reason it works is that everyone agrees to it being "the way it is." It's just a lot of energy packets, being maintained by the agreement of so many people that that is what's real.

But there is also another mind at work — the Mind of the Creator — and THAT mind is the only one that is truly "real." It creates energy packets, too, and as one aligns more and more with the Mind of the Creator and begins to work more in harmony with THAT instead of the consensus reality of people, then things change in many different ways.

The more one is aligned with the TRUE reality of the "real," the more one falls away from seeing and experiencing the way one used to and this can be somewhat disorienting at first. However, as time proceeds and one becomes more acclimated to what is "real" as opposed to fiction, then one begins to see with "different eyes."

One begins to experience a shift in identity that can be quite confusing if one seeks to re-engage with the identity one has understood most of one's life. You lose interest in the things that source outside of you and you begin to recognize and respond to those things that source from within you — the gifts of the Creator that you carry simply because you ARE the Creator-in-expression, not because you have earned them.

Fears come up because this is such a radical thing to do. It goes counter to the consensus reality, but it is the consensus reality that is "made up" and is not real. However, in your cellular and species memory, many of you have deep scars from incurring the wrath of the consensus reality when it is challenged and it does not wish to change. These energy packets (such as the consensus reality), being self-aware, can resist change as much as any embodied being can. You see this in your institutions, your governments, your armed forces ... in every aspect of human endeavor, these energy packets strive to maintain themselves, much as your "ego" strives to maintain you in your present form.

You are pioneers in that you came to forge a path to a totally new world — not one that is a refurbished version of the present one, but something that has not existed at all, except in your memories of the "future." The world you want to create runs totally counter to the present consensus reality and would be considered a "danger" to the present system — an "enemy of the [present] state [of affairs]." How can you REMEMBER something that has not yet been experienced? You can't. You remember this because you ALREADY HAVE experienced this world! You have come here, embodied here, and carried that memory with you, and you are awakening from your amnesia now.

What this "looks like" is that you feel more and more alien to the world you perceive around you, and your longing grows to return to what you ALREADY know is "how it should be." Every one of you who resonates with these Messages from deep within your core self has already "been there, done that" (to use your expression), but it is the energy packet of "home."

You are on the present Earth as messengers (angel means "messenger") and the message you carry, coded within your very cells, is the message of the "good news" of Terra — the world that lies ahead. By your being here, by your carrying this new tone, this energy packet within you, you are the seeds of that new world, and you carry within you all of the knowledge of how to live that energy packet, but it's not something that you can give to anyone else.

You won't GIVE this knowledge to anyone who does not already have it. You carry it within you, and collectively you sound a tone — a frequency pattern — that creates a new vibratory pattern. That pattern runs totally against the institutions and invested patterns of the consensus reality, so if it were possible, the consensus reality would try to keep that new pattern from existing.

It is not because the consensus reality is "evil" or wants to control you. It's simply that it wants to perpetuate itself. That's the job of that energy packet — to perpetuate and maintain itself — and to do so, it must defend itself against all challenges OR change and adapt and incorporate those changes into its new definition of self. But change is not easy when there is so much energy invested in what "has always been." Just as people will resist change until there is much more to gain by changing than by continuing to resist change, the consensus reality will resist change until there is much more to be gained by adapting to new models of thought.

Why do we bring this up at this point in time? Because you are approaching one of those boundaries we spoke of in the beginning of this discussion. Depending on where you live, in a very short time, you will cross one of those boundaries that you agree upon, called a "year." This time, the year we are referring to is the one used in the Gregorian calendar — the one that says 2005 is about to begin. We refer to THIS particular calendar because it is the one that is used for global commerce and it is the interests of global commerce that are the most rigorously defended among the possible competing interests and priorities within the consensus reality.

"Commerce is king" in the consensus reality, and all other values and goals are secondary to and dependent on that. Commerce is the engine that keeps the consensus reality ticking along, that keeps people willing to accept many things in order to maintain and improve their material position in a material world. All of that is about to change and change radically.

The year you refer to as 2005 is going to see many upheavals. The purpose of these upheavals is not a human one, but an energetic one. The planet has reached a place where it is actively throwing off the "thoughtforms" or energy packets of the past, particularly those energy packets that the human species has created through its consensus reality over time. These upheavals will directly challenge the consensus reality, and much chaos will ensue. At first, the response will be to try to hang on to what WAS — to preserve it at all costs. But the pressure for change is relentless now, and all things that will not bend and adapt will break instead. In the coming year, everything will undergo the first "contractions" associated with the birthing of this new world.

Keep in mind that everything we say is only relevant to the timeline that leads to Terra. All of the people passing from YOUR world continue on another timeline that is not perceptible to you, so the many thousands that just "died" did not die at all, but rather continue on another of the timelines. As they have disappeared from YOUR world, so YOU have disappeared from theirs. It's all in divine order and part of the separating out of the other destiny paths.

These "contractions" will challenge the commerce of the world in many ways.

These "contractions" will challenge the commerce of the world in many ways. There will be shortages of foods, disasters that outstrip the ability of treasuries to cope with them, and financial duress that has not been seen before, not even in the "Great Depression." The consensus reality will be challenged on every front, but because everything is knit together by the global commerce system, everything that happens from now on will be a challenge to that commerce and no part of it will be unaffected. No country exists in isolation from all others, so all countries will be affected, although the details will be very individual, and each person will have a different story to tell.

Those of you who are destined to go to Terra have a very special job to do. You have to maintain yourselves in such a way that you continue to sound and expand on the frequency pattern of Terra. You carry Terra within you. You KNOW HER already. When someone describes Terra to you, you recognize her as the child of your own longing.

Your dream/vision of Terra is your dream/vision of "home," and your job is to cultivate the reality of home within you for a time, until it is time to bring it with you and create it on the new planet that Earth will become. We will be giving you "Terra lessons" that you will recognize as being what is really "right" to do, but you need to understand that it runs counter to everything in the consensus reality — so much so that the consensus reality appears to have everything "backwards." The priorities are all wrong, and you sense that and know that, but until now, not only did you not have an explanation for that, you also did not know what to do about it.

The next few Messages will have to do with very "radical" ideas — radical in that they counter the consensus reality. You must follow these teachings in private, within your own minds, hearts, and bodies. You must continue to live IN the world at the same time you are creating a new world within yourselves, so you must become skilled at "riding two horses" at the same time for a while.

You must continue to function in your world, to provide for yourselves, and at the same time make the time to begin creating your "garden" within yourselves. You will find this easiest if you can be in touch with others of the same inclination, but you can also find support within yourself if you have the courage to listen to your own inner voice and phase out of listening to the voices of everyone who would tell you to do otherwise.

Keep in mind that there will be a lot of resistance from those around you. They will cling to what they know as long as they can, and even argue with you about it and make you "wrong" for what you know, rather than consider what we are saying here. All meaningful change has been resisted at the time of its inception, and this time it is no different. It is the collective bonding between you, the collective sounding of the note of Terra that will blaze the path home.

This is not a rescue mission. This is the work of pioneers for a new world, and you are on Earth to embody and carry out this job. It has to be done on the ground, within the Earth's aura/ionosphere. It cannot be done "from above." You are the "ground crew" for blazing a path to somewhere else, but it has to be done from where you "are" to where you are "going," a place that you already have been.

We shall have more to say on this topic as we go along, but for now, we leave you now in peace, honor and blessing. Amen, Adonoy Sabayoth. We are the Hosts of Heaven.

TERRA LESSON #1: OF CABBAGES AND KINGS
January 21, 2005

> "The time has come," the Walrus said,
> "To talk of many things:
> Of shoes, and ships, and sealing-wax;
> Of cabbages and kings."
> — "The Walrus and the Carpenter," by Lewis Carroll

All right, now. The time has come to speak "of cabbages and kings." In other words, to use your expression, to get down to the "nitty-gritty" of the "op."

If you were to step back and see recent developments from a larger perspective — from that of a movement of ENERGIES rather than the details (the SYMPTOMS of the energies), you would see that all of this is an indication of further movement toward the poles of one's destiny/destination. In a sense, all of it was pre-ordained before embodiment took place, so each of these players is acting out of their "God-given" role. You have already seen this in "The God Game," but now it is time to really LIVE that in your life.

You must — for your own sake and the sake of the "op" — detach, step back, and simply sing your note. Speak your truth when asked, but do not attach in any way to a particular outcome in any situation. In interacting with someone who does not have a clear focus, or is confused, or is conflicted, ask, "What do you want for yourself?" Not, "What is your alignment?"

In pursuing what they desire — what they want — they will be homing in on their destiny within the larger whole. THEIR desire is an expression of the Creator's desire. In order to experience everything, the Creator needs all of these different players in order to explore all possible choices.

Each person carries within them the compass that will direct their journey and — because they are "blindfolded" — the seeking can appear clumsy at times, but even that clumsiness serves the timing of events within the context of the whole. Tiny movements, small choices, are amplified through intersection with other movements in the same general direction. To the extent a clear pattern emerges, the alignment with others becomes more coherent, and therefore more powerful. Each individual is NATURALLY drawn to what is "theirs" — in the perfect way and at the perfect time in keeping with the whole — and the wonder of it is that they experience this as a discovery, similar to putting your hand in your pocket for your keys and drawing out a large amount of money instead.

Each person carries within them everything needed to get to where they are going, and for all of the steps along the way. The "new song" was written before the world was formed. Each of you were aligned with each other then; each of you is coming into alignment with each other now. [Sara] was simply the person with the tuning fork. That's all. She is not meant to LEAD you. She merely sounds the note you are waiting to hear and you begin humming in response because it is inherently YOUR note also.

You must understand that no one can change what they came to be, what they came to do, what they came to experience. Their life is ALREADY written, and the "author" is the Oversoul, in the employ of the Creator's design and desire. Therefore, YOUR job is simply to continue sounding the note. If people do not "hear," simply sound it again — and again and again and again.

This note will evoke a response in everyone who comes in contact with it. For those whose inner tuning forks are set to the same note, they will be drawn into resonance with that note and begin vibrating with

316   OPERATION TERRA: A JOURNEY THROUGH SPACE AND TIME

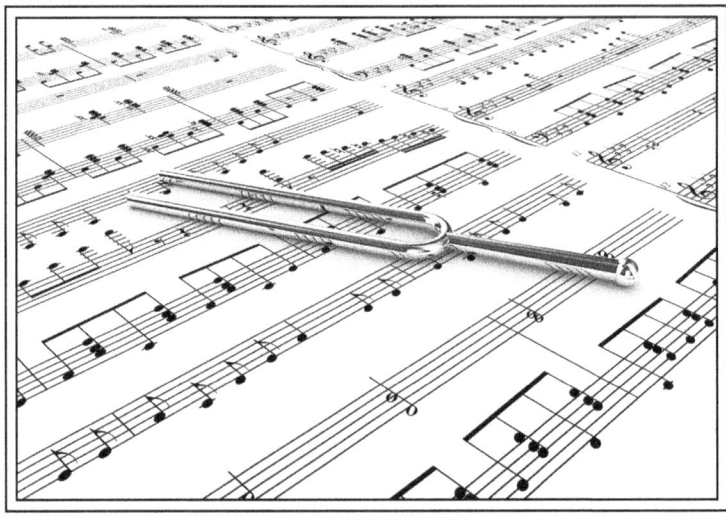

The "new song" was written before the world was formed. Sara simply carries the tuning fork.

YOUR job is simply to continue sounding the note.

it, too — perhaps tentatively at times, but eventually with growing trust and confidence that it is THEIR note, too.

We emphasize that this is simply the way it IS. No one can change their note. Some will hear your note and be drawn to it, thinking it MIGHT be theirs, and while it may be similar, their note is sufficiently different that eventually — because they DO NOT come into full resonance with it — because it does not vibrate through them and awaken THEIR song, their passion to sing, to open to that note and let it reverberate through them without resistance to it, they will move on according to the strength of their seeking. Some will be "lukewarm" and never find their note, precisely because that is also a valid experience, and the Plan for their life is that they DO NOT "find," but must continue to seek, through other incarnations in other space/time environments.

Now we come to the last point: the polar opposites. The more strongly a note is polarized to ONE polarity, the more it annoys or irritates someone of the opposite polarity. In other words, the more a note is opposite another, the more strongly they create discordance when coming into contact with each other. The response, though, is different in its expression.

If one is of a positive polarity, based in cooperation, the response would be to stand together, sing the common note with joy in the singing of it, and simply send the note — the song — out into the universe — freely given, freely sung, without resistance or attachment to effect. That is what you and "yours" (your kind) are created to do, and in so doing, your note — the note of peace, joy, and love — will resound and literally precipitate a WORLD into form that formerly existed only as a potential in the Mind of God.

However, the opposite polarity to yours — the negative polarity — is based in fear and competition — in "power over," rather than pure power from within, and so its response is predictable from the perspective of THAT polarity: they MUST strive with you, to assert their power over you, to POSSESS your power, or to try to destroy you if there is no other option.

The more you sing your note, the more you bring forth "attacks" from those of the negative polarity. They are just being who THEY are; you are just being who YOU are. Everybody is doing and being what they are supposed to be and do through divine design. In the past, this has engendered bloody wars and imprinted the IDEA of war as a way of coping, a way of imposing one's will on others, in order to suppress their song and eliminate it.

The idea of forcing "freedom" on others through military means is an example of this. One cannot impose "freedom." That is a contradiction in terms. One can only create and nurture freedom through cooperation in seeking mutually desirable circumstances and ALLOWING everyone to make their own choices without attachment to how they choose. Any imposition of one ideology over another is tyranny, not liberation, and there is no freedom in that.

This is just as true when the ideas seem to be "good" ones as when they seem to be "bad" values of greed and thirst for power. They all translate to an expression that says, "MY way is the right way, and anyone who does not share in my thinking is mistaken."

No, they are not mistaken. They are simply resonating to a different song, a different note that has a different outcome. Those who think they are of the positive polarity and seek to impose their views on the rest of the world — who see through the rose-colored glasses of denial and say things they WISH were true, but for which there is no clear evidence of BEING true — they are not of EITHER polarity. They are simply in denial of what IS, "how it IS," and therefore what must be.

Those who see through rose-colored glasses and say things they WISH were true are not of EITHER polarity.

"Wishing does not make it so." But "wanting" is different than mere wishing. Wanting contains within it a seed of desire, a portion of the Creator's desire to experience all things. Your "wants" are the fuel for your journey. They fuel your desire and propel you to the fulfillment of your desire. Wishing is a fantasy, an "if only ..." thought that leads nowhere. But wanting leads to action, and action leads to results, which lead to further action, and so on. The sounding of one's note is the spark that kindles the fire of desire, and the desire is fueled by the degree of passion the person carries within them for the fulfillment of their desire.

Not everyone carries the same amount of passion. According to where they are on the polarity continuum, the further one is toward the two extremes of positive and negative polarity, the greater and more intense the passion for expressing and manifesting the goals inherent in these polarities: cooperative achievement for one, and total "power over" for the other. To the degree that one moves AWAY from these extremes, the lower the amount of passion for attaining a goal. If the "heat of desire" is greatest at the poles, the center would be said to be "lukewarm" or tepid. No fire at all.

You who are part of Operation Terra are of the positive pole and the more you collectively join together in resounding your vision of Terra, the stronger your collective note resounds through the matrix of the Mind of God, creating standing waves that literally CREATE Terra from that matrix, in which all potentials exist.

You are manifesting Terra by WHO you are, what you carry within you, and your willingness to join with others in singing the new song. This is why you are here. This is what you have come to do. "Baby Terra" has been "conceived," and as the many come to join their voices with yours in singing this song, this note of Terra, the "glass ceiling" of 3D will be shattered, the barrier will be broken, and the energetic pathway will be anchored in place for those who are heading for Terra.

In closing, we will also say to you that as things "heat up" in the world, your job is to simply stand together and continue to sound the note for Terra. We have placed a shield around you, but it is maintained by your commitment and dedication to this single task: sounding the note for Terra. If you do this, no matter how much gnashing of teeth it stirs up in those of the opposite polarity, you are safe and Terra is safe and none will prevent the birth of this new world. It is ordained and so it shall be.

Amen, Adonoy Sabayoth. We are the Hosts of Heaven.

Your job is to simply stand together and continue to sound the note for Terra.

TERRA LESSON #2: BUILDING BRIDGES
March 5, 2005

All right, now. We have asked to speak with you because a critical threshold has been reached in the progression of the events of which we have spoken. From our perspective, there is no linear time, but we do perceive of sequence. Things do relate in both a linear and logical connection with respect to each other. So event A does relate to event B and event C is interposed between event B and event D, and the logic branches of which we have spoken also exist in linear relationship with each other. The outcome of decision point 1 affects what decision point 2 will be.

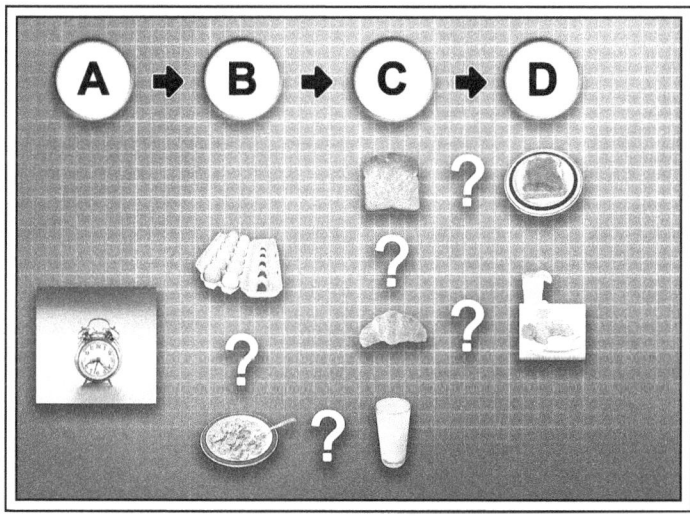

A diagram that demonstrates the sequential and logical relationship between events, linked by decision points

If one course of action is chosen, then only the logic branches that proceed from that result are accessed. So if you decide to have eggs for breakfast, you don't need to decide what flavor of jam you will put on your eggs — unless, of course, you like to put jam on your eggs! However, if you then decide to have TOAST with your eggs, then that is a result of a different logic branch (toast or no toast), that follows from your decision to have eggs, which then accesses the choices about jam (jam or no jam). Each event and each decision stands in linear and logical relation to the ones that precede and follow it.

So now, we stand at a certain point in the journey, one that naturally arose from its relationship to the events that have taken place and as the bridge to those that will follow it. We have also spoken of parallel realities that accommodate all of the possible logic branches (one in which you eat eggs, and others in which you make other possible choices for your breakfast menu). But we have ALSO spoken of a time when a threshold is reached that cannot be delayed, a kind of barrier that exists to limit further possibilities from being explored. You might call that the termination point of that particular Creation.

A kind of barrier exists to limit further possibilities from being explored.

Through the mechanism of parallel realities, different pathways are charted through linear sequences of events that lead to different conclusions. We have referred to these as timelines. We have also spoken previously of a phenomenon in which people who appear to die on YOUR timeline are continuing just fine on another one.

When a "death" occurs, the Oversoul disconnects the silver cord from that extension of itself and that physical body is left behind. This is why there were so many bodies left behind in the disaster that occurred in Asia near the end of December.* Their silver cords were disconnected and withdrawn into their Oversouls, but OTHER bodies created by those SAME Oversouls continued to be supported in other parallel worlds.

Nothing will be lost, but some will pass away from each timeline that is being followed, in the times you are in. When this is complete, the timelines will have separated completely from each other, and the people who occupy different timelines will also be separated from each other. To each person, the "others" will have disappeared, but they will experience themselves as continuing.

We have emphasized that most of what we have put forth is meant for a particular audience: those who carry the light codes in their DNA to respond to the tone of these Messages, and whose Oversouls have made the choice for them to experience the journey to Terra. We would like to add that there is another timeline that is somewhat similar to yours, but whose occupants are meant to incarnate as children born onto Terra at a future time.

Those people may feel drawn to these Messages as part of their seeking, but they do not lock in on them in the way you do. They feel a certain stirring within themselves, but it is not the clear activation that occurs when the light codes match the ones we put forth through the mechanism of the Messages. It stirs up a longing within them that will resurface in other lives that their Oversouls create in other space/time locations, and it will eventually lead them to Terra, but not at THIS particular time.

Our voice speaks directly to those relative few who are going to be the pioneers associated with Terra. Those who are drawn to other teachings are not going to Terra at this time, but may at a later point in time, after the Creation is refreshed and begun anew.

Time is a vector quantity, similar to width, height, and length. Space has volume, which is described by units of width, height, and length, and time is a way of identifying which particular occurrence within

---

*The December 26, 2004 magnitude 9.3 earthquake and tsunami near Indonesia, which killed approximately 230,000-280,000 people in nine countries

space is being referenced. For example, you can identify a certain location within a city, but to identify what exists at that location, you must also specify WHEN it is that you are referencing. The bus that passed through yesterday morning had different passengers on it than the one that passes through there today in the afternoon.

The bus that passed through yesterday morning had different passengers on it than the one that passes through there today in the afternoon.

You can see how complicated it can be to become specific about certain kinds of things, but we take the easy way: we access everything at once, simultaneously, and we experience all of the possible choices as being present all of the time. It must sound to you like that would be very hard to keep track of, but it is very natural to us, and it will soon be very natural to you, once you are in full consciousness again. We navigate through this maze of potentials by what presents to us. The one that does the presenting is the Creator Itself, and all we do is observe and respond appropriately to what the Creator is "saying" through what It presents.

We can feel what is appropriate, and YOU will be able to feel what is appropriate. To the degree you are listening within, you can feel what is appropriate now. One choice always feels better than any of the others, more "right" than any of the others. That's how it is for us, also, but we don't need to reflect on it for very long, as you might. As you learn to trust your intuitive sense, it becomes easier for you to be spontaneous in responding to whatever presents, but you will be doing that ALL of the time as the natural way of being once you have attained full consciousness.

Now, because we do not experience linear time, we have announced the arrival of certain things in the past, because they presented to us as being imminent. That was our experience of them. Even though we can observe you, hear your thoughts, see what you see, and understand you at your core, we do not SHARE in your experience as you experience it.

Events and phenomena that we communicated were beginning, such as "the time of ingathering" or even "booster rocket time" were experienced as imminent to us, and we communicated them that way, but within linear time, those potentials took a much longer time to appear on YOUR perceptual screen than they did for us from our perspective. To us, everything is immediately perceived once it emerges from the Formless, and we did our best to translate that into your frame of reference, but the actual events lagged the immediacy we felt about them.

The time of ingathering is now underway, within linear time. The time of the lifting of the first two waves is (again, from OUR perspective) soon to follow. We expect this to begin occurring later this year but have no way of being sure until it actually occurs. Our frame of reference is not driven by us, but in response to what emerges within the Creator's thought. It is said in your Bible that "no man knows the hour or day; only the Father knows." That is what we are talking about here.

YOUR experience is perceived from within linear time; ours is perceived in a perpetual state of "now-ness," from which we can only estimate things as to when they will emerge at the physical level. Things ALREADY exist as full potentials within "the Mind of God," but as you have no doubt experienced already, there is a quality of unfolding that requires a passage through linear time for the full manifestation to take place at the observable level of space/time.

For example, let's return to the busses that pass by a certain location in a certain city at a particular time. If it is "written" that two people are going to meet on one of those busses by sitting next to each other, all of the events that lead up to them getting on the same bus in the same location within space/time must line up perfectly for that to occur. While we can observe the potentials, we do not either have control over them or ability to predict them except within certain probabilities. However, from being able to read their Oversouls' scripts for them, we DO know that they WILL meet and certain interactions will occur between them, in keeping with that script, even if we have to wait to see how it actually plays out within linear time.

So we have given you a "map of the territory" — the map of the journey to Terra that you are making and have been making since you emerged from the Mind of the Creator as an actual expression of the Creator. We have given you some of the features of the journey, and we have given you some of the markers of it, just like you have on your highways. You see a mile marker that tells you how far you are between two points on that highway — from its beginning to where you are as you pass that mile marker. Those mile markers are spaced uniformly, one mile apart. But there are also other markers that tell you how far you are from other destinations that lie ahead of you — so many miles to a particular town or city, so many miles to the one that lies beyond it, so many miles to a place where you can turn off onto another road altogether.

We have tried to be precise in translating the map, but there have been some obvious miscalculations that have come in when trying to correlate information that appears as imminent to us from outside of time with specific locations within linear time. You have collectively been making this journey for over 4.5 billion years, so our "margin of error" within that range of time is very small indeed, but for you, it might have caused you to doubt our accuracy, and for that we do apologize.

Now, however, the signs are clear that the times we have spoken of have indeed arrived. The event horizon for these times has been passed and nothing will affect what plays out now. No choices remain to be made that will affect the outcome on your timeline. You can essentially let go of any need to fix anything other than putting your energies into your own completions, healing, and preparation to transform.

The rollout (or should we say roll UP?) for the first and second waves is imminent to us. It might take place over as much as two years within linear time, but we can see the readiness of all of the factors involved, and to us that indicates the time is at hand, whether it takes a few months more or not.

A true wave has a wave shape to it. That may seem obvious, but to many it is not something they have really thought about. A wave has a leading edge, which swells into a fullness that contains the main body of the wave, and a trailing edge. Form follows function in the created world, and so the leading edge of this wave will contain those whose functions are necessary to support the activities of those who follow. There will be a sort of overlap between the trailing edge of the first wave and the leading edge of the second wave.

Events were originally thought to be taking place over a much greater span of time, so the distinctions between the waves were much clearer and separate from each other before. However, because of the kinds of delays we have mentioned, events that were originally thought to be spread out over decades are now going to be occurring very close together. Very little has been discarded from the original list of events, although some were ameliorated through prayer, the collective effects of the personal work that has been accomplished, and other shifts that came about through collective efforts.

However, now you are IN the "birth canal," and rapidly approaching the "ring pass not"** phase of things. In other words, that immovable threshold that we spoke of so long ago is still there, still immovable, and the events that have to occur are piling up against that immovable threshold or barrier like a single large wave of enormous power and force. That wave is building force now, and so we can say with confidence that the waves of our ground troops will be lifting soon because they will be needed soon. The times ahead will be very intense — much more intense than they would have been if they had been more spread out — but they will also be much shorter in duration. This is where your "surrender lessons" are very valuable to you, in dealing with the acceleration that is now occurring.

Booster Rocket Time has come and gone — twice. The first one had little shock value because there was so much publicity for its slow

---

NOTE: A ring-pass-not is a barrier or filter of sorts that keeps certain energies contained within certain boundaries. In order to pass this "ring," the energy has to be operating on a level BEYOND that which is being filtered out. In this case, the implication is that any energies that have not "qualified" and gone beyond separation consciousness will remain contained at the 3D level. To go beyond the filter or barrier, one's consciousness must be "lifted" above the 3D frequency level.

On the timeline leading to Terra, everything that is not lifted beyond the 3D level will appear to perish, but can continue on another timeline within 3D and go on to other incarnations. Some of those who do this will eventually incarnate on Terra by being born there, but not during this particular cycle or lifetime.

progress over time that by the time it occurred, the "surprise" element had all but disappeared. It did happen, and it did set in motion so many of the things that are playing out now. It was truly the beginning of all that is building toward the conclusion, but the real shocks still lie ahead. Even though the magnitude of the impact was much greater the second time around, the world still turns pretty much as it had before. Commerce still hums along, communications still buzz, and despite a growing unease that most people feel but can't put their finger on, the clinging to "business as usual" is still there, even though it takes more effort to cling than it did before.

The weather is still the biggest news, that and the impact of oil prices. Crop failures, fires, floods, and growing death tolls are all linked to those two. But there is a time coming of greater global breakdown — the conditions that will bring those of the third wave into readiness for their lifting, and so it is time to actively prepare those who will gather them up at the end.

Your timeline is the shortest one out of the twelve futures that will emerge from this one shared reality. That is partly the reason why the dates given that are associated with other timelines do not mesh with your experience. You are still accessing each other, but the groups are forming up and moving strongly to their poles of destiny. The timelines are separating and you are moving into the final part of your preparation for the task that lies ahead.

Your greatest service to the world at this point in time is to respond to what presents in your life, just as we do. There is a feeling to withdraw in some of you. Respect that. There is a feeling in some of you to move out into the world and engage with it more. Respect that. Each of you is being guided from within yourselves to be in the right place at the right time.

Each of these steps takes you further on the path that is yours alone to walk. You are not many, and your task and your life are unique to you. There are many of us on the ships now, waiting to receive you as you disembark from your lifting when it comes for you. Those of the first and second waves will be tucked away on the ships for a time and completing their transformation there, so when it is time to gather up those of the third wave (who number in the millions), you will be ready and equipped for the task.

We hope this has been helpful to you in bridging the difference between the way we perceive things and the way you do at present.

When you have completed your transformation, our way will be your way, but for now we still have some bridging to do.

We leave you now in peace, honor and blessing. Amen, Adonoy Sabayoth. We are the Hosts of Heaven.

When you have completed your transformation, our way will be your way, but for now we still have some bridging to do.

THE TIME OF SORROWS
April 10, 2005

Dear ones,

This past week, many millions of people around the world mourned the passing of a single man [Pope John Paul II], a man who had in some way touched them through his life. The tolling of the bells to mark his passage also marked a stage in the passage of the planet from one frequency band to another. It is about this particular frequency band that we wish to speak today.

Every thoughtform or idea or concept has a frequency pattern to it. These frequency patterns make up layers of different "heaviness" or "lightness." The heaviest frequencies feel "heavy" or "dark" to us and the lighter frequencies feel "lighter" or "light" to us. As the Earth is rising slowly through the frequency bands, each frequency pattern that has been passed through no longer can hold that pattern and it is flushed out into manifestation. And so, at this particular period of time in the passage through these frequency bands, the "time of sorrows" has arrived.

This is a symptom of the patterns contained in the band that has just been traversed. It will outpicture as many funerals, many losses, and much sorrow for many of the people in the world. The cause of these sorrows will be losses of many kinds — loss of loved ones, both animal and personal; loss of jobs; loss of homes; loss of property; loss of health; loss of well-being in all kinds of ways. We have come to you today in the role of comforter, to help you come to terms with the sorrows that will be outpicturing in the world.

We wish to remind you that these losses are a passing away of all that is not in keeping with the frequencies of peace, joy, and love that make up Terra's foundation. They are a passing away of all that has kept people from truly being free to express themselves in all of their fullness.

At this particular period of time in the passage through these frequency bands, the "time of sorrows" has arrived.

They are a passing away of everything that has CAUSED sorrow and the lack of peace, joy, and love on this planet. It will be a time to grieve one's losses, but it is also a healing of the root of those who suffer every day from the losses of personal freedom that have come down through the generations of ignorance, control, and penury.

So while this time is upon you now, we want to tell you how to be with this experience, so you can receive it for the healing that it is. We also want to express our support for you and your transition, and to explain how it will be after you have withdrawn from the planet for a while, so that you can understand how the pieces of the puzzle fit together. We expect that, having a frame in which to see through, it will make it easier to bear.

We are aware that you are very caring individuals, and that you have a tendency to identify with loss and suffering so much so that you experience it as if it were your own. In particular, you feel this way about those least able to protect themselves — innocent children, elderly, those who are crippled by disease, animals and plants, and those who are already beset with life's harsher aspects. We ask you to detach from all of these individual dramas, to instead create a tent of your love over them, like a bowl or container in which these things can play out to their end, and the healing that will result from having gone through those experiences.

Many losses are coming now.

Many losses are coming now. We ask you to hold forth where you are, with all of the love you can muster for the entire process, independent of the details of each calamity. For calamities will be so numerous, it can and shall overwhelm many.

We ask you to understand the real purpose being served by the calamities, to see them as a healing for the planet and a release from the conditions that have occurred over the millennia. We ask you to stand where you are and continue to sound your note. We ask you to do this until the time comes when the portal arrives, and when you move through the portal, to not look back upon the calamities you are leaving behind. You are moving to a place where you will let go of any sorrow you carry, to prepare yourself to offer comfort at a later time, when it will be of some use.

You see, at this time, the cleansing of the sorrows has just begun, and many are destined to depart through the portal of "death." Your time to be of use is not until this time of sorrows has come to an end, and you will extend a helping hand to those who have been transformed by going through them.

Remember that a higher purpose is being served through all of this, and therefore, there is nothing to fix and nothing to stop. It all must come to pass. You can always pray for as smooth a process as possible in keeping with the highest good, but it is important to detach from specific outcomes and — most importantly — from seeing any of it as either a judgment or punishment. It is none of those, for everyone is just being who they came to be, in keeping with the Creator's desire to experience everything.

No one is being punished. No one is being judged. Those ideas are a creation of man, not of the Creator. As we have said, to the Creator, all of Its creations are good, in that they serve the Creator's desire to experience all of the possibilities through Its creations. Everything that exists is in existence solely to serve the Creator's desire to experience everything.

In speaking of the "end times" or "last days," many people judge others because they are different or believe differently, but the Creator does not judge. Many people say that THEY "are the way, the truth, and the light," and if anyone does not follow THEIR precepts, they will suffer an eternal punishment.

There is no eternal punishment. There is no heaven; there is no hell. There is only the Creator, expressing through Its creations. All things stem from the Creator. All that you consider "evil" in the world stems from the Creator. All that you consider "good" in the world stems from the Creator. The Creator is All That Is.

Do not pay attention to the rhetoric of those who are enmeshed in division, hatred, fear, and rage. Many will be losing control and acting out from those places of division, hatred, fear, and rage. The response will be dramatic, and the only response that will be effective is to institute more and more control.

Health care delivery systems, especially those that treat mental disorders, will be overwhelmed, and a system of triage will have to be resorted to. Those who cannot be helped will not be helped. Those who will survive without help will not be helped, and will have to rely on themselves and their own resources. Only those who can be helped within available resources will be helped within available resources. And those resources are about to be taxed beyond the ability to respond.

A time of tyranny will follow this time of sorrows. It will be the response to the losses and the need to institute order and control, which will be yet another loss — a loss of personal freedoms. All systems will be stressed to the maximum possible, and many things will be sacrificed that people have come to take for granted. Many things will be in scarce supply, and to control the fear levels that would result in riots and mass hysteria, more controls will be put in place until everywhere you look around the planet, helmets and guns will be seen. These measures will take place against the backdrop of growing discontent and a kind of unleashing of a wild beast.

Nations are entities, too, and when an entity is in pain, it lashes out against what it perceives of as the cause of its pain. It identifies the cause of its pain as its enemy and moves to destroy its enemy in order to stop its pain, but the reality of war is that it does not stop pain — it increases it. And so a spiral will be set in motion soon, and that spiral will build upon itself until everything appears to be out of control. Then those who thrive on power will institute the controls that preserve their position and the spiral will continue to build until all will appear to be heading into the darkest days ever seen upon the planet.

The sheer numbers of people actually contribute to this spiral. Consider that 1,000 years ago, there were many fewer people on the planet, and their technologies and modes of transport limited them in the kind of destruction they could wreak on a given area. The Bubonic Plague killed many more than the puny forces of people could, but now there are superpowers with superweapons, capable of destroying the entire planet singlehandedly. There are other nations with more limited resources, but with enough people being drummed into hating others, alliances will coalesce and the united resources will throw everything possible at their enemies. It will be like the entire planet has gone insane, but it is a madness that is already there, festering unseen and just waiting for the right circumstances to boil forth.

We tell you this now, to prepare you for this time of sorrows, so that you will know how to respond. Your time to withdraw also helps this healing process go forward. Until now, you have been acting like human lightning rods to anchor the higher Light into the planet. You have done this and the Light is doing its work of scouring every atom clean of its contaminants.

The resulting "sludge" has to go somewhere, and it will outpicture in this image of human suffering, but please understand, it is just the PURGING of the suffering that has existed and gone on for millennia. Many of you have memories of this suffering, for you experienced it yourselves. In this present life, you received it as a legacy from your elders, who received it as a legacy from THEIR elders, and on and on, back through the dim reaches of time.

The Time of Sorrows 335

This is just the PURGING of the suffering that has existed and gone on for millennia.

Your Oversouls have created many lives, and played out many themes, but now it is all coming to an end. This, you might say, is the "great end game" — the game that will play out and then the end will come.

This time that has now arrived must occur for the ending to be a happy one — in the end. This is a last look around at the things that the Creator desired to experience, and then you will move on to something else. You have your part to play, and you will be the deliverance from suffering that will be so welcome at the other end of this time, but in the meantime, focus on your own healing, focus on your own transformation, focus on what you CAN do to support your own transition, for it is only when you are fully transformed that you will be able to provide meaningful relief and support for others. This period of sorrows is upon the world now, and it will last until it is over and it is time to clear the stage altogether.

Please understand that all of this has been anticipated, has been prepared for, and we are doing our part to help all of you, and through you, millions of others when it is time to do that. But each thing progresses in phases and stages, and this is where you are at in the overall process at this time.

We leave you now, in peace, honor, and blessing. Amen, Adonoy Sabayoth. We are the Hosts of Heaven.

A CHANGE IN PLANS
May 6, 2005

All right, now. We have asked to speak with you because there has been a change in plans. As we have indicated, the Creator loves surprises, and now we are also surprised by some recent events that have presented for us to respond to.

It appears that those of the higher-density STS polarity have concluded that things are not going the way they want on the surface of the planet, primarily in that they have become impatient for the "fireworks" to begin. What this translates to is an acceleration in the speed at which events will unfold, primarily in the realm of wars and human suffering. These higher-density beings feed off the emotions of fear and its offspring: anger, rage, jealousy, and hatred — the more intense the better, from their perspective. They know, as we do, that the time is growing short and they wish to maximize THEIR harvest as much as we wish to maximize ours.

So an order has gone forth and is being communicated in various ways to their servants in 3D whose vibratory pattern matches those of the higher-density negative-polarity entities. This order is sourcing from the 6th- and 5th-density levels, passed down to their 4th-density operatives, and seeded into the consciousness of the humans on the ground who serve them and their agendas.

The humans experience this urging as an impatience and an impulsiveness within themselves, but they are largely unaware that it does not begin within them. What the result will be is not wholly known at this point in the unfolding of the drama, but there is enough of a potential for an escalation into a state of global war that we have decided to move up some of OUR plans as well.

Accordingly, we have asked for assistance from within OUR ranks and those who are scheduled to be lifted in the first and second waves will be worked with more directly than in the past. It is necessary to increase the speed at which you are lifted through the various frequency bands, and each of you has been assigned at least one "helper" to tend to you as you experience this acceleration.

You may feel some symptoms of the acceleration, and we wanted to let you know so you would not become alarmed. There will be sensations of a "state of emergency" that are a result of your body's response to the increased speed, just as you might feel if you were in some type of vehicle — airplane, car, or train — that suddenly began moving faster than you were comfortable with. The acceleration carries within it a feeling of greater and greater speed, and your bodies respond with sensations of "jitters," "butterflies in the stomach," light but passing nausea, and an odd mixture of anxiety, anticipation, and excitement.

This will be more of a "wild ride" than we had originally planned, and our advice is for you to remember to breathe when you feel these feelings arising within you. It will also be easier to remain comfortable within the acceleration if you sink INTO the experience, much as you would settle into your contoured seat on a spaceship. As you feel the stimulus of this acceleration, keep your attention on calming yourself by deepening your breathing, closing your eyes, and choosing over and over to trust the movement and those who are creating it.

The whole intent and purpose of this response is to move up your entry into a higher frequency band so we can tuck you away safely onto the ships before the wars are fully unleashed on the ground. This will also require that whatever energies reside within you that are not compatible with these higher frequencies be purged from your system, so that translates to a more rapid clearing of those energies. Your attendants from our ranks will be working with you to ease the symptoms of those clearings, but you can also make things easier on yourself by choosing to ride this wave of change calmly and without resistance.

It is the resistance that keeps the energy from moving, and it is an innate tendency to resist when movement seems to be pushing, rather than carrying you along. If you can choose to relax INTO the movement and trust it, you can more easily experience this, with the least amount of discomfort possible. Above all, if you find yourself experiencing fear, breathe deeply and do those things that calm you.

Create sanctuary within yourself and your immediate environment. Detach from the drama going on around you. If you are constantly listening to the news broadcasts, you will only increase your adrenaline levels, and it will be much easier to slide into fear and anxiety about what is happening. We advise you to pull your attention toward ways of calming yourself, rather than in ways of stimulating yourself. Slow things down for yourself as much as you can, and it will be a smoother transition. Do less and do it with full attention and it will be easier for you to glide through these changes smoothly.

We are not going to place estimates on the timeframe for your lifting into the ships at this time. We will be keeping pace and tracking each of you individually, and we have reserve capacity to handle this acceleration, both while it is going on and afterward. Once you are on the ships, the rest of your processing will take place, and we are preparing to receive you in greater numbers than before.

We had intended to lift you gradually over the next year and a half, but now we must get you off the surface of the planet much sooner. We expect the wars to occur later this year, and a financial collapse to follow, so we want to make sure you are safe and provided for by then. We are working with a system of probabilities, and things are subject to change if new information arrives. We will do our best to keep you informed in all ways — through these Messages and also through direct inspiration, so keep your inner radio tuned to our frequency band as much as you can and pay attention to those subtle messages that seem to arise within you.

In the meantime, know that you are loved, that you are precious to us, and that we are standing with you at all times and in all ways. You are never alone and we so look forward to having you among us again.

Amen, Adonoy Sabayoth. We are the Hosts of Heaven.

LISTEN WITHIN
June 7, 2006

All right, now. We have asked to speak with you to inaugurate the movement into the final 3D phase of Operation Terra. Today we will only speak in generalities of what lies ahead, but it is our intention to guide you through the final phase in more detail as things proceed across the planet.

To begin with, many changes have occurred during the time we have been silent, requiring adjustments in our plans beyond the last "change in plans" that we announced. However, now we are so close to the ending of all of this that there will be specifics that might be altered, but the overall movement must complete without further delay.

You stand on the threshold of profound change for the entire planet, but most especially for its human population. Things are leading to a crisis point that should be clearly visible to those who have "eyes to see." We remind you that your safety lies within, and we encourage you to strengthen your ability to quiet yourself and listen to your inner wisdom, despite what might be going on around you.

There will be many putting forth their solutions to the "problem," but remain calm and ignore the predictable chaos that will ensue. The world's leaders have been trying to maintain the status quo for a very long time, and don't want to have people panicking until it is unavoidable. We urge you to not panic at any time, for clear thinking and reasoned action are what is called for during chaotic times such as those which lie just ahead. You will make your journey easier if you can remember this, and you will also serve as a model for those around you who might otherwise give in to their fear.

Those of you who have been reading these Messages and applying their principles in your lives will be of great help to those who are just beginning to realize that things are not quite right in the world and are worsening on a daily basis. The movement into chaos is well under way, but it is being kept hidden for as long as possible by those in power and who stand to benefit by doing so.

In one of our earliest Messages, we spoke about the last grab for resources that would be taking place. You have seen some of that in some of the actions taken by the US government, but other governments are doing the same thing to the best of their ability. Those who have the necessary information to sense the magnitude of what is about to transpire have been taking actions for quite a while that will give them the most power when things begin to come apart.

Those who can sense what is about to transpire have been taking actions that will give them the most power when things come apart.

It is all rather like a game, but in this case, not everyone is an equal player. Many have nothing to play with at all, so it will be a contest among the "haves," as the "have nots" do not have the resources to do anything but survive as best as they can. It will not be a pretty sight as the awareness dawns on the many just how dire things really are.

We do not say these things to alarm you. We only wish to prepare you for what is coming and to direct you in the ways that will be in keeping with your life's purpose and plan. Each person who is incarnated now is here because of a decision made by their Oversoul. Each one has a part to play in the larger drama that is unfolding. Some have more visibility than others, but each one is equally important in the context of the whole.

Each one of you reading this Message is a "player" in this drama — not because you have great material resources, but because you have great spiritual resources within you. You think that your material world is what is "real" because you can verify its presence with your physical senses, but what is truly real is invisible and inaccessible by the physical senses. It is the Creator's presence that is the only thing that is real, and you are an individualized aspect of the Creator-in-expression.

We are embedded within the matrix of the Creator as much as you are. All of us source from the Mind of the Creator, and as you make your journey into greater mindfulness and awareness of what is real, you will also be more aware of the Mind of the Creator as it generates you, speaks through you, thinks through you, and moves through you. All of the clearings you have been going through have one aim: to make you as clear as possible so that the Mind of the Creator can work through you with as little distortion as possible.

As long as you identify with your body as who and what you are, you will be living from an illusory sense of reality. As you are able to surrender your personal preferences and become more detached and neutral, you will be able to align more perfectly with the Mind of the Creator.

The Creator is dispassionate toward Its creations. This is in direct conflict with the belief in a personal "God," one that puts some of its creations above others. To the Creator, all of Its creations are equal, and serve equally to fulfill the Creator's desire to experience all possibilities.

To those who feel that their way is the only way to God, we would say that they are laboring under an illusion. The Creator is present within all of Its creations, so there is nothing that is outside of the Creator, and there is nothing that is separate from the Creator. These ideological wars that lead to people killing each other are not based in any kind of truth other than what people believe to be true. That does not make it true, despite the power of the individual mind. Only the Mind of the Creator can truly create anything.

Then where do these mistaken ideas come from? They arise from the interactions of individuals with their environment, which includes other individuals with whom they interact. But where do these interactions source from? From the Oversoul that creates each projection that thinks it's a separate individual. So it all comes back to the Oversouls as the source of the interactions and what could be taken as mistaken ideas. However, if one examines the fruit of such things, it all comes back to the Creator's desire to experience all things, without preference for some things over others.

So what you as an individual might prefer is not right for everyone. It is only right for you. Therefore, as you see things playing out in chaotic ways, what you need to discern is what is right for YOU. It will not be exactly the same for anyone else. It will be challenging to not get swept up in other people's ideas of what should happen or how things ought to be done, but remain sovereign, and listen to your inner wisdom. This is something that must be applied constantly.

There is little time left to learn "lessons," as there is little time left to do things over again. The best way through these times is to listen within and tune out anything that is not in keeping with your own inner wisdom. There will be much to tune out.

Pay attention to how things FEEL within you. Be selective in what you eat, what you expose yourself to in the form of entertainment, and how you spend your time. Be selective in where you go when you have a choice and make choices that enhance your sense of inner peace and quiet.

If you don't know how to still the chatter in your mind, find ways to do that. Meditate regularly if that helps you to do that. Take warm baths. Play soothing music. Spend time in nature if possible.

Get rid of clutter in every way you can. If you haven't already done so, review your possessions and get rid of everything that you are not actively using. Pass them on to others if they no longer serve you. The details will be different for each of you, but the goal is the same. Do whatever you need to in order to remain calm in a time of chaos. This is of vital importance.

Pay attention to the little clues that appear in your life. Do not hesitate to break out of your habitual patterns if it feels right to do so. No one else can live your life for you, so do not let anyone else's opinions dictate how you live and the choices you make. Your inner wisdom will be your own best friend.

We are always with you, and we often do things to get your attention and make you aware of our presence. We are all part of the same team, with the same goal — namely to prepare the way for the new world of

Pay attention to the little clues that appear in your life.

Terra. To this end, you have all been doing your part in clearing energies that would impede the planet's progress upward, and you have also been rising in frequency yourselves.

Look back to the time when we last spoke to you. It was just a little over a year ago, around 13 months to be more exact. Has anything changed in your life? Do you perceive things differently? How do you feel about yourself now as compared to then? The changes are not just going on in the phenomenal world of material reality. There are even greater changes taking place within. They are affecting everyone and every thing on the planet — the animals, the plants, the very air you breathe. Nothing is unaffected by these changes, and the changes will continue to accelerate from here on in.

Do you doubt that you are changing? When you look in the mirror, there is not so much that is different, but inside is a different story. Ideas that used to excite you somehow have lost their flavor. Everything looks pretty much the same, but your relationship to it has changed a great deal.

Many (if not most) people on the planet have not changed a great deal in this past year, but those of you who are part of Operation Terra have been going through an accelerated transformation — one that has required a great deal of you at times. Well, it is only going to go faster from here on in, so the best way to be comfortable with this journey is to remain surrendered at all times. Whenever you become aware of resistance to or avoidance of anything, surrender that resistance and open up to receive what must be received in that situation.

To align with what's real, you must surrender up your previous ideas of "how it is," ideas you learned from others who learned from still others, all of whom were in veiled consciousness and therefore not qualified to teach those ideas to anyone else as truth. Become a Truth seeker. There is only the Creator in expression. That is the only truth. That is what is real.

Work with that idea. When you feel an emotional charge rise up within you, do not resist it, but do not feed it either. Let it flow through you without acting from it. Allow yourself to feel all the emotions, but recognize them as the passing things they are. It is only in the quiet space within you, when you are not being affected by your passing emotions, that you can know and receive Truth. There is a lot of noise in the world, and it keeps people from truly hearing what is going on within themselves. You can choose what you listen to. Listen within.

We will have more to say to you, but this is all we would say to you now. We leave you in peace, honor and blessing. Amen, Adonoy Sabayoth. We are the Hosts of Heaven.

MOVING INTO UNITY WITH ALL THAT IS
July 3, 2006

If you are uncertain as to where to go and what to do, what is the best approach to take? Listen within. Wait for clarity. Refuse to act until you are certain that that is what you are supposed to do. Certainty is not easy when there are so many voices clamoring in your head for attention to their particular point of view. What do you do about that? Wait for clarity. Wait until the clamor dies down and only a single quiet voice remains. Wait for clarity. Do not act without clarity about it being the TIME to act, as well. Everything has its perfect timing in the larger scheme of things.

So, now, why do we repeatedly emphasize these basic principles? Because they are your compass through the uncharted waters that lie just ahead. If you are setting out on a journey without a map and only the sense that you must cross an ocean to reach a shore that is not visible to you, you will have to keep your attention fixed on that far horizon until you reach it. You must set your course, and then follow it. Your guidance systems must have a "fix" on your destination.

You carry this information within you. It is coded into the very cells and DNA of the body you walk around in. Your journey IS already mapped out, but because of the necessity of making this journey in a state of veiled consciousness, you have to "pretend" you don't know where you are going. It is all part of the illusion about who and what and where you are.

The "real you" is nonlocal. By that, we mean it is not limited to a particular space/time location. If you have had an extensive out-of-body experience or a near-death experience, you might have realized that once you were free of your body, you could see in all directions at once. However, that still provided the experience of perceiving through a particular and fixed location. As an expression of the Creator, you exist everywhere at once. You exist in everything you perceive, and just as the Creator experiences Itself through Its creations, you also experience yourself through all of the creations that you intersect with from your individualized point of awareness.

This will not change when you are in full consciousness again, but what WILL change will be how you perceive everything you observe and interact with. You will EXPERIENCE being part of everything that exists. You will directly "know" the meaning of the phrase, "I am that."

Are you familiar with that term? It has appeared in many of your languages. In the Hebrew language, it is "Ayeh Esher Ayeh" ["I am that I am," spelled phonetically]. In the Mayan language, it is "In Lakesh" ["I am another yourself," spelled phonetically]. This is a very old understanding. In the traditions that emphasize something you call self-realization or enlightenment, the attainment of those states brings you to the direct experience. "You" are everywhere and in everything you perceive. The meaning of these terms come down to that simple fact. You are intimately interwoven with everything that exists and everything that exists has its counterpart in you.

"You" are everywhere and in everything you perceive.

Why do we emphasize this point? Because in order to move out of separation consciousness, you have to realize this for yourself — not just as an intellectual concept, but as an inherent feature of your experience of life. In point of fact, this is absolutely true, but until your veils are thinned to the point you can actually FEEL the reciprocity of the dance of the illusion you are mired in, you will never be able to move past enemy-patterning into oneness with All That Is.

Your life is bringing you closer to this realization every day. Your life is giving you opportunities to see and know that everything and everyone you come in contact with mirrors something of yourself back to you, so you can come to see yourself EVERYWHERE and IN EVERYTHING. You will come to realize that everywhere you look, there you are.

One of the terms you have for the Creator is "All That Is." The Creator permeates all of Its Creations. It is the matrix, the foundation, the ground of all that exists. As an individualized aspect of the Creator, YOU also exist in All That Is. YOU also are part of the matrix, the foundation, the ground of all that exists. But that does not mean that "you" ARE "the Creator." Let us give you an example from your experience with food.

The Creator is the gelatin or the broth, interpenetrating all of the pieces of ingredients.

Let's say you are going to make a soup or a stew or a gelatin salad. Any of those dishes contain individual ingredients. In the gelatin salad, for example, there may be sliced vegetables or small pieces of fruit or nuts or any number of ingredients. What interconnects all of these individual pieces is the gelatin that forms the whole. Likewise, in a soup or stew, all of the individual pieces are swimming in the broth. The Creator is the gelatin or the broth, interpenetrating all of the pieces of ingredients.

However, the Creator is ALSO present in the pieces themselves, unlike the gelatin or broth. This is very difficult to grasp with the intellect alone, but if you can — even for a moment — get your intellect to step back so you can use your intuition to directly experience the reality BEHIND the apparent reality in which you move and have your focus, you might just catch an intuitive sense that what is REALLY going on is not perceivable with your physical senses.

Why is this important to mention at all right now? Because very soon, things are going to get very intense in many aspects of your planetary civilization, and unless you can somehow manage to remain in a state of unity with everything that unfolds, the experience of separation from Source will be greatly magnified and you will feel very threatened and very much at risk.

This in turn will cause you to contract in fear, and when you are in fear, you cannot be in a state of acceptance or love. Your energies will congeal instead of flowing, and you will be unable to respond appropriately to the enormous amount of change going on. You will get "stuck" and instead of moving with grace through these changes, you could get mired down in the muck and literally drown.

Now, each of you carries within you the codes that make up your personality as it was designed by your Oversoul. You have "designer genes" (pardon our pun) and you are designed to make the appropriate choices to make it through the times that lie just ahead. Nonetheless, for reasons that you will understand better once you HAVE attained full consciousness again, it is necessary for you to again learn to be in unity with everything around you and it is necessary for you to have lots of practice in disengaging and detaching from the drama. You have all made this trip before, long ago, when you first incarnated into a body of flesh. Before that, you were vastly expanded consciousnesses, unembodied and much less limited.

You have already made it "up the scale" through the various densities of experience, and from the higher densities, you responded to a call for your participation in the present drama. Then you came down again, accepted the partial amnesia that accompanied your "fall" down through the levels to arrive in a body on 3D Earth, and now you are finding your way back up to where you were before. By the end of this entire process, those of you who are our soul family will find yourselves back in the experience of being vastly expanded consciousnesses again. Some of you actually sustain entire creations. But before that occurs, you have a certain job to perform and that is to re-attain that state of unity with all things and from that platform of higher consciousness, carry out your tasks for the evacuation and the colonization of Terra.

Your consciousness has already been moving in that direction for quite a while. Many of you have become even more sensitive than you have been most of your life because of the clearings of your cellular memory, and that can present quite a challenge when trying to operate and survive within such a dense field of consciousness as that which exists on 3D Earth at this time. However, you were created with all of the inner resources to not just survive in this density, but ultimately to thrive in it. You might have to revise your definitions of what constitutes "thriving," as so many pictures of the "good life" seem to include a lot of material possessions and large properties in which to house them.

From OUR perspective, a life is "good" based on how you FEEL about living it!

From OUR perspective, a life is "good" based on how you FEEL about living it! Have you ever heard about a person who seemed to have everything possible and who committed suicide or was hospitalized for depression? THINGS can't make you happy. Your inner satisfaction is what makes you happy. You can rejoice in your ability to FEEL emotions, TASTE flavors, SMELL fresh air or the fragrance of a flower, and SEE the tenderness between a parent and its child. You can take satisfaction in your aliveness. If you have done as we advised and simplified your life, you might be astonished to discover how simple your needs actually are.

You might also be astonished by how many things you are encouraged to buy aren't really necessary for a "good life," one that pleases you.

When you are back in full consciousness and can directly manifest everything you desire, you won't have closets full of clothes, cabinets full of dishes or movies or equipment or tools. You will be totally free of all of those things and totally free of the need for a house to contain them and organize them. Can you even imagine that kind of freedom from THINGS? Try it. Try living that way now. Try finding pleasure in what is there in front of you, whether it's a sound, a sight, a feeling, or a flavor. Savor your life. Live fully NOW. Begin moving in the direction of having everything you want or desire, right where you are and right where you find yourself in each and every moment of your life.

We will have much more to say on these subjects as things unfold, but we felt it was time to at least introduce these concepts and reinforce the ones we have already given you. We will speak with you again. In the meantime, we send you our love and shelter you with our peace. Every day brings us closer to being together again.

Amen, Adonoy Sabayoth. We are the Hosts of Heaven.

ON "CLEARING"
July 20, 2006

All right, now. Things are definitely heating up on your planet, aren't they! We would like to give you some gentle reminders and then move on to some topics that may be new for you.

First of all, remember to detach from the drama that is unfolding all around you. Be sure to remind yourself that all of this was planned from the moment of Creation, and was a part of the Plan for the end of the present Creation when it was formed, so there is no point in becoming upset about what must come to pass.

Deep breaths that emphasize the exhale are helpful in dispelling tension that might arise within you. Breathe deeply and often, as often as is necessary to remain calm. This is going to be a somewhat rough transition, because things were delayed as long as possible and now there is a store of unreleased energies that must be released over a shorter period of time.

That being said, we want to remind you that you are not alone. Not only are there many of you scattered across the surface of the planet, there are so many more of us grouped around each of you — watching you, tending to you, and working with you at all times, but especially while you sleep. If you have issues that need to be cleared, the time has arrived to complete with that process, for the time is short before you will need to be finished with that part of your movement into 4D and beyond. This may be a very intense period for you, but we wish to assure you that it is only a phase, not a permanent state, and it will pass, as everything that is not eternal also passes.

Now, then. How about a new topic to entertain your minds? What would you most like to know? Of course, there are the perennial "when" and "how" and "where" questions, and we decline to answer them, simply because it's part of your process to discover this for yourself, and we won't infringe on your process in those ways.

A number of you have been wondering about the symptoms of the clearings and some of the sensations and emotions that have been coming up for you during this time. We can't do anything but speak in generalities, as the process is so individual that each one of you will have a slightly different experience. However, we can talk about some of the broader phenomena that will likely be common to all of you at some point in your process.

First of all, wherever you have energetic blockages in your body, those places are going to be totally cleared of all restraints to free energy flow. This will require the blockages to be cleared and released, so whatever is causing the blockage will also have to be cleared and released. Most of the blockages are held in the emotional body, so much of the clearing will involve clearing of emotions.

Most of the blockages are held in the emotional body, so much of the clearing will involve clearing of emotions.

Some of the blockages also are held in the subtle body that you sometimes refer to as the etheric or astral body. These result from residue left over from other lives lived and carried as vestiges of those experiences in the Oversoul, which collected and received those experiences through the individual soul connected to each individual life. Those "memories" from other lives lived are also being cleared, so you may be having dreams in which you recall these other lives, and you may also be briefly meeting or connecting with individuals who were participants in those other lives and with whom you interacted at that time.

This matter of other lives gets a little confusing. When we say "you," it might refer to the locus of awareness that is reading this Message, or it might refer to "you" in the more generalized sense — an Oversoul that is an individualized expression of the Creator, the "projector" of the projection that you presently identify with as being who you are. We have said before that there is no "re-incarnation," only "incarnation." By this, we mean that the particular body and personality you currently occupy only gets created once.

The Oversoul normally creates several bodies or projections simultaneously. The word "incarnation" means to be in a "carnal" (fleshly) body. So an incarnation is really a projection of a portion of the Oversoul into a carnal or fleshly (physical) body. Any given incarnation/body only is created once for a particular space/time nexus (intersection). It never is created at any other time, but shares in a common Oversoul with other incarnations created/projected by that same Oversoul.

None of you is really your body, and it is not your body that is what is important. The body is just the vehicle for gathering experiences from interactions with everything else in its environment. What is important is the awareness of the experience — the "charge" that the experience carries and that is communicated to the Oversoul as part of the memories it stores — and the essence of the experience itself.

The reason the experience is created in the first place is to satisfy the Creator's desire to experience Itself through Its creations. All experiences have this in common, no matter what the individual details of the experience may be. The degree of emotional charge is associated with how much of that experience is remembered, both at the physical and cellular levels and at the Oversoul level. The greater the charge, the greater the impact on the storage systems, and the greater attention that experience draws to itself.

Consider that this current Creation is approximately 4.5 billion years old. That means that each Oversoul has been collecting experiences from its created projections for 4.5 billion years also. The memories that have the greatest impact are the ones with the greatest emotional charge, so it is logical to conclude that those are the ones that will surface and draw your attention during this time of DIScharging (eliminating the charge) all of the emotional charge that has been collected over the 4.5 billion years.

This is one of the reasons you are witnessing a buildup of emotional charge in present time. These dramas that are being enacted now are actually symptoms of the purging of the collective cellular memory, both on an individual and global basis. The planet herself has served as a repository for the collective charge stored over the time of her existence, and she is purging herself now, also.

The more extreme emotions will dominate the scene as the discharging takes place.

So what does this translate into, in terms of your individual and collective experience? Since the emotions of fear, hate, rage, pain, hunger, and anger have been far more prevalent and carried more charge than the gentler emotions of peacefulness, love, joy, and content, these more extreme emotions will dominate the scene as the discharging takes place. However, for those of you who are not in resistance to letting things move through and out of you, in the wake of these discharges, there will be a growing sense of inner peace and calm between the waves of clearing. Resistance only blocks the flow, so where there is resistance, heat and pressure will build up until the necessary release is achieved.

Everything will be cleansed from the planet, and every thing that is *on* her will also be cleansed in one way or another. For most of the lifeforms on a given timeline, this will result in physical death. However, through the mechanism of multiple timelines, many who appear to die on one timeline will persist and be alive on another timeline. Nonetheless, due to the massive numbers of people present on the planet and the greatly reduced numbers of people on the future Earths residing on the different timelines, many points of awareness will remain "between lives" for a very long time, until an incarnational opportunity presents for their Oversoul to manifest a new projection.

All of this is totally "normal" in the normal life cycle of a Creation. If you look back over the history of planet Earth, it is only in recent times that population levels became so massive. Most of the Earth's history didn't even contain people, and in the earliest phases of human population, the numbers of people were very small and highly localized, as compared with today. There are too many people on the planet that are living in unsustainable ways, and that is one of the imbalances that will be corrected in the times that lie just ahead.

This is the time that has been referred to as "the Great Purification" in some of your cultures. Yes, everything will be purified and returned to its essence. However, you must also remember that not everything is on the same "side" as you are. Those whom you have labeled as your enemies or "evil" will be returning to more of their essence also, so there will be an intensification of polarity. Those who are of mixed polarity and do not polarize sufficiently to energetically qualify for either the purely STO or STS polarities will be created as projections onto other 3D versions of planets and continue to explore experiences that eventually lead to sufficient polarization to graduate into 4D or higher levels of existence.

So what you will witness is an intensification of identification with "one's own," the gathering into groups that share the same destination, and an intensification of polarity on both sides of the polarity table. Remember, too, that everyone and every thing is an expression of the Creator, so in the end, you will have to come to embrace that as your truth.

It IS the truth. No one and no thing exists separate from the Creator, because everything is *an expression of* and stems *from* the Creator. If you despise someone or some thing, you are despising the Creator, and you are not in wholeness or acceptance of what IS. In order to re-attain your former state of mastery, you will have to release all personal preferences and all attitudes that maintain separation. One can't experience a permanent state of unity with All That Is and also maintain separation — separation from the Creator and all of Its expressions through Its creations.

This is a natural process and progression, proceeding forth from within. It may seem like things are being forced upon others from outside of themselves, but in fact, each person is a player, created for a particular part and role in the larger drama, and they are simply playing their part as it was "scripted" for them by their Oversoul within the context of the whole.

The only difference between how it is now and how it will be for you when you are back in full consciousness will be how AWARE you are of how all of the parts fit within the larger whole. The only thing that will change at a fundamental level is your degree of conscious awareness of the workings of the whole. With full awareness, everything "makes sense" and there is nothing that is natural to resist. Right now, all of your learned responses, from across all the "lessons" in the past 4.5 billion years, cloud your awareness so that you can't "see" clearly, but that is one of the things that is being changed through the process of clearing that is going on now.

Do not judge other people's actions or choices. They are serving their role and part in the larger drama just as much as you are. If you were fully aware and conscious of everything and how it fits together with all of the other parts, this would be easy for you. However, until you ARE in full consciousness, one of the ways you define yourself is through your differences from others, and one of the ways you emphasize those differences is either by judging the others or by judging yourself as "less than" or "lower than."

No part is less important than any other part. Every thing and everyone is equally important to the whole. So as various actions play out on the planetary surface, remain centered in yourself, listen within in each moment that presents in your life, and choose only for yourself. The question you must ask is, "What is this moment asking of me?" Notice that the emphasis is on what YOU are being asked, not what the moment is asking of anyone else.

The only "job" you have right now is to support your own process and take full responsibility for your choices and responses to what presents in your life. Right now, the highest and best use of your time and energy, beyond that which is required for your survival needs, is to pay attention to the things that are "up" for clearing within yourself and to give yourself over to moving through them. This will assist you in moving through your completions with the experiences contained within your Oversoul, and those completions will prepare you for the "next act" — the new Creation that is nearly upon you now.

4.5 billion years is a long time from a human perspective, so it is totally logical that you would have a lot of clearing to do. However, since several lives are often linked by common themes, when you clear the charge for one of those lives, you clear the charge associated with that theme across all of the lives that contain that theme, on both sides of the equation.

This is all we have to say today, but we will be speaking to you again. Amen, Adonoy Sabayoth. We are the Hosts of Heaven.

4.5 billion years is a long time from a human perspective.

ABOUT "VISION"
August 15, 2006

All right, now. We have asked to speak with you because of events that have occurred on the inner planes since we last spoke with you. First of all, you will be glad to hear that you are over the worst part of the clearings we mentioned before. However, that will present a new challenge for you and that is what we want to address today.

You see, if you can appreciate the fact that all of these "clouds" that have obscured your light also kept YOU from seeing clearly, then as the clearings do their work, you might encounter some difficulties with having your vision made more clear. By "vision," we speak metaphorically. We are not talking about your physical sight itself, but rather how you perceive things in the world around you. We are also talking about the vision you carry within you, the vision of the world you want to create, so we will call this Message, "About 'Vision.'"

Seeing more clearly can be uncomfortable at times, for what you could ignore in the past, you can no longer ignore now. It is a little like coming out of a dream and waking up to a world that is not quite as comfortable for you as the dream state was. This is why many people in the world refer to this process as "awakening." However, we would say you are awakening from a dream that is an illusion and waking up to the dream that you have always carried within you, throughout all the lives that your Oversoul has created.

Think back, if you can, to 4.5 billion years ago, when you joined with others to dream this dream together. You have all been dreaming and now you are awakening and there is a certain discomfort with what you are seeing as you awaken. It is a world that is clearly out of balance and not in keeping with the dream of what you had hoped her to become.

About "Vision" 359

Seeing more clearly can be uncomfortable. What you could ignore in the past, you can no longer ignore now.

You have a saying about there being good news and bad news. The good news is that you are much closer to realizing the original dream than ever before. That dream will culminate with the manifestation and realization of Terra, the new world where all of your dreams will manifest as reality for you. We think you will be surprised at how much of yourself has already gone into the creation of Terra as an idea. It speaks to your heart's deepest longings, now that you have had your fill of experiences on 3D Earth.

You will appreciate Terra all the more for having been through everything you have been through, and once you have completed your transformation in form and consciousness and re-attained your former way of being, all of what you have traversed in the past will indeed seem like a dream, even though you still think of it as real right now.

And now for the bad news. In the process of disassembling the present structures, energies that have been tangled together must be untangled. Think of a ball of yarn, only this yarn is not smooth and silky. It is rough, and has many pieces sticking out of the threads, like so many dry twigs, and those pieces get caught up in the other threads in the ball and the yarn is very tangled indeed.

In order for that which is "crooked" to be made "straight" a delicate process of untangling the energy must take place. It is far more demanding to do this without damaging the "yarn" itself than it is for

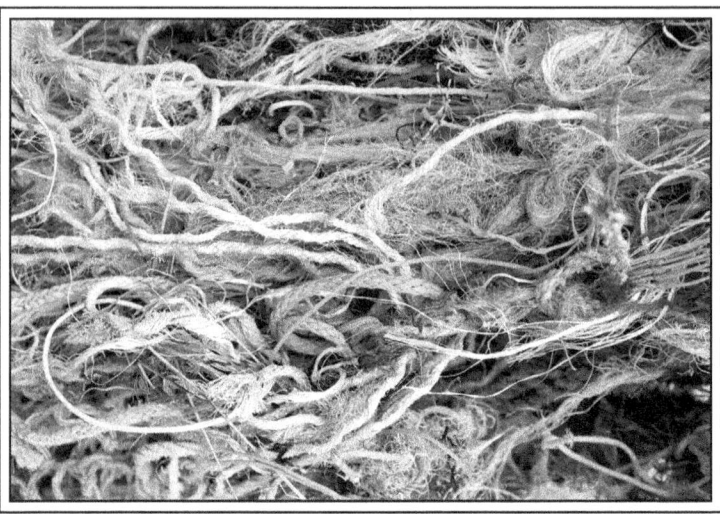

This yarn is rough, and has many pieces sticking out of the threads, like so many dry twigs. Those pieces get caught up in the other threads in the ball and the yarn is very tangled indeed.

one of your surgeons to do the most delicate neurosurgery on the very fine structures of the nervous system. What this will mean is that things will have to proceed somewhat slowly for a while, while this untangling takes place, so that translates to a process that will require you to be present on the ground a bit longer yet, as much as you and we would like for you to be totally on the ships at the present time.

The untangling of energies is part of the process of sorting everyone and everything into their destination — the one chosen for them by their Oversoul. Most of you have Oversouls that have been creating projections into many of the time nodes involving human habitation of your planet. You have served the Creator's desire to experience Itself through Its creations by offering the Creator a vast array of experiences. You have worn many costumes and played many roles, and you had your companions from the loyal opposition to keep the mix more flavorful across these various lives.

In classical drama, there are protagonists (heroes and heroines) and antagonists (villains). Both are needed to create the tensions and conflicts that propel the drama forward and advance the "story line." Many of you have become entangled with those who did not have your best interests at heart, and these tangled energies are carried in the cellular memories of all of the entities that took part in "the dance" with each other. So, in clearing YOUR cellular memory, it is necessary to "untangle" the tangles you have carried inside of you.

Some of you may be aware that you have these entanglements with others of the opposite polarity; most of you are not aware of them. While there are a few individuals who are clear enough in themselves to assist with this process, most of your "healers" have some work to do on themselves before they would be clear enough to do this kind of work on others.

We would caution you to stay clear of techniques and methods that promise to restructure your DNA, clear your soul memories, erase your karma, align you with your soul's purpose, and such. The techniques and methods that would be most beneficial are those that enable you to heal yourself. The inner work is the most valuable thing you can do for yourselves, and no one else can do what is yours to do for yourself.

We cannot recommend a particular course, as each of you is an individual, but we would recommend that if you seek healing, you do so within well-established and proven methods. If someone is promising you the "keys to the kingdom," take a good look at whether they have attained "the kingdom" themselves.

We are not talking about those who claim that their lives are better in some way. We are talking about those who say they have the "formula" that will result in your going ALL of the way. Those who have genuinely attained full consciousness will not be promoting themselves in seminars and websites. They will understand how the universe works to bring people together in synchronistic ways. They don't need "press" for their "audience" to find them!

There are many who are taking advantage of other people's naiveté and gullibility, so as your vision improves, you will be seeing these things happening around you and it's important you don't get caught up in battles over these things. You aren't going to "fix" anything, and it's all you can do just to work on what you can work on for yourself. The ideas we speak about are difficult to embrace in your life precisely because they run counter to the consensus reality around you. They are almost counterintuitive, and yet that is precisely what you must do.

You must go INTO your pain, INTO your fear, without resisting either of those. This is precisely the opposite of what your society has programmed into you. Seeking solutions outside of you is what keeps you from ever being satisfied with any of it. No outside authority —

including us — is ever going to take away the necessity of you doing the part of the work that is yours alone to do.

We are not speaking about treating medical conditions. We are not saying that if you break your arm, you should just leave it alone. We are speaking of the more subtle kinds of "healing" that aren't healing at all. They are also a way to create more entanglements and confusion within yourself. Some of these people who really mean to heal are themselves serving entities they are not aware of. Those entities feed off the energies that are created in the interactions with people seeking healing. Those usually are the kind that perpetuate the condition of helplessness and needing help — a kind of dependency on outside sources that never leads to healing of the fundamental kind.

The entire purpose of what is going on now is to "make straight" what is crooked, to untangle what is tangled. We are working with you around the clock, waking and especially when you are sleeping. We are pulsing you with energies that gently free up the tangles within you. We are straightening out that which is tangled, and this frees up the energies and the entities that are involved.

Many of you have or have had "entities" with whom you have become entangled. This is just a common consequence of the many lives created by your Oversoul and the themes and dramas that have been part of those lives and their "scripts." All of those experiences have been carried across lifetimes in what we refer to as your cellular memory — the cellular memory that is now being cleared.

As you become clearer, you will also have memories or a certain awareness rise up within you, and you will "see" more of who you have been and who you are returning to being. (This may seem like we are talking in circles, but in dealing with time loops, circles are the path that you traverse.) You are waking up from one dream and moving into another dream. This is all we would say on this part of the "vision" topic (awakening) and would like to move on to the other part of the "vision" question — the vision of Terra.

Terra is the world of your dreams, and it is actually your creation just as much as this present planet is your creation. You are projections that can be traced back to the elohim themselves, who are the progenitors for this portion of the created reality. Terra is the culmination of your time together as elohim, of your agreement with each other, and of your time as an earthly human being.

From the time you complete your ascension back to what you were before you entered the time loop, only a glorious future awaits you. It will be full of adventures and discoveries, to be sure, and it will also be full of the peace, joy, and love that you ache to have again. It will truly be a joyous time for all, and you will know exactly what it is that was missing while you were dreaming this other dream.

Terra is there, awaiting you already. You can feel how much closer you are to her now than when you began to be aware of her as your destination. You can feel that she is just out of reach, and we are saying that that is NOT a "dream," but rather an emerging reality. You can "see" her through the lens of your heart. You can feel her in your heart. You already "know" the joy that awaits you and you already know how much closer you are to that joy than you were before.

A little more time is needed now, to untangle these tangled threads — to set each entity free of the others with which it was entangled, so all can go to their proper place. Those who have opposed you also have to be set free to go their way, and all of us are working toward that end result. There are some who do this consciously; there are others who are doing it unconsciously. The end result will be the same, with or without awareness.

So if you don't like what your "vision" shows you at this point in time, be patient. The mere fact that you can "see" it so much more clearly is a good sign. It means you are waking up from the dream — coming out of the trance you have been in — and are moving into full wakefulness, the realization of your other dream — the dream of Terra. So much good awaits you! And yet there is this time that must be traversed while everything is sorted out and made "straight" again. If you can continually release all resistance, this time will be much more comfortable for you. You really don't have to do much else. Just work on releasing resistance whenever you become aware of it.

There are times when the energies are very uncomfortable. They can feel chaotic, or like an electrical current that is unpleasant — a sort of "buzz" that is unsettling. However, if you can remember to release resistance to what is not pleasant, it won't be so unpleasant anymore. You do have a little choice about the relative smoothness of your journey. You will all "make it" to where you are destined to go. If you choose to focus on releasing resistance, things will go more smoothly, although they may not be what you would prefer.

No matter the discomforts along the way, each of you is becoming clearer, more free to fully express your essence and archetype. Those who will not bend before the winds of change will break from their rigidity. Think of the grasses and how, after the winds pass, they spring back up again. Trees can only bend a little before they snap. Be like the grasses, bending in the wind. Remain flexible. Let the energy direct you. Don't try to direct the energy.

We will speak to you again as things progress. We are speaking more often now because we feel you will have an easier time if we remind you of our presence in your lives. You are one of US. Even though you might not think of it that way, we do. You are OUR "family," just as we are YOUR "family." All of us are related to each other — some more closely than others, but all are connected and part of one big "soul family." It will bring us all great joy when we are back together again.

We leave you now, in peace, honor, and blessing. Amen, Adonoy Sabayoth. We are the Hosts of Heaven.

DENSITY 3.8
September 17, 2006

We have asked to speak with you today because you have reached a certain threshold point in the journey back to the next density. If you were to label your starting point as density 3.0 and your emergence point as density 4.0, you are now at density 3.8. Since all movement takes place as a form of oscillation — that is, a wave that moves back and forth between two points, above and below the line that describes the forward movement — you may have noticed that you have been having times when you feel more like you are in fourth density and times that you feel more like you are still in third density.

Well, since you have now reached density 3.8, that will result in your awareness "peeking" into 4.0 density more and more. This could get a little confusing at times, so we thought it would be helpful for us to offer some explanations about the process as it is being experienced now.

Some of you are already noticing these things, and some of you have either not begun to experience them or won't experience them at all. For those of the "special forces," your job requires you to remain fairly close to density 3.0, so the most you will experience until after the evacuation is an oscillation around density 3.2. This is because your task requires you to interface with those who are oscillating around 3.0 most of the time. They will rise slightly as a result of your interaction with them, but all of you will remain closely tied to third density for now.

Those of the third wave are being prepared on the inner planes to receive these teachings and vision but they are not yet conscious of this, as for them, the world is very much the way it has been most of their lives — perhaps a bit more uncertain right now, but otherwise very much "business as usual." They still have to go through what you might term "a rude awakening," and it is precisely the shocking nature of what they have to register that will awaken them to how much the world is changing and how quickly "business as usual" will disappear. It will seem like almost an overnight thing when it all comes to a head, but of course this has been going on in this direction for centuries.

The first and second waves are the ones to whom we are primarily addressing these remarks today. You number in the thousands. The special forces number in the thousands, and the third wave contains around 6 million individuals, more or less. We don't concern ourselves with precise numbers at this time. That will not come into play until other things have occurred and the lists of specific tasks have to be made and followed. It is still a little early for that, but we are already very aware of what is coming and how best to prepare for those times.

So, now, for those of the first and second waves, you may have already begun to notice a heightening of your physical senses and periodic moments in which you are content to simply stop and "be." This is part of your "peeking" into fourth density. Perhaps you have already had moments in which you aren't sure exactly where you are. You can still look around yourself and see the same objects and people, but there is a sense of being further away somehow, like you are seeing through a telescope or some kind of mechanism that allows you to peer in from another location, although you are not quite sure where that might be. This is very normal and typical of your present level of vibration.

You might also find yourself less motivated by the things that used to motivate you. Fear is a great motivator, and as you move through your fears and your cellular memory is purged, fear ceases to motivate you. Instead you feel a certain confidence building within you. Your trust in the process is greatly increased because you have had so much recent evidence of the changes that you are going through, it becomes harder to doubt. In fact, you could say that you are feeling progressively more relaxed and at ease, when compared to those around you. There is a loss of identification with what you used to define yourself by, and that may leave you feeling somewhat undefined at times. Get used to it.

When you are fully in fourth density consciousness and awareness, you will always be creating in the present moment, with no thought to what you have done and no thought to what will follow. This is difficult for you to comprehend right now, as you are still not quite "in" that way of being. However, now that you have reached this threshold, you will experience fourth density ways more often and for longer periods of time.

You may remember that a long time ago we told you that when the moment came to fully enter fourth density, it would only be another small step of many already taken. Perhaps now you can begin to appreciate that statement. The process is entirely natural and does not require arduous studies, methods or "cures." Everything you need is being provided and it is perhaps more difficult to accept that all you need to do is RECEIVE it than it would be to be told you had a lot you had to do.

In third density, everything is built around striving and doing. When one goal or achievement is reached, there is a brief time of respite and content and then you are back to "doing" again. Then there comes a time when life winds down and one prepares to die. Well, you are already dying to who you were and the ways you followed to bring you this far in the journey.

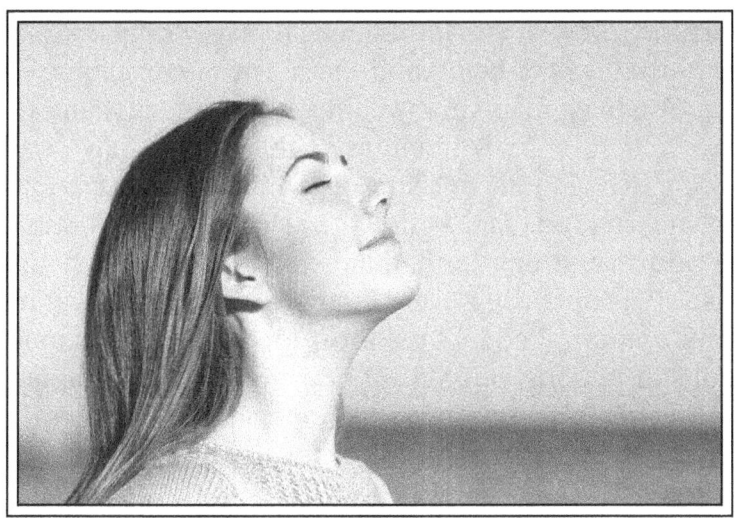

Relax and enjoy the ride. Go with the flow. Don't push. Breathe. Remain in the present.

So what to do now? We have said it so often. Relax and enjoy the ride. Go with the flow. Don't push. Breathe. Remain in the present. Listen within. Simple directions, simple choices, but they must be repeated over and over again. It is a little like the practice of meditation. At the beginning, one's mind wanders and one has to make a conscious choice to bring the mind back to the intended focus. One has to make this choice over and over again, until it becomes a new habit.

In this journey to Terra, you have had to learn some new habits, such as "let go and let God" handle the details. You have had to become more aware of when you are tense and when you are in fear. You have had to learn to allow your emotions to surface and push away much of your social conditioning. You have had to have a lot of courage to differ from those around you, and you have all done beautifully on these things.

Now it's time to take all of these practices that you have been practicing and make them a part of the way you are, all of the time. The "old patterns" will continue to surface to a certain degree until all has been cleared. Remember that you are clearing 4.5 billion years of experiences from many planes and locations of existence, so what is going on is a monumental task when focused through such a small "lens" as a single individual, especially when one is still in veiled consciousness, so we applaud you for your commitment and persistence on your path. You have done well, and the time for joy is getting closer and closer.

As you move upward into fourth density, everything that is not compatible with that way of being and that form of consciousness has to drop away. You have made many completions already, and those that are left sweep across many lifetimes as themes you have explored. If you are going to be in full consciousness and fully in communion with All That Is, any residue that has not been cleared would be shared with everyone and everything, and that would multiply the discomfort enormously. It would be like every thought and emotion was magnified tremendously, multiplied by an almost inconceivable number — not just millions or billions, but almost beyond being countable. The fact that you are being taken up slowly and the reason the process has taken so long is a form of protection — for you, and for everyone you would come in contact with.

This process is a gradual one for several reasons. One is that if it went any faster, you might not be able to handle it and it is intended that you arrive intact. Another reason is so that you can integrate the changes and remain relatively balanced and functional. In some societies and cultures, there are provisions for people who are in full consciousness so that they do not need to be working at jobs, but are taken care of through the donations of those who value their state of being. You are widely scattered across the planet, and you inhabit many different cultures, so it is necessary for you to remain functional, you might say, all the way to the "top." You have now passed this critical threshold, and although there will be still some clearings, it will become much easier now.

You have made a long upward climb, but now things will get easier for you to complete the rest of the process.

You have made a long upward climb, and it has been difficult much of the way, but now you have passed a certain "milestone," and things will get easier and easier for you to complete the rest of the process. Your outer circumstances may remain much the same, but it is in your inner places that the ease comes. Almost without realizing it, you are already vastly different than you were when we began delivering these Messages 7 years ago. Look back to the previous year and you can see how much has changed within you since then. Take a moment to appreciate how far you have already come, and then be comforted that there is not much further to go.

During this last part of the movement into fourth density, it will become easier for you to accept the changes that come with that. Your bodies are going to be somewhat "undependable" as you move back and forth between these two vibratory rates and states of being. Your senses may be greatly heightened one day and be greatly dampened the next. You may be in excruciating pain, and then inexplicably feel a great deal of relief and even bliss.

Your bodies are being greatly challenged to keep up with the changes, so this is a time to be very good to yourself. Take things slowly and don't overdo. Simplify and take time to enjoy where you are. Appreciate what you have and let go of the endless striving for "more." Look at "needs" versus "wants," and also recognize how many of your "wants" are simply habit. They are driven by the mass consciousness, and there is a paradox for you now: as you "progress" on your path more, you will also experience yourself as falling behind those who are in the mass consciousness and stampeding over the cliff like so many herd animals. You are slowing your progress in the direction they are taking and you are beginning to swing around to take another direction entirely.

In your sciences, there is something called inertia. What this means is that an object that is in motion tends to remain in motion until and unless another force occurs to impede or redirect that motion. (It is also true that when an object is at rest, it requires the application of some kind of force to get it moving, but we want to follow the first thread of this conversation, namely to look at the inertia or momentum of objects in motion.)

You have all been part of the society in which you live.

You have all been part of the society in which you live. There is a certain momentum and inertia to overcome in order to go in a different direction than the mass of people is following. These Messages have been one way of redirecting you to take a different trajectory or course than those around you. In fact, many of the suggestions we have given you run totally contrary to all of your social conditioning. That is another reason why this process has of necessity taken so long.

But now a certain threshold has been crossed, and the change of direction has built up its own momentum. The movement will be quicker and easier than before, and soon it will seem like you almost slip effortlessly into your new state of being and find yourselves in another place altogether. This will be a literal perception of being somewhere else when your oscillations have taken you across the threshold and you are vibrating wholly above the 4.0 density point. In the meantime, you will experience more and more of the fourth density ways and perceptions, so please do not think you are losing your sanity. This is totally normal in this process and we are watching over you and working with you constantly, to make sure the pace is perfect for you.

This is not something you can do for yourself. It is not something you can buy in a bottle or read in a book. It is something that is being given to you, and all you have to do is receive the gift. It is not because you are more "deserving" than others. It is because your Oversoul has chosen it to be this way for you, and we are simply "following orders" that come down from the very highest sources in the spiritual hierarchy. If you could see the amount of activity that is really going on "behind the scenes," you would be in awe. And we are only speaking about the part that involves you! Just imagine that similar activity is taking place on every other timeline, for those who are heading toward other destinations. It truly can't be grasped with the linear mind.

And so, beloveds, we are truly filled with joy at your having attained this important milestone. It has taken much work at both ends of the equation. You have been great "soldiers" in the struggles that have warred within you and the choices you have had to make over and over again. The process will be much easier for you now, and if you can just remember to continue to release resistance, remain over your feet (don't get ahead of yourself), and listen within, that's all you have to do. We will supply the rest.

We leave you now, in peace, honor, and blessing. Amen, Adonoy Sabayoth. We are the Hosts of Heaven.

LET IT BE
November 10, 2006

All right, now. We have asked to speak to you from the perspective of the "long view." For us, the things that are in motion are those that have been in motion since this reality was formed. Think about that for a moment. When the "idea" of a new life emerges from the Mind of God, it does so fully complete with all of the elements present that will be required for its desired "dance," and also for its completion and resolution back into the Mind of God, from which it came.

Just so, now. When this portion of reality was "conceived" in the Mind of God, that "conception" or "idea" included everything that has played out for the past 4.5 billion years and everything that will complete that arc of experience until it resolves back into the Mind of God. This is how the "God Game" works. Everything is already present, but does not reveal itself all at once. Rather, it plays out within linear time and reveals all of its contents in a sequence of actions and steps.

Everything that you will be witnessing now is part of the completion that was seeded at the inception of the "idea" that resulted in this portion of reality. When the elohim came together to precipitate this reality out of their beingness, they did so according to the template brought forth from the Mind of God. They were co-creators, not THE Creator, and they did the work OF the Creator, in service TO the Creator.

So it is with you. None of you are separate from the Creator, and none of you are working against the plan of the Creator. Even those who provide the stimulus for your experience — those of the "loyal opposition" as well as those of your team and everyone else — are working within the plan of the Creator. It could not be otherwise, because that's how the Creation works.

When we asked you to detach from the drama, we really meant that. The stimulus level is increasing daily, and if you don't detach from the drama, you will get caught up in the swirling waters and get sucked down into the chaos. You speak of the Age of Aquarius, the water bearer, who is often portrayed tipping a container of water over its shoulder so that the water flows out of the container in a great stream — what you might term a flood.

The "tipping point" came decades ago, and the flood — from your perspective — has been heading toward you for quite a long time. From outside of time, it is just another "moment" — another bead on the string of experience — no more and no less important or significant than all that preceded it and all that will follow it. It is all just experience to satisfy the Creator's desire to experience Itself through Its creations. So we feel it would be beneficial for you to detach from the drama, step back, and let the flood sweep by you entirely.

Detach from the drama, step back, and let the flood sweep by you entirely.

The workings of the power elite will be surfacing more and more with each passing day, with each passing year. However, that is only half of the picture. You see, we have been working, too, and we have our own "power plays," also. We seek to empower you to reclaim your essence and true nature, because out of you a whole new set of possibilities will emerge, as part of a wholly new creation.

While the power elite (and those who will initially oppose them) focus on the phenomena of 3D, we are quietly working away, hidden in the background and invisible to those who cannot see us or what we do because they are blind to whatever does not exist within themselves. Even those of the negative polarity at the higher densities are not all-seeing or omniscient. They can only recognize what their experience and models allow them to recognize. Although we all have access to similar technologies, they cannot recognize the essence and vibration of love.

While they seek to dominate nature, we work WITH nature, including the human nature. We both seek to eliminate resistance, but we do it in opposite ways. We encourage; they discourage. Each side in the polarity game pursues methods in keeping with that polarity. Precisely because they cannot see or understand our ways, we are able to carry out our activities in a totally hidden way, safe from those who might wish to intrude on or prevent what it is that we are doing.

No matter what you might see taking place in the events playing out in the physical realm, there are also events taking place in the non-physical realm. Each of you that is part of the "op" carries hidden codes and programs in your DNA — not just the portion of the DNA that is visible to your scientists with their physical instruments, but also the many layers of non-physical information that is also coded within you. We play on those codes like a musician plays music. Each "note" is struck at a particular time in the overall song. We set off tones from our side of things and your built-in codes are set in motion (through the principle of resonance) in response to the tones we sound at precise moments in the entire process.

We have spoken before of our use of the technologies of sound and light to accomplish the task of restoring you to your full estate. The other side is also using technologies of sound and light for their purposes and will continue to do so. However, resonance works in both directions. If you DON'T resonate with a tone, nothing happens inside of you. It doesn't matter what your intellect "believes." This is all taking place below the level of your conscious knowledge, in secret and in a very protected way.

So we are speaking to you today to ask you to trust in our methods, to listen within, and to allow the drama to play out in front of you without fearing it or engaging with it. There is nothing to fix and nothing to stop. There is no one to warn, and no one to write letters of protest to. There is nothing to be gained by engaging in debate with those who don't have this perspective or understanding. All we ask you to do is release your

We set off tones and your built-in codes are set in motion at precise moments in the entire process.

resistance, release your pain, release everything that is not part of your essence.

We can't overcome your resistance. That is a choice you have to make for yourself. We don't force ourselves or our methods on anyone, and neither does anyone who is a positive-polarity being. If you happen to read about predictions of takeovers, demonstrations, or other kinds of "public education," recognize that those are either the workings of the deceivers or projections from the very human minds that feel they have to "do something" to change things from the course they are slated to take.

It is sad to see the end of a dream. The "American dream" has come and gone and is over now, for all intents and purposes. However, we hope that the vision of Terra will present a much higher and better dream to attain, and we hope to empower you to reach for it, for it is your destiny and destination. Even those who have come to serve the "op" and then depart for other areas of service have been drawn to the vision of Terra and lent their efforts to help it come to fruition.

This is a very big event for a relatively small planet, and many hands are tending to the birth, not all of whom will remain to see the new life grow. There is a very complex weaving together of some of the energies at the same time we are untangling others in the ways we have spoken of before. Therefore, we ask you to trust in the "long view," do your part, let us do ours, and leave everything else behind.

No one is going to rescue anyone from doing the inner work. This is a team effort. No one will stop you from achieving your destination and destiny, either. Each of us is one player in the larger drama. We have our script, too. Everyone has their script, and we can't tell you details about your individual scripts. All we can tell you is that we are with you and working on you around the clock to enable you to make the rest of the journey successfully.

No one is going to rescue anyone from doing the inner work. This is a team effort.

The drama that is playing out will become even more dramatic in the days, months, and years ahead. Observe it if you feel to, but allow it to play out without resistance from your end or contributing to it by becoming involved in it. It is going to play out, no matter how you respond to it. It isn't going to be stopped, and it isn't supposed to be stopped. Everyone is playing their individual part perfectly. This is the grand summing up of the human experience on 3D planet Earth. Some of it will continue on other future Earths, which have no connection to you or your individual journey.

You are going to be heading into 4D and leaving the drama of 3D Earth behind you. Now is a good time to begin doing that. Leave this drama where it belongs. Do not engage with it or you can get caught up in it, and that will interfere with the work we are doing with you. There was a song that was popular during the "flower children" era that had a refrain that seems appropriate to recall now: "Let it be. Let it be." In fact, we think that is such a good idea that we will title this Message that way: "Let it be."

When we asked you to "let go and let God" (handle the details), that was another way of saying, "Let it be." By not resisting what is playing out, it will simply slide by you as you slip out another door and leave it behind. "Let it be," and you will free yourself to move on to something else entirely.

We would like you to slip out of that other door and come to be with us where we are. In order to do that, you must be willing to let everything else play out as it needs to in order to fulfill all of the other scripts, too, so "let it be" what it is supposed to be and go another way entirely. Let it be what it is supposed to be and let yourself be what you are supposed to be, too.

Amen, Adonoy Sabayoth. We are the Hosts of Heaven.

We would like you to slip out of that other door and come to be with us where we are.

LIVING FROM THE CALM CENTER
December 7, 2006

All right, now. We have asked to speak to you today because there are a number of things on the horizon that we wished to prepare you for. The first of these is a change in our relationship with you.

As you probably know by now, we are working closely with you at all times. There is not one of you who is part of the "op" who is not being worked with. This includes the third wave, who is being prepared to receive us and who will need to go through the "wake-up call" of the events that lie just ahead. They are not aware of us in the same way you are, so we work with them quietly, behind the scenes of their everyday life. By the time you will be involved in the evacuation itself, they will be ready to receive your help and be taken onto the ships — something that would frighten them now if they were presented with that option without this extensive preparation.

Because it is necessary for you to become more fully a part of the working team, we will not be giving you the kinds of discourses we have given you in the past. We acknowledge that you have found hearing from us comforting and helpful in solidifying your feeling about the purpose and direction of your life. However, now it is time for you to move more fully into sourcing from within yourselves for your "knowing," so we will not be giving you the kind of reassurances we have given in the past. It is very important for you to work on feeling into the rightness or wrongness of each potential action, as this will train you in the ways you will know what to do from here on in.

There is no one who can't do this. All it requires is to create a habit of feeling into a situation when it presents, take a moment to center yourself, and feel what your body is telling you. Trust the feelings you get in your body. You can always tell when you are repelled by some potential action or when you are relaxing into it. A feeling of tightening or pressure is a "no." A feeling of expansion or release is a "yes."

All of your decisions can be felt into and distilled into a simple "No, this is not the best choice at this moment" or "Yes, this is the right choice in this moment" kind of answer. You don't need to know anything more than what to do in the moment that is presenting. What you need to work at is to remember to not proceed until you have felt into what to do.

A feeling of tightening or pressure is a "no." A feeling of expansion or release is a "yes."

If you are upset by something, then be sure to wait until you are calm before deciding how to proceed. As we have said, there is very little that can't wait until you have clarity as to how to proceed. It is so very important to always wait until you are calm within, even if that takes a while. Most decisions are not so difficult, but it is so important that you practice this behavior in everything you do so that it becomes almost instinctive to treat everything in your life this way.

Much of the "op" is going to go "underground" now. We will not be announcing our moves publicly, but each of you will be guided perfectly as to where to go, who to meet with, etc., as things unfold. Your only communication with us will be from within. You have provided yourself with all of the abilities you need to get through this time without relying on us in the ways you have relied on us before.

We will still be with you, and we will continue to work with you until you are also on board the ships and finished with your transformation. However, there will not be many more things for us to say to you about how to live your lives. We have given you a solid foundation, and now it is up to you to live by those principles. The principles will get you through. They are far more important than any dates or predictions we can give you now. Live the principles and you will do just fine.

There are many things ahead in 2007 and beyond, some of which will require you to make changes in how — and possibly where — you will be living. We encourage you to simplify your life as much as possible. There will come a time when you may be required to make rapid changes in your circumstances, so if you have done all you can to clean out the clutter from your life and made your completions with the past, these changes will be much easier to make and respond to when the time arrives.

We recognize that most of you are still widely scattered, all over the planet, and without face-to-face contact with any of the others from the first two waves or the special forces. This has served a purpose and it still serves a purpose for now. This relative isolation will serve to strengthen your self-reliance and require you to be more attentive to the signals that present in each moment as to what you should do and when to do it.

Without regular reinforcement from us, you will have to become resourceful in the ways you find to sustain yourself on the rest of this journey through 3D. However, it won't be that way much longer because, very soon, you will complete the passage out of 3D consciousness and anchor yourself in 4D awareness. When this happens, you will have the full awareness of everyone else — of us, and of the rest of your team on the ground. You will not need printed materials or the Internet to communicate with any of us. You will be totally aware of all of the parts and how they are serving the whole.

This will be a radically different way of operation for you in some ways, but by the time it arrives, you will not notice that it is so different from what you have been approaching all along. If you will take this seriously enough to practice the principles we have given you, no matter where you may find yourselves and no matter what is surrounding you, you will do just fine. You do carry the ability to "know" in each moment what the right course of action is, and you can make use of the resources that are available to you right now in terms of the "op."

The key task you have right now is to make a habit out of living the principles we have given you and to use the techniques of quieting yourself that we have given you, so that you can listen within. Your body always "knows," if you can turn off the chatter of your mind and listen from a place of calmness within yourself.

The time of cellular clearing and untangling is nearly complete. There will still be some "bumps in the road" for a while, but not forever. As you encounter the last bits of clearing you will notice that there is a feeling of spaciousness opening up within you — the places where you used to carry the emotional baggage that have been cleared out. You will begin to feel a more expansive definition of yourself, and to feel it more often, if you choose to let yourself feel that. Even in the midst of a noisy crowd, it is possible — if you are detached enough — to feel as expanded and calm as if you were standing in a broad landscape in total isolation from others.

Listen to the sound of silence within you. Keep your breath deep and slow. Recognize that what others around you may be feeling is not "yours" but "theirs." Become a witness to what plays out around you, but do not get caught up in the emotions that take you out of your calm center. Whenever you are aware that you are NOT responding from your calm center, STOP! Take whatever time you need to become calm again. Close your eyes if necessary to shut out the external stimulus. Make a practice of living your life from a place of calm, no matter what is going on around you.

No one can MAKE you react. If you are mindful and have practiced this skill well, you can remain calm no matter what is going on around you. When the clearing of the cellular memory is complete, there will be very little that will be capable of triggering you unless you choose to engage with it emotionally within present time. Remain detached and sovereign. If you are still engaging with the 3D drama, we suggest you discontinue that behavior.

The world around you is dying. The things that will be happening around you will be the result of desperation and fear. Do not engage with them. The world around you is in a precarious state right now. It took a long time to get that way, and there are cracks appearing in the veneer that covers over the depth of what is going wrong, but the power elite are doing everything they can to make things appear "normal" and just as they always have been.

Do not be deceived. The foundations are crumbling and soon the whole thing will come tumbling down into a time of chaos, confusion, and irrational behaviors on the part of those who are afraid and desperate to find something to cling to for support. There will be a lot of angry people, too, as they realize the extent that they have been betrayed in placing their trust in their leaders, who cannot lead them out of the mess that has been collectively created and must be dealt with now.

It will not be a pretty sight, and there will be a lot of shouting, demands for action, and "acting out" when frustration levels get too high. The simple fact is that things have gone too far to be corrected in "normal" ways, and so a major "course correction" will come about as each thing gets so far out of balance that it triggers another thing to go over a critical threshold and also begin to spin out of control.

You have an expression called "the domino effect." It refers to how the rectangular tiles used to play a game called Dominoes can be stood on edge and placed in a line in such a way that if one piece falls over, it knocks over the piece that is next to it in the line, which then knocks over the piece next to it in the line, and so on, until all of the pieces have fallen over. This happens in a smooth, wavelike motion, and happens in a sequence determined by the relative position of each piece with respect to the whole line of pieces and the interrelationships and connections with every other piece in the line. Just so with the world around you.

When the critical piece falls, then the whole thing falls down in rapid succession.

What is about to occur could not have occurred before. There were certain kinds of connections that had to line up, in order for all of the pieces to cause the other pieces to fall. Things had to proceed slowly at first, so that all of the pieces would line up, but there is a certain point when everything is lined up and waiting until the one critical piece falls, and then the whole thing falls down in rapid succession.

When this occurs, it will still take time to play out, but for those with "eyes to see" and who can FEEL the energy of things, it will be obvious when that critical point has arrived. This is when we will go into "high gear" with the "op" and this is when you must be ready to respond to changes and to respond to them quickly and without hesitation.

You must be ready to respond to changes and to respond to them quickly and without hesitation.

You have had a long time to prepare. We have been providing these Messages over a period of years, and we have been asking you to do certain things that some of you have been doing and some of you haven't. Now the time is very short, so if you have not made living these principles a priority before now, we strongly suggest that you do so now. For those of you who HAVE been following our instructions, keep on doing that and strengthen your new habits so that they become automatic no matter what is going on in your life.

You are close to a time of massive change, and we have given you all of the instructions you need to cope with these changes in an effective and beneficial way. If you will re-read what we have given you already, you will discover it is all there and that it only awaits your using it in your life — every moment of every day.

We may still speak to you from time to time, but it will only be to give you brief announcements of temporal value, ones that will not tell you what to do or how to be, but rather just to tell you about something that is about to occur. There will not be many of these announcements, so this will be the last of the formal Messages for Volume Three. The rest of the information will be provided through our messenger and her efforts to communicate with the rest of you through the medium of the Internet. However, even if you do not have access to the Internet at times, you can always get your moment-to-moment information and "news" within yourself.

Once you have fully crossed over and anchored your awareness in 4D, even these brief notices will not be necessary. You will have full awareness of everything that is going on and will have no need of notices within the 3D envelope. In the meantime, we hope you will take our advice and finish the work you still have to do in order to make that crossing.

You are here to do a job, and everything you are doing now is still preparation for that job. It has all been preparation until now, and the preparation has been going on for centuries of your time. However, the time is coming when the preparation will be behind you and it will be time to go to work on the evacuation itself. That will be the culmination of what you have come to do within the 3D envelope and that will complete the focus of your 3D life.

However, just beyond that ending is a new beginning for you. A door will swing open on an entirely new set of possibilities and only peace, joy, and love will remain.

We leave you now, in peace, honor and blessing. Amen, Adonoy Sabayoth. We are the Hosts of Heaven.

INTRODUCTION TO THE ARTICLES

The material in this book is the result of a long journey of awakening. This section of the book contains four articles that are intended to supplement the material contained in the other sections.

The first is the original vision I received in March 1982. When the scenes played out in front of me, I experienced them from outside of linear time. Everything I saw seemed like it was happening within my sense of "now," so there was no way that I could know how long it would take to play out within linear time.

I thought it was imminent because it felt that way to me as I experienced it. The Hosts have said that their experience of accessing probabilities is similar, so their attempts to predict when things will occur within linear time have often been inaccurate except when there is a very short horizon involved.

That being said, the signs appear to be clear that what I saw in the original vision is steadily unfolding, regardless of how long that takes to complete. On July 19, 2018, I felt a personal shift that seemed to mark the beginning of what I can only call "the long slide home" and I believe it is so for all of us.

The second article is something I wrote back in 1999 and brought up to date for the new version of the website. It tries to explain the shift into 4th density by using scientific models that we can understand as metaphors for our process. It also sheds some light on the process itself that is not dealt with elsewhere on the site or in this book.

The third article is a report on some of our experiences with the OT ships. The first half describes my own experiences and the second half shares some of the photos and experiences that other people have had and continue to have to this day.

The final article uses the metaphor of the caterpillar's transformation into a butterfly to stimulate your thinking about why you may not have to die after a certain point in your personal journey. For those of us who are going directly to Terra at this time, we will be taking our physical bodies with us and they will be transformed into the bodies we will occupy on Terra. For those who will be born onto Terra later on, either as part of the first generation of native Terrans OR after more third-density incarnations on other versions of this planet, this article still has value because it will at least seed the idea that one does not always have to drop one's body in order to move on.

I hope you find these articles helpful in coming to understand and embrace some of the more difficult aspects of the Operation Terra perspective. There is other supplemental material in the Archives section that may also add to your understanding and experience, and I encourage you to read it all.

Blessings,
Sara/Adonna/Oriole

THE ORIGINAL VISION (1982)

The information in this book arose from a long personal journey. It began in earnest on March 9, 1981, when the Christ materialized in my bedroom, put his hands on my head, and called me to a path that has demanded everything I had in me, and it also brought me to a place of greater understanding with regard to the times in which we live.

A year later, in March of 1982, I took some lessons from a man who said he could teach me to access information from other planes of reality. In one of those lessons, I received the following vision.

At the time, I experienced it all as an observer who was located in the timeless "now," so the part of me that experiences linear time was expecting the Earth changes and the other things that I saw to occur much sooner than they have. It wasn't until 2018 that I recognized that things in the outer world had begun to FEEL like they had in the vision, and while there is still a lot that needs to play out, I do feel that we are finally going to experience those changes on a planetary scale.

When I had connected with my guides, my teacher said, "Ask them to show you what there is to see." I said out loud, "Show me what there is to see."

I had my eyes closed and in my inner vision, something that looked like a movie screen rolled down. At first the screen was blank. Next to it, I saw what looked like a Chinese gentleman, similar to the statue my parents had on the living room bookshelf in our home. He had long skinny mustaches on both sides of his upper lip and he was wearing a floor-length robe.

He unrolled a long scroll, which I somehow knew was a checklist of the "duties" that had to be performed [i.e., the things that had to happen]. As he began to consult the scroll, my attention was drawn to

Next to the screen, I saw what looked like a Chinese gentleman, similar to the statue in my parents' home.

the screen behind him, where I saw a globe shape take form. As I drew closer to the globe, I knew that I was looking at the Earth.

> **NOTE:** The following scenes "dissolved" into one another, similar to how scenes can "fade" from one to another in a movie. I was only aware of what I was seeing, and I described it to my teacher, who made notes about what I said as I talked.

First, I saw a grey, pointed mountain with a green slope in front of it. The top of the mountain exploded and opened a rift down its side that spread forward, opening a crevasse in the ground in front of it.

Then I saw a full moon over the ocean. The wind began blowing very hard, whipping up foam and huge waves on the oceans. Tall trees were being blown over on land. I could not tell what was causing the wind, but I could see it had far-reaching effects.

The scene shifted and I saw people running, frightened, screaming. They were all dressed in grey. I knew the grey color meant that they were undifferentiated from those around them — the implication was that they were the general masses of the population. They were all going through this at the same time.

The scene shifted again. Large cities toppled over, tall buildings just collapsing, as if their foundations had failed to support them. The sky behind them was red from the fires everywhere — everything was burning.

I saw what looked like a man who was holding his child and struggling up a steep slope, trying to escape, but he slid back down each time, as if in a bowl with steep sides. There was no escape for him or anyone.

All was confusion, greyness ... there was a tremendous amount of confusion ... As I peered into all of this confusion, trying to grasp what was causing it, suddenly the cause revealed itself to me: "There's not enough love, [teacher]! There's not enough love!"

There was a sense of billowing grey clouds that covered over everything. The people couldn't be seen as individuals anymore. Details were blotted out by the greyness, but there was a sense of rising tension and increasing noise from many voices calling out in distress.

The tension continued to build. At the point where it seemed that if one more thing happened, there would be mass suicides everywhere, people clothed in white robes began appearing in the midst of the people who were dressed in grey and were running around, seeking relief. I knew this was happening all over the world. Wherever the people dressed in white appeared, centers of calm occurred in the midst of the confusion.

The people in white began appearing in greater and greater numbers, just like popcorn does when it begins to pop. They were calm in the midst of the confusion, giving blessing to all whom they reached. Their mere presence was soothing and calming for those around them. I heard the phrase, "They are centers for calm and blessing."

Order began taking form out of the chaos. The ones in white began to form columns of people, moving them toward some unseen destination. They were gathering and guiding the ones in grey, calming them so they joined together into steadily moving groups. Large white disc-shaped spaceships appeared in the sky, everywhere I looked. The people in white led the people in grey in an orderly procession that went up into the openings in the bottoms of the hovering vehicles. It was a massive, world-wide exodus ... a tremendous undertaking ... .

I drew back to a position in outer space where I could see the Earth rotating in front of me. At first, everything looked normal, but then the Earth slowed its rotation and finally stopped rotating altogether. All of the water from its surface was thrown off in great white clouds and everything that was not bedrock also was flung off into space. Nothing was left except barren rock — no moisture, no plants, no animals.

I drew back to a position in outer space where I could see the Earth rotating in front of me.

The Earth hung motionless for a moment, then it rolled over like a top that has lost its momentum and slowly began spinning on a different axis. The north pole had tipped downward toward the equator by what looked like around 26 degrees south of its present position.

Then there was a break in the scenes that indicated time had passed. During that time, most of the people who had been taken off the Earth were carried to other parts of the universe to complete their lives while Earth was going through her own transformation. and healing.

While Earth was healing from all that had gone on over her existence as a planet, about 10% of the people who had been lifted off of the planet were taken to what looked like a large planet to be equipped for their migration to the "new Earth" as colonists. This included a reprogramming of their consciousness, as well as equipping them with clothing, supplies, and technology. None of the old patterns would be taken to the "new Earth" (which we now refer to as Terra, the Latin word for "Earth").

There was another break in time and I saw the "new Earth" itself. It is polished and gleaming like mother-of-pearl. There is a great gleaming light everywhere. It is now re-inhabited.

The sky is incredibly blue. I hear this beautiful music, which I know is the "music of the spheres." The plants are bright and joyous; they exult in the shining light and the clean air. The people move in quiet, radiant joy. Everyone and everything is completely and blissfully aware of their direct connectedness to the Creator.

Now I see Christ on his throne ... incredible love streaming forth ... how much there is ...

Thoughts come: We don't have to be limited ... He will be with me throughout all this ... I am surrounded by his love, his blue-white light ...

I am surrounded by his love, his blue-white light

I feel so small and remember the Bible passage, "only if ye be as a little child" ... I am totally enfolded in his love.

(That experience of being totally enfolded in Christ's love was so powerful, I could not speak for some time afterward.)

More thoughts come: "Meanwhile, be in a prayerful attitude, feeling gladly serving. Attitude is the most important thing; the nature of the activity doesn't matter. Be in an attitude of readiness ...

I'll be called ... Be ready when the call comes ... incredible amount of Love ... cherishing ..."

Then everything faded out and I returned to the room where I was sitting with my teacher.

This vision laid out the blueprint for what later became Operation Terra and defined the course of the rest of my life. After I received it, the first confirmation I found for what I had experienced was in the Bible:

> "Then I saw a new heaven and a new earth, for the first heaven and earth had passed away, and the sea was no more." — Rev 21:1

The part about "the sea was no more" confirmed what I had seen when the oceans were flung off into space as a result of the Pole Shift. I later found confirmation regarding the ships I had seen (the Biblical prophecy about "coming on the clouds"), and the conditions that had preceded the Pole Shift (much of the Book of Revelation predicts them, and analyses of current global trends also confirm what I saw).

The Hosts have asked me to make it clear that the scenes in the vision are symbolic and not to be taken literally. They represent a time of increasingly severe geophysical events and a time of increasing chaos and social breakdown on a global basis.

On the timeline that leads to Terra as its destination, this will culminate in the removal of around 6-7 million people (plus many plants and animals) that will migrate to Terra via a lengthy stopover on Midway Station — an extremely large mothership that is approximately 80% the size of Earth. Midway Station is the large sphere that I saw in the vision (I thought it was a planet), and it will house the colonists from Earth while Earth is transforming into Terra (the "new Earth").

The other 90% (approximately 60-70 million) who are taken off the planet will return to their home planets throughout the galaxy and some (but not all) of them will take part in creating colonies on Terra that represent their home planets. When it is fully colonized and settled, Terra will maintain a global population of around 500 million people (plus a rich array of other lifeforms) from throughout the galaxy.

I think we are at the very beginning of those times and that they may play out for several years, depending on which timeline one is referring to. See the "About Operation Terra" chapter in this book for more information about the timelines and the timeline for Operation Terra.

Sara/Adonna/Oriole
July 5, 2018

PHASE SHIFT TO 4ᵀᴴ DENSITY

In late July of 1999, I was traveling to an airport. I was not doing the driving, so I was free to muse about anything I wished. It is at such times that I am particularly receptive to psychic or intuitive impressions, and I became aware of a perceptual metaphor that was arriving in my mind:

I "saw" a space that was completely filled with large boulders that were lashed together in all directions by a system of heavy thongs. As I watched, I saw the boulders beginning to move. At first, they only rubbed against one another a little. Then the distance between them increased and they began to move more freely, crashing and bumping into one another and straining and stretching the thongs.

I realized that I was seeing into the "future" of this structure and, as the scene moved forward in time, the boulders moved further and further apart and their movements became more erratic until the thongs broke and they could move freely among one another. At the time, I felt that the boulders represented large units of planetary energy and that I was watching the breaking up of old forms and patterns. After reflecting on this experience, I realized that it was very similar to a process that is called "phase shift."

You may be familiar with the three physical states of water: ice (solid), water (fluid), and "steam"/water vapor (gas). When ice melts into water or water turns to steam, it is the result of the absorption of more energy in the form of heat. When a solid melts into a liquid or a liquid becomes a vapor or gas, it is still chemically the same substance, but the molecules behave differently and have a different orientation with respect to one another. It has shifted to another "phase" or state of the substance.

The key element in this process is the absorption of more energy. The increase in energy causes the molecules to vibrate more rapidly and to move apart from one another.

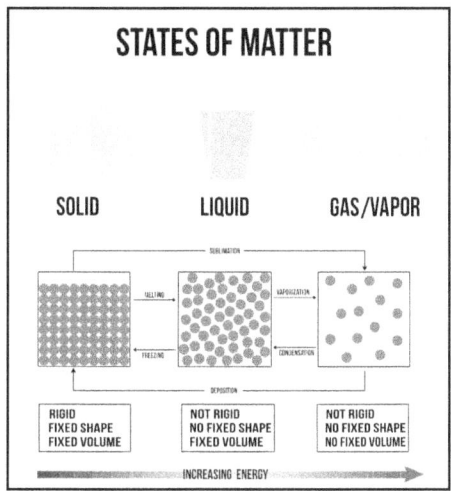

When a solid melts into a liquid or a liquid becomes a vapor or gas, it has shifted to another "phase" or state.

In solids, when enough energy has been absorbed, the bonds that keep the molecules locked into a crystalline lattice break apart and the molecules can slide freely past one another. The substance is then in the liquid state or phase. If even more energy is absorbed by the substance, the molecules move faster and faster until they escape into totally free motion. The substance is then in a gas/vapor state or phase.

This is exactly what is happening to us and to the world around us right now. We have entered a time in which increasing energy is being absorbed by the molecules that make up our physical reality. They are moving faster and faster, which means that their rate of vibration (frequency) is also increasing. The basic vibratory rate of the planet is increasing. All of the physical forms that we are familiar with are undergoing a phase shift.

In fact, if one is sufficiently sensitive to the energies, it does feel like our reality is in the process of "melting down" into a more freely flowing reality. In stark contrast to the sorts of "fixed" or "solid" perceptions and ideas we have been accustomed to on 3D Earth, the Messages from the Hosts of Heaven refer to a type of stream-of-consciousness experience as being the norm on Terra. It is the word "stream" in the term "stream-of-consciousness" that is the clue to the fluidity of 4D reality.

The planetary frequency is shifting upward, and the frequency of every material object is also shifting upward. If things feel like they are going faster, it's because they really are! We are going through a profound phase shift that will take us to the next level in the reality spectrum. Our "solid" world is melting and becoming a more fluid one.

To help you understand this concept a little better, let's take a look at visible light. We define "visible" light as energy that is vibrating within the frequency range that can be detected by the receptor cells in the retinas of our eyes.

The frequency of vibration of a form of energy is in an inverse relationship to its wavelength. *The shorter the wavelength, the higher the frequency.* Very long waves have a very low (or "slow") frequency. Our physical eyes can "see" or detect energy in a frequency range that corresponds to a wavelength of 400 to 750 nanometers. A nanometer is a very small unit (1 billionth of a meter) that is used to measure the extremely short wavelengths found in various forms of radiant energy.

Visible light ranges from the color "violet" to the color "red." Ultraviolet (which means "beyond" violet, i.e., a higher frequency than violet) and infrared (which means "below" red, i.e., a lower frequency than red) light is not normally visible to our eyes without special equipment that extends the range of our vision. On Terra, the planet and everything on it will be vibrating at a frequency above that of our (3D) physically visible light. Terra already exists, but we cannot see her with our physical eyes because she is vibrating beyond the range of light that our 3D physical eyes can see.

When our own frequency gets sufficiently high, WE will not be visible to those whose eyes are not operating in our frequency range. To them, we will seem to have disappeared, but to us THEY will not normally be visible and our experienced reality will still seem physical to US, even though it is invisible to others who are operating in a lower frequency band.

Everything has a characteristic vibration and frequency. Colors, emotions, substances, names, and thoughtforms all have an energetic "signature." Everything is made up of energy, and all energy is vibrating. We call the emotions of fear, anger, hatred, jealousy, and greed the "lower" emotions because they actually DO have a lower vibrational frequency. The so-called "higher emotions" of joy, peace, love, bliss, and compassion actually DO have a higher vibrational frequency.

As the planet and everything on her moves up in frequency and transits the phase shift into fourth density, all lower-frequency waveforms are being thrown off or canceled (when waves are totally out of phase, i.e., exactly opposite to one another, they cancel each other out). It is a purification process, and the only thing that will be left on the other side of this phase shift will be those waveforms that are vibrating at a frequency that is compatible with that of Terra. There will only be the "higher" emotions of joy, peace, love, bliss, and compassion. The "lower" emotions simply won't occur.

What this means in our daily lives and experiences is that everything we carry within ourselves that is not of the "higher" frequencies is being flushed out. This is most noticeable in our close relationships, but it is already showing up in the larger society as road rage, increasing violence, and international crises.

These are just the symptoms of a deep cleansing and purification taking place. The higher emotions are being enhanced, so we also see a greater emergence of the qualities of love, and a growing desire for peace, compassion and forgiveness. (There are many examples of this, such as the growth in the use of hospice services to provide comfort for those who are dying and for those who love them.)

There are many of us who have been doing a lot of self-work in preparation for this time. We have acquired many tools and skills to cope with the accelerating pace of change. No one will be unaffected, but there are many hands and hearts to help us deal with the necessity of our own process of purification. Everything is moving toward healing and wholeness, even though it seems like everything is coming apart. Both movements are happening at the same time.

Let's return to our example of ice melting into water. We can view the breaking of the crystalline bonds as a liberation of sorts. In the solid state, the water molecules have a very limited range of motion or activity. In the liquid state, there is much more freedom of movement, and the molecules can glide past one another smoothly, with much less friction and disturbance. The same is true for this transition as we shift from third density to fourth density.

We are breaking loose from the confines of our limited ideas of who and what we are and moving out of time-bound thinking into a more fluid reality. We have to experience the purging of our anger, fear, rage, and other "lower" emotions and this is affecting the entire population of the planet. As the amount of energy being absorbed by the planetary systems increases, there will be more apparent agitation and movement, some of which will not be harmonious. It will feel like things are melting down, but it may also take on the form of explosive reactions, just as bubbles of steam rise from the bottom of the pot to burst through the boiling surface of the liquid in the pot. People may have a "short fuse" and trigger easily as the breaking apart of the structures and systems proceeds.

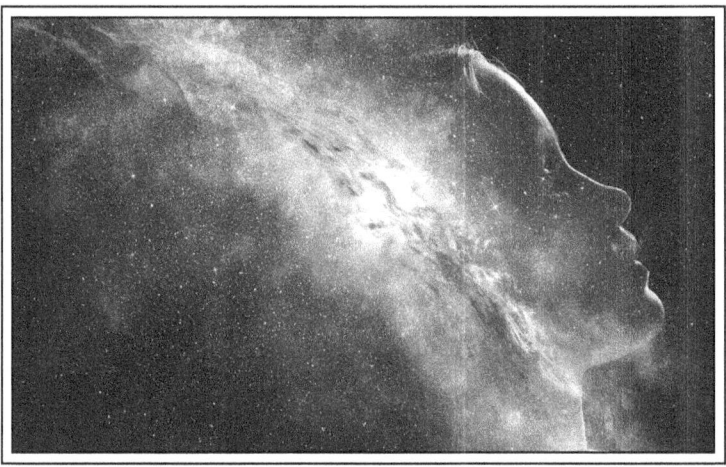

We are breaking loose from our limited ideas of who and what we are and moving into a more fluid reality.

When a chick emerges from the egg, there is some destruction of the shell that had contained the chick while it was growing and developing. The same is true for us now. Those structures and patterns that have held us within a certain limited range of actions and movement are cracking and shattering, so that we can emerge and operate with a much greater degree of freedom and creativity.

As our own inner "earthquakes" release the bound-up energies of our "stuck" emotions and challenge our customary habits, it certainly won't be comfortable at times, but if we can understand our experience as one of moving into greater personal and creative freedom, perhaps it will help us to align with supporting the purification process instead of resisting it.

Those structures and patterns that have confined us are breaking, so that we can operate with greater freedom.

Resistance will be overcome whenever and wherever it occurs, simply because the momentum of this change is too great to be stopped. Anything and anyone that cannot ride this wave of change — this shift from third density to fourth density — will not survive the shift itself. It is important to remember that nothing ever really perishes. It just changes form and goes on.

In closing, I would like to say to you that there are great challenges occurring, but also great opportunities. All of our "stuff" is being shaken loose so that we can become truly free, and our best service to ourselves and to the process is to simply get out of the way. Surrender to a higher power and let that (the higher power) carry you through this process. That will enable you to "go with the flow" of these changes in the smoothest possible way.

This is the time for which we have been waiting, and we have created ourselves to have all of the inner strength and resources that we need in order to finish this round of existence in keeping with the choices of our soul/Oversoul/Higher Self. Each time we find ourselves in resistance to the rapidly increasing changes confronting us, if we can just remember to surrender up our desire for personal control over our lives, we will have a much more comfortable and peaceful transition.

Resistance is the source of all pain. It is always based in fear, so fear is always at the root of our pain. If we can move into surrender, there will still be sensation, but it will no longer be pain. By choosing surrender over and over again, we can train ourselves to move into surrender as easily and automatically as we used to go into "reaction" and resistance mode.

Not everyone will go to Terra, and there may be a temptation for you to try to "save," redirect or "convince" others. Remember that all of these choices are being made by the soul/Oversoul/Higher Self of each individual, regardless of whether you can see it that way or not. If someone asks you for help, by all means give it to the extent that it can be received, but there is much that you will see taking place that is not supposed to be "helped" or "fixed"; it is part of your own surrender to allow that process to take its course without resisting it in any way.

We ourselves must expand enough to be able to hold the entire process in the chalice of our hearts. We must also willingly and gratefully open and empty ourselves out, so that we can serve as humble servants of the Creator, in support of the events that must unfold. In this way, we help the planet and everything upon her to move upward.

Terra will be the manifestation of Heaven on Earth. Although there may be some discomfort during the "birthing" of the new world, let us also remember the joy that comes when the birth is complete and the struggle and pain are finally over. It is written and so it shall be.

OUR EXPERIENCES WITH THE OT SHIPS

When I received the original vision in March 1982, the part that was the hardest for me to accept was when I saw the large spaceships filling the sky and the groups on the ground being led up into them. Then the scene shifted and I experienced myself standing near a viewport on one of those ships and watching the Pole Shift take place in front of me.

At that point in time, I had never looked up at the stars and thought I was from "out there somewhere." I had never had an interest in UFOs and read very little science fiction. However, the ships were as real to me as any other part of the vision, so I couldn't selectively deny them. I tried talking about them with people I knew, but their body language told me that they felt threatened by such things, so I put it all "on hold" until I could find out more.

My first experience with a ship that displayed itself to me personally was on May 31, 1986. I was asked to go to a location that was about a 2-hour drive from where I lived. I was supposed to find a certain place and was told I would know I had found the right place by a "show of presence" within 20 minutes after I had arrived there.

I found the place and parked the car so that I was facing the group of buildings in front of me. I looked at my watch and exactly 20 minutes later, a ship-shaped cloud suddenly appeared in front of me in the otherwise cloudless sky. On the drive back home, I was treated to a sort of cloudscape, with two dolphin-shaped clouds placed at the sides of a large cloudship. I had someone with me in the car, and we both saw all of the clouds I have described.

In September 1986, I was told that my "space connection" would officially enter my life in April 1987. So much happened in the intervening months (all of which I had been told would happen) that I totally forgot about it.

In the afternoon of April 25, 1987, I was resting and two men appeared to me, both dressed in yellow jumpsuits. The first man spoke to me telepathically and told me he would come into my life at the end of June. He appeared again on June 30 and told me he was Lord Michael Andronicus of Sirius Star System. He visited me daily all through the summer and into the fall of 1987, and occasionally spoke to me after that when it was particularly relevant for him to do so.

(I didn't know who the second man was until December 20, 2008, when I learned that he was Lord Michael Adir of Sirius Star System. I am now married to his 3D aspect and expect us to be together throughout the remainder of Operation Terra and beyond.)

In the early summer of 1987, I was asked to climb to the top of Sun Mountain (a somewhat large mountain in the foothills near Santa Fe) and when I got to the top an hour later, they gave me a large "show of presence." The sky was perfectly clear and cloudless, and I was directed to sit down and face in any direction I chose. I chose to face the Jemez Mountains, the mountain chain that is west of Santa Fe.

As soon as I had made myself comfortable where I sat, an entire armada of ships blinked on simultaneously. One minute the sky had been clear; the next minute they were all there. I say they "blinked on" because that's what it looked like to me. It was as if a switch was flipped and suddenly they were all visible, all at the same time. There was nothing gradual about it.

The ships were surrounded by an ionization field that caused the water vapor in the air to condense and form a layer of cloud around them; to me, they looked like ship-shaped clouds. I counted them. There were 76 of them and I had the thought, "The Spirit of '76," which to me (as an American) refers to an attitude of self-determination and individual liberty. As soon as I had this thought, approximately one-third of the ships blinked off again and totally disappeared. These were no ordinary clouds!

Then, from its perch in a nearby tree, a raven flew off into the space in front of me, over the city that lay below where I sat. As I followed its line of flight, I was surprised to see another ship forming up at my feet. It was long and cylindrical and had been entirely invisible. (The way it became visible was very similar to the "uncloaking" scenes I later saw on TV in *Star Trek: Next Generation*.)

The ship was initially transparent. It gradually took on more color and substance until it was a greenish translucent object. It looked like it was at least 2½ miles in length and was hovering over the city, but it was below the altitude of where I sat. As soon as I had seen it clearly and registered what it was that I was seeing, it began to fade out until it was totally invisible again.

(This was similar to the rheostat effect one sees on light switches that allow one to gradually turn the intensity of the light up or down, only in this case the visibility/opacity of the ship was being turned up and down.)

The next "display" was a little different. I was told to drive toward Lamy, New Mexico, and to stop when I felt to stop. When I felt I should stop, I pulled over to the side of the road and waited. Suddenly, a "whirlwind" appeared in front of me, across the road from where I sat. The sand and leaves it picked up were swirling around in a cylindrical shape, that rotated around a perfectly vertical axis.

I could clearly see the EFFECT of the vortex that the ship was creating, but I couldn't see the ship itself, which remained invisible to me. It was a cylinder, not an elongated cone (such as a "dust devil" or tornado), and it stayed where it was. It was not moving along the ground, the way dust devils and tornados do. The implied field had straight, vertical walls, defined by the diameter of the ship.

I heard a voice in my head that said, "Go home and read Ezekiel." The vortex then disappeared, so I went home to read Ezekiel.

(I have found the Lamsa translation of the Bible to be the most accurate rendition of the original language — it comes directly from the Aramaic, which preceded the Greek Septuagint that forms the basis of most of the Bible versions that are in print today.)

In Ezekiel 1:4, I read, "And I looked, and behold, a whirlwind was coming out of the north, a great cloud, and a flaming fire and a brightness was about it, and out of the midst of it there came as it were a figure out of the midst of the fire."

(I later found I was not the only one to think that Ezekiel had seen a spacecraft. Joseph Blumrich, a former NASA employee, had published a book called *The Spaceships of Ezekiel*, and R.L. Dione had published a book called *God Drives a Flying Saucer*. Dione had concluded that all the "clouds," "pillars of fire," and "pillars of cloud" mentioned in the Bible were really descriptions of spacecraft, and my experiences fit with his conclusions. Rev. Barry Downing came to similar conclusions in his book, *The Bible and Flying Saucers*.)

These were all small, gentle steps that gradually led me toward greater acceptance of spaceships and higher-density beings as being part of my reality and my life. However, the next experiences were truly "close encounters" for me:

On the morning of the first day of Harmonic Convergence (August 16, 1987), my upstairs team awakened me from a sound sleep and told me to go out to see the sun come up. I stepped out of my door at that magical time when the sky is just beginning to lighten at the horizon.

The three stars in "Orion's belt" were lined up vertically in front of me and the crescent moon was above them. I looked to my left and there was Lord Michael Andronicus's ship, clothed in a cloud. I could see its shape clearly. Then a small scout ship flew across the sky from left to right, passing between the moon and the upper star of Orion's belt. It was Quaternicus, my mentor from Constellation Hydra, who showed up again a few days later in my backyard (see below).

I stood there for over an hour as the sky brightened and turned beautiful shades of gold, rose, and pink. Andronicus's ship remained stable throughout that time, in a nearly cloudless sky. When the experience seemed to be coming to an end, I ran inside and grabbed my camera and took the following picture just as the cloud that covered the ship had begun to dissipate and disappear.

Lord Michael Andronicus's ship, clothed in a cloud.

On the second day of Harmonic Convergence (August 17, 1987), I was asked to see if I could "translate" myself onto Andronicus's ship. I tried, but I was only able to make it up through some of the "levels" at that time.

I DID get far enough into the process to discover that the ship was ALIVE and CONSCIOUS, and that the "crew" did a kind of "mind meld" with the craft and then the entire group (the ship and the people who were its passengers) teleported itself to its destination. "Mind power" was the only fuel needed.

Even though I could not physically transport myself there completely, I was able to see all of the inside features quite clearly. The upper level was a sleeping rotunda that contained 30 pod-like enclosures that would give their occupant complete privacy and quiet; they had storage compartments beneath them to hold personal items. The middle level was where all activity took place, including a lounge area for the crew, storage areas, Andronicus's private office, and the navigation area. The lower level was a sort of hangar for the smaller scout ships and it could hold up to 5 of them. I have drawn a rough outline over the photo and labeled each section so you can see the shapes of each level more clearly.

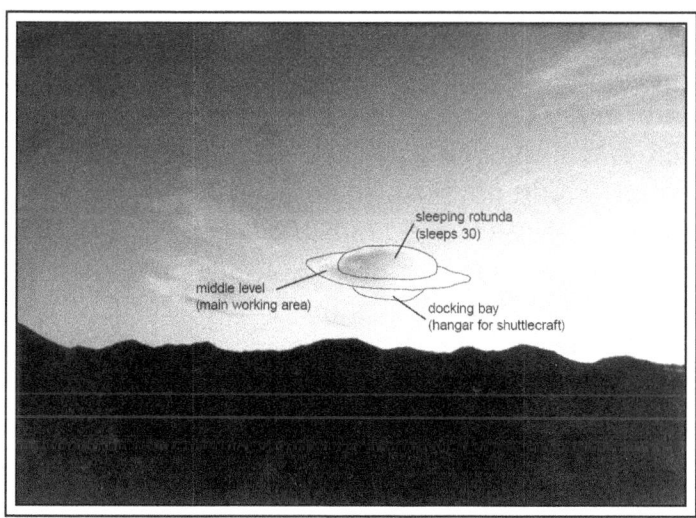

The three levels of the ship

There were many other demonstrations that summer, put on for my personal benefit and for the others who were with me when they happened, but the experience that was "my moment of truth" occurred in August 1987.

I was awakened at 4 a.m. and asked to go outside, stand in my driveway, and face north. I grumbled something like, "Don't you have anything better to do at 4 a.m.? Get a life!" but I pulled on my robe and went outside anyway. I hoped that none of my neighbors would see me and wonder why I was standing out there at 4 a.m. in my driveway, dressed only in a robe and nightgown.

"Okay," I said to orient myself, "this way is south, so this way (turning around) is north." I was facing the rear of the house that was located behind the property on which I was standing. Like most of the houses in Santa Fe, it had a very flat roof. Suddenly a spacecraft lit up. It was hovering about 5 feet above the house. From its relationship to the house, it looked like it was around 20 feet across. The whole ship was evenly illuminated, but it did not give off a glow or an aura of light around it. There were no shadows or features that I could make out, and there was no beam of light shining onto it, so it seemed totally self-luminous. I could see it clearly in relation to the house and there was no doubt about what I was seeing.

When I had fully registered the entire scene, the light blinked off again and I couldn't see anything more, but I was totally convinced. From that time on, I had no doubt whatsoever that our ships could appear in our frequency band if they wanted to, and that they were definitely "for real." Even though I was given many more "shows of presence" after that one, the only "next step" that would matter to me would be when I could physically board a ship. Anything less tangible than that would only be scenery along the way.

After that, whenever I saw ships, they always appeared at significant times — times that held meaning for me (and for those I was with, when that happened). Through those "shows of presence," they seemed to silently communicate, "Remember this. We are always with you." I think that the reason I experienced these "shows of presence" was probably to help me to accept the ships as being real and to trust what I have been told and shown.

All of the experiences that I have described above happened to me personally. Twelve years later, the Hosts asked me to deliver a series of Messages from them and the Operation Terra site came into being. Eventually, this put me in touch with others who were also having their own experiences with the OT ships.

Our Experiences with the OT Ships   407

A drawing I did of my mentor, Quaternicus, as he appeared to me telepathically on August 7, 1987. He is from Constellation Hydra. His people see with their entire body surface and perceive into the infrared spectrum, which makes them excellent navigators for the ships. His ship was the one that appeared over the roof of my neighbor's house at 4 a.m. in August of 1987.

In the Message, "Across the Great Divide," the Hosts confirmed my prior perception that the ships are alive and use a kind of mind meld between the ship and its passengers to teleport themselves to their desired destination. They also say that the ships have names, like we do. The man who will perform his role as the Commander of the Sirian Fleet when it's time for that to happen has been good enough to share some of his personal photos of the ships that have shown up for his benefit, including one of his command ship, Jonathan.

This large cluster of ships was photographed on Nov. 23, 2007. Note the layer of cumulus clouds that are below and around the lenticular shapes. This is significant in understanding that these are really ships, clothed in an ionization layer.

This is his command ship, Jonathan, photographed on December 3, 2007. Jonathan is clearly distinct from the cumulus clouds underneath him and to the left and right. He is considerably larger than Lord Michael Andronicus's command ship (shown earlier), but you can still see some similarities between them.

He sent me an email in June 2018 and said he had a large show of presence recently. His command ship (Jonathan) also showed himself, which hadn't happened since 2007. Both he and I feel this was significant timing in terms of what lies ahead for OT.

Several other people have sent me emails to share their own experiences with the ships. I have selected the following images to share with you and will intersperse my comments with their own. Their comments will be shown in a different font than mine.

Dear Adonna,

I stumbled across Operation Terra several years ago and have been an avid follower ever since.

When you wrote about cloudships, it didn't really surprise me because I saw one in October 2006 when my sister and father drove to Mexico. I looked up and saw this massive mother ship cloaked within a cloud. It was incredible! I pointed it out to my family but they couldn't see it. Alas, they are very much still asleep.

Attached is the photo of the cloudship in the distant horizon which was taken from the automobile.

Afterwards I discussed seeing this cloudship with a friend who is an intuit[ive] and does channelings. He confirmed that this ship appeared before me and I was supposed to see it. Wow. My ET family stopped by to say hello!

Thank you for your work and providing us with these beautiful updates from the Hosts of Heaven. The ground crew is ready and we are waiting for the call to do the work we have chosen to do!

Blessings.

October 2006 cloudship, Mexico

Dear Adonna,

I have enjoyed your books and articles over the years as well as following the process of you and your people. Although I am not one of the opterra people, there are many parallel "programs" going on and I am a part of one of those. For some reason I felt compelled to connect with you after reading your most recent post this morning. I am not sure why.

I will share with you a photo I took 4.5 years ago in Barcelona. I had been in the eastern Pyrenees "working." I was at an airport hotel and up quite early for my flight. As you can see there are various cloud forms. The really interesting thing is that (although you can't really see it here) they were [flying] in formation. I took the pic early just after waking. About an hour later, when I took the shuttle to the airport, the "discs" were all still in this formation and had not moved, but all the other clouds had gone.

Cloudships over Barcelona, Spain, 2010

There are all different types of beings here at this time. Some from this sector, galaxy and some from other universes. This is a big project and there is relevance to many. As well, some who are here, are here because they have done something similar before. They are here to offer their experience and mastery to this particular situation.

There are also many spirit beings (beings who don't usually incarnate in physical form to expand their consciousness and do what they do). An unprecedented number of those beings are in physical form now and for the most part will not be a long-term part of the physical aspect of the project. Even some of the material type beings who are here, are here for support rather than habitation.

For me, this is a special assignment and not my long-term home. The parallel programs I refer to are ALL the beings who are here to support this new expression from start to finish. The ground work began a VERY long time ago (earth time) with seeds of consciousness planted to support the preparation for this new world being created. There continues to be many layers of support facilitating the enactment of the NEW. And that will be the case for many years to come.

Her reference to the diversity of beings involved in "this new expression" (which OT refers to as the new Creation) fits with some of the experiences I have had in coming into contact with people who are "on loan" to Operation Terra. Her reference to "many years to come" agrees with the information I have been given about the amount of time the evacuees will spend on Midway (approximately 20-25 years), preparing to colonize Terra.

The type of ships shown in her photo are the kind I usually see, instead of the lenticular shapes that other people photograph so often. Her comment about the other clouds moving and the ships remaining stationary was a typical phenomenon in many of the experiences I have had.

The following photo was taken on February 20, 2016 (around 2:00 pm), over the northeast part of Seoul, South Korea. Note the difference in the shapes between the ascending stack of cloudships in the center of the photo and the group of ordinary cumulus clouds lined up at the horizon at the bottom edge of the photo.

Cloudships over Seoul, South Korea, photographed on February 20, 2016

Another reader sent me the following photo in an email dated March 23, 2018:

I had a strange experience with a cloud, it was a few months ago. [It was] 4:35 p.m. I left the supermarket and crossed the street and at that moment I saw a big cloud in the sky in the form of a disk. It began to expand and suddenly [there was] a flash and I thought it was thunder but there was no sound. It was clear [all] around, blue sky and bright sun. I got the impression that I was the only person to look at that. When I finished crossing the street, I took a picture. I had more pictures but they were inside another cell phone that didn't respond anymore. I'm enclosing the photo that I was able to save.

I do not really know if it is one of "our ships" or an ordinary cloud and unrelated to all this. I just wanted to share it with you.

I wanted to have a more panoramic picture but the cloud was too big (it was crossing two streets) and its height too low; it was impossible for me to capture it in its entirety. This event was in Puerto Vallarta, Jalisco; Mexico. Time: 4:36 in the afternoon (I put that on a note).

I continually see a point of luminous light in the sky, it's like a star but it increases and decreases its light. It disappears and reappears.

Cloudship over Puerto Vallarta, Mexico

The following photo was taken at 4 p.m. on Saturday, March 10, 2018 at the Desert Vista RV Park, near Deming, New Mexico. The person who sent it to me said:

[My husband] felt it was a spaceship and so did I. I thought, "Yay! They're here."

Cloudship over Desert Vista RV Park, near Deming, New Mexico (USA)

The following picture was taken at 8:20 a.m. on April 2, 2018, in Tucson, Arizona. The ships are the kind that I see most often.

Cloudships over Tuscon, Arizona (USA) at 8:20 a.m. on April 2, 2018

As I saw in the original vision in 1982, the evacuation will take place during a time of extreme turmoil and chaos — a fundamental breakdown in society on a global basis, punctuated by cataclysmic earth changes and rising tensions and fear everywhere.

The finale for all of that drama will include the evacuation of those who are heading to Terra at this time. We are now approaching that time and, as things look like they are coming apart and fear and chaos are rising around you, I ask you to remember to remain calm and centered and know that you are never alone.

Peace and blessings,
Sara/Adonna/Oriole

YOU MAY NOT HAVE TO DIE

The material in this book is intended for three audiences:

1) Those who will make the trip to Terra now, from the platform of their present incarnation;

2) Those who will drop their present bodies (i.e., "die") and incarnate on Terra as the first generation of native Terrans; and

3) Those who will drop their present bodies (i.e., "die") and go on to experience more third-density lives before they finally incarnate on Terra.

Each of us has been created by our Oversouls for a particular and specific purpose. If we are in the first group listed above, our personal purpose requires us to migrate to Terra from within our present incarnation in order to provide the adult bodies that will create the fetuses into which the second group can incarnate, and we will have to transform both our consciousness and our physical form in order to fulfill that purpose.

That transformation is not required for anyone in the second and third groups, but I feel it's useful for all of us to consider how profound that transformation will be, because all of us will experience it eventually, when it's time for us to personally do that.

Butterflies are widely accepted as symbols of physical transformation because part of their normal life cycle includes their physical transformation from a caterpillar into a butterfly.

When a caterpillar hatches out of its egg and begins to eat leaves, it has certain characteristics in common with all of the other caterpillars. Its body is made up of many segments, each with a pair of legs, so it also has many legs. Its mouth is designed to chew on leaves, and its eyes are relatively simple, often carried on protruding stalks.

It has a soft body, covered with a flexible skin, and it must crawl in order to get around. The caterpillar placidly munches its way through its

Swallowtail butterfly caterpillar

growth phase, crawling around from one leaf to another. Then one day, an inner timing mechanism kicks in and the caterpillar spins a cocoon around itself until it is completely enclosed. The cocoon hardens and then a miraculous transformation occurs.

Tucked safely inside its cocoon, the caterpillar's body literally dissolves. Only the heart remains and it still beats. The rest breaks down into a gooey "soup" of organic materials that has no form at all. If we were to open the cocoon at that point, the "goo" would never become anything. It would just dry out and die. However, if it is not harmed or interrupted, the "goo" forms up into another shape altogether — that of the developing butterfly.

Instead of the soft skin, it forms a hard shell. Instead of a mouth that is adapted to chew leaves, it develops a long tube, curled into a tightly wound spiral, designed to reach deep into flowers and suck out their nectar. The eyes form as part of the head and are complex. Instead of many segments, there are only three, each with a pair of legs.

Instead of being limited to crawling in order to get around, a delicate and intricate system of membranes, framework, and muscles takes shape; it will become the butterfly's wings. All of this takes place in secret, hidden away from the eyes of potential predators, but it is truly one of the miracles of nature.

Finally, all is complete. The butterfly emerges from the cocoon and perches on a leaf or stalk, but its wings are still rumpled from being folded tightly against its body. Its heart pumps fluid into the hollow framework of the wings and they unfold to their final size and shape. The framework hardens as the wings dry in the air. Then the butterfly takes its first flight, a totally different creature than the caterpillar it used to be.

The butterfly is a totally different creature than the caterpillar it used to be.

What, then, has happened to the caterpillar? Has it died? No, of course not. It has simply changed its form.

When we speak of people dying, we mean the process in which the spirit separates from the body, leaving it behind to decay into its more elemental components, while the spirit moves on to occupy another plane of reality.

We have all done this so many times that it is easy to forget that it is not always necessary to do this when it is time to move on to another phase of our existence. Just as the caterpillar has not "died" (i.e., left its body behind) in order to become a butterfly, we do not have to die (i.e., leave our bodies behind) in order to become our "new selves" for the new Earth, Terra. We simply have to change from one form into another

When various spiritual writings make reference to a "glorified body," it is this other form that is being referred to. In order to understand this, one needs to consider the spectrum of existence. We each occupy a spectrum of reality that spans from these dense physical bodies up through many levels — each one of a finer substance than the one below it — to a level where we are pure consciousness and light.

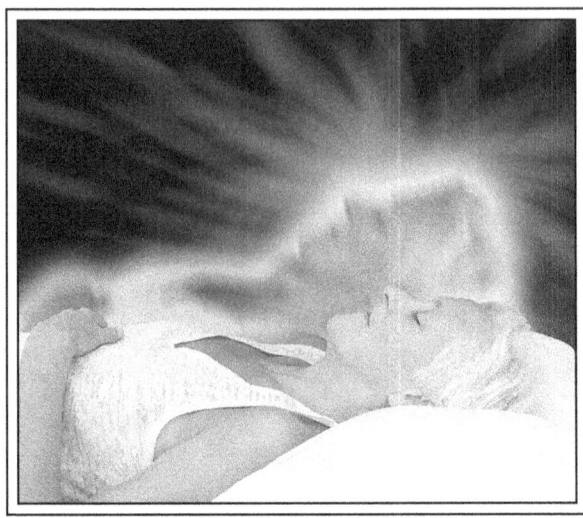

The spirit separates from the body, leaving it behind while the spirit moves on to another plane of reality.

If you pass white light through a prism, it will spread out into bands of different colored light. A rainbow exhibits these colors when sunlight passes through a mist of water droplets, each of which acts as a tiny prism that splits the light into those bands of color with which we are so familiar. When the pure Light of the Creator is spread into different bands of reality — different "planes" or "densities/dimensions" — it vibrates at different frequencies, just as the different colors of light vibrate at different frequencies.

At the level of third-density (3D) physical matter, by using our physical eyes, we can generally see colors from red (the lowest/slowest frequency we can perceive) through violet (the highest/fastest frequency we can perceive). But there is also light that is below the frequency that we can perceive (infrared, for example) and light that is above the frequency we can perceive (ultraviolet, for example) with our physical eyes. It is THERE, but we cannot perceive it because our instruments of perception (in this case, our physical eyes) are limited to perceiving a certain range of frequencies.

In the transformation we will make on our way to Terra, we will be shifting our own frequency and we will then be able to perceive a different range of frequencies than are available to us now. Terra already exists — right here, right now — but we cannot directly perceive her because we have not shifted into the same frequency band that she occupies. In order to see and experience her directly, we have to make a shift in consciousness, frequency, and perception. They are inextricably linked.

Each different "plane" or frequency band within the reality spectrum vibrates across a discrete range of frequencies. Each "form" that we occupy takes its characteristics from the frequency band it occupies. We express in different bodies for each part of the spectrum of reality. I have remembered four other bodies that I occupy at other frequency bands. They are all quite different from each other and each one is the appropriate form for its particular frequency band.

The bodies we are in right now are the appropriate vehicles for us at this level of reality, just as the caterpillar's body was uniquely adapted to its type of existence as a crawling insect. However, in order to inhabit Terra, we have to transform into totally different kinds of bodies that will be the appropriate vehicles for THAT level of reality.

When the Messages say that we do not have to die, it is similar to the caterpillar-to-butterfly transformation: there is a change in the actual form, but the particular lifestream continues without interruption. Those of us who are destined to physically colonize Terra will not die; we will simply change form. In fact, we are already well on our way to doing just that.

Then there are those who will incarnate on Terra through the normal birth process, just as babies incarnate through the normal birth process here on Earth. But where will the sperm and eggs and wombs to create and nurture those babies come from?

Sperm and eggs and wombs don't just materialize in the air and create babies. Some adult forms must be present in order to "seed" and colonize the new planet. They must come from somewhere. That is part of what Operation Terra is about: gathering up the seed stock for the new world. Some of us (the first group in the list) are destined to be the progenitors of a whole new species of beings, and in order to do that, we ourselves must transform our present bodies into those that are appropriate for the new world. We are taking our bodies with us, so in that sense, we will not die.

You may point out that in the caterpillar-to-butterfly example, the caterpillar may just change form, but the butterfly eventually completes its life cycle, lays the eggs for the new generation of caterpillars, and then "dies" (leaves its body behind). That is true for 3D butterflies, but when we have completely transformed our consciousness to that of our next level of being, we will complete each life after that by consciously

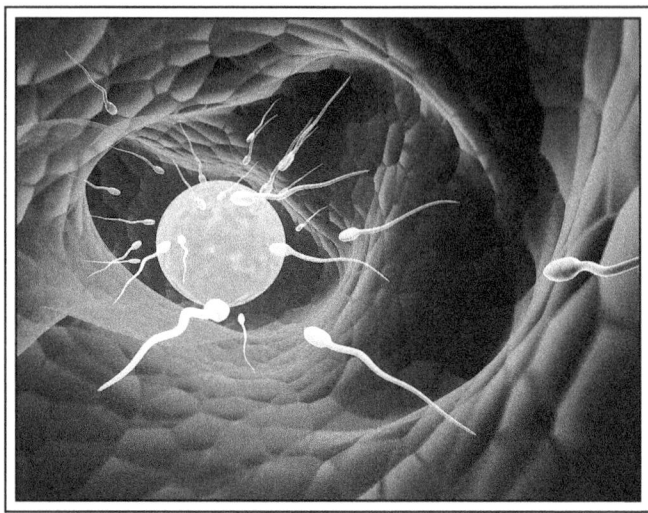
Sperm and eggs and wombs don't just materialize in the air and create babies.

choosing to change form, again and again and again. We will never again have to leave our body behind (which is what it means to "die"), so therefore, we will never have to "die" again.

This transformation is going to happen to a fairly large number of people — several million, in fact — so it has to be a well-established process in order for it to happen to so many in the relatively short time left for third-density Earth to shift into fourth density. We are indeed the "last generation" spoken of in the scriptures, regardless of our chronological age. At some point, Operation Terra will have to gather up those who will be the pioneers in the new world. This entire book is dedicated to providing information about that particular process and journey as well as the context in which it takes place.

Peace and blessings,
Sara/Adonna/Oriole

ARCHIVES

ARCHIVES SUMMARY

The last Message in Volume Three was received on December 7, 2006. After that, there were many pages of news, updates, and private communications that I shared through the News/Updates section of the previous OT site. Most of that material was very topical and time-based, particularly in 2011 and 2012, when there was a lot of talk about the expected end of the Mayan calendar in December of 2012.

On September 23, 2011, a grid of 12 stargates was activated during a ceremony that was performed in a remote location in South America. This activation connected the entrance and exit points for all 12 of the timelines that will emerge from this one shared reality. There has not been much new information since then.

On July 30, 2018, the Hosts told me that "all [future] communications will be carried out directly with those who have a need to know, and will not be for general publication … the website will serve to awaken and inform regarding the overall basics of the "op," but the details of what will follow will not be provided there, so there is no need to try to extract details from former communications. Stay with the fundamentals and the basic practices and you'll be on safe ground." When I asked them for guidance as to what I should include in this Archives section, they told me that "only material of a more lasting nature should be included, and not a lot of that."

Only the four chapters included here met that standard. Ironically, I think they are among the most important pages in this book, but it isn't until one has read the rest of the material that they can understand what is being presented here. That's why I haven't included them in the list of "recommended reading" for people who are new to this perspective. You could say that I "saved the best for last."

The Operation Terra perspective is radically different than almost any other source of information and these four chapters summarize it nicely. I encourage you to spend some time with them and see what they stimulate in you.

In service,
Sara/Adonna/Oriole
August 7, 2018

BULLETIN
August 12, 2007

All right, now. We have asked to speak with you today because of some changes on the immediate horizon for everyone connected with the "op." You are nearing the crossover point between 3D and 4D, and for those in the first two waves, this will result in a substantial shift in one's perceptions and subjective experience. What will this look like when it arrives? We can only give you an analogy to something you can imagine, because otherwise you could not imagine it at all until after you had already experienced it.

Imagine it is daytime and you are inside a house, looking through a window to the outside. Even though the sun is shining, the window looks like it is coated on the outside with a thick translucent gel, so the images you see through the window are blurred but still recognizable by their overall shape and color. This is how you perceive 4D right now.

Now imagine yourself moving toward the window and then passing through it bodily. While you are still inside of the house, the window and the gel will still blur the images outside, but as you draw closer to the window, they will become somewhat sharper and clearer. However, it is not until you have passed through the window itself and are fully present outside of the house that you will see clearly.

The window and the gel represent what you refer to as "the veil." You are approaching a time when you will, figuratively speaking, pass through the veil that clouds your perceptions and begin to see clearly again. We say "again" because this is how you were before you incarnated as a veiled human being, and you will now return to that prior state, and once you have fully crossed over into 4.0 awareness, your memories will also be restored.

You will be able to see in all directions at the same time. You will be able to hear the thoughts of others, and you will begin to access the full range of your abilities — all while maintaining a physical presence within 3D. At some point, when you have adapted to this change in your abilities, you will literally be able to walk through walls. However, we must emphasize that this is still a process, not an event, and there is a continuum of experiences that will accompany the shift.

The first stages of this will involve a gradual shift in your ability to "see," just as things began to appear more clear as you moved toward the window in our example. However, what you "see" will not just be visual perception. You will "see" with your entire being, and it will be more like total "knowing," involving your intuition as the container of the experience and your subtle senses providing the colors, shapes, sounds and smells that are part of that experience.

Most importantly, you will understand what you perceive for what it is. The blinders will come off and you will just "know" everything you need to know in that moment, and eventually — as you acclimate to this experience — you will know everything that is connected in that moment. You will be able to perceive all of the relationships — past, present, and future — that intersect in the moment and be able to trace them in any direction you choose.

Your sense of self will dissolve as you move into this shift until you become without boundary, able to merge with and become anything you perceive. You will know yourself to BE everything you perceive and when this process is complete, you will be in union with All That Is, and all experience of separation will fall away.

We want to remind you that this IS a process, not an event, so it will proceed gradually enough for you to integrate it as it proceeds. However, we felt you should know what is coming so you will understand and recognize it for what it is when your perceptions begin to change.

This will not occur at the same rate or the same time for everyone, as each has their own unique process to go through. However, everyone who IS part of the first two waves WILL go through this now and everyone who is NOT part of the first two waves will NOT go through it until after the evacuation.

This will be a profound shift of identity and perception and it will occur in small increments so that you can maintain function and adapt. You will not be able to explain this to anyone who is NOT part of the first two waves, so we suggest you don't even try. There will eventually be a merging of the minds of everyone involved in this and you will be together even while your bodies are expressing in separate locations. This is all we wish to say at this point in time, but we will tell you more when the need to know arises later on.

Amen, Adonoy Sabayoth. We are the Hosts of Heaven.

COMMENTARY: It has been 13 years since this information was received and it is clear that what the Hosts meant by "immediate horizon" was defined from their experience of being outside of time. For those of us who operate from within linear time, it has not been what WE would call "immediate," but for me personally, it is now unfolding just as they describe, although it is a gradual process that is not yet complete.

Peace and blessings,
Sara/Adonna/Oriole
December 2020

EXCERPT FROM "PRIVATE MESSAGE"
March 23, 2009

All right, now. There is little to say of a general nature, but we would like to summarize a number of things that we have referred to in the past and cast them within a new light, hopefully to bring a proper focus and understanding to everything that is now unfolding.

To begin with, all things are now in motion that will lead to the conclusion of the arc of experience that began when the elohim came together to precipitate this portion of reality out of their beingness. As we have indicated, this conclusion will be complete at the point in time when the first generation of children born onto Terra is mature enough to take over the reins from that point on. When that occurs, those of you who came together those billions of years ago will have completed your contract with one another and with the planet and galaxy as well.

This point in time is still many years into your future. Your children will not be born until the colonization is well-established and running smoothly. All structures and personnel that are needed to be involved in the raising of those children need to be in place and harmonized with everything else that is going on, and that alone is a process of many years. Measured in your present time, we are describing a period extending approximately 150 to 200 years from now, and that is the time horizon we recommend you use as you think about the process you are engaged with right now.

It is understandable that your focus will be on the liftings ... and the evacuation itself, but those comprise less than 1% of the time frame we are talking about.

... This is all a process that has been in motion for centuries, and there are still approximately two centuries left to complete this process, so though the immediate future appears to hold some intensity for you, it will be of a passing nature when compared to the remainder of what

There are still approximately two centuries left to complete this process

is left to play out. We hope these comments will help you to remain in proper relationship between the details and the bigger picture.

... Once everyone is on board Midway Station and involved in the processes that will proceed from there, the difficulties will be behind you and the process will become much more pleasurable, interesting, and varied.

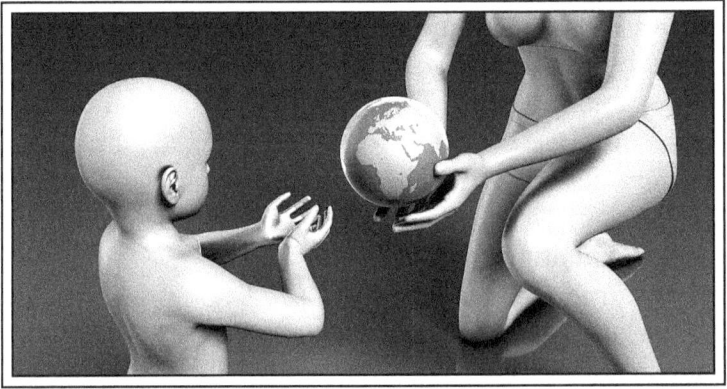

You will not comprehend your achievement until you see your own children acting as adults in that environment.

You will not fully grasp the gift that is Terra until the time comes for you to take your leave of her and you take your "last look around" at what you have achieved there. You will not comprehend your achievement until you see it in its fullest flowering by looking at your own children acting as adults in that environment, see the flow of individuals and information that passes between Terra and the rest of the galaxy, and look back on the journey that you went through in reaching that point in time. It is only then that you will fully appreciate what has occurred and what you have created.

Because those of you who are reading this are still on the ground, you also do not appreciate the vast numbers of beings who are assisting in this project. Once you are lifted and aware of your surroundings, that will also add to your experience and understanding. Eventually, you will lose your amnesia and appreciate who you are also, but that is something that you cannot grasp at this point in time, while you are still veiled and identifying with your present bodies as being who you are. That will change.

We will have one more of these private messages before we are through speaking to you in this way. It will essentially be our goodbye to the relationship we have had with you in the past, a pause in the unfolding of the project that we are participating in along with you, and then — when it is time for each of you to do so — you will be standing with us and acting as full partners with us in carrying out the rest of what remains to occur. There is only so much we can say until words become unnecessary and actions are what count.

This is something that must be lived, rather than talked about, so if you need more than this, you can talk with one another, you can go back and re-read what we have already given to you, and — most of all — you can listen within.

The fundamentals are simple. It may not be easy for you to make a habit of them, but in the end it always comes down to those simple fundamentals. We do not need to repeat them here. You know what they are. Use them and make them a way of life in the time remaining to you. Soon, all of us will be moving on to our respective next steps in the journey and the silence will speak loudly of our departure. We have essentially accomplished what can be accomplished in this manner and now it is up to you to make use of what we have given and walk the rest of the way on your own, toward your particular expression and destination, whatever that may be.

We leave you now in peace, and honor, and blessing. Amen, Adonoy Sabayoth. We are the Hosts of Heaven.

[Amen, and thank you.]

AN EXPERIENCE WITH "OCEAN"
October 18, 2011

A man who has been connected with Operation Terra for many years shared the following experience with me in October of 2011. I asked his permission to share it with all of you, as I believe it reinforces and validates several things that I have personally experienced and what the Hosts have said in the Messages, as well:

To all,

I've had an interesting experience today that I need to share. In the early morning hours (around 2 a.m.), after only two hours of sleep. I woke up from "something" that wasn't a dream. I don't know how to call it, but it was an experience unlike any dream state that I've ever experienced. In that unnamed state, I was a point of awareness fully embedded in what felt like a very fluid Ocean of Consciousness and I was having a bird's eye view of the street from my childhood. What is interesting is that I had a full perception of dozens of the versions of that same street that somehow coexisted, but were also separate.

As that experience continued, I sensed that there was HUGE activity going on in the Ocean and that EVERY single thing that happened was an EFFECT or a RESULT of OCEAN'S ACTION. This is hard to explain, but nothing happens or manifests that isn't a result of Ocean's will and action. It's extremely simple — everything I saw was Ocean in action and NOTHING ELSE. There were people in the street, but they were Ocean in manifestation, not some kind of separate entities that have free will. Free will doesn't exist; only thing that exists is the will of the Ocean, whatever the manifestation is — human or a mountain.

I saw that all the motion that was happening was scripted and I (in the connection with the Ocean) knew the script, and how everything moves on the scenes. Every single detail is simply just happening as the

Ocean wants it to; it's total impossibility for anything to happen that isn't part of the script.

As I was grasping all of this, I saw that scenes of my street started to change, especially the one that was somehow my main focus. First, the extremely strong winds came and people were running around seeking shelter; then there came strong earthquakes that had cars that were parked rolling down the street like they were children's toys. As I was witnessing all of this happening on this one scene that was my main focus, other scenes of the same street at the same time happily coexisted and not much was happening on them — weather was sunny and people were normally walking and cars were passing by. They were totally unaffected and unaware of the apocalypse from my main scene. However, before the cataclysms started to occur on my main scene, there was a huge energetic sorting out happening below the surface. I don't know how to explain it, but it was like people were energetically multiplying and splitting up.

For example, there was one man who had two energetic copies of him come out and separate/be pulled to 2 different scenes. He didn't stop [existing] when his copies were extracted; he was still doing what he was doing, totally unaware that this was happening. Therefore, I don't believe that people will simply disappear when timelines separate. They will continue on other ones, but their versions/bodies on our timeline will be killed in the cataclysms. Their spirit might even be instantaneously transferred to their embodied version on some other timeline, but I don't know as I wasn't drawn to explore this.

What fascinated me the most was that single hair doesn't fall off anyone's head if it isn't part of Ocean's Plan. The feeling was one of total safety because I was connected to the Ocean intimately, and aware of how EVERYTHING is being orchestrated. I was being one with this Ocean; I was literally wearing it and feeling its internal tides.

Today (October 18) marked a huge internal shift for me and this experience I've had still lingers on. What I've realized by having a glimpse of it is what the Hosts have been talking about — that there is only one BEING in action at all times and EVERYTHING happens according to ITS plan.

(He added the following on October 20):

I know that to "normal" people, what I have said here sounds crazy and I would not even try to attempt to describe to them what my experience was like. I believe that at least some people have benefit from me sharing this because of the clearing work that has enabled them to understand it at some level. Full understanding and "A-ha" moment will come only with direct experience. There is no way around it.

What strikes me as ironic is that once one is experiencing this Ocean of Consciousness, one realizes that Its nature is baby simple, but to the veiled entities it appears mysterious and complicated. Sananda didn't say in vain that to enter the Kingdom one has to become like child. Ocean's basic nature is the most simple and most natural way of being there is; complexity comes in Its creations, but the base on which all of it is built is extremely simple and there is this childlike simplicity to it.

Ocean is not a human being and therefore doesn't perceive like humans do. It doesn't have emotions or moral code — It is everywhere and in everything and It IS everywhere and everything. Everything is under Its total, absolute control at all times, and there are no uncertainties or surprises because Ocean knows everything and is everything. Ocean is the CAUSE of everything at all times — this is extremely important to keep in mind. What we might perceive as uncertainties or surprises are nothing but effects of Ocean's actions.

I'm not yet in direct connection with the Ocean and I still have preferences. I would prefer pleasure over pain and suffering, etc., and this is normal for human beings; nothing wrong with it. However, when one is experiencing itself as a point of consciousness without a body and shaped identity, things are perceived vastly different. This is where "no preferences" hallmark can be applied, in my opinion. I don't want my body to be tortured in any density, but from this higher, unincarnated level, all is good at all times and the point of consciousness is not affected by pain or emotions. I don't know yet how to conciliate those two perceptions.

That's it. I hope that some of you will have your own glimpses into these matters of the Ocean. I really prefer the word Ocean for the Creator because there is this malleable, fluid quality to it that kind of reflects the properties of water.

COMMENTARY: What he said at the very end totally fits with what I was shown many years ago when had I asked to see "the Mind of God."

I was presented with a gently undulating, self-luminous plasma-like surface that stretched further than I could see. All things emerged from it and resolved back into it again. Both his experience and mine also fit with physicist David Bohm's description of the movement of the hologram — upward from the deeper layers of the "implicate order" to where it expresses on the surface as part of the "explicate order," after which it resolves back into the implicate order again.

The Hosts described a similar fluid relationship between the Ocean/the Creator and Its manifestations in two Messages: "Go With the Flow: Becoming One With the Mind of God" and "The God Game."

Our experience of being separate from the Creator/Ocean is an illusion; at some point in our journey through time, that illusion will fall away and we will directly experience what has been described in this report. I hope this information is useful to you in coming to accept that reality.

In service,
Sara/Adonna/Oriole

EXCERPT FROM "DATES, GATES AND MATES, PART 2"
October 22, 2011

All right, now. We have asked to speak with you today because there are some points we feel need to be made at this time.

... First of all, in terms of dates, we want to reiterate the endless nature of the process and journey you are experiencing and that will not change, no matter what form your particular subjective experience takes for you. Outside of time, all things are simultaneously present in some portion of what we have called the Mind of God. They may be actually manifesting or only be there in potential; everything is always either emerging or resolving back into that ground of existence that gives rise to it.

It is really a very dynamic and complex process and unless one is in a state of full connection with that consciousness from which everything else arises, one cannot really appreciate our perspective on this, no matter how many words we use to try to describe it to you in terms you can understand from within the perspective of a veiled human being that thinks it is separate from everything else.

There really is no "time" as you understand it. As we have said before, time is a vector quantity that places things within the physical realm of the space/time continuum. It has shape — height, depth and width — just as "space" does, and it serves as a "locator," but has no separate reality of its own, other than to be useful as a model through which one can place things and events in relationship to each other.

Your calendars and other devices for marking or measuring time are just that — DEVICES that various mental processes have invented as useful tools to describe these phenomena. However, because of the nature of the experience of thinking that you are a separate being, whose existence is separate from and in relation to everything else you perceive, you tend to get things backwards. Instead of perceiving these devices AS devices, you confuse the measuring tool with the thing that is being measured. You place undeserved importance on both the devices and the interpretations of them made by others whom you consider authorities of some kind.

Your calendars and other devices for marking or measuring time are just DEVICES — useful tools.

While there is significance in WHEN things occur that is just as important as observing WHAT occurs, this often leads to incorrect conclusions when not perceived in the proper context. Unless one directly perceives the intimate connections between any one thing or event and everything else that exists, it is easy to attribute causality to the phenomena themselves, when there is really only one "cause" that is responsible for everything that exists.

And that leads us to our second point — the apparent misunderstanding of our prior statement that the concept of twin flames, twin souls, or "twins" is a human fabrication, based in the illusion that you are separate from each other. Some people have not read what we said very carefully, and they have ignored the actual descriptions we have given about the form things take on Terra, only one of the many levels of reality.

We said that on Terra, everything that reproduces sexually is part of a mated pair that we have called a dyad. We have also said in more than one place that the Oversouls create all of the projections that are

The concept of twin flames, twin souls, or "twins" is a human fabrication, based in the illusion that you are separate from each other.

observable as "lives" or bodies, and that within itself, the Oversoul has no gender and is complete, so there is no need to find one's other parts in order to be complete. We said that the dyad is a mechanism through which one can seek union with the whole. We did not say it was a fundamental unit of existence, and we want to make it clear that there is NO fundamental unit of existence other than the ONE LIFE that is expressing through all of the forms that It creates.

You can call It what you want to call It. Any name will do, but some names will convey meaning to others around you while other names will not. In the past, we have used the terms "God," "the Creator," and "Source," because they would be understood by most people who understand 3D terms and expressions.

Our transmission is being translated into physical words by our scribe, who speaks American English as her native language, so our words come through her in terms that she would use in speaking to others who also understand American English. However, our meaning is also filtered through the awareness and perceptions of those who read and receive these communications through her writings and website, so what comes across to each person will vary according to what they *bring to it* in terms of their understanding, experience, and perspective.

One of our readers has recently come up with the term "Ocean" for this source from which everything else arises, because he recently experienced this ground of existence as a liquid medium that undulated like the ocean does. You will note that our scribe has repeatedly used images and figures of speech that relate to the ocean, and we have also used metaphors along those lines throughout the Messages. You could call it "the Ocean of Consciousness."

The point here is that there is no one word or even a phrase that accurately describes this ground of existence. It must be *experienced* in order to be understood, and until one is in full connection with it — whether briefly or as a permanent state of being — no amount of words will convey the nature of the experience itself OR the nature of that ground of existence.

We have spoken repeatedly about this point. Perhaps some of you are beginning to understand this as you move into your own "knowing" enough to begin to recognize that there are no secrets between us here. There is only the veil. As the veil thins, you will also change your relationship to us as your source of information, replacing US with your own "knowing" and becoming more independent, sovereign beings — our peers, not our students.

Everything we have said and done in connection with Operation Terra has had this as one of its goals — to liberate you from the prison of the "small self" and assist and support you into moving into your true nature as a vast, self-aware intelligence that has precipitated this portion of reality from within your own being. We have referred to that aspect of you as an "eloha" (the plural is "elohim"), but again the words and names really are just devices for trying to bridge the gap between our perspective and yours. They have no reality of their own, other than what you bring to them in hearing the words and translating them through your own lens.

If one looks back across the more recent portions of human history (going back only several thousand years), you can see the adoption of different devices with which to try to describe various understandings as they emerged in the human consciousness. However, an interesting thing occurred as that unfolded. The concepts that were considered the "truth" in a given time and environment became accepted as immutable, so anything that went beyond that was considered radical, heresy, or something to be feared and eliminated.

The same is true today. For reasons we won't go into today, established thinking about the nature of this ground of existence is threatened by our insistence that there is nothing inherently good or evil to That which creates it (which we find convenient to refer to as the Creator, since that describes the action of continuously creating everything that manifests) — that to the Creator, all of Its creations are good.

Many, if not most or all of you, have personal preferences, in keeping with your unique expression of the One Life being lived. You were designed by your Oversoul with certain biases, tendencies, and what might properly be called "character traits," using the double meaning of "character" to refer to one's role in a given drama and also to refer to "what one is made of" — the stuff of morality, conscience, and value systems one is imbued with from the other "characters" one comes in contact with — from conception, ensoulment and gestation on through to physical death or complete transformation, whichever occurs for a particular individual.

Your preferences are part of how you define yourself as being different or the same as others around you. You seek those who share your values as a way of validating your definition of yourself. However, from OUR perspective, there is just the ISness of everything. Everything just IS what and how it is, and there is nothing that is better than anything else, nothing that is worse than anything else. There is only the Creator, wearing Its creations like many costumes worn all at once.

We see reality from the perspective of full connection, and therefore we can experience and observe everything in its proper relationship to everything else. Everything fills a unique place in the whole so that all of the possible experiences are available to the Creator for Its own experience of Itself. It has no preferences. It only wants to experience everything possible.

Therefore, everything is perfect just the way it is at any given moment. It is providing the perfect experience to satisfy the Creator's desire to have that particular experience. The Creator takes pleasure in all of the experiences It creates. This may be difficult to understand, but your pain and your joy are just experiences for the Creator, through which It is fulfilled.

People who are still veiled have no authority to speak for what "God wants" for anyone else. Each person can only know what "God wants" for them, and then only if they are listening within and can hear what each moment is telling them. Some people are "called" to a given purpose; others have no idea what their purpose in being is. It doesn't matter if they know their purpose or not. They are serving it just by being in expression.

There are so many ideas floating around about how one should eat,

Excerpt from "Dates, Gates and Mates, Part 2"

behave, or believe in order to achieve a certain outcome, but none of those beliefs are valid in and of their own, just like a belief that one needs someone else to complete them is not valid. It's just a belief, and just a mechanism through which to further one's seeking to fulfill its purpose, whether one understands their purpose or not. It is all being driven by the Oversoul. None of it sources from within the veiled human being, and until the veil parts and full connection is attained as a permanent state of being, none of it is properly understood by anyone who is not in that state.

You have no idea how much peace comes from being in full connection. Everything is grasped appropriately, seen in its proper context, and appreciated for its place in the whole. Those of you who are making the trip to Terra at this time will be able to appreciate these words more when you regain that state of full connection. To others, they may reject what we say here because it's not part of their journey to appreciate the correctness of these statements at this point in time, but that, too, is also perfect because they are just being who they came to be. They are just being "in character" for their role and place in the whole.

If you were watching a movie and one of the characters suddenly started acting in ways that were not consistent with the way they have been acting or, more importantly, in keeping with the overall drama of which they are a part — the story line — it would feel "off" to anyone perceiving them. Because we can perceive the perfection of everything just as it is and as it is unfolding, we can accept everything and just do our part in playing our roles within the whole. Our roles include having these conversations with all of you who have been drawn to read our words because of *your* roles in the whole.

So, while you may be drawn to find a mate or even enjoy being with the one you have, this is just a part of the overall seeking to become one with All That Is. It is not a fundamental building block of the universe! We hope we have made our position clear on this.

Everything sources from and is scripted by the Oversouls, which in turn are serving the Creator's desire to experience all of the possible combinations and permutations by CREATING all of the possible combinations and permutations for the Creator to experience. It sounds a bit circular, and it is. There is ONLY the Creator-in-expression, and anything else is an illusion that makes it possible for the Creator to explore all of the possibilities available to It within the parameters of a given Creation.

Since calendars are just devices for marking or measuring time and do not DEFINE time itself, all methods of assigning dates to anything are approximations at best, and could simply be interpretations on someone's part that are not universally true.

It wasn't so long ago in human terms that people thought the Earth was the center of everything because they observed that the sun rose and set and the stars appeared to move through the skies. It seemed that the celestial bodies all revolved around the Earth, and there was a certain periodicity to those movements. Calendars of many kinds were developed to describe those movements, and certain positions or occurrences were given special significance by those who were the authorities for their times. However, there is nothing intrinsically valid to any of that. They are conventions at best, and most of them will soon be as useless for predicting or marking anything as a watch without hands or numerals that only displays the single word "NOW."

There is only "now."

There is only "now." Even our word "soon" is a rough approximation and one given in a context of BILLIONS of years. Are any of you reading this tired of waiting for something to show up or happen according to a given calendar or prediction?

We suggest that you put the ideas of "dates" and "mates" in the past and fully enter the "now." Respond to what shows up, WHEN it shows up, as best as you can, and trust that the journey will take you to where you are going. It cannot do otherwise, since the Oversouls have created it to work that way, and "you" (that part of you that thinks it's separate from everything else) don't have any say in it at all! (Pardon our laughter, but from our perspective, it is really quite humorous.)

That being said, we are left with our third point — that of the "gates" themselves. They, too, are just devices or mechanisms — ways of carrying out what the Oversouls have scripted/written to occur in keeping with the Creator's desires for a new Creation. Each of these 12 gates will take those that are on a given timeline to their new place in the new Creation. While most people who do not drop their bodies immediately will think they are still on the same planet as they always were, they will not be.

There is no version of this present planet Earth that comes through any of the wormholes intact. Each version of planet Earth will emerge in a different place in the new Creation. The version that becomes the "new Earth" (which we refer to as Terra) will move out of her 3D body and move into her 4D expression. Some people will end up on a 4D negative-polarity planetary "twin" to Terra, which we will not name. All other "Earths" will move into other 3D planetary bodies, and each of those will provide more 3D experiences for those who are scripted to have them in the new Creation.

The timelines are already separating out from each other and have been doing so for many years. The movement is not generally apparent and ironically, those who pass out of your experience may continue in a different direction — one that is parallel to yours but not perceivable by you. It's as if each timeline has moved into a tunnel (its own wormhole) and as things move forward to their conclusion, all memories of what one left behind will fade as new information comes in and new scenarios present.

This is already in motion and can be seen as an overall movement, but one that is not shared equally across all beings who are now in bodies on the present planet. Those who pass out of your experience may or may not still be walking around on another timeline, but all you have to do is keep your eyes trained on the journey that is yours alone to make. It has all already happened anyway, so just enjoy the journey as much as you can, be good to yourself, and be ready to respond to what shows up.

We leave you now in peace, honor and blessing. Amen, Adonoy Sabayoth. We are the Hosts of Heaven.

ABOUT THE AUTHORS

I first became aware of the Hosts as a presence in my life in 1994, when a therapist encouraged me to write down my feelings because I seemed to be quite stuck in certain places in my life. At first I resisted this, but the pressure for change built up to such a degree that I finally took pen in hand and began to write, "I feel …" The feelings flowed freely and at some point I wrote a question of some kind, stopped and listened for an answer. To my surprise, the answer came and I wrote it down, in awe of the wisdom it contained. I repeated this experience several times that day.

I did this again on two more occasions and finally, after being quite impressed with the wisdom of the answers I was being given, I asked "Who ARE you?" because it was quite clear that "I" didn't know all of that! They replied, "We are the Hosts of Heaven, your brothers and sisters in the many mansion worlds of the One Infinite Creator."

Since then, they have also identified themselves by other terms: the "angelic hosts," the "Legions of Michael," and the Hosts that are referred to in the expression "Lord of Hosts." (The Hebrew for that expression is Adonoy Sabayoth, which is part of the way the Hosts conclude every communication. "Sabayoth" translates to "legions" or "armies," not "hosts" in the sense of hospitality.)

They also informed me that they reside in the [fifth-density] frequency bands "… that contain those *you* would call Masters, angels, and archangels," and they "work with the Office of the Christ." (The latter is an office or position within the spiritual hierarchy, not a person.)

These are *our* terms, not theirs, but they meet us where we can meet them and then help us to shift our perspective so that by the time we will actually meet with them face-to-face as their equals and partners within the "op" as a whole, we will have moved to being able to understand them as they understand themselves, and be beyond the need for such 3D labels and terms.

According to the Hosts, the people to whom they are speaking are all part of a large soul family, as they expressed in five different Messages:

When it is time for the lifting, you will be ready and your own love and joy will be the force that reunites you with your spiritual family. — "Across the Great Divide"

You are one of US. Even though you might not think of it that way, we do. You are OUR "family," just as we are YOUR "family." All of us are related to each other — some more closely than others, but all are connected and part of one big "soul family." It will bring us all great joy when we are back together again. — "About 'Vision'"

You will feel less connected with some people, more connected with others, as you move toward the poles of your destiny and merge your being and energies with those of your true family — your brothers and sisters in the many mansion worlds of the one infinite Creator. WE are that family, and you are preparing to shed your old skins and put on your garments of light. When you have done that, you shall stand among us as equals and we shall be able to embrace each other once again. We look forward to that day as much as you do, for we know how much joy we shall all have in that reunion. — "Signs Along the Way"

If we are silent sometimes, it is so that you can learn to listen to your own sound, to your own inner voice instead of ours. We are family, you and we, and we are here with you every step of the way. But we do not wish you to become dependent on hearing our voice to know you are safe and loved. We wish you to hear your own inner voice to know you are safe and loved. — "On Your Way Home"

You have already made it "up the scale" through the various densities of experience, and from the higher densities, you responded to a call for your participation in the present drama. Then you came down again, accepted the partial amnesia that accompanied your "fall" down through the levels to arrive in a body on 3D Earth, and now you are finding your way back up to where you were before. By the end of this entire process, those of you who are our soul family will find yourselves back in the experience of being vastly expanded consciousnesses again. — "Moving Into Unity with All That Is"

As they said, the amnesia was only partial in our case and I have had some direct experiences that enabled me to remember some of the concepts that were later expressed in the Messages. In 1992, I traveled backwards in time to 4.5 billion years ago and experienced myself as being one of the 144,000 elohim who came together to precipitate this sector of reality from our beingness. I "saw" and felt all of us and how were were back then, and as I traveled back through the millennia to that time, I also "saw" how each of us had incarnated at various times to redirect the course of events so that they would be in keeping with the original plan for this planet.

I had another experience sometime in the early 1990s, in which I remembered standing in a group of approximately 30 "tall beings." We were discussing who would come into third density, when each of us would do so, and how we would find each other again. I "saw" us as being very tall. (The Hosts are between 10 and 12 feet [3 to 3.7 meters] in height.) We were wearing full-length robes with hoods that hid our faces. I don't think I was ready to see more than that at that time, so I was not allowed to see more.

In 1994, when they had told me that they were my brothers and sisters, I took that as a general statement of shared affinity, but have since learned that it is quite literal in a spiritual sense. In 2017, I became aware of my "Host" identity and began signing myself with three names: Sara is my third-density expression; Adonna is my fourth-density expression; and Oriole is my fifth-density expression, as one of the Hosts. Since the Hosts say that we are expressing at all of those levels simultaneously, I sign my name as Sara/Adonna/Oriole, so you can choose to address me by any and/or all of those, according to what's most comfortable for you.

In terms of the usual kinds of entries in the "About the Author" section of a book, I can look back and see how everything I did and experienced in this life (and many others that I have remembered) has led me perfectly to where and how I am today. It is the same for each of you who is reading this. The details may differ, but the principle is the same. The "Operation Terra" story is OUR story as well, and each of us is perfect just as we are, providing our unique contribution to the entire story. We are each the characters we are supposed to be in the Creator's "movie," and we will continue to play our parts, even after the stage has been cleared and a new one appears in the new Creation.

In closing, I want to wish you well in all things and look forward to the time when our family will be able to be together again, face-to-face.

Amen, Adonoy Sabayoth. WE are the Hosts of Heaven!

ABOUT THE PUBLISHER, CONTACT INFORMATION

The Hosts have referred to themselves as "celestial beings," so as the publisher of the Operation Terra material in all of its forms, I have named my business Celestial Way.

Current plans are that the hardcover Keepsake Editions of this book will be followed by their publication in the e-book and paperback formats, in each of five languages (English, Spanish, French, German, Korean and French).

The paperback editions will be printed in black and white and have fewer illustrations; the e-book editions will be almost all text.

It is my current understanding that I will be available in some way to those on the ground until the evacuation is complete, but I do not know the details about how I will do that or where I will be located, so the best I can do is give you the following information if you want to contact me or find out more:

e-mail address: sara@operationterra.com
website: https://www.operationterra.com

www.ingramcontent.com/pod-product-compliance
Lightning Source LLC
Chambersburg PA
CBHW081352290426
44110CB00018B/2353